Getting Started with Citrix XenApp® 7.6

Install, configure, and support your XenApp® systems with the power of Citrix XenApp®

Konstantin Cvetanov

BIRMINGHAM - MUMBAI

Getting Started with Citrix XenApp® 7.6

First published: November 2015

Production reference: 1281015

Published by Packt Publishing Ltd.
Livery Place
35 Livery Street
Birmingham B3 2PB, UK.

ISBN 978-1-78439-423-3

www.packtpub.com

Notice

Credits

Author
Konstantin Cvetanov

Reviewers
Markus Darda
Shankha Mukherjee

Commissioning Editor
Usha Iyer

Acquisition Editors
Manish Nainani
Llewellyn Rozario

Content Development Editor
Kirti Patil

Technical Editor
Rahul C. Shah

Copy Editor
Sonia Cheema

Project Coordinator
Kranti Berde

Proofreader
Safis Editing

Indexer
Mariammal Chettiyar

Production Coordinator
Nilesh Mohite

Cover Work
Nilesh Mohite

About the Author

Konstantin Cvetanov is a principal architect at ProSys Information Systems, which is one of only ten Citrix National Partners in the United States. He designs, implements, and supports enterprise virtualization systems and end user computing solutions for Fortune 500 companies across a variety of industries. Before he joined ProSys, he worked for Citrix as an escalation engineer, fixing production outages on a daily basis and participating in the development and testing of the latest Citrix product releases and patches. Besides his experience inside and outside the Citrix organization, he has his own technical blog at http://www.pvsguy.com, where most frequently, he writes about Provisioning Server, XenApp, and XenDesktop.

From the rest of the Citrix products, he is very passionate about NetScaler. Beyond this, he is a cloud enthusiast with a strong passion for automation and troubleshooting methodologies. He is very interested in the transition from private to hybrid and public clouds. In his spare time, he enjoys reading about robotics and artificial intelligence.

About the Reviewers

Markus Darda is the owner of MD Consultancy (Germany) and DaComp GmbH (Switzerland). As a Senior Citrix Engineer and Architect, he works for enterprise customers in Europe where he designs and implements Citrix (XenApp and XenDesktop) environments based on different hypervisors. As a Citrix and Microsoft trainer, he also teaches about Microsoft server and Citrix products to customers who reside in Europe. He works for Citrix as a subject matter expert (SME) for different courseware and exams as well.

He has worked for German companies, such as LANXESS and T-Systems, Koenen en Co in the Netherlands, and companies in Switzerland, Sweden, and Norway.

Markus has worked on different Citrix courseware and has also reviewed Citrix XenApp 7.5 Desktop Virtualization Solutions.

Shankha Mukherjee has over 8 years of experience in the IT industry. He is currently working as a Windows L2 engineer at Accenture Services Pvt. Ltd., supporting client infrastructure for Windows, Citrix, and VMware architecture. He is currently working on a project to migrate and transform the applications/servers/databases from legacy to new generation datacenter environment for clients.

He has a BTech degree in information technology. Previously, he reviewed *Getting Started with Citrix XenApp® 6.5* and *Citrix® XenApp® 6.5 Expert Cookbook*, both by Packt Publishing.

I would like to thank Packt Publishing and its team for providing this wonderful opportunity and I definitely look forward to more such opportunities. A special thanks to Kranti Berde for her cooperation and for patiently bearing me.

www.PacktPub.com

Support files, eBooks, discount offers, and more

For support files and downloads related to your book, please visit www.PacktPub.com.

Did you know that Packt offers eBook versions of every book published, with PDF and ePub files available? You can upgrade to the eBook version at www.PacktPub.com and as a print book customer, you are entitled to a discount on the eBook copy. Get in touch with us at service@packtpub.com for more details.

At www.PacktPub.com, you can also read a collection of free technical articles, sign up for a range of free newsletters and receive exclusive discounts and offers on Packt books and eBooks.

https://www2.packtpub.com/books/subscription/packtlib

Do you need instant solutions to your IT questions? PacktLib is Packt's online digital book library. Here, you can search, access, and read Packt's entire library of books.

Why subscribe?

- Fully searchable across every book published by Packt
- Copy and paste, print, and bookmark content
- On demand and accessible via a web browser

Free access for Packt account holders

If you have an account with Packt at www.PacktPub.com, you can use this to access PacktLib today and view 9 entirely free books. Simply use your login credentials for immediate access.

Instant updates on new Packt books

Get notified! Find out when new books are published by following @PacktEnterprise on Twitter or the *Packt Enterprise* Facebook page.

To my wife, Ljubinka - I am forever grateful for your love and support.

To my daughter, Yoana - daddy is truly blessed to have you in his life.

To my brother, Daniel - your youth is your gift…make it count.

Table of Contents

Preface

Getting Started with Citrix XenApp® 7.6 is a beginner's book that is based on the latest version of the Citrix XenApp product. It is aimed at providing an introduction to application virtualization and is a step-by-step implementation guide for Citrix administrators, system engineers, and consultants. Leveraging his expertise both as a consulting architect and a former Citrix escalation engineer, the author takes an end-to-end approach to the XenApp deployment by incorporating components, such as NetScaler and Provisioning Services, to lay the foundation for an enterprise-focused solution.

What this book covers

Chapter 1, Why Citrix XenApp® – Making the Case for App Virtualization, aims at explaining the benefits of Citrix XenApp in the context of the latest trends in the field of virtualization technology. It will help you adopt the ideas presented to you and justify the Citrix solution to your management team.

Chapter 2, Designing a Citrix® Solution to Fit Your Needs, explains that even though system architecture is suitable for a more advanced-level book, some design knowledge is needed in order to be able to build a relevant XenApp system that meets the needs of your IT enterprise. In this chapter, you will learn how to create a simple design of a Citrix solution that meets your business needs.

Chapter 3, Preparing Your System for XenApp® Deployment, explains the various methods of deployment and system requirements that need to be in place before deploying XenApp.

Chapter 4, Installing and Configuring Citrix XenApp®, covers how to install the Citrix XenApp solution and perform initial configurations.

Chapter 5, Installing and Configuring Citrix® StoreFront™, provides a walkthrough of the steps needed to install and configure StoreFront in order to present XenApp resources to end users.

Chapter 6, Installing and Configuring NetScaler Gateway™, provides a walkthrough of the steps needed to install and configure NetScaler Gateway in order to provide end users with remote access to their published applications.

Chapter 7, Load Balancing with Citrix® NetScaler®, provides a brief overview of Citrix NetScaler and how a load balancing implementation fits into the XenApp deployment.

Chapter 8, Building Your First XenApp® Farm – Machine Creation Services, covers the first steps involved in deploying a XenApp farm using the Machine Creation Services method.

Chapter 9, Building Your First XenApp® Farm – Provisioning Services™, covers the first steps involved in deploying a XenApp farm using the Provisioning Services method.

Chapter 10, Administering a XenApp® Environment – Application Management, introduces an IT administrator to the XenApp administration (specifically, application publishing and management of the newly built XenApp system).

Chapter 11, Administering a XenApp® Environment – Server Management, introduces an IT administrator to administration and maintenance of XenApp servers and Delivery Controllers.

Chapter 12, Printing, is dedicated to explaining how printing works in a XenApp environment and deploying Citrix Group Policies to satisfy printing needs.

Chapter 13, Troubleshooting Tools, Tips, and Tricks, introduces basic and advanced troubleshooting techniques and teaches you how to leverage Citrix and third-party tools to support the XenApp environment.

Chapter 14, The Big Day – Going Live with Citrix XenApp®, provides a prelaunch checklist and best practice recommendations on rolling the XenApp environment out to production.

What you need for this book

This is based on the Citrix XenApp 7.6 Platinum edition and all its associated components, including StoreFront 2.6, Provisioning Services 7.6, and License Server 11.12. As part of an enterprise deployment, important products, such as NetScaler 10.5 and SQL Server, are explored. In order to conduct an implementation, in addition to the XenApp 7.6 installation media, you will need access to Microsoft Windows 2012 (trial versions are acceptable for a temporary Proof of Concept).

Who this book is for

This book is intended for IT administrators and consultants who want to build application and desktop virtualization solutions for their employers and customers. No prior knowledge of Citrix technologies is required.

Conventions

In this book, you will find a number of text styles that distinguish between different kinds of information. Here are some examples of these styles and an explanation of their meaning.

Code words in text, database table names, folder names, filenames, file extensions, pathnames, dummy URLs, user input, and Twitter handles are shown as follows: "Create a new folder called `C:\SSL` on the Delivery Controller and save the file there."

A block of code is set as follows:

```
[default]
sp_configure 'show advanced options', 1;
GO
RECONFIGURE;
GO
sp_configure 'Agent XPs', 1;
GO
RECONFIGURE
GO
```

Any command-line input or output is written as follows:

asnp citrix.*

Get-BrokerHypervisorConnection

New terms and **important words** are shown in bold. Words that you see on the screen, for example, in menus or dialog boxes, appear in the text like this: "Upon launching the VM creation wizard, under **Template**, scroll down and select **Windows Server 2012 (64-bit)**."

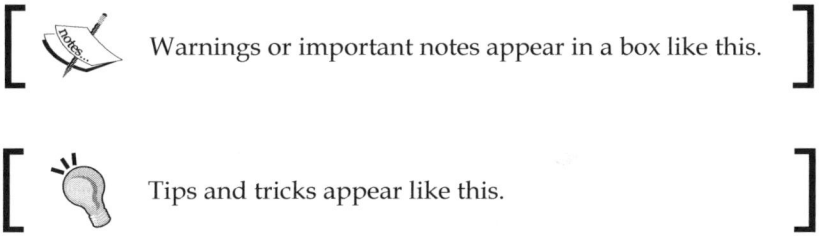

[Warnings or important notes appear in a box like this.]

[Tips and tricks appear like this.]

Reader feedback

Feedback from our readers is always welcome. Let us know what you think about this book — what you liked or disliked. Reader feedback is important for us as it helps us develop titles that you will really get the most out of.

To send us general feedback, simply e-mail feedback@packtpub.com, and mention the book's title in the subject of your message.

If there is a topic that you have expertise in and you are interested in either writing or contributing to a book, see our author guide at www.packtpub.com/authors.

Customer support

Now that you are the proud owner of a Packt book, we have a number of things to help you to get the most from your purchase.

Errata

Although we have taken every care to ensure the accuracy of our content, mistakes do happen. If you find a mistake in one of our books — maybe a mistake in the text or the code — we would be grateful if you could report this to us. By doing so, you can save other readers from frustration and help us improve subsequent versions of this book. If you find any errata, please report them by visiting http://www.packtpub.com/submit-errata, selecting your book, clicking on the **Errata Submission Form** link, and entering the details of your errata. Once your errata are verified, your submission will be accepted and the errata will be uploaded to our website or added to any list of existing errata under the Errata section of that title.

To view the previously submitted errata, go to https://www.packtpub.com/books/content/support and enter the name of the book in the search field. The required information will appear under the **Errata** section.

Piracy

Piracy of copyrighted material on the Internet is an ongoing problem across all media. At Packt, we take the protection of our copyright and licenses very seriously. If you come across any illegal copies of our works in any form on the Internet, please provide us with the location address or website name immediately so that we can pursue a remedy.

Please contact us at copyright@packtpub.com with a link to the suspected pirated material.

We appreciate your help in protecting our authors and our ability to bring you valuable content.

Questions

If you have a problem with any aspect of this book, you can contact us at questions@packtpub.com, and we will do our best to address the problem.

1
Why Citrix XenApp® – Making the Case for App Virtualization

Whether we like it or not, change is upon us. The evolution in technology has changed the way we work, learn, and live. In fact, the world has become so data driven that we can subscribe to any type of data we want and receive it through our laptop or mobile device at any given location and time. In order to make all of this possible, something else had to be transformed—information technology. Nothing amazes me more than the change we've experienced in IT over the past 15 years. With the advancement of wireless communications, virtualization, cloud computing, and software-defined networking, IT organizations have had to adapt faster than ever to new demands from end users and management teams alike, while getting accustomed to a permanently steep learning curve. Amidst all these changes experienced in the technology sector, a company called Citrix (formerly known as Xitrix in the early 90s) took a simple and very intuitive concept and transformed it into an industry standard—and this is the mobile workstyle. Enabling companies to allow their employees to work from anywhere (and eventually on any device they want), while saving big on hardware *and* without compromising security—sounds too good to be true? Well, it's here to stay. The big question is how you transform your existing IT infrastructure that has no Citrix software installed on it into a complete and production-ready Citrix solution that will boost the productivity of your users, save unnecessary expense for your management team, and minimize administration efforts for the IT department. Hopefully, you will find the answer you are looking for in this book, and you will enjoy the journey in the meantime.

In this chapter, you will learn about the following topics related to Citrix virtualization:

- Hardware and application virtualization
- Introduction to Microsoft Remote Desktop Services and Citrix XenApp
- Design changes and feature enhancements in XenApp 7.x
- Application delivery methodologies in XenApp 7.x
- Microsoft and Citrix licensing models
- Citrix components used for networking and web access
- The XenApp supportability matrix and important product lifecycle dates
- Citrix certifications needed to advance your career

Understanding virtualization

Before we dive into application virtualization with Citrix XenApp, it is important to make sure we have a fundamental understanding of virtualization. This is not meant to be a by-the-book definition, and generally, most definitions in this book will target your common sense and intuition rather than your ability to memorize dry material. If you are an experienced virtualization engineer, feel free to skip this section.

So, what is hardware virtualization? In a broader sense, it is the unlocking of the OS layer from the underlying physical hardware, making it possible to run multiple OSes (also referred as guest OSes) on top of a single hardware entity. Let's take, for example, a rack server. In a traditional IT infrastructure, we would ship the rack to our data center (or server room), install Windows 2012 R2 on it, and enable **Internet Information Services (IIS)** to run a web server. In this one-on-one relationship, we run a single instance of an OS and a single server role on a physical machine. So, if we require twenty web servers to manage our website, in a traditional environment, we would need to purchase twenty physical servers. Instead, if we decide to virtualize our workloads, we can install a piece of software, known as a hypervisor, onto our rack server that can run multiple guest OSes or VMs. We can now scale up and build many web servers on this single hypervisor, provided that it has sufficient processors and RAM. Since we have installed this software into bare metal and not on top of another OS, this is known as a **Type-1 hypervisor**. Citrix XenServer and VMware ESX are examples of Type-1 hypervisors. However, our options do not end here. If we decide to install a traditional OS, such as Windows 2012 R2 or Linux RedHat, onto our rack, we can then place a hypervisor on top of the OS and run multiple VMs. This is defined as a Type-2 hypervisor. Sun VirtualBox and VMware Workstation are examples of Type-2 hypervisors.

Most hypervisor platforms have a **Graphical User Interface (GUI)**, which makes administration of guest OSes extremely efficient as you have your entire environment in the palm of your hand. Examples of management consoles are XenCenter (for Citrix XenServer), vSphere (for VMware ESX), and SCVMM (for Microsoft Hyper-V). Hypervisor installation and configuration is beyond the scope of this book. VM configurations, however, will be covered in *Chapter 2, Designing a Citrix® Solution to Fit Your Needs*, to the extent that they are relevant to the Citrix XenApp design. The following diagram illustrates the layout of Type-1 and Type-2 hypervisors:

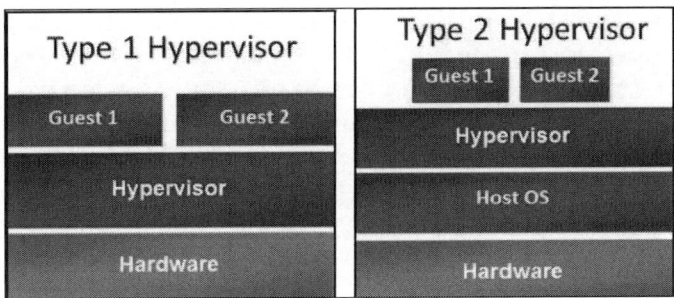

Application virtualization

Now that we have a better understanding of hardware virtualization, we can focus on application virtualization. App virtualization is similar to hardware virtualization in the sense that the upper layer is separated from its underlying components. The former, however, entails the isolation of an application from its original OS and the application itself is presented to the end user as if it were native to their device regardless of the OS in use. For instance, Betty can launch a Windows-based accounting app from her Linux home computer, but this app actually runs on a server in the data center and not locally on her machine. This way, she can use any device she wants in order to fill out her spreadsheets and this application never gets exposed to any potential security threats from her device because it never actually executes on her machine. This is the key concept behind application virtualization that is addressed by the Citrix XenApp solution in an enterprise environment. One of many other use cases is running 32-bit apps on a 64-bit endpoint OS. This comes in very handy for financial services companies and healthcare institutions that rely heavily on legacy applications that are not being updated on a regular basis. However, what if Betty wants the full desktop experience instead of individual application instances? In this case, IT can assign a Windows 2012 R2 desktop to her that multiple other users share at the same time. Technically, this is referred to as desktop virtualization; however, in the context of Citrix and Microsoft, it is accomplished by the same product suite—Citrix XenApp in conjunction with **Microsoft Remote Desktop Services** (formerly known as **Terminal Services**).

Understanding Remote Desktop Services

Remote Desktop Services (RDS) from Microsoft is an essential platform and a requirement for app virtualization via Citrix XenApp. It is a role in Windows 2012 Server that enables users to share a physical or virtual desktop located in the data center over the network via the Microsoft proprietary RDP protocol. Every user in an RDS environment needs an RDS license in order to use a remote desktop or application. RDS licensing can be per user or per device. These are also known as **Client Access Licenses (CALs)**. Commonly, organizations employ a per user license, which allows one user to have access to all the instances of a particular product (for example, RD hosts), while device licenses make sense in an environment where multiple users connect to a single RD Host from the same computer (for example, shift workers using kiosks, and so on). So, you may find yourself wondering why you need Citrix in the first place when you can deliver remote apps and desktops to your users by simply configuring RDS on a Windows 2012 server. A lot has been said about the two products and the main arguments in favor of Citrix XenApp are the level of granularity involved in configuring and administering the environment, the security of the Citrix proprietary **Independent Computing Architecture (ICA)** protocol, and the endpoint device support. Currently, 95% of Fortune 500 companies use XenApp to deliver applications and desktops to their end users, and Citrix has been focused on developing its virtualization portfolio for well over a decade with cloud networking and mobility products recently acquired to complete the circle of workspace transformation.

Introducing Citrix XenApp®

XenApp 7.6 (formerly known as Presentation Server, MetaFrame, and WinFrame) is an application virtualization software built to deliver a secure and highly-customizable set of applications and desktops to end users regardless of their location or endpoint device type. XenApp's **Virtual Delivery Agent (VDA)** is installed on an RDS-enabled Windows Server OS, while the XenApp environment (also known as a farm or site) is managed by a Delivery Controller installed on a separate non-RDS Windows server. The applications can be installed on the XenApp VDA server, and a client software called Citrix Receiver needs to be deployed on the user's endpoint device to enable application launching. We will explore the XenApp architecture in further detail in *Chapter 2, Designing a Citrix® Solution to Fit Your Needs*, but, for now, it is important to remember (much like other enterprise software) that there is a management component (also known as a controller or broker) and a delivery agent. The communication between the two is vital for an operational environment. The following diagram illustrates the conceptual architecture of XenApp:

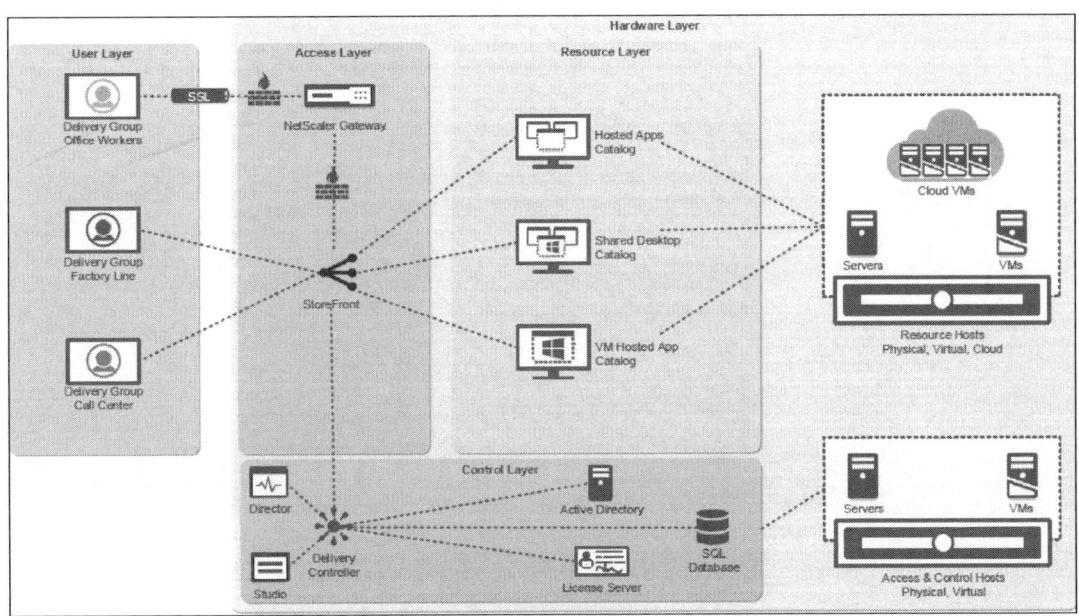

The XenApp conceptual architecture available at http://www.citrix.com/. © Citrix Systems, Inc.

XenApp 7.6 uses a proprietary Citrix communication protocol called ICA. ICA transmits data intercepted by XenApp from an application running on the server to the Citrix Receiver on the client device over standard network protocols, such as TCP/IP and, formerly, IPX/SPX. From the client side, when a user interacts with the application (for example, a mouse movement or keyboard input), the Receiver software on the client device circulates the traffic back to the application running on the XenApp server. Multiple virtual channels exist within the ICA protocol, such as multimedia, printing, USBs, smart cards, and others. These virtual channels define various functions within the ICA stream and different settings can be applied to control their impact based on the requirements of the environment. In *Chapter 11, Administering a XenApp® Environment – Server Management,* we will go into further details regarding Citrix group policies that can be implemented to manage application security and user experience. The following diagram illustrates the ICA protocol and virtual channels:

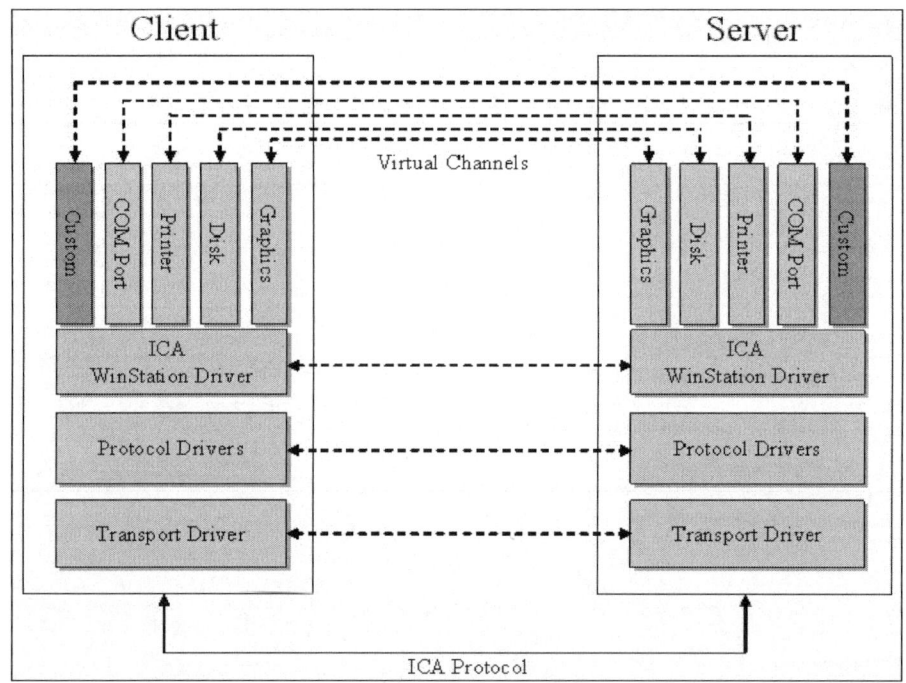

ICA protocol and virtual channels available at http://www.support.citrix.com. © Citrix Systems, Inc.

Citrix XenApp 7.6 uses the **FlexCast Management Architecture (FMA)**, which is conceptually the same model used by Citrix XenDesktop. In fact, in 2013, Citrix merged the XenApp and XenDesktop technologies into a single delivery platform under the umbrella of XenDesktop 7.0. Starting with XenDesktop 7.0, you could deliver both applications and **Virtual Desktop Infrastructure (VDI)** from a single pane of glass. However, less than a year later, Citrix reintroduced XenApp as a standalone licensed product, which once again used the same integrated management model as XenDesktop FMA. You do not have to purchase XenDesktop licenses in order to use XenApp. The latter can also be deployed on both virtual machines and physical servers depending on the nature of the existing infrastructure.

Design transformation in 7.x

Older versions of XenApp, such as 6.5, have a completely different design than 7.x releases. Pre-7.x XenApp uses **Independent Management Architecture (IMA)** as its operational platform. Citrix has since moved away from IMA and onto FMA, which is a more service-oriented multiproduct platform. If you've had previous experience with XenApp, you will find that 7.5 and 7.6 have a completely different look and feel than older versions. There have been significant changes in administration as well. Here are some examples of architectural modifications in 7.x:

- **Server management**: Application delivery and farm administration is no longer managed from the XenApp server itself but rather from the Citrix Delivery Controller. Application and desktop configuration can also be configured by a server with the Citrix Studio console installed. The Delivery Controller's only unique roles are user access and optimization of connections.

- **Graphical User Interface (GUI)**: Citrix Studio (formerly known as Desktop Studio) has replaced the AppCenter and Delivery Services Console.

- **Database**: XenApp no longer uses a local host cache, mirroring the data from the primary SQL data store to a local access database. FMA relies on the high-availability features set in the SQL server instead.

- **Provisioning methods**: **Machine Creation Services (MCS)** can now be leveraged to provision XenApp servers from a single master image. Previously, they could only be deployed as standalone machines on a hypervisor or via Citrix **Provisioning Services (PVS)**.

- **Agent software**: The **Virtual Desktop Agent** has replaced the XenApp 6.5 software installed on a XenApp image.

New features in XenApp® 7.6

XenApp 7.6 offers features that were either absent in 7.5 but present in 6.5 or nonexistent in previous versions altogether. Here is a list of the main new functions that can be enabled in 7.6:

- **Session PreLaunch (available in 6.5)**: This refers to sessions that are launched before users request them

- **Session Lingering (available in 6.5)**: This refers to sessions that are not terminated when a user disconnects from an application

- **Anonymous logon**: This refers to credentials not being required in Citrix Receiver or StoreFront, and users can authenticate directly at the application level

- **Connection leasing**: This refers to session information that is cached locally on the Delivery Controller so that if a SQL server outage occurs and the Delivery Controller loses connectivity to the site database, users who request new sessions can be connected to their applications and desktops

- **Cloud integration**: This refers to XenApp servers that can be deployed and managed by cloud solutions, such as Citrix CloudPortal, **Amazon Web Services (AWS)**, and Microsoft Azure

Application delivery models in XenApp® 7.6

Citrix enables you to deliver resources to end users in a variety of ways. Which model fits your environment best will depend on the business purpose of your solution. There are three methods for application delivery via XenApp—hosted apps, streamed apps, and hosted shared desktops. Let's have a look at them:

- **Hosted apps**: With this model, the application is installed on the XenApp server and will execute there as users launch instances of it on their client devices. The application will consume CPU and RAM on the server and multiple instances of the same process will appear in **Task Manager**.

- **Application streaming**: In this delivery model, apps are packaged and streamed to the endpoint device via Microsoft App-V as part of the XenApp store. With this method, apps will execute and consume the compute resources of the endpoint device instead of the XenApp server.

- **Hosted shared desktops (HSD)**: This model is the right approach if the requirement of the environment is to present a full desktop to users instead of individual apps. With the hosted shared model, the XenApp server itself is presented to the end user as a full desktop launched from their Citrix Receiver and it can be shared among multiple users at the same time. The number of users that can utilize the desktop simultaneously is determined by the compute resources allocated to the server and the nature of the applications being run within this desktop. In *Chapter 9, Administering a XenApp® Environment – Application Management*, you will learn how to deploy the different models of application delivery with Citrix XenApp.

The XenDesktop model allows a user to have a dedicated OS and not share resources with other users by delivering a desktop to the user. The desktop can be pooled or private. Pooled desktops are nonpersistent and any changes made by the user outside of their profile are not retained upon reboot. Dedicated desktops are also assigned to a single user. All changes made by the user to the underlying system are retained after a reboot much like a physical computer when a personal vDisk is configured for users. Bear in mind that this approach is only available if you have a XenDesktop concurrent or user/device license.

The user logon process

In this section, we will explore the user logon process in XenApp in a hosted app scenario. As explained earlier, the true power of XenApp is that a user can launch a variety of remote applications running in a server environment at any time on any device. This is a brief overview of how the traditional logon process in XenApp 7.6 works:

1. A user launches Citrix Receiver on a client device or opens a web browser and navigates to a web portal supplied by an IT administrator.

2. The user types in their credentials in Citrix Receiver or StoreFront.

3. Upon successful authentication, the user is presented with an app store showing the applications and desktops assigned to them by the administrator.

4. The user clicks on one of the applications or desktops available in the store.

5. Within a few seconds, the application runs on their workstations and they are able to use their business application as if it were local to their device. For customers who cannot have the Receiver client installed on user devices, Citrix has included the Receiver for HTML5, which is configured on the StoreFront server and runs a virtual session inside the web browser.

Now, let's take a look at how the Citrix infrastructure makes the aforementioned transaction possible on the backend:

1. Upon user login, either Citrix StoreFront or NetScaler Gateway (depending on the frontend solution used) passes the credentials to Active Directory (AD), which validates them and passes the information over to the Delivery Controller.

2. Delivery Controller polls back AD and checks in the SQL database to determine what resources are assigned to the user.

3. Hosted applications and desktops are enumerated in the user's Receiver store.

4. When the user clicks on an app, StoreFront transmits an ICA file to Citrix Receiver on the client device. Receiver then uses the file to establish an ICA session.

5. When a session is granted by the Delivery Controller and the application is launched, a Receiver progress bar is displayed on the endpoint and during this phase, the user profile is loaded and group policies and any logon scripts are applied for this particular session.

With XenApp 7.6, the session prelaunch and lingering features can be leveraged to reduce wait times for the application to start by shifting profile load, GPO processing, and logon scripts to an earlier time. The benefits and functionality of these features are demonstrated in *Chapter 10, Administering a XenApp® Environment – Application Management*.

Citrix® licensing

An entire book can be written on licensing a Citrix environment, its underlying components, and how to make the best decision on what license to purchase. To sum up, three product editions are available for XenApp—Advanced, Enterprise, and Platinum. Advanced offers a basic set of features required to build an application virtualization solution, such as the ability to publish apps and desktops. Enterprise and Platinum provide a rich set of functionalities, such as image management via PVS and comprehensive monitoring tools that are needed to operate a large environment with business-critical applications and no fault tolerance.

Visit `http://www.citrix.com/go/products/xendesktop/feature-matrix.html` for the most up-to-date Citrix product matrix.

It is important to note that the XenDesktop Enterprise and Platinum editions include XenApp, so if you were to purchase XenDesktop, you would have the flexibility to publish applications and shared desktops as well as dedicated end-user OSes. XenApp licensing is based on a session concurrency model where each user needs to be granted a license when a session (running application) is initiated. This license is returned to the license pool when a session terminates. The next time the same user launches an application, they are granted a new license. In other words, a license is not permanently tied to a user or a device, but is rather granted for the current session only.

After purchasing Citrix licenses, license files need to be installed on a Citrix license server version 11.12, which can reside on a Windows 2008 or 2012 OS, and it is also available as a Linux-based VPX (virtual appliance) imported directly to the hypervisor. The license service software can be downloaded from http://www.citrix.com/. During the first deployment presented by this book, you will learn how to work with Citrix license files and troubleshoot a Citrix licensing component.

Microsoft licensing

Most big vendors have a licensing structure that is often times a bit more complicated and cumbersome than we would like it to be. Furthermore, it can lead to unnecessary costs if not carefully analyzed upfront. Microsoft is no exception and the combination with Citrix can sometimes cause confusion as to what type of licenses are needed to build a new XenApp environment or expand existing systems. For Citrix to work on Windows, you will need to license two components—the operating system and **Remote Desktop Services (RDS)**. Here is a list of licensing options from Microsoft that support virtualization at the time of writing this book:

- **Operating system**: The following types of servers are supported:
    - **Virtual servers**: The following virtual servers are supported:
        - **Windows Server Standard Edition**: One license is required for every two virtual machines (guest OSes).
        - **Windows Server Datacenter Edition**: One license is required per hypervisor host, granting unlimited VMs (guest OSes) running Windows within a particular host.
    - **Physical servers**: The following physical servers are supported:
        - **Windows Server Standard Edition**: One license is required for every single-processor server, and two licenses are required for every four-processor server.

- ○ **Windows Server Datacenter Edition**: One license is required for every single-processor server, and two licenses are required for every four-processor server (same as Standard).

- **Remote Desktop Services**: A license is given per user or device (also known as CAL), and in the context of Citrix, one license is required for each user to connect to a XenApp server; the license will be tied to this user.

With regard to an OS, today, many companies use a **Key Management Service (KMS)** server to manage the volume licensing of their enterprises. KMS is supported by Citrix as a central licensing authority for Windows and Office and is by far the most popular method for license activation. It is always beneficial to have a conversation with your Microsoft sales representative or a Microsoft reseller to ensure that you get the best licensing mix for your budget.

Other components

The purpose of this book is to build and showcase an enterprise-ready Citrix solution. As such, other Citrix products and components will also be involved in the implementation. For example, Citrix StoreFront is a component of XenApp and XenDesktop that presents users with the Receiver store or website where they can subscribe to their applications. StoreFront, which is a required component, is part of the XenApp installation media and needs to be installed on an IIS-enabled server.

In *Chapter 6, Installing and Configuring NetScaler Gateway™*, and *Chapter 7, Load Balancing XenApp® with Citrix® NetScaler®*, you will learn how to implement load balancing with Citrix NetScaler VPX, and how to frontend your XenApp environment with NetScaler Gateway. NetScaler is a multipurpose appliance developed by Citrix and is widely used for load balancing backend server connections on a variety of communication protocols, such as HTTP, SSL, and FTP and other functions, such as network security and traffic optimization. In fact, NetScaler is such an enormous platform that a dozen books have been written about it. If you would like to dive deeper into full-blown enterprise implementations of NetScaler, I personally recommend you to go through *Implementing NetScaler VPXTM, Marius Sandbu, Packt Publishing*. My book only focuses on what is necessary to build a basic load balancer and gateway and no advanced configurations are covered. NetScaler is not required for XenApp to function properly. However, load balancing your StoreFront (Web) servers is highly recommended in a production environment, which is why it is included in this book.

In *Chapter 9, Building Your First XenApp® Farm – Provisioning Services™*, you will learn about Citrix **Provisioning Services (PVS)**. PVS is an enterprise-ready UDP-based streaming technology that is designed to deliver an OS over a network to the **Preboot eXecution Environment (PXE)**-enabled physical or virtual clients. At this time, PVS is included with XenApp Enterprise and Platinum editions and it can be leveraged for the provisioning of XenApp servers from a single virtual disk providing tremendous scalability over traditional standalone machine deployment.

In *Chapter 4, Installing and Configuring Citrix XenApp®*, you will learn about Citrix **Universal Profile Management**. UPM is another add-on product for XenApp and XenDesktop that Citrix offers in order to facilitate integration of user profiles. UPM can be used instead of Microsoft roaming or mandatory profiles and a rich set of group policies is available through an **Administrative (ADM)** template to enforce granular profile settings. UPM also works in conjunction with **Microsoft Folder Redirection**, which can come in handy if your environment requires user files to be stored in a separate location from the profile.

XenApp® supportability

Most paid software nowadays have some type of support agreement to provide technical resources to customers in case issues are experienced with the product itself or as a result of its operations. Vendors generally offer phone support, e-mail, newsletters, whitepapers, and even on-site assistance for critical issues. Typically, Enterprise Technical Support is subscription-based and there is an annual fee associated with the contract. Citrix provides different levels of support agreements. At the time of writing this book, Premier Support has gained a lot of popularity due to their 24x7 phone assistance and unlimited tickets. It is recommended that you engage your Citrix sales representative or an authorized reseller to get the most up-to-date information on technical support.

Each Citrix product version has an **end-of-life (EOL)** and **end-of-maintenance (EOM)** date. EOM is when a product is no longer maintained by developers, but you can still get assistance from a technician. EOL is when technical support is no longer offered for a particular version, and you are strongly encouraged to upgrade your software to the next supported version. Some product editions have **end-of-extended-support (EOES)** dates after the EOL, so if you have an extended support contract with Citrix, you will continue to receive assistance until EOES is met. Currently, XenApp 7.x (all subversions of 7) is maintained and supported until June 30, 2018. The following screenshot illustrates the XenApp product supportability matrix:

Product/ Component Name	Version/ Model	Language	NSC*	EOS*	EOM*	EOL*	EOES**
XenApp	7.x	All	31-Oct-13	N/A	N/A	30-Jun-18	14-Jan-20
XenApp for Windows Server 2008	5 and FP	EN, DE, FR, ES, JA	26-Oct-12 CTX122442 ☑	N/A	13-Jul-14	13-Jan-15	14-Jan-20
XenApp for Windows Server 2008R2	6.0	EN, DE, FR, ES, JA	26-Oct-12 CTX122442 ☑	N/A	24-Feb-16	24-Aug-16	14-Jan-20
XenApp for Windows Server 2008R2	6.5	EN, DE, FR, ES, JA	26-Jun-13 CTX122442 ☑	N/A	24-Feb-16	24-Aug-16	14-Jan-20
Presentation Server for Unix	4.0	EN	TBA	N/A	TBA	TBA	N/A

The XenApp product supportability matrix available at http://www.citrix.com/support/product-lifecycle/product-matrix.html. © Citrix Systems, Inc.

XenApp® certifications

IT certifications have become an important part of the career development of IT professionals. A recent study conducted by InformationWeek showed that IT managers listed certifications as two and a half times more valuable than an MBA degree. Recent evidence shows that a certified professional can make up to a 40% higher salary than their noncertified counterpart. Many administrators, engineers, and consultants seek to obtain a Citrix certification as proof of technical proficiency in the Citrix stack. At the time of writing this book, Citrix has recently completed an overhaul of their previous exam structure.

Currently, three certification paths are available to customers—Apps and desktops (virtualization), networking, and mobility. The virtualization suite includes three certification exams—**Citrix Certified Associate (CCA-V)**, **Citrix Certified Professional (CCP-V)**, and **Citrix Certified Expert (CCE-V)**. The CCE-V certification is an architect-level certification that validates the ability to design and implement enterprise systems based on XenApp and XenDesktop 7.x. Obtaining a Citrix certification can greatly increase job security and influence career advancement.

Summary

In this chapter, you learned the fundamentals of virtualization from both the hardware and application perspective. With regard to hardware, we took a hypothetical example to demonstrate the benefits of virtualization and learned how to differentiate between Type-1 and Type-2 hypervisors. From an application and desktop standpoint, we introduced two major platforms that work together—Microsoft RDS and Citrix XenApp. The latter was classified into three categories—hosted applications, streamed applications, and hosted shared desktops followed by a brief summary of desktop OS virtualization with Citrix XenDesktop. We also explored a user logon process in XenApp as seen by the user and as executed on the server. On the vast topic of licensing, we explained current offerings from Microsoft and Citrix in terms of OSes, RDS, and XenApp as well as benefits derived from various product editions. Required components, such as StoreFront for web access, and recommended options for load balancing and external authentication, such as NetScaler and NetScaler Gateway, were reviewed and more content will follow as they become more relevant in later chapters. From the supportability point of view, we looked at the lifespan of XenApp and the maintenance duration and current vendor support offered by Citrix. Last but not least, we provided insight on Citrix certifications paths to help you solidify your Citrix skillset and advance your career.

To sum up, we briefly touched on the high-level aspects of the XenApp software, its requirements, and its use cases.

In the next chapter, we will analyze some use cases from real-world field implementations. As we enter the design phase, we will start laying the foundation of our XenApp solution. Stay tuned...

2
Designing a Citrix® Solution to Fit Your Needs

This is one of the most important chapters in this book. I say this because without proper planning and an assessment of requirements, implementation would imminently fail to meet your business needs, which could lead to financial losses to your company. To avoid this, sufficient time needs to be allocated to building a phased approach, starting with design. The following topics will be covered in this chapter:

- Project planning
- Reference architectures
- Collecting data from existing systems
- Defining boundaries and peripherals
- Analyzing and testing core applications
- Architecting Citrix XenApp and other components
- Real-world examples from the field

Project planning

If you are reading this book with the intention of building an IT business solution for your company, then you are probably already involved in a project or some type of initiative with clear objectives and metrics in order to achieve success. Every successful IT project requires a great bit of attention to detail in planning and architecting a solution that would have a substantially positive impact on business operations. Many consulting companies take a phased approach when working with their client on projects. Usually, a project manager creates a project plan with a schedule chalked out to complete tasks or milestones. Projects can vary in terms of size and resources. On a very basic level, the lifespan of a project can consist of several phases:

- Design
  - Conducting the analysis of an existing environment
  - Defining business requirements and limitations
  - Architecting an IT solution according to specifications

- Implementation
  - Building a solution based on design specifications
  - Documenting an environment and all the steps involved in deployment

- Testing and piloting
  - Forming a test group of users to participate in a pilot
  - Receiving and reporting feedback
  - Resolving issues discovered during the pilot phase

- Go-live
  - Requesting a maintenance window via change control
  - Ensuring visibility within an organization
  - Bringing systems online

- Post-implementation knowledge transfer and support

During the design phase, architects usually study the existing environment and collect data to plan the steps needed to accomplish the goal of a customer. During this time, they gather requirements from stakeholders (management, IT, users, and service providers) and define any limitations that may present themselves during the deployment. For example, an application that runs on a 32-bit OS can be challenging to implement on a 64-bit OS and will be defined as a limitation. Another type of limitation is a company's financial budget. A project can only be completed successfully if the company can afford the necessary software, hardware, and professional services involved in the implementation. Once sufficient data has been gathered and clear goals and limitations have been set, the architect can begin designing the new environment with the desired results in mind.

After the design is completed and has been cleared and a detailed reference architecture exists, the next phase of the project is to implement the system that was designed. Multiple resources can be involved in the implementation, including solution architects, systems engineers, support engineers, and others. The key focus during implementation is to execute the project plan within the deadline defined by the business and to ensure that all milestones are met and documented properly.

Once the environment is deployed, it can be placed into a pilot where a relatively small user group is designated for testing, and vital feedback on functionality and performance is collected from users. The goal of testing is to report and mitigate any issues in the environment and ensure that performance of the newly deployed system is acceptable for the business.

If all issues are properly resolved and users validate good performance and functional levels, the environment can be rolled into **production**. In enterprise operations, **production** is a frequently used jargon to describe actively used systems that are critical to the well being of the company. There is an inherent sense of caution and urgency whenever **production** is discussed and all IT resources are mobilized during the go-live process to ensure that rollout of the systems is successful and if there is an issue, a rollback plan should be in place and ready to be executed.

Once the new environment is online and users start doing their day-to-day activities on it, the project can be concluded and post-implementation support begins.

In this section, we've only described one of many ways a project can be rolled out. The scope of such an engagement largely depends on the company, technology, and the parties involved. For example, a government agency will have project guidelines that are very different from those of a private sector company due to compliance standards applicable specifically to public institutions. Some phases will also vary based on the type of solution being deployed and its impact on business operations. Replacing a core switch, for instance, would most likely require downtime that would affect a large number of users, while updating QuickBooks would only affect the accounting department. These are factors that must be carefully evaluated during the design phase.

Reference Architectures

A **Reference Architecture (RA)** is a technical document designed to showcase a software or hardware solution. RA very often serves as a template for standardized computer system deployments and is widely used by administrators and consultants to assess infrastructure requirements, perform benchmark testing, and obtain knowledge about product features. Typically, vendors release RA papers on a regular basis whenever a new version is released or a third party product is tested. For example, on their website, Cisco has an RA for a Citrix XenDesktop system built on UCS blade servers, Nexus switches, and VMware ESXi. Of course, this is only a basic foundation of a single configuration that has been tested by vendors, and actual systems deployed in the field will vary according to the business needs of the end customer. Most RAs contain a business scenario and a documented approach to accomplish this goal, including a proven combination of hardware and software and multiple diagrams to visualize a concept or communication model. The following diagram is a great, simplified example of an IT infrastructure built entirely with the Citrix Workspace Suite (XenDesktop, XenApp, XenMobile, NetScaler, CloudBridge, and ShareFile), and illustrates how the different components in the environment connect with one another:

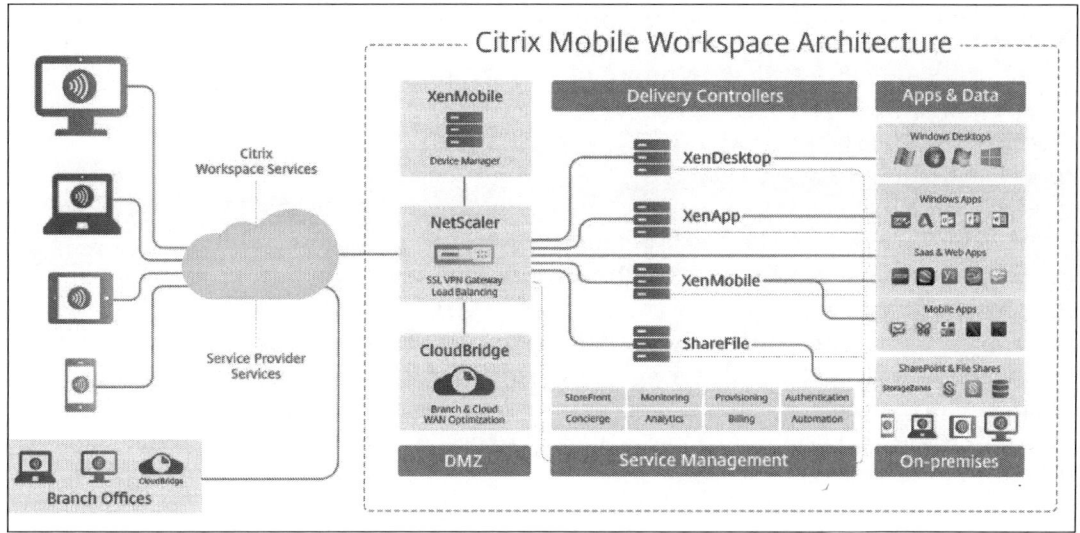

A Citrix all-in-one RA diagram by Alexander Ervik Johnsen, which is available at www.ervik.as

In conclusion, the RA approach provides a benchmark to build best practice deployments, and is an important resource when designing a Citrix solution.

Designing XenApp® for an enterprise

Now that you are familiar with what RA is and how a planned approach works, you will be able to design your own architecture that will fit the unique needs of your company. The real purpose of this chapter is to arm you with the right tools and guide you through the process to accomplish your goals. In this book, we'll build a solution from scratch, but whether this is true in your case or you are just looking to expand your existing environment, the best way to start is by setting a goal and defining what we know already.

Goals

It's your first day as a system admin. Your boss calls you in her office and tells you that due to high work volume, your training has been cancelled and you are being placed on a project. She says the CIO of the company has become increasingly concerned with recent security breaches in the industry and wants to prevent any sensitive data from leaving the corporate premise. He also insists on being able to manage business-critical applications for the accounting, sales, and human resources departments, respectively, from a centralized system to reduce administration costs (you are thinking, "Wow! XenApp must've been an easy sell!") Your boss tells you that since the company has already deployed several hypervisors to virtualize Domain Controllers and SQL servers, you can use the existing XenServer hosts, which are underutilized, to build out a XenApp environment. Since you are the go-to person for XenApp now, she also wants you to come up with a list of all the licenses that need to be purchased beforehand.

Users

IT has to walk a fine line between satisfying management requirements and user needs. Very often, what users really want differs from what the management can allow. You have to take this into account when designing a XenApp architecture, and ensure that your solution is compliant with the guidelines that are given to you while delivering the best possible experience for the user within these boundaries. Your user base is what determines the end goal of the environment and being able to define it is critically important during the design phase. In this particular scenario, the first question you need to ask is how many users are in Accounting, Sales, and HR. In a large environment, there will likely be **Organizational Units (OUs)** or other containers in **Active Directory (AD)** where you can check the members of each group if you have access rights, but to be on the safe side, you need to always consult with your manager (or customer, if you are a consultant) on how many users really need to use the Citrix environment. For the sake of simplicity, in this book, we will assume that there are 600 users (200 in each department).

Concurrency rate

Until now, the math was pretty straightforward. However, what if only 50% of all 600 users use an environment at any given time? Would the number of concurrent users impact the design at all? The answer is a big fat YES. Concurrency changes everything. If you know that only 300 people will ever be connected to XenApp at the same time, wouldn't it be an overkill to build an environment for 600 users? If you can get by with twice as few XenApp servers, you can save a ton of time and resources. The concurrency rate also matters a great deal for Citrix licensing. If you are using the XenApp Concurrent licensing, a license is checked out every time a user requests a session on a single device and returned to the pool when this session terminates. So, if you are absolutely sure that the most people that would ever be logged in at the same time is 300 and none of them would be launching sessions from more than one device, then, it would make perfect economical sense to purchase only 300 licenses. In reality, though, you would want to have some extra licenses in case of rapid growth or multidevice sessions. For RDS, on the other hand, concurrency does not matter at all. When you purchase RDS licensing, you need to take into account that any user who will ever need to connect to an RDS-based session will need a license. So, for this scenario, we would need at least 600 RDS licenses to ensure that every user will be able to connect to the RDS hosts. XenApp can also be licensed as part of XenDesktop on a user/device model.

Active Directory considerations

Part of defining your user base is understanding how users are currently grouped within the Active Directory domain of your organization. Groupings will largely depend on the hierarchy of your organization. For example, everyone from the accounting department might be a member of the same logical function-based container or they might be part of a more location-oriented structure. How your users are grouped and the type of software that is to be published will ultimately determine the number of Delivery Groups in XenApp and how Citrix policies will be applied to them. Studying the AD and GPO infrastructure of your domain is a necessary step in laying the foundation of your XenApp environment.

User location

Last but not least, you need to define the connection type of your users. From a networking standpoint, connections to the XenApp environment can be categorized as internal and external. An internal session request is one that originates within the company's **Local Area Network (LAN)** inside an internal firewall. Examples of internal users include any personnel that use the company's internal Ethernet and Wi-Fi. An external session (for example, third party vendors) request is one that originates from a device on an outside network and is usually filtered through one or more firewalls that form a **Demilitarized Zone (DMZ)**. NetScaler can be placed in the DMZ to load balance connections to backend servers and the gateway feature can be leveraged as a first point of authentication for external users. Examples of external users include telecommuters, remote contractors, traveling sales personnel, and others. Determining the ratio of external to internal connections is key to providing the most efficient experience for your employees. Prior to 7.x, XenApp had a zoning feature that allowed servers to be separated geographically with a dedicated **Zone Data Collector** assigned to each zone and users could be directed to the zone closest to their region for optimal performance based on priority. Since XenApp 7.6 uses the **FlexCast Mangement Architecture**, the zoning feature is no longer available and best practice dictates that if a deployment has to span across multiple locations that introduce high latency, a separate XenApp site should be configured for each distinct physical location. For instance, a data center on the West Coast would have its own set of highly-available Delivery Controllers, SQL servers, and VDA images that are independent from the ones on the East Coast. If Citrix **Provisioning Services (PVS)** is in use, the farm-based hierarchy of PVS allows for multiple sites to reside under the same farm, but often times, it makes sense to also separate PVS sites into their own individual farms to avoid sharing the same SQL server in high latency scenarios.

Devices and peripherals

Knowing about endpoint device types and their OSes will empower you to create a consistent experience for your users. You can create session policies in NetScaler Gateway to apply specific filters based on the device type (for example, Windows, Mac, iPhone, Android, and so on). Almost every endpoint has one or more peripherals. Some peripherals already have virtual channels and can readily be mapped into a user session. For the ones that do not have virtual channels, you can leverage USB redirection policies configured on an Delivery Controller. Citrix has made XenApp 7.6 USB 3.0 ready, so any USB devices based on the 3.0 standard can be used within a XenApp session. Other examples of peripherals that have virtual channels in XenApp 7.6 are nonspecialty keyboards, mouse, microphones, speakers, webcams, CD/DVD, and smart cards.

Networks

In this book, we will use a traditional enterprise network layout for our XenApp deployment that consists of the following three main components:

- **External network**
- **DMZ**
- **Internal network**

An external network is any network that is outside a corporate LAN. DMZ is the Demilitarized Zone between an external-facing firewall and an internal firewall. An internal network is where all your backend servers (such as XenApp, StoreFront, Exchange, SQL, and Active Directory) exist. Let's take a moment to review the following diagram that puts a combined Citrix solution in the context of an enterprise network:

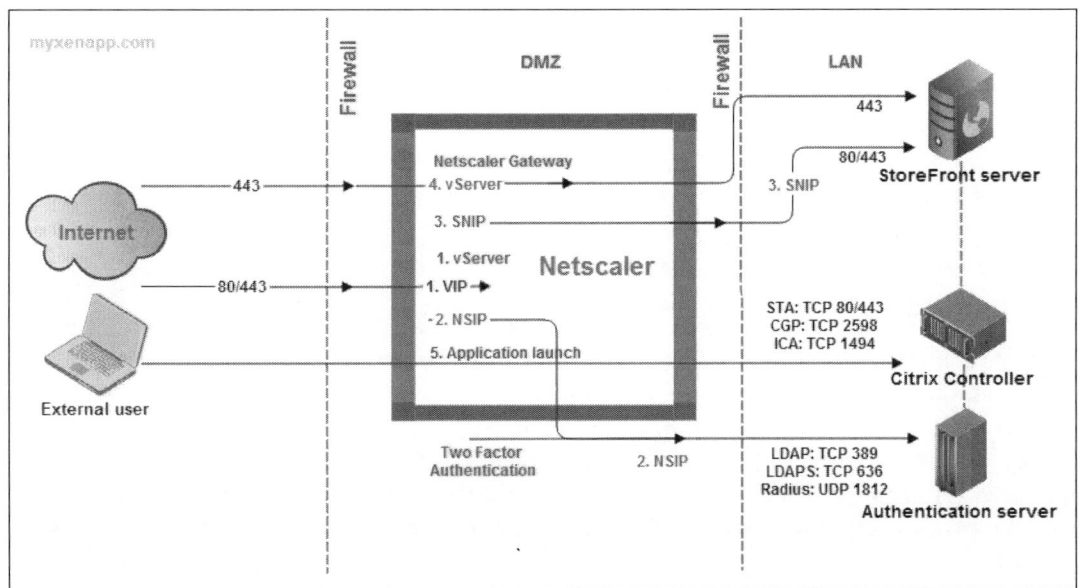

A network layout (External-DMZ-Internal) by Murugan B Iyyaooan, which is available at www.myxenapp.com. © Citrix Systems, Inc.

An external user is given a URL, such as `https://access.yourcompany.com`, which resolves to a public IP, that is NAT-ted to a NetScaler Gateway virtual server IP in the DMZ on port `443`. This vServer presents a user with an authentication page, and once credentials are validated, it passes the connection to the backend server. If load balancing is enabled on the NetScaler, the connection to the StoreFront server is load balanced by a traffic management vServer that can be configured to terminate SSL on an appliance. It can also use port `80` to send the connection to the internal environment, or it can serve as a proxy and pass the SSL connection along port `443` for end-to-end encryption. NetScaler uses a **Subnet IP address (SNIP)** to communicate with internal networks.

There are many other possible scenarios that may be a better fit for your environment, such as double-hop DMZ for which Citrix has released several articles. However, for the purpose of this environment, the assumption of External/DMZ/Internal will hold true throughout the book.

Having some knowledge about the routing and switching of your network can also help with the design, especially with regard to NetScaler and load balancing in general. The NetScaler will typically reside between two firewalls in the DMZ. Some smaller companies that don't actually have a DMZ might deploy it directly on the internal network. When designing your Citrix architecture, you should have frequent discussions with your networking team to ensure that your design will actually be feasible on your company's network.

Storage

Storage can present bottlenecks that are very hard to deal with, so it is important to understand the implications of running XenApp in an enterprise environment. This book will not advocate any particular type of storage and what you have today largely depends on your company's existing infrastructure and budget. Fibre Channel (FC), iSCSi, NFS, and even local storage all have their advantages and disadvantages, and XenApp is mostly agnostic to which type of storage you choose as long as you have a thick enough pipe to handle the increased I/O from **Machine Creation Services (MCS)** and PVS target streaming. In terms of storage devices and tiers, you will almost always have faster performance with **solid-state drives (SSDs)**. Most industry recognized storage vendors offer all-flash arrays or a combination of flash and spinning disks for performance intensive workloads. The following table reveals the supported storage types and protocols depending on the hypervisor in use as noted in the Citrix product documentation. The items marked with asterisks are recommended in this documentation:

Virtualization resource	Local Disks	NFS	Block Storage	Storage Link
XenServer	Yes	Yes *	Yes	No
VMware	Yes (no vMotion or dynamic placement)	Yes *	Yes	No
Hyper-V	Yes	No	Yes * (requires Cluster Shared Volumes)	No

Storage types that are supported by XenApp 7.6 , which are available at edocs.citrix.com. © Citrix Systems, Inc.

In this book, for ease of deployment, we will use a storage that is local to the hypervisor. However, if you attach LUNs from SAN and create datastores on your hypervisors, the Delivery Controller will see them the same way as it sees local disks—as just another storage repository.

Profiles

The next step in the environment discovery process is to identify the type of profiles that are configured for existing users. Whenever a user establishes a new XenApp session, a profile is created for them on the XenApp server. There are four profile types in Windows—mandatory, roaming, local, and temporary. In an enterprise domain, depending on security requirements, users are typically assigned either mandatory or roaming profiles. A **mandatory profile** is a template profile assigned to each user when they login to their physical machine or virtual instance, which is deleted upon logoff and all user data generated during the session is erased. Many healthcare and financial institutions use mandatory profiles because of their simplicity and significantly smaller administration overheads as compared to other types of profiles. A **roaming profile**, on the other hand, is one that retains user data upon logoff and stores it on a network share. This type of profile follows the user, and during logon, it loads settings and transfers any files stored on the profile share for use within the session. Roaming profiles provide greater flexibility to the user as they can store important data inside their profile system, but they increase administration and bandwidth overheads as files have to transverse the network when users log on. If no profile policy is defined, a user will be assigned a **local profile** based on the default user profile in Windows on each XenApp server that is accessed. While this would allow changes to be retained on each machine individually, the profile would not be synced and would not be accessible on a new server. As far as temporary profiles are concerned, they usually get created when an error condition prevents the user from getting their regular profile. Citrix XenApp comes bundled with **Citrix Profile Management** (also known as UPM or Universal Profile Management) that can optionally be configured on the Delivery Controller to enable the centralized management of user profiles.

Citrix® Profile Management

UPM is a customizable solution tailored specifically to Citrix environments (such as XenApp application delivery, XenDesktop VDI, and physical desktops). UPM is not a requirement for XenApp but is rather a tool that can be leveraged to take over profile management from Microsoft. Admins have experienced numerous issues over the years with profile corruption and inconsistencies and these are exactly the points addressed by Citrix. In contrast to Windows roaming profiles, UPM only writes back modified settings to the profile share instead of all settings, which prevents a setting from being overwritten in simultaneous sessions. The following diagram illustrates a multisession scenario without UPM:

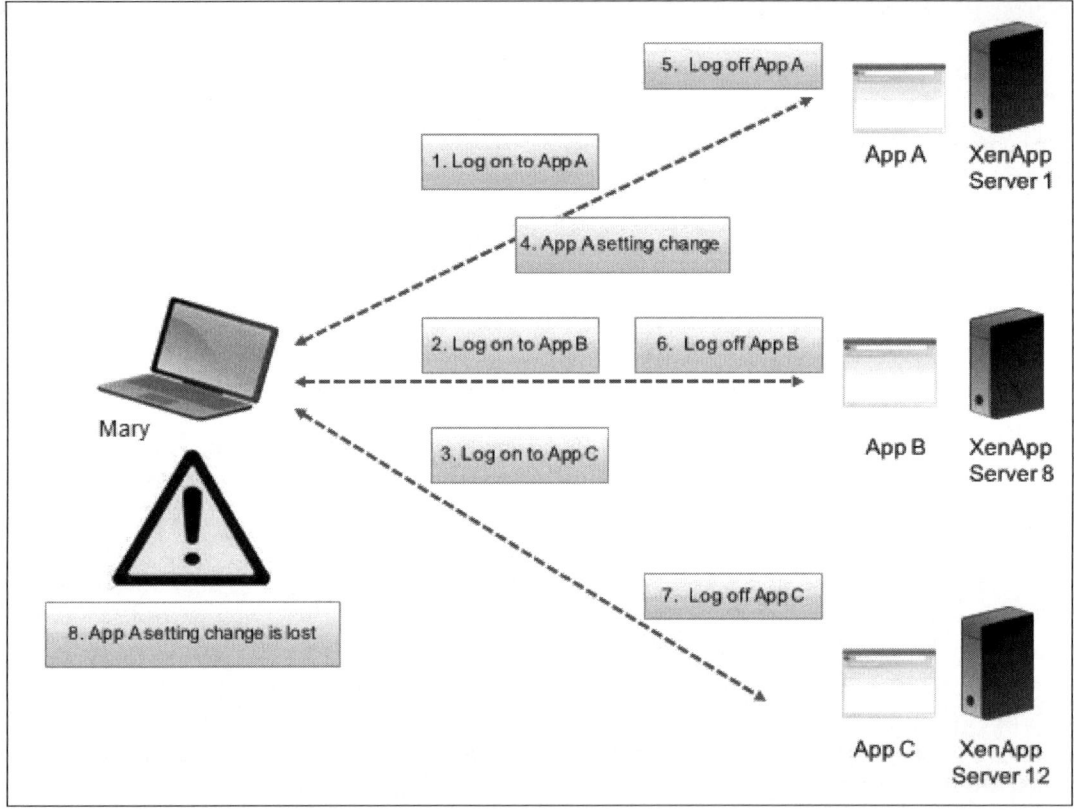

A multisession scenario without UPM, which is available at www.support.citrix.com. © Citrix Systems, Inc.

Another benefit of UPM is that it can be configured to reduce profile bloating. Many times in the past, I've seen profiles reach gigantic sizes due to users constantly saving data in their profiles or applications and browsers storing cache files in them. To alleviate and avoid this issue, exclusion lists are available in the UPM administrative template in Group Policy where administrators can exclude certain items from being synchronized back to the profile share, and are thus dragged along with the user. The ADM template contains multiple Group Policy settings that can be used to configure UPM and profile behavior with the desired level of granularity.

Folder Redirection

To minimize the user profile size, Citrix also recommends using **Folder Redirection** (**FR**), which allows you to isolate user folders, such as Documents, Pictures, and Music from the user profile and save them to a dedicated UNC share separate from the profile. With UPM, you can integrate existing Microsoft FR settings or completely delegate FR management to XenApp by configuring Citrix-based group policies in Citrix Studio.

In *Chapter 4*, *Installing and Configuring Citrix XenApp®*, you will learn how to configure Citrix Profile Management with both mandatory and roaming profiles as well as FR. Ultimately, it will be up to you to decide which profile type is the best fit for your environment. However, this chapter should give you a good baseline to find the right solution.

Core applications

The ultimate goal of the XenApp software is to deliver published applications and desktops to end users at any time, anywhere, and on any type of device. To achieve this, the discovery of all business applications that your users work with today needs to be conducted and a list of requirements needs to be compiled for each department (accounting, sales, and HR). These applications will then be installed on a master image (also referred to as a golden image) from which several XenApp server agents will be deployed in **production**. In this case, accounting will need QuickBooks, sales will get IE10 with a preconfigured **Software-As-a-Service (SaaS)** URL to their salesforce.com login, and HR will get UltiPro. In this book, we will demonstrate how to publish single application instances as well as a full desktop experience via hosted shared desktops.

Printing

Printing in a large enterprise can be very complex and a major pain point for IT administrators. Keeping track and providing the right printers to the people who need them, while maintaining print drivers and connectivity are just some of the everyday challenges faced by admins. To centralize printer management and standardize driver maintenance in the XenApp environment, we will be taking advantage of Citrix **Universal Print Server (UPS)** and **Universal Print Driver (UPD)**. With UPD, we would not need to install any drivers on the XenApp servers as it supports most major business and consumer printer brands. We will also demonstrate working with both local and network printing. In Citrix terms, network printing is also referred to as session printing. Due to the critical importance of printers in a Citrix XenApp environment, *Chapter 12, Printing*, is dedicated to this topic and will discuss Citrix policies and printer administration in detail.

Creating your first architecture

Now that you have conducted an assessment of all the relevant components in your existing environment, it is time to create your first architecture design. This will be composed of Citrix XenApp, StoreFront, Provisioning Services, XenServer, and NetScaler, and it will attempt to resemble real-world scenarios as closely as possible. Some components, such as NetScaler, are optional, albeit strongly recommended and will be marked as such throughout the book. So let's start with creating a description of the specifications of the environment. You can skip the next subsection on physical hardware if you already have a hypervisor in place.

The host hardware

To host hypervisors, you can use any enterprise servers that are certified by your hypervisor vendor. Citrix, VMware, and Microsoft have a Ready program that thoroughly tests and certifies hardware (visit http://www.citrix.com/, http://www.vmware.com/, or http://www.microsoft.com/ for more information). Typically, larger companies have long-term relationships with certain vendors and this is what determines their hardware preferences. Some popular and well-established server brands are Cisco **Unified Computing System (UCS)**, Dell PowerEdge, HP ProLiant, and Lenovo System X (formerly by IBM). Here are the generic specifications for the physical server that will host your hypervisor platform sustain 600 XenApp users:

- Four physical servers (three active and one passive to help achieve *N+1* redundancy)
- Dual 12-core Intel Xeon E-series processors

- 96 GB of RAM per server
- Two or more 1 Gb or 10 Gb NICs
- Two 300 GB 15K RPM SAS drives (this is optional if you're not using local storage)

Keep in mind that specs can vary based on the type of workloads that these servers are used for as well as your personal preference on scaling up versus scaling out. This is only to be used a basic starting point.

The VM infrastructure

The VM infrastructure indicates a breakdown of the number of VMs needed per hypervisor host and the function of each VM in a Citrix environment. In this design, 12 XenApp Server OS machines are planned to account for 300 concurrent users (out of a total user base of 600). Every environment is different and thorough testing should be performed during proof of concept, and third-party vendor documentation should be leveraged to identify CPU and memory requirements for the applications being used. As an example, if 25 users launch applications from a single server and the corresponding processes in **Task Manager** average 500 MB per user, then the total amount of memory expected to be utilized by only these apps is 12.5 GB per server. You should always allow extra resources in order to avoid reduction in performance.

Host A

The following resources are required for Host A:

- One XenApp 7.6 Delivery Controller
- One StoreFront 2.6 Server
- One Citrix Provisioning Server 7.6
- Four Windows Servers with VDA installed
- One NetScaler VPX (optional but recommended)
- One SQL Server (not needed if SQL is already in place)
- One Citrix License Server

Host B

The following resources are required for Host B:

- One XenApp 7.6 Delivery Controller
- One StoreFront 2.6 Server
- One Citrix Provisioning Server 7.6
- One XenApp Master Image
- Four Windows Servers with VDA installed
- One NetScaler VPX (this is optional, although recommended for HA)
- One SQL Mirror Server (this is not needed if SQL mirroring is already in place)

Host C

The following resources are required for Host C:

- Four Windows Servers with VDA installed
- One Citrix Universal Print Server

Resource allocation

Each environment is different and the amount of resources for each will vary greatly based on system utilization and the nature of user applications. In this deployment, we will use the following resource allocation scheme:

- XenApp 7.6 Controllers (two vCPUs, 4 GB RAM, and 48 GB hard drive)
- StoreFront Servers (two vCPUs, 4 GB RAM, and 48 GB hard drive)
- Windows Servers with VDA installed (six vCPUs, 20 GB RAM, and 48 GB hard drive)
- NetScaler 10.5 Virtual Appliances (one vCPU and 2 GB RAM)

Microsoft licensing

We use Microsoft licenses for the Windows Server OS and RDS. The following resources are required for this:

- Four Windows Server 2012 Datacenter licenses
- 600 Remote Desktop Services licenses
- Volume Microsoft Office licensing (KMS)

Citrix® licensing

We use Citrix licenses for XenApp and NetScaler (optional). XenServer Standard Edition is available for free and Enterprise is paid. However, most Enterprise features, such as GPU virtualization and **Dynamic Workload Balancing**, are included in the XenApp entitlement. These are the available licensing models:

- XenApp 7.6 Platinum Edition
- NetScaler VPX Platinum Edition

Examples from the IT field

Before we go ahead and conclude this chapter, I would like to provide some real-world examples from consulting projects that I've been heavily involved in, which demonstrate use cases for Citrix XenApp from the field.

- A nationwide transportation company implemented hosted shared desktops via XenApp for its fleet division to use locally installed applications. Lock down policies were put in place to ensure that no administrative changes could be made by users to the shared desktop image.

- A leading credit institution implemented hosted applications via XenApp for its teller workforce in branch locations in order to be able to work with legacy banking apps that are no longer supported in later OSes, such as Windows 7 and 8.

- A major hospital in the Southeast U.S. implemented XenApp to host performance-intensive **Electronic Medical Records (EMR)** software. High-capacity XenApp servers were dedicated to an individual application that was published for end users (a method formerly known as **application siloing**).

Summary

In this chapter, we laid the foundation for your first XenApp deployment. We defined the existing components of your environment and how they would fit into the Citrix stack. We examined infrastructure components, such as network, storage, Active Directory users, profiles, and printers. We also defined endpoint devices and peripherals that users operate with for their day-to-day activities. Being aware of the existing environment and the requirements for the future system allowed us to project what specifications will be necessary to build it from a hardware and compute (CPU and memory) perspective as well as software licensing for Citrix and Microsoft. In this case, we allocated enough resources to the physical hosts to allow for future growth, and we assigned specific processor, RAM, and hard disk specs to support core applications for accounting, sales, and human resources. The design was conducted as part of an IT project plan that is regularly employed in consulting engagements.

Now that we have designed the architecture, and we have a clear goal for the environment, we can move forward with deployment preparation. In the next chapter, we will explore specific system requirements for each component of the Citrix solution and ensure that we cover all prerequisites before the implementation project is started. Stay tuned!

3
Preparing Your System for XenApp® Deployment

As we approach the beginning of the XenApp implementation, there is a list of prerequisites that have to be met to ensure that the Citrix software will install and function properly. Building on the architecture designed in the previous chapter, we will deploy Citrix VMs on top of a hypervisor (in our case, XenServer). The entire Citrix infrastructure will use Windows VMs (both server and client side, except for NetScaler), so the first step is to create the VMs outlined in the previous chapter, design your hypervisors, and install an OS on them. In this chapter, we will use a layered approach to examine the system requirements for all Citrix components. The following layers will be analyzed in detail:

- Access layer
- Resource layer
- Control layer
- Hardware layer

Each layer in the Citrix infrastructure has a function to either deliver, manage, or access published applications and desktops. By ensuring that all the required components are in place prior to deploying Citrix XenApp, you can avoid costly delays during installation and configuration that can slow down the project. The system requirements described in this chapter are largely based on the Citrix product documentation (also known as Citrix eDocs), so you can always use the content at http://support.citrix.com/proddocs/ as a reference. However, what this chapter does differently from the eDocs is that it provides additional comments for each section, detailing not just the *what*, but also the *why* and *how* of each component. The following diagram illustrates the infrastructure layers of XenApp 7.6:

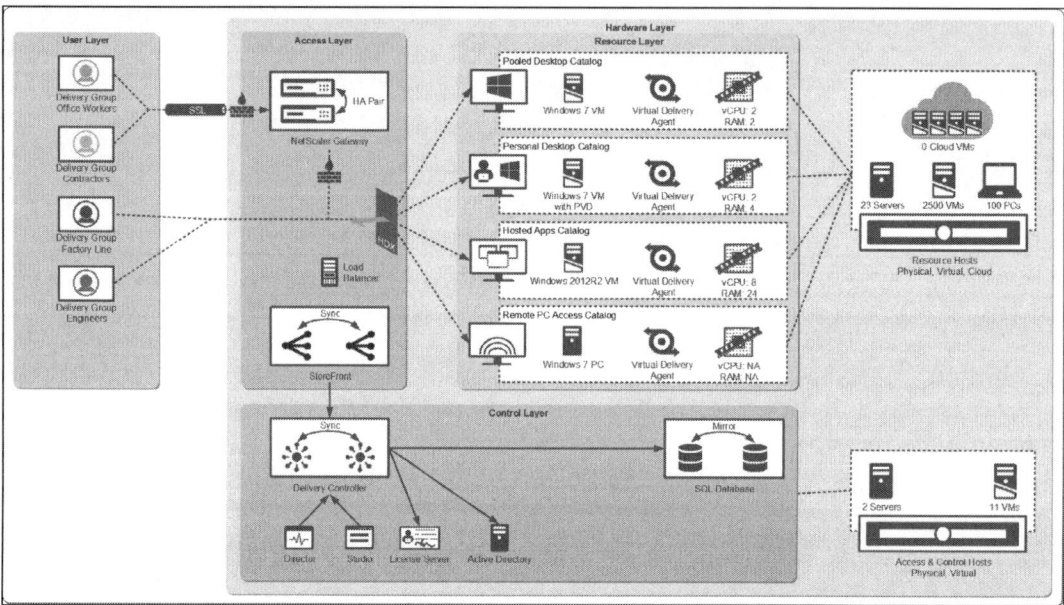

The infrastructure layers of XenApp 7.6, which can be found at http://blogs.citrix.com/. © Citrix Systems, Inc.

Control layer

The control layer in a Citrix environment consists of the Delivery Controller, License Server, Active Directory, and SQL server. Citrix Studio is the management console on DDC, and Citrix Director is an integrated monitoring tool with a web console. Both Studio and Director are considered part of the control layer. Let's take a closer look at the system requirements for the components of the control layer.

XenApp® Delivery Controller

XenApp 7.6 **Delivery Controller**, previously known as **Desktop Delivery Controller (DDC)**, supports the following OSes:

- Windows Server 2012 R2 (Standard and Datacenter)
- Windows Server 2012 (Standard and Datacenter)
- Windows Server 2008 R2 SP1 (Standard, Enterprise, and Datacenter)

As you can see, under the newest version of XenApp and XenDesktop, Windows 2003 is not supported for DDC. The Windows 2003 OS became obsolete on July 14, 2015 and vendors are quickly dropping it from their product lines as well. If you are deploying a brand new XenApp or XenDesktop 7.6 environment from scratch, then you will only have the option of using one of the supported platforms. However, if you are building a new environment to migrate existing workloads, you will need to consider the impact of implementing newer OSes in your infrastructure. For instance, some apps cannot run on Windows 2012 because of legacy code.

The following Windows components are required for DDC:

- Microsoft .NET Framework 3.5 SP1 (for Win2K8 R2 only)
- Microsoft .NET Framework 4.5.1 or 4.5.2
- Windows PowerShell 2.0 (on Windows 2008 R2) or 3.0 (on Windows 2012 and 2012 R2)
- Visual C++ 2005, 2008 SP1, and 2012 redistributable packages
- 100 MB of disk space as a minimum requirement (without connection leasing)

Citrix® Studio

Citrix Studio is a management console on the XenApp Delivery Controller. As a component of DDC, Citrix Studio can run on the same OSes that are supported for DDC. However, because it can be run remotely, it also supports Windows 7 (Professional, Enterprise, and Ultimate editions), Windows 8 (Professional and Enterprise), and Windows 8.1 (Professional and Enterprise). The requirements for the underlying components include:

- A minimum of 75 MB disk space
- Microsoft .NET Framework 4.5.1 or 4.5.2
- Microsoft .NET Framework 3.5 SP1 (for Win2K8 R2 and Win7 only)
- Microsoft Management Console 3.0 (built in for all supported OSes)
- Windows PowerShell 2.0 (included with Win2K8 R2 and Win7) or 3.0 (included with Win2012, 2012 R2, 8, and 8.1)

Citrix® Director

Citrix Director is an integrated monitoring tool included in the XenApp software bundle to help administrators track user activity and identify performance bottlenecks early on. The following OS platforms are currently supported for Director:

- Windows Server 2012 R2 (Standard and Datacenter Editions)
- Windows Server 2012 (Standard and Datacenter Editions)
- Windows Server 2008 R2 SP1 (Standard, Enterprise, and Datacenter Editions)

The following specifications are required for the software to install and run properly:

- 50 MB of hard disk space.
- Microsoft .NET Framework 4.5.1 (4.5.2 is also supported).
- Microsoft .NET Framework 3.5 SP1 (Windows Server 2008 R2 only).
- Microsoft Internet Information Services (IIS) 7.0 and ASP.NET 2.0. If these are not already installed, you are prompted for the Windows Server installation media, and then they are installed for you.
- Supported browsers to view Director are listed as follows:
  - **Internet Explorer (IE)** 11 and 10. IE compatibility mode is not supported and can lead to problems while accessing a web console. The default settings should be applied when installing IE.
  - Firefox ESR.
  - Chrome.

Citrix® License Server

Upon purchase of XenApp or the XenDesktop software, you will receive a link to your MyCitrix account where you will be able to review and download Citrix license files. License files need to be imported to the Delivery Controller during the XenApp site configuration or later from a licensing node in Citrix Studio. In order to be able to use these licenses, however, a Citrix **License Server (LS)** is required. The LS component is part of the XenApp Delivery Controller installation media and can be installed either locally or on a dedicated server. To reduce overheads on the Delivery Controller, a separate machine is recommended for licensing. The minimum supported version for XenApp 7.6 is Citrix License Server 11.12.1, and we will install this on a VM that is designated for licensing.

SQL Server

DDC requires a SQL database to actively store and access data about the XenApp site structure and user activity. SQL Express is supported for product evaluation purposes only and is not recommended in production due to its limited functionalities. A dedicated SQL server is recommended, and the following SQL versions for a **site configuration database** are supported:

- SQL Server 2014 (Express, Standard, and Enterprise editions)
- SQL Server 2012 SP1 (Express, Standard, and Enterprise editions)
- SQL Server 2008 R2 SP2 (Express, Standard, Enterprise, and Datacenter editions)

If the Controller does not detect a supported version of an existing SQL software, it provides an option to automatically install SQL Express 2012 SP1.

Citrix best practice dictates that every XenApp and XenDesktop environment should have a highly available SQL database solution by leveraging one of the following supported features of SQL:

- SQL Server mirroring
- SQL Server clustered instances
- SQL Server 2012 and 2014 **AlwaysOn Availability Groups**

SQL Server mirroring

SQL Server mirroring is a Microsoft SQL feature that enables High Availability by maintaining a standby copy of a database (frequently referred to as a **mirror database**) of a production database (also known as a **principal database**). In case of a failure of the principal database, SQL mirroring provides an option for the mirror database to become active and workloads to be failed over almost instantaneously. Typically, the mirror database resides on a secondary SQL server known as the **mirror server**. There are three operating modes in a mirrored environment: high-performance (asynchronous), high-safety without automatic failover (synchronous), and high-safety with automatic failover (synchronous). The latter requires a third server called a **witness server**. Since it's only synchronous with the witness server, which provides automatic failover, Citrix recommends using this model to ensure minimal impact on user connections during a database outage. The following diagram illustrates the process of SQL Server mirroring:

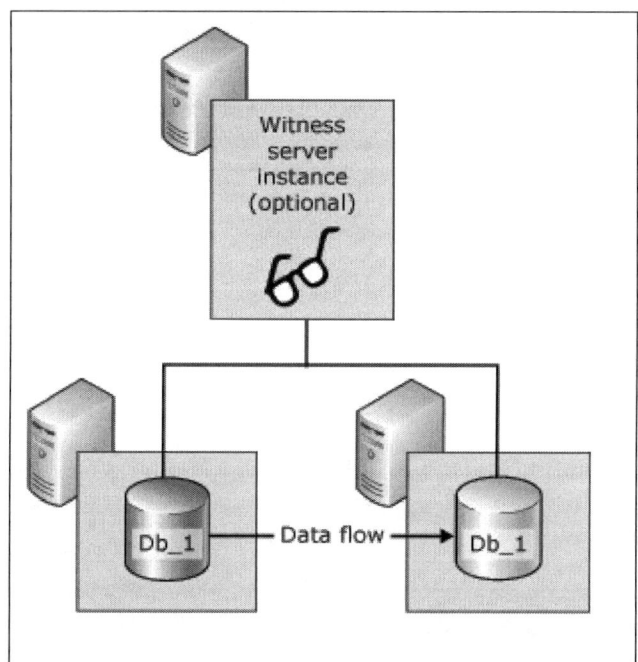

SQL database mirroring (synchronous), which can be found at www.msdn.microsoft.com

SQL Server clustered instances

Another method of ensuring **High Availability (HA)** for the XenApp site database is to employ SQL Server clustered instances (also known as **AlwaysOn Failover Cluster Instances**). In a clustered scenario, a single copy of the database resides on shared storage, and the **Windows Server Failover Clustering (WSFC)** feature is used to enable a **failover cluster instance (FCI)**. Even though FCI appears as a single SQL instance to a user, it actually represents multiple SQL nodes, and if one node fails, FCI provides redundancy by failing over workloads to another node that is available to serve the database. Traditionally, Citrix has recommended mirroring over clustering due to the simplicity of the mirroring setup.

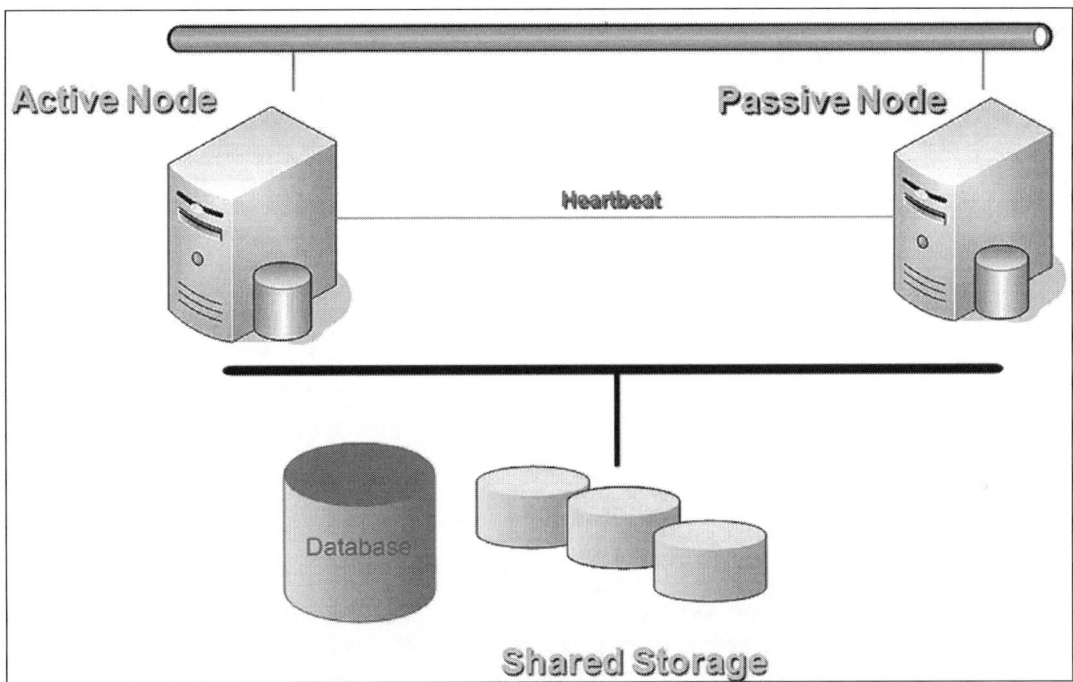

A SQL failover cluster with WSFC, which can be found at www.mssqltips.com

AlwaysOn Availability Groups

The third supported option to achieve HA for the XenApp database is to implement the AlwaysOn Availability Groups feature, which was introduced by Microsoft in SQL 2012. Much like the SQL Server FCIs, AlwaysOn Availability Groups leverage the use of WSFC. AlwaysOn, however, generally does not depend on shared storage. An **Availability Group** is a predefined set of databases that can fail over at a replica level where each SQL instance has a local copy of an availability database that corresponds to an Availability Group. The following diagram illustrates the basic structure of WSFC and AlwaysOn Availability Groups:

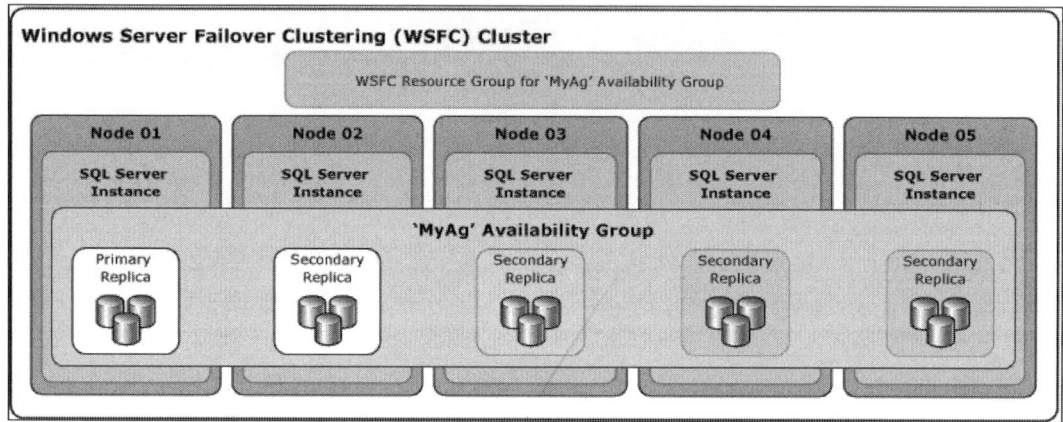

Windows Server Failover Clustering (WSFC) and AlwaysOn Availability Groups, which can be found at www.msdn.microsoft.com

Database permissions

Certain permissions are needed for XenApp services and administrators to be able to perform tasks on the XenApp database in SQL. Two types of permissions exist in XenApp 7.6 — **administrative** and **runtime**. The most routine operations on the XenApp Delivery Controller are executed by one of the XenApp services at runtime, and each of these services communicates with the SQL database through the machine account of the Controller. For example, if the local Controller's **Fully Qualified Domain Name (FQDN)** is xadc.pvsguy.com, then the machine account entry in SQL would appear as PVSGUY\XADC$. Since the XenApp services running on the Controller are created automatically when the XenApp software is installed, there should be no need for the manual assignment of machine account permissions. Examine the following table for a detailed outline of the runtime permission model:

Database Role	Corresponding XenDesktop Service
ADIdentitySchema_ROLE	AD Identity Service
chr_Broker chr_Controller	Broker Service
ConfigurationSchema_ROLE	Central Configuration Service
DesktopUpdateManagerSchema_ROLE	Desktop Update Manager Service
HostingUnitServiceSchema_ROLE	Hosting Management Service
MachinePersonalitySchema_ROLE	Machine Personality Service

The XenApp database runtime permissions, which can be found at http://support.citrix.com/article/CTX127998. © Citrix Systems, Inc.

Administrative permissions are ones that enable a user to perform administrative tasks in Citrix Studio, including the initial XenApp site creation. For this type of operation, the user needs to be assigned access rights to the SQL server by the person in the organization who manages the SQL infrastructure (usually the database administrator). This user will need to have both server roles and database roles. Examine the following table for an exact reference of administrative permissions:

Operation	Purpose	Server Roles	Database Roles
Database Creation	Create suitable empty database for use by XenDesktop. See note [1] below.	dbcreator	
Schema Creation	Create all service-specific database schemas and add first controller to site.	securityadmin	db_owner
Add Controller	Add controller (other than the first) to site.	securityadmin	db_owner
Add Controller (mirror server)	Add controller login to the database server currently in the mirror role of a mirrored XenDesktop database.	securityadmin	
Remove Controller	Remove controller from site.	See note [2] below.	db_owner
Schema Update	Apply schema updates/hotfixes.		db_owner

XenApp database administrative permissions, which can be found at http://support.citrix.com/article/CTX127998. © Citrix Systems, Inc.

Database collation

Database **collation** is a set of rules that define how characters are represented in bits and how they are sorted and compared. For the XenApp and XenDesktop 7.6 SQL database, the supported collation is Latin1_General_100_CI_AS_KS. This is created for you if you use Studio to automate the XenApp site deployment. However, if you are using database creation scripts in SQL, you need to ensure that this is the collation set in the script.

All in all, it is critically important that prior to starting the XenApp deployment, we have met all the database prerequisites as this will help us to have a smooth installation and configuration of the XenApp site.

Citrix Provisioning Services™

Provisioning Services is a Citrix technology designed to deliver an operating system to endpoint devices or virtual machines over a network via an optimized UDP streaming protocol. PVS uses the **Preboot eXecution Environment (PXE)** capabilities of a client's network card to carry out a boot sequence in which the client gets an IP address from a DHCP server and uses a bootstrap file to connect to the PVS server farm. After this, a read-only OS image (vDisk), which is contained in a VHD file, is streamed to the clients. Upon reboot of the client, any changes made to the target device OS are discarded and a new image is loaded on the next boot. PVS allows IT administrators to manage a single vDisk and update it on the fly without any downtime for users. In fact, PVS is such a crucial technology in today's Citrix enterprise environments that the entirety of Chapter 9, *Building Your First XenApp® Farm – Provisioning Services™*, is dedicated to the installation and configuration of Provisioning Server 7.6. This provisioning methodology is an alternative to **Machine Creation Services (MCS)** on the Delivery Controller, but device collections are still integrated in to DDC as machine catalogs.

PVS 7.6 has console, server, and agent software. The console and server software are installed on a virtual or physical machine with a server-class OS, such as Windows 2008 R2 or Windows 2012/2012 R2 and the Microsoft .NET Framework 4.0 is required similar to many other applications developed for Windows. The Agent is installed on the master image where the VDA software is present, which is then converted to a VHD via a built-in tool called P2PVS.

Access layer

The access layer in a Citrix environment is the infrastructure that connects users to their applications and desktops on a corporate network. In a typical deployment with external, internal, and a DMZ network, users coming in from the outside connect to a NetScaler Gateway vServer on the DMZ, which, upon successful validation of credentials, sends the connection over to a load-balanced StoreFront vServer on the NetScaler (again in the DMZ). The HTTP or HTTPS vServer then uses a SNIP to connect to the internal network where the actual StoreFront servers are, and through a load balancing algorithm it chooses which StoreFront server to hand the connection to, so that the user can be presented with their assigned resources. In the case of a user who's requesting access from the internal network, the browser (Receiver for Web) or Receiver stores URLs hit by the user. These can be set up to resolve to the load-balanced HTTP or HTTPS StoreFront vServer on the NetScaler directly, so that you can bypass the NetScaler Gateway. Once the user is in, StoreFront obtains the application and desktop assignments from the Delivery Controller and presents them to the user.

Citrix® StoreFront™

Citrix StoreFront is a component of the XenApp and XenDesktop installation that provides an access point for users to applications and desktops delivered by the XenApp and XenDesktop solutions. StoreFront aggregates resources into stores that users can access via a software deployed on their devices, called Citrix Receiver, or using Receiver for Web by browsing a web store. StoreFront was developed to replace Web Interface, which has been widely used in the past as a resource aggregation tool and is still supported by Citrix until 2016. Web Interface, however, is based on the J# programming platform, which has been deprecated by Microsoft, and thus, Citrix has moved away from it in favor of the more versatile StoreFront. The software is a component of the XenApp and XenDesktop installation media, and it can be installed on the same machine as the XenApp Delivery Controller or on a dedicated Microsoft **Internet Information Services (IIS)** server. In *Chapter 5, Installing and Configuring StoreFront™*, we will use two dedicated machines for the StoreFront software, which are recommended in enterprise environments to ensure High Availability. The following OSes are supported for Citrix StoreFront:

- Windows Server 2012 R2 (Standard and Datacenter Editions)
- Windows Server 2012 (Standard and Datacenter Editions)
- Windows Server 2008 R2 SP1 (Standard and Enterprise Editions)

 If multiple StoreFront servers are deployed, they have to run on the same OS version.

Since StoreFront is a web server, the Microsoft IIS role is required along with the .NET Framework. The following ports need to open on corporate firewalls for the StoreFront communication:

- TCP 80/443 are required for HTTP/HTTPS connections from an external to an internal network, and an internal to an internal network.

- TCP 808 is required for management communication between StoreFront servers on the internal network.

- A random TCP port is assigned from unreserved ports to use for communication between StoreFront servers in the same server group. A Windows firewall rule is automatically configured when StoreFront is installed, allowing access to the StoreFront executable. Check the rule after installation and make sure that firewall appliances outside the Windows VM don't block access on a randomly assigned port.

- TCP 8008 is required by Receiver for HTML5 for local users on the internal network to communicate with their respective StoreFront servers for clientless access.

The latest StoreFront version 2.6 supports both IPv4 and IPv6 networks as well as mixed IPv4 and IPv6 network stacks:

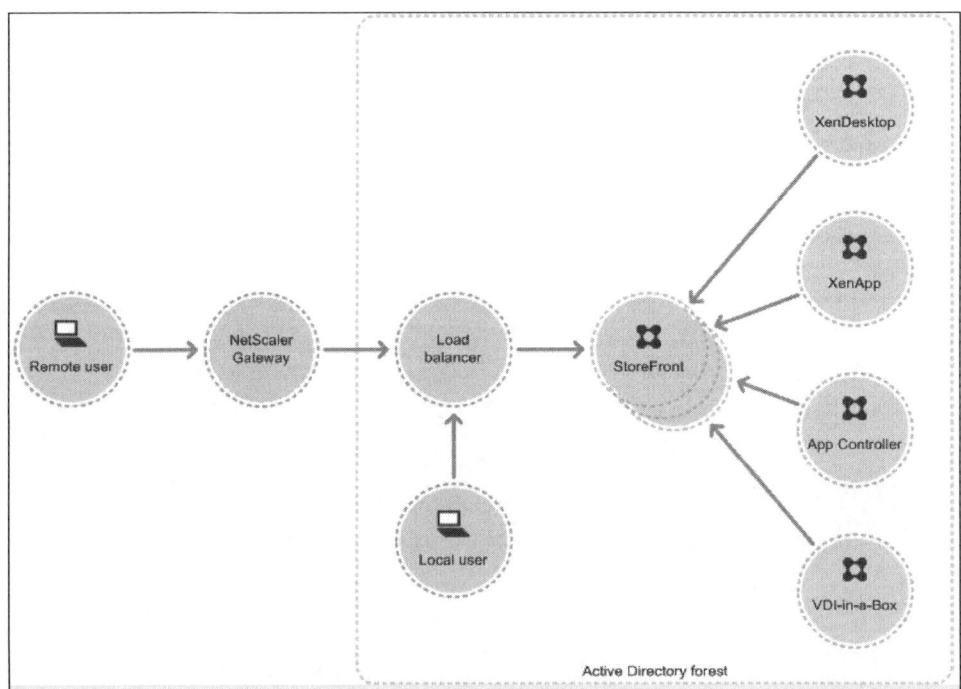

The Citrix StoreFront deployment (simplified), which can be found at www.support.citrix.com/proddocs. © Citrix Systems, Inc.

NetScaler VPX™

To load balance the connections going to the StoreFront servers, we will implement a highly available Citrix NetScaler VPX 10.5 Platinum Edition solution. VPX is a virtual appliance available for XenServer, VMware, and Hyper-V. NetScaler is also available as a standalone physical appliance with the MPX and SDX models, where MPX offers hardware acceleration for SSL offloads and SDX provides the opportunity to deploy multiple VPX instances on a single physical server. In *Chapter 6, Installing and Configuring NetScaler Gateway™*, and *Chapter 7, Load Balancing XenApp® with Citrix® NetScaler®*, we will build a Gateway and a load balancing solution for the XenApp environment. NetScaler can be used to load balance various protocols, such as HTTP, HTTPS, FTP, DNS, TFTP, and others, and it is widely employed in enterprise environments to optimize web and application server traffic for Citrix and non-Citrix (third party) workloads. Besides the features, the NetScaler licensing cost is based on throughput levels, and thus, it is very important to plan the type of workloads you will be leveraging NetScaler for ahead of time to ensure that you are licensed for the throughput you need. You also have the option to upgrade throughput licensing as needed:

Performance	VPX-10	VPX-200	VPX-1000	VPX-3000
HTTP throughput	10 Mbps	200 Mbps	1 Gbps	3 Gbps
SSL encrypted throughput	10 Mbps	200 Mbps	1 Gbps	1 Gbps
HTTP compression throughput	10 Mbps	200 Mbps	750 Mbps	750 Mbps
Application firewall throughput	10 Mbps	200 Mbps	500 Mbps	500 Mbps
Max concurrent TCP connections 2	5 million	5 million	5 million	5 million
New SSL requests/second	500	500	500	500
Max concurrent SSL VPN users 3	300	300	300	300

The NetScaler VPX performance throughput levels, which can be found at www.support.citrix.com. © Citrix Systems, Inc.

In this particular deployment, we use an HA active-passive pair of two NetScaler VPX-1000 lab appliances.

Citrix Receiver™

Citrix Receiver is a piece of software that runs on the user's client device in order to enable access to applications and desktops delivered through Citrix XenApp and XenDesktop via the ICA protocol. Receiver offers support for a wide variety of operating systems and endpoint devices, including Windows PCs, Linux machines, Mac, Android, BlackBerry, Chrome OS, iOS, and Windows phones (I am sure that I'm missing some, so always refer to the Citrix documentation for an updated list of supported devices). Receiver can be pushed out via StoreFront so that when first time users log on to their store, they are offered to download the software through **Group Policy Objects (GPOs)** or **System Center Configuration Manager (SCCM)**. Receiver for HTML5 provides the ability to run applications and desktops within a browser without the need to install any software locally on a client. Receiver for Windows provides the ability to configure **Single Sign-On (SSO)** authentication so that users do not have to type in their credentials every time they need access to their store:

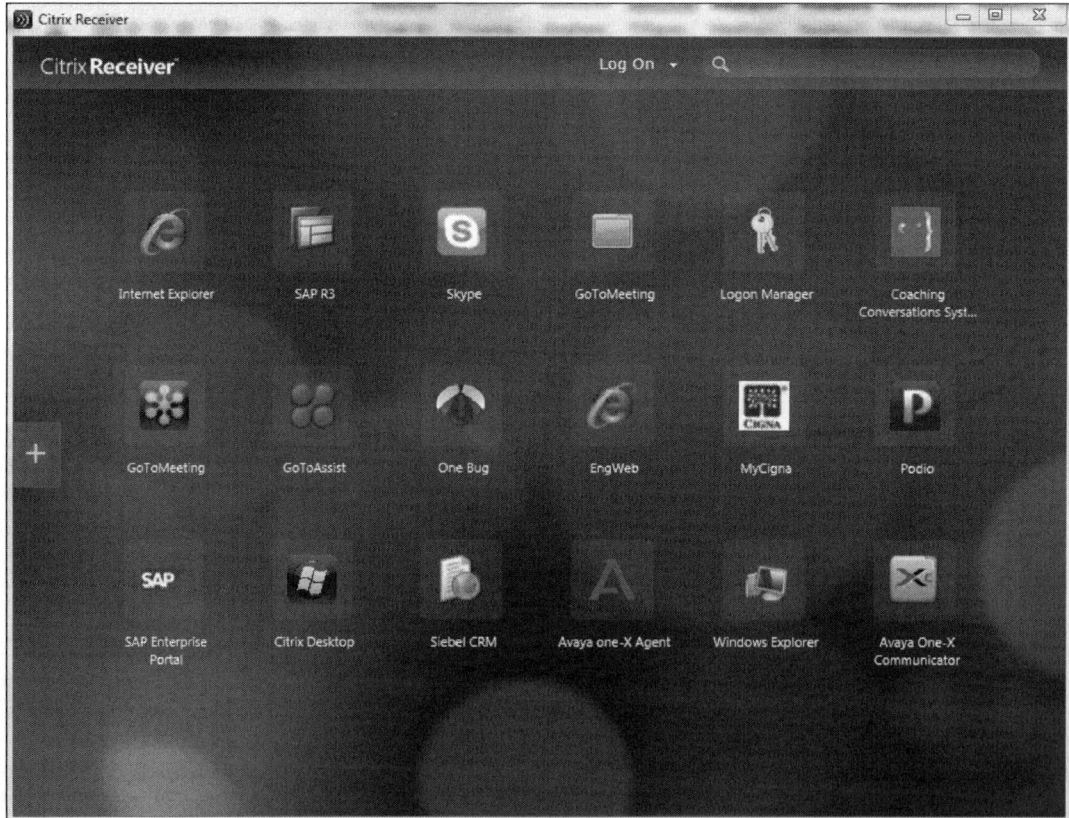

The User Store in Citrix Receiver for Windows

In this book, we will use Citrix Receiver for Windows to connect to a published application from a laptop. Receiver for Windows can be installed on any OS from Windows Server 2003 (both 32 and 64-bit) all the way up to Windows 2012 and also from Windows Vista to 8.1. It also supports Windows Thin PC without the **Self-Service Plugin** (**SSP**). In this particular deployment, we will use the latest version of Receiver for Windows 4.2.

Resource layer

After we've determined the system requirements for the control layer, it's time to define the resource layer. The resource layer is a set of applications, virtual desktops, and data that each user group in a XenApp environment is assigned to. For example, the accounting department will need access to QuickBooks, so the application will be virtualized on a server OS VM that has the Citrix **Virtual Delivery Agent** (**VDA**) installed on it. In this case, QuickBooks is part of the resource layer.

Server OS VDA

Citrix VDA is a component of the XenApp software that needs to be installed on a master image, which is used to deploy RDS-enabled XenApp servers. The VDA turns on communication from the agent machine to the Delivery Controller via the **Windows Client Foundation** (**WCF**) protocol, and also enables connectivity from client devices via the Citrix ICA protocol. The following OSes are supported for the VDA:

- Windows Server 2012 R2 (Standard and Datacenter Editions)
- Windows Server 2012 (Standard and Datacenter Editions)
- Windows Server 2008 R2 SP1 (Standard, Enterprise, and Datacenter Editions)

Similar to the Delivery Controller, note that Windows Server 2008 without the R2 SP1 is not supported as an underlying OS for the VDA. If not present already, the following components are deployed by the VDA install package:

- Microsoft .NET Framework 4.5.1 (Note that version 4.5.2 is supported as well)
- Microsoft .NET Framework 3.5 SP1 (if Windows Server 2008 R2 is the underlying OS)
- The Microsoft Visual C++ 2005, 2008, and 2010 32-bit and 64-bit runtime packages

You can either enable **Remote Desktop Services (RDS)** on the master image prior to installing the XenApp VDA or you can let the latter enable the RDS role automatically. In addition to RDS, if multimedia acceleration features, such as HDX MediaStream Windows Media Redirection are needed, the **Microsoft Media Foundation** feature needs to be turned on in **Server Manager**. We will configure and test HDX policies in *Chapter 11, Administering a XenApp® Environment - Server Management*, where **Media Redirection** settings will be examined in more detail.

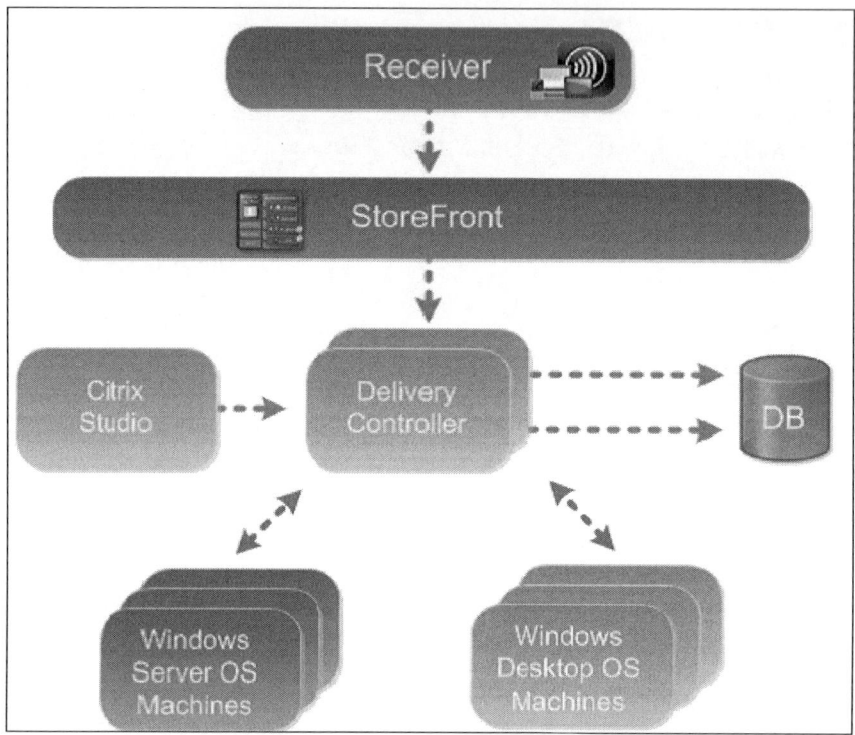

Windows Server OS machines with VDA as part of the Citrix Stack,
which can be found at www.blogs.citrix.com. © Citrix Systems, Inc.

The way in which we will deploy the VDA after we install and configure the XenApp site on the Delivery Controller is by creating a standalone virtual machine on the hypervisor that we will refer to as a master image. On the master image, we will install Windows 2012 R2 SP1, update the OS with the latest patches, and deploy the VDA from a XenApp ISO. Once this has been completed, we will create VMs from the Delivery Controller using MCS and from the Provisioning Server using PVS, to demonstrate both these methods that are available in XenApp 7.6.

Hardware layer

In a Citrix XenApp environment, the hardware layer is the sphere that contains a hypervisor and its underlying physical hardware. The hardware layer participates in the XenApp infrastructure by running the OS resources and keeping VM workloads highly available.

Host requirements

Since we've mostly focused on building a virtualized environment in this book, the entire Citrix infrastructure will reside on virtual machines running on a hypervisor. In this deployment, the XenServer hypervisor (version 6.2 SP1) will be used, but you can leverage your existing host infrastructure to build a XenApp solution as long as it is supported by Citrix. The following host platforms are currently supported for XenApp 7.6:

- XenServer
    - XenServer 6.5 (plus the latest hotfixes for maximum stability and performance)
    - XenServer 6.2 SP1 and 6.1

- VMware vSphere
    - VMware vSphere 5.5
    - VMware vSphere 5.1 Update 2
    - VMware vSphere 5.0 Update 2

 Note that the vCenter Linked Mode is not supported by Citrix at the time of writing this book.

- Hyper-V and SCVMM
    - SCVMM 2012 R2
    - SCVMM 2012 SP1
    - SCVMM 2012

XenApp 7.6 is also available for cloud deployments on **Amazon Web Services** (**AWS**) and Citrix CloudPlatform. For AWS, applications and desktops can be implemented on server OSes (XenApp model) only. AWS does not currently offer desktop OS builds (XenDesktop model). Also, **Amazon Relational Database Service** is not supported and SQL Server 2012 Enterprise is not offered on AWS.

For Citrix CloudPlatform, the following prerequisites need to be considered:

- As a minimum, CloudPlatform 4.2.1 with hotfixes 4.2.1-4 need to be in place
- There is no support for Hyper-V hypervisors
- VMware vSphere 5.5 is only supported with CloudPlatform 4.3.0.1

Domain infrastructure requirements

The Citrix XenApp and XenDesktop 7.6 software are tightly integrated with a domain environment and **Active Directory (AD)**. XenApp requires an Active Directory environment with DNS. All the components of the Citrix stack, including Delivery Controllers, server and DDAs, Provisioning Servers, StoreFront servers, and NetScalers, are connected to AD in one way or another. All components except NetScaler reside on Windows machines on a corporate network and, as such, they are required to be part of the AD domain. NetScaler is based on the FreeBSD computer OS and can be configured for AD authentication using an LDAP vServer. Citrix supports the following AD forest and domain functional levels:

- Windows 2000 native
- Windows Server 2003
- Windows Server 2008
- Windows Server 2008 R2
- Windows Server 2012
- Windows Server 2012 R2

Summary

In this chapter, we analyzed all the components of the Citrix XenApp design and reviewed their system requirements. To achieve this, we divided the Citrix infrastructure into four distinct layers: control, resource, hardware, and access. The layered approach allowed us to examine the role of each component from both the administration and end user perspective. We also discussed the supported XenApp database configurations and HA solutions for SQL in an enterprise environment.

At this point, you can finally sit back and relax because the theoretical part of this book is over! In *Chapter 4, Installing and Configuring Citrix XenApp®*, we officially launch our implementation of Citrix XenApp, which is probably what you've been waiting for all afternoon! Hopefully, with the knowledge acquired thus far, you are one step closer to not only installing, but also architecting your own environment.

4
Installing and Configuring Citrix XenApp®

We are finally here and ready to deploy Citrix XenApp in a virtual environment. In this chapter, we will install and configure the software in a guest OS on a hypervisor. The following step-by-step approach is undertaken during the installation:

- Creating a VM in XenServer
- Installing Windows 2012 R2 on a VM from a CIFS share
- Configuring networking and joining a machine to the domain
- Mounting the XenApp ISO image and installing the XenApp 7.6 software
- Creating another machine and installing Citrix License Server 11.12.1
- Configuring the XenApp site

Creating a VM in XenCenter®

Before we start deploying a XenApp environment, we need to create the VMs that the XenApp components will reside on. For this exercise, we will use Citrix XenServer as the underlying hypervisor. However, if you are already running VMware vSphere or Microsoft Hyper-V in your environment, you can build the XenApp infrastructure on top of those platforms, and the steps are very similar. Creating a new VM in XenCenter is a simple albeit very important task because that is when we define the CPU, memory, and disk space available for the machine and adapters that it will use to connect to resources on the network. At this point, we will build a new VM for the XenApp Delivery Controller, which is the main component of the control layer. You can always refer to *Chapter 3, Preparing Your System for XenApp*® *Deployment*, for a detailed list of system requirements, but in short, Citrix supports a minimum of 3 GB of RAM for the controller. It is always a good idea to assign more since this is a critical component of the XenApp environment. In this case, we go with 2 vCPUs and 4 GB of RAM, but if memory is not a constraint, 6 or 8 GB of RAM is also recommended to ensure that the Windows processes have enough RAM to operate and the OS is stable. Windows 2012 R2 will be the operating system used, but the Delivery Controller software supports 2008 R2 as well. We will now perform the steps that will allow us to create a VM in XenCenter, but if you already have a VM spun up and ready for XenApp installation, you can skip this section:

1. Open XenCenter and log on using `root` or another account with administrative access.

2. Next, right-click on the XenServer host and select **New VM...**:

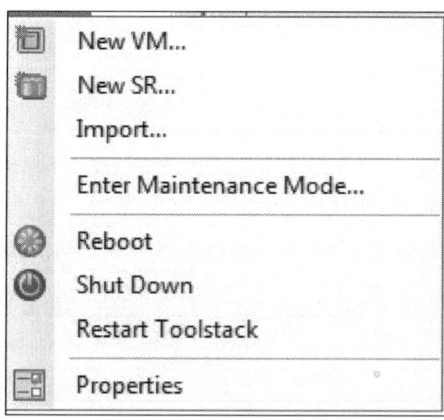

3. Upon launching the VM creation wizard, under **Template,** scroll down and select **Windows Server 2012 (64-bit):**

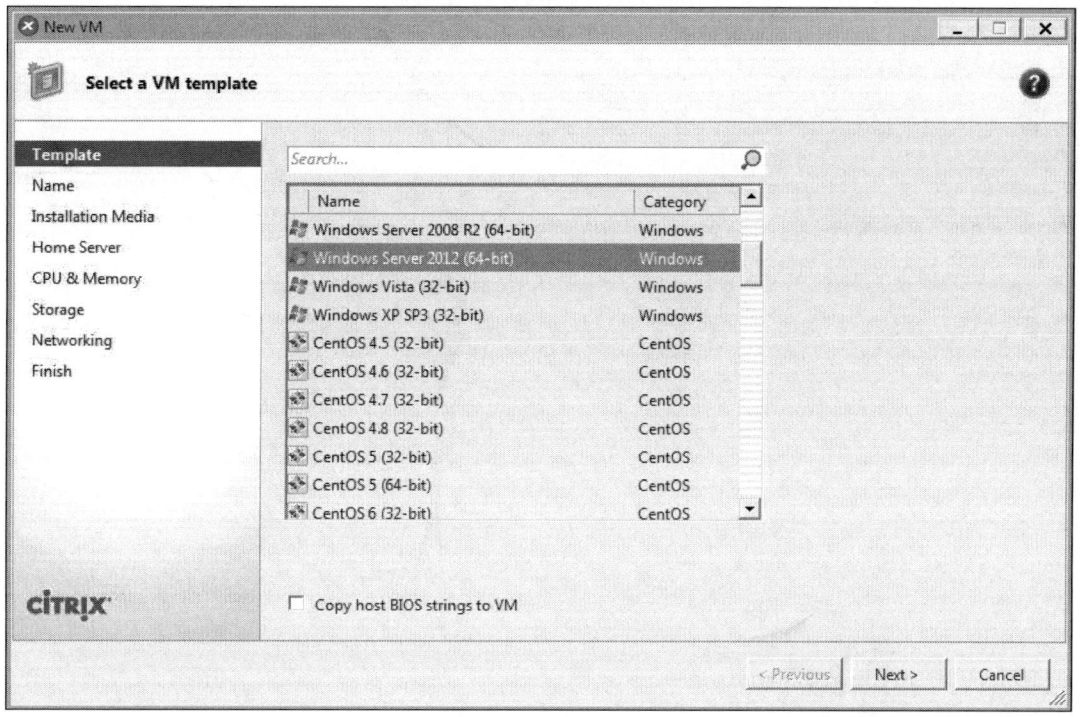

4. Under **Name**, type in a descriptive name for the new VM. I personally like to use what would be the hostname of the machine. In the **Description** field, you can enter more information about the role of the VM in your environment:

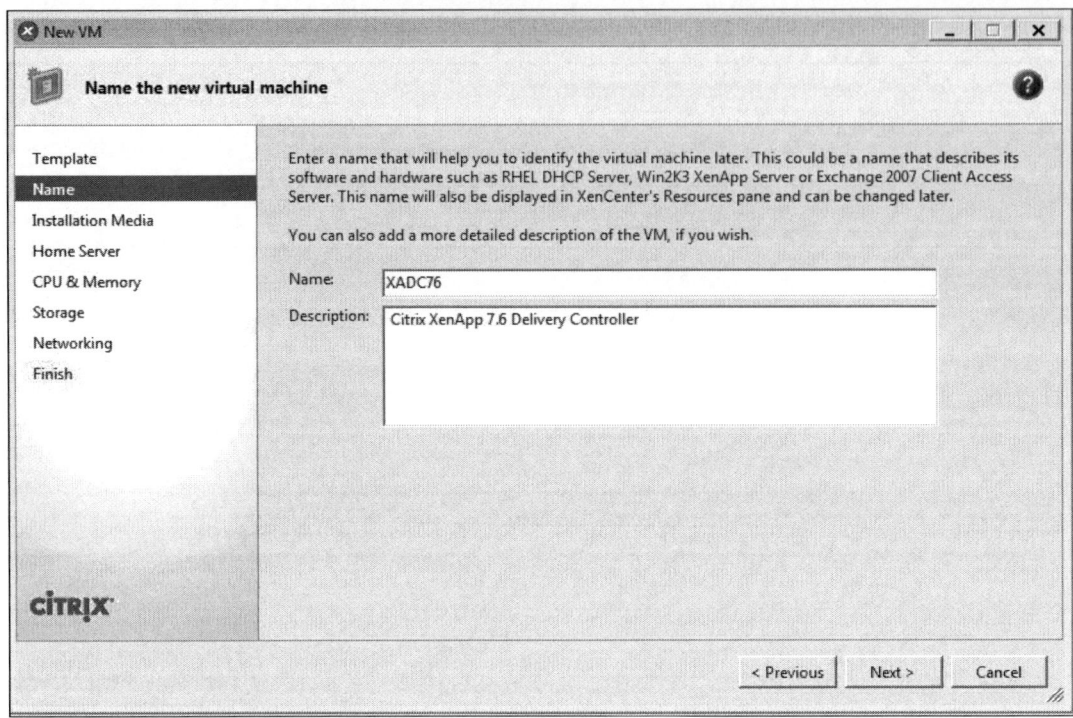

5. Under **Installation Media**, select the Windows 2012 R2 ISO image, that you downloaded from Microsoft from the CIFS share:

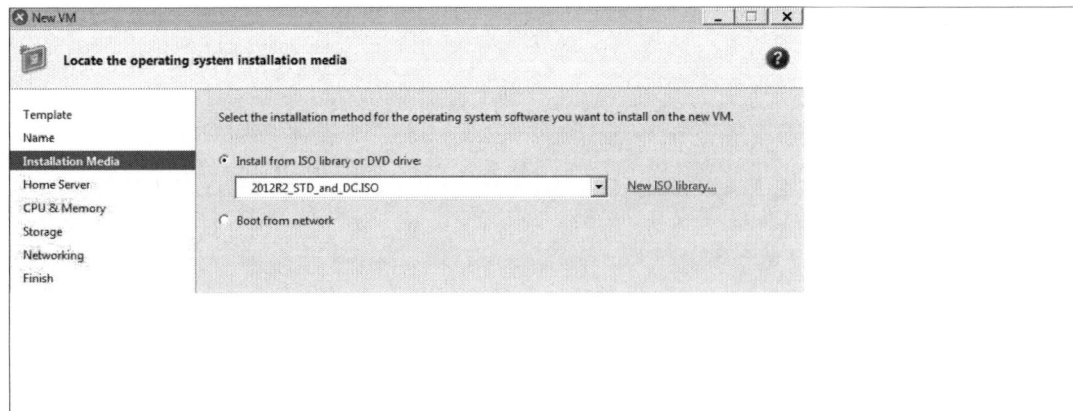

6. Next, under **Home Server**, select the hypervisor host you want this machine to reside and be powered on when possible. If you use shared storage, you can choose not to assign the VM to a specific server and leave XenServer to decide which one to use, based on resource availability:

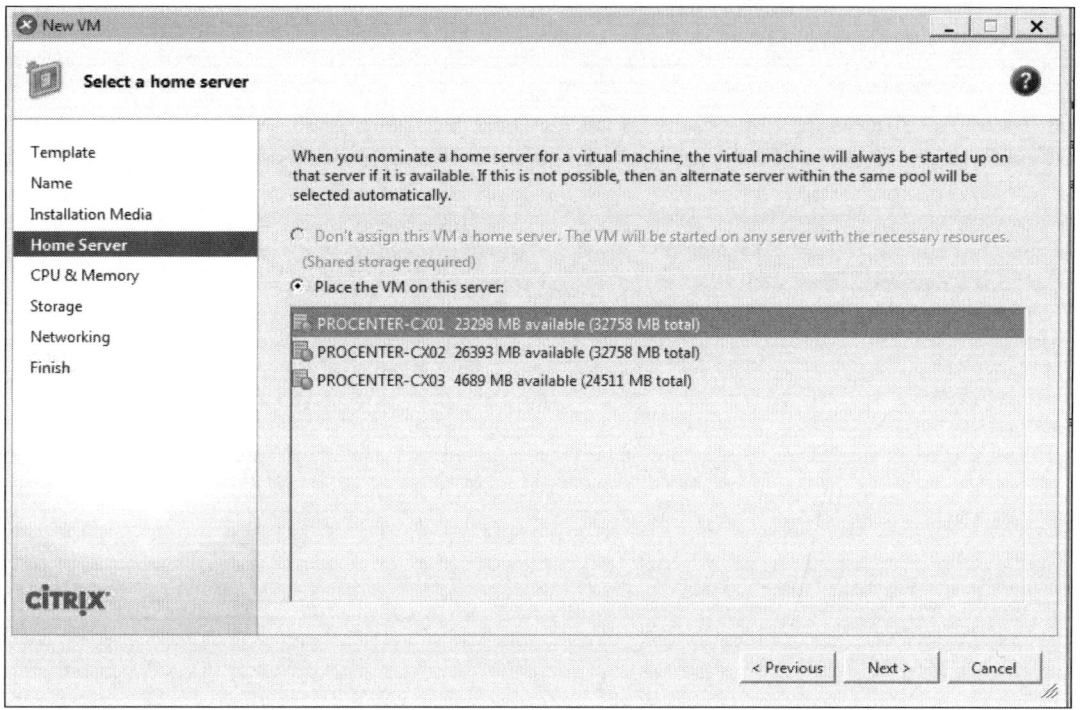

7. The next step defines the resources available to the VM. Under **CPU & Memory**, increase the value of the **Number of vCPUs** option to 2 and the value of the **Memory** option to 4096 MB. The default is 1 vCPU and 2048 MB of memory:

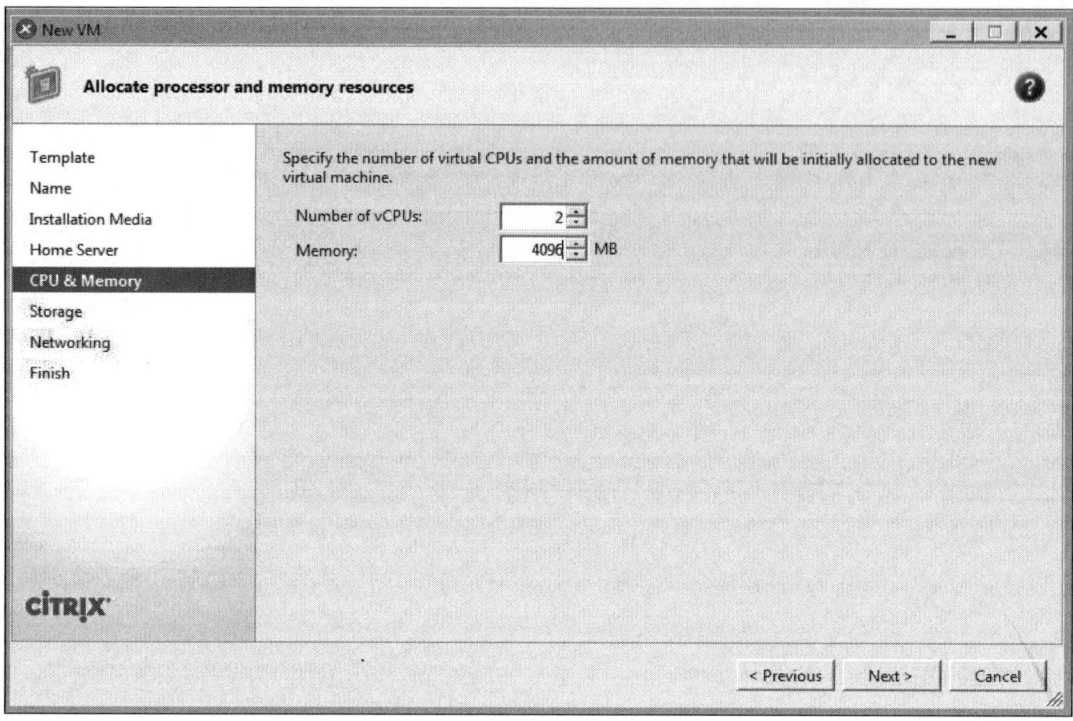

8. Under **Storage**, choose **Use these virtual disks**. Select the storage repository you want the VM's hard disk to reside on and click on **Properties**. Increase the size of the disk to 32.000 GB (default is 24), make sure the correct storage location is selected, click on **OK**, and then on **Next**:

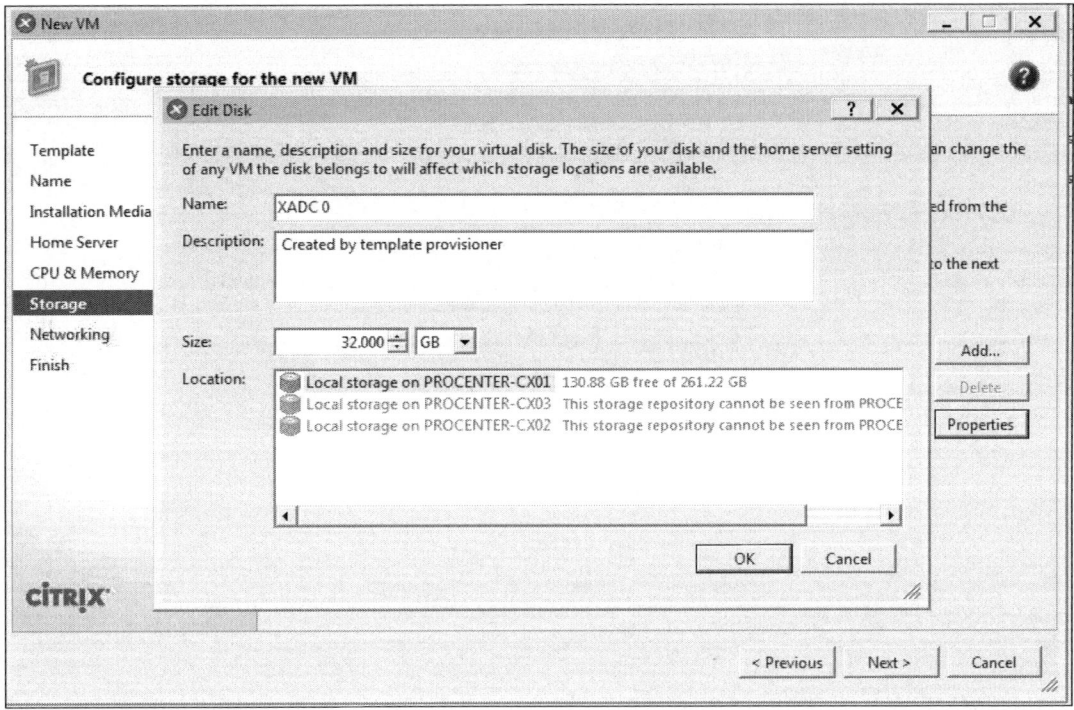

9. Under **Networking**, select the virtual **Network Interface Card (NIC)** for this VM and delete all the NICs that will not be in use. In our case, **Network 0** is selected with an autogenerated MAC address. If you would like to assign a static MAC address, you can click on **Properties** and enter one manually. Also, a QoS limit can optionally be enabled to limit the bandwidth consumed by the selected interface:

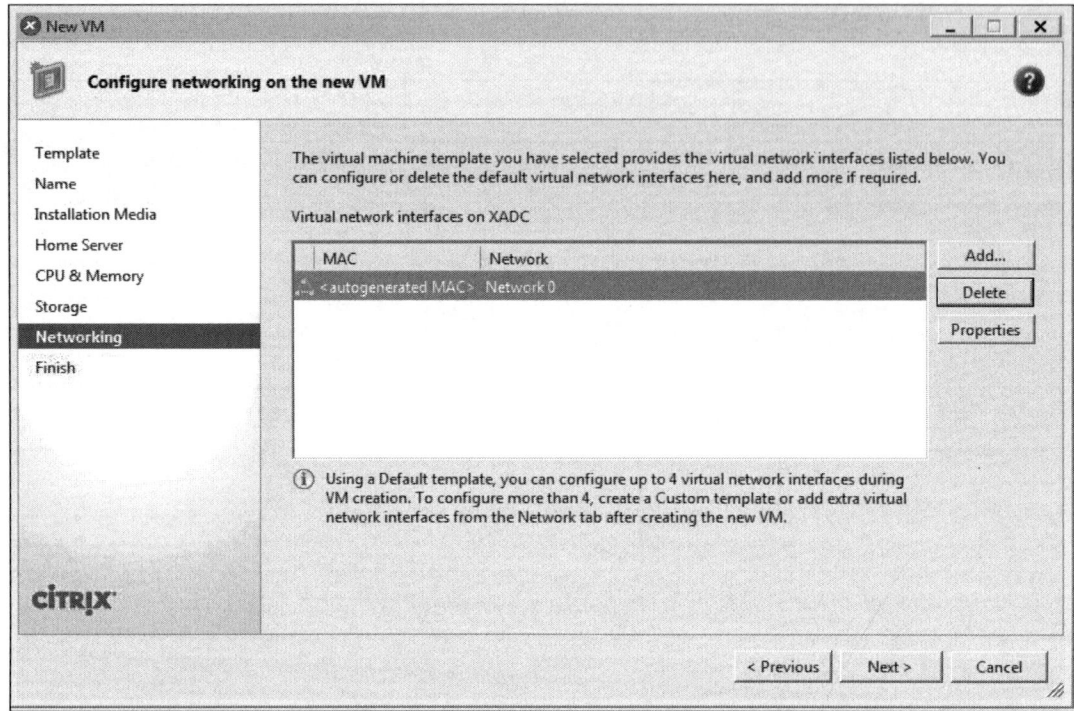

10. Click on **Next** and under **Finish**, review all the settings configured for this VM. Verify that **Start the new VM automatically** is selected and then click on **Create Now**:

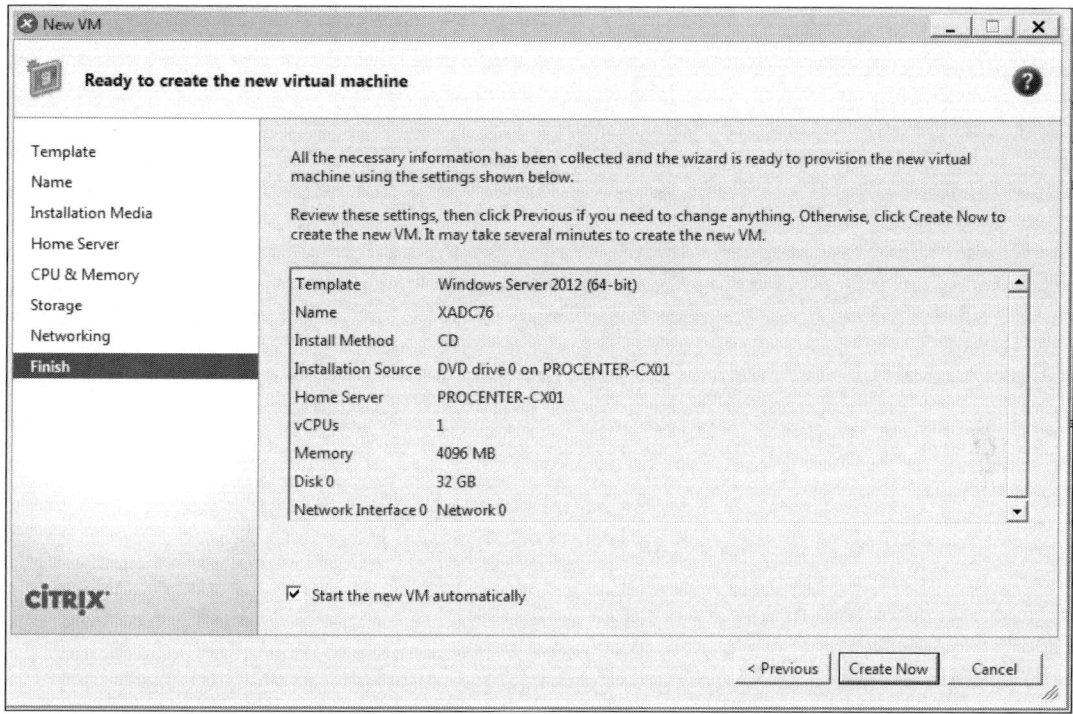

Depending on the resource availability of the host, the process can take a few minutes. In the **Logs** tab of the specified host in XenCenter, you can monitor the progress of the VM creation activity.

11. Once completed, the machine will show up in XenCenter, as shown in the following screenshot:

12. Once the machine is powered on, the Windows 2012 R2 installation will start automatically from the ISO media mounted on the CD/DVD drive of the VM. Go through the installation steps as you would normally do on a physical computer (for more information, follow the installation guide from Microsoft at `http://blogs.msdn.com/b/msgulfcommunity/archive/2013/03/06/installing-and-activating-windows-server-2012-step-by-step.aspx`).

13. Once completed, reboot if required and install the hypervisor tools by mounting the XenServer tools ISO to the CD/DVD drive of the VM, as shown in the following screenshot:

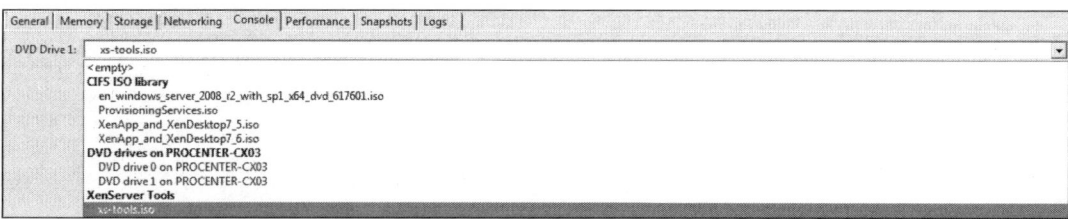

14. Complete any pending Windows updates on the VM for optimal performance and security and reboot if prompted.

15. Once the OS has completed all the installation and update tasks, assign it a **static IP** address by navigating to **Control Panel | Network and Internet | View network status and tasks | Change adapter settings | Properties** of Network Adapter | **IPv4 Properties**. This will ensure that your Delivery Controller has a constant IP address that the XenApp site will be associated with. This is very important in order for XenApp to function properly and avoid major outages. In **Computer Properties**, assign a **hostname** for this computer that follows the naming convention employed in your domain environment.

16. The next step after assigning a static IP address is to join the machine to the Active Directory domain. Use **Computer Properties** or **Server Manager** to perform that task and type in your domain administrator credentials when prompted. Once completed, reboot the machine if required.

Installing the Citrix XenApp® 7.6 Delivery Controller

In this section, you are going to install the Citrix XenApp 7.6 Delivery Controller onto the freshly-created VM on your hypervisor. For easier navigation, enable **Remote Desktop** in the Windows system settings of the VM to be able to logon via RDP. Use the following steps for installing the Citrix XenApp 7.6 Delivery Controller:

1. From the CD/DVD drive dropdown in XenCenter, mount the XenApp 7.6 ISO image. Browse D: and double-click on AutoSelect to launch the installer:

Name	Date modified
Citrix Receiver and Plug-ins	9/22/2014 9:20 PM
Documentation	9/22/2014 9:17 PM
Support	9/22/2014 9:20 PM
x64	9/22/2014 9:20 PM
x86	9/22/2014 9:20 PM
AutoRun	5/7/2014 8:24 AM
AutoSelect	9/4/2014 11:05 AM
ProductVersion	9/22/2014 9:20 PM

2. A new window should appear on the screen to select **XenApp** or **XenDesktop**. Right next to **XenApp**, click on **Start**:

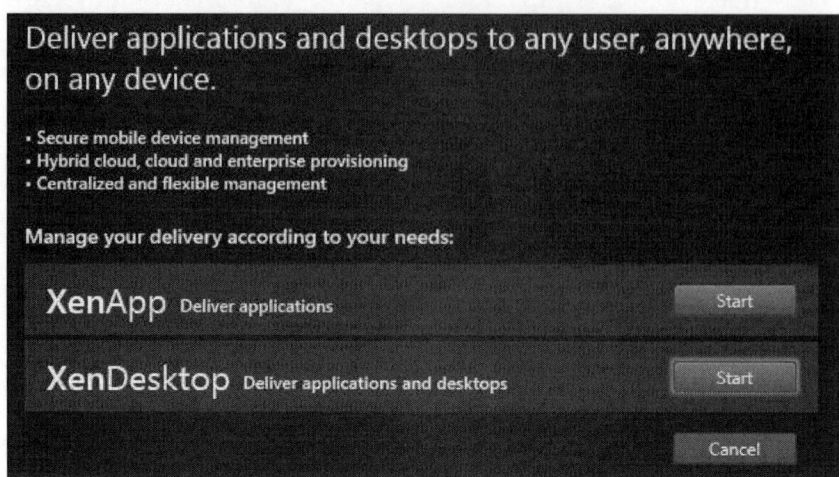

3. An installation menu appears on the screen where various options are available to install different components of the XenApp infrastructure. Since this machine will serve as the XenApp Delivery Controller, under **Get Started**, click on **Delivery Controller** to launch the installation wizard:

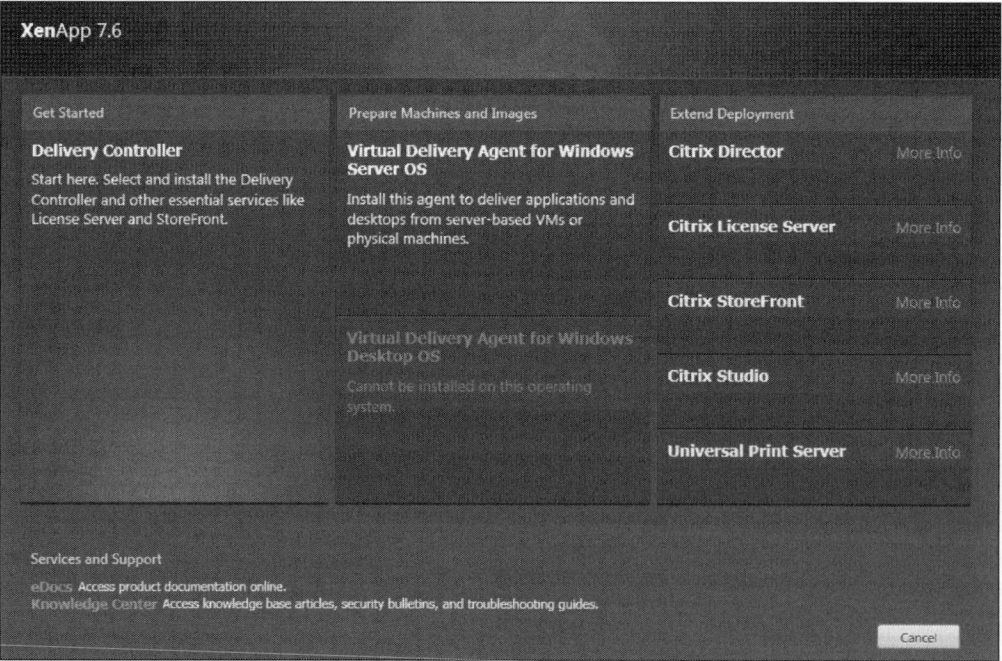

4. Read **CITRIX LICENSE AGREEMENT**, select **I have read, understand, and accept the terms of the license agreement,** and click on **Next**:

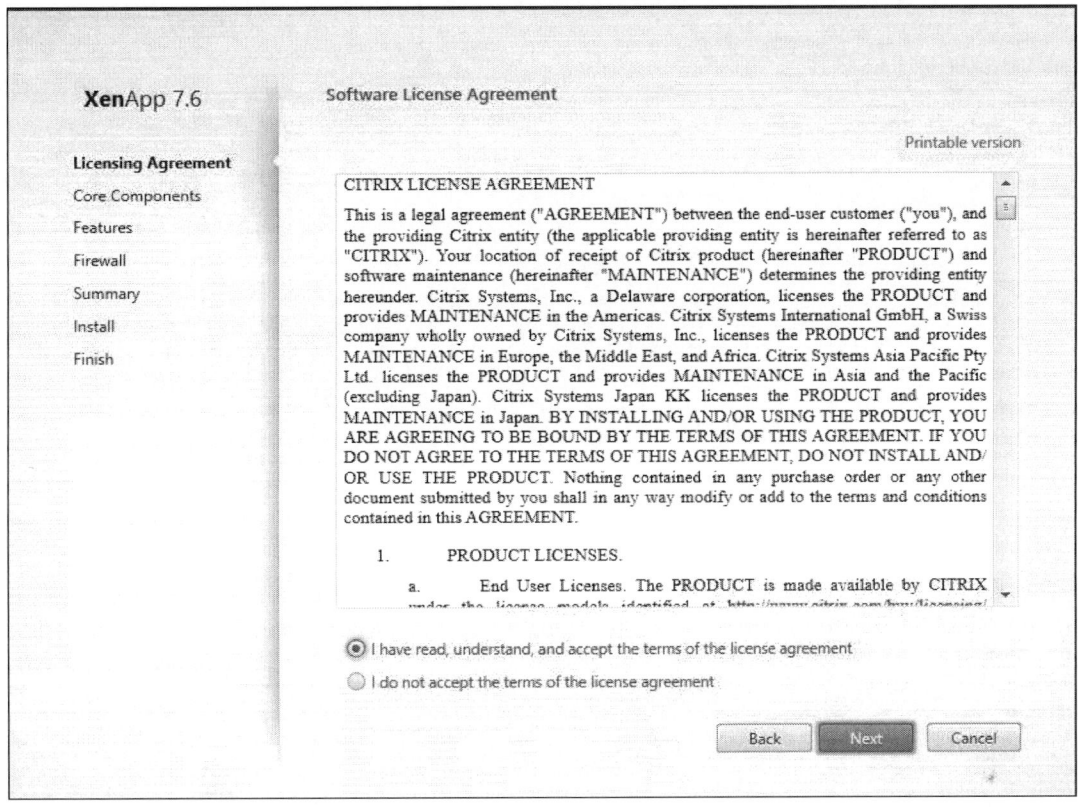

5. Under **Core Components**, select **Delivery Controller** and **Studio**. Uncheck **Director** and **License Server** as they will be installed on a separate, dedicated VM. In an enterprise environment, to build a fully redundant solution, it is recommended to use different machines for the various components of the XenApp software. This also reduces overhead on the Delivery Controller, allowing its resources to be concentrating on executing the core controller tasks. Now, click on **Next**:

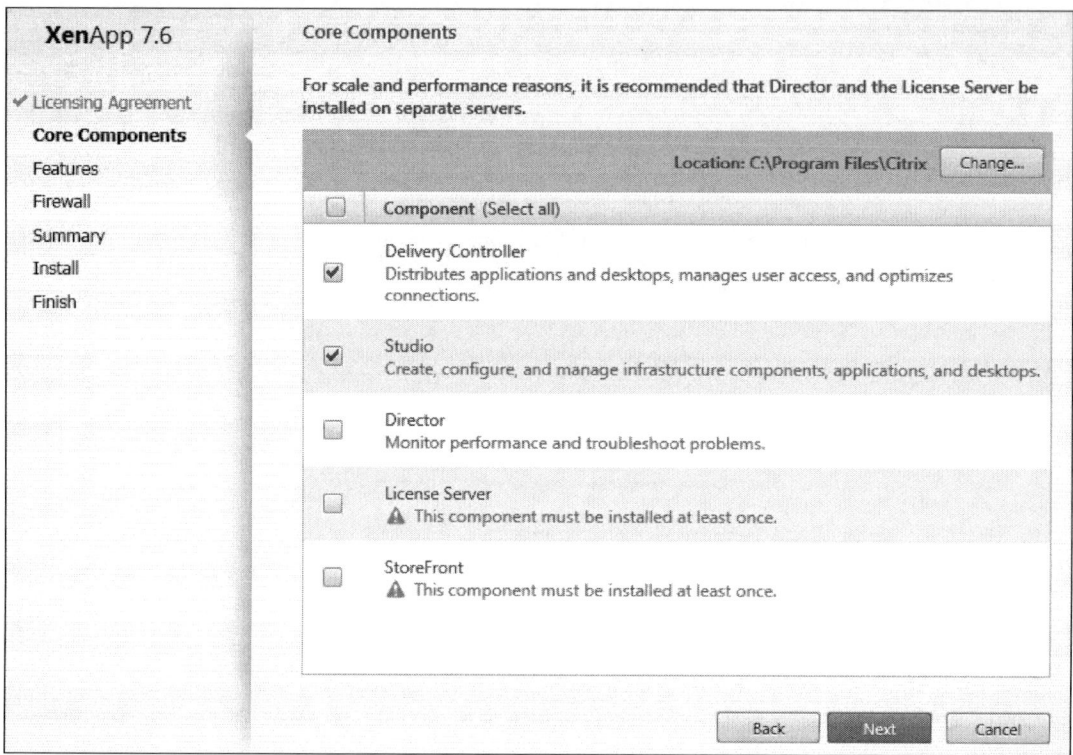

6. In **Features**, uncheck **Install Microsoft SQL Server 2012 SP1 Express**. SQL Express Edition is *not* recommended in production environments and is generally supported by Citrix for Proof of Concept and lab environments only. You can use it if you are deploying one of the latter two scenarios or just testing the XenApp product. Now click on **Next**:

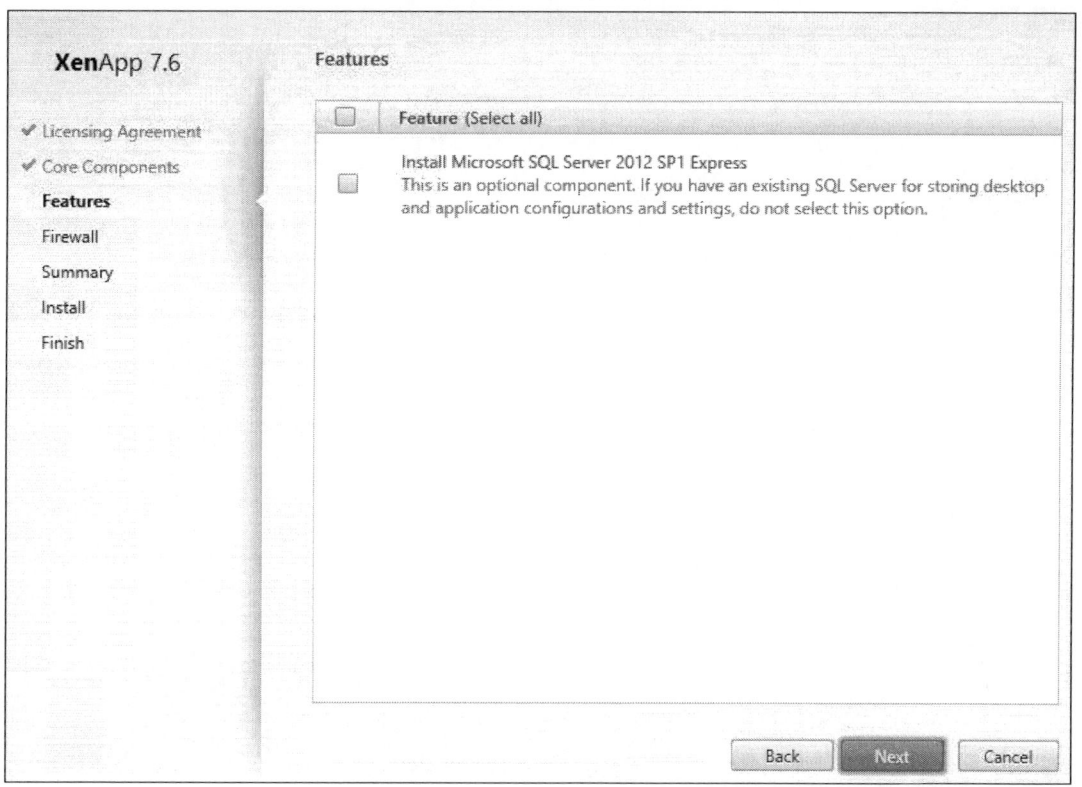

7. Next, make a note of the firewall ports and protocol information if you are configuring firewall rules manually. Otherwise, choose **Automatically** and click on **Next**:

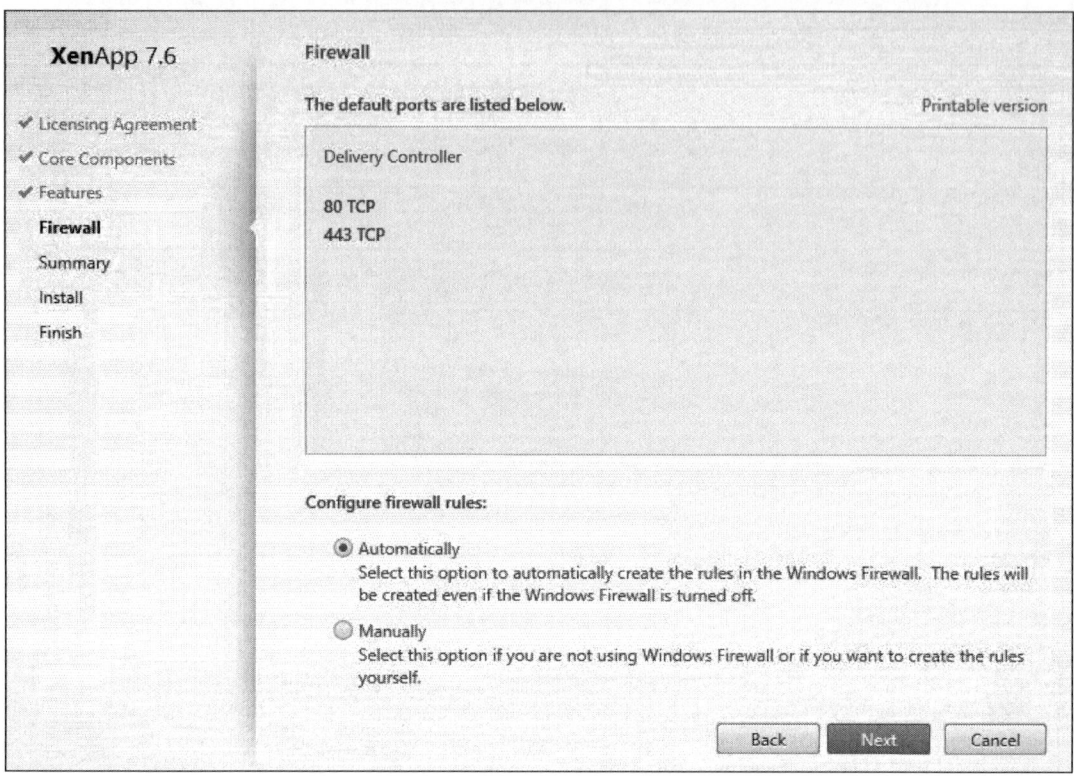

8. Review the **Summary** screen and ensure that the information is correct. Note
    that XenApp will install Microsoft .NET Framework 4.5.1 and Microsoft
    Visual x64 C++ 2008 Runtime as prerequisites if they are not already present
    on the server. When done, click on **Install**:

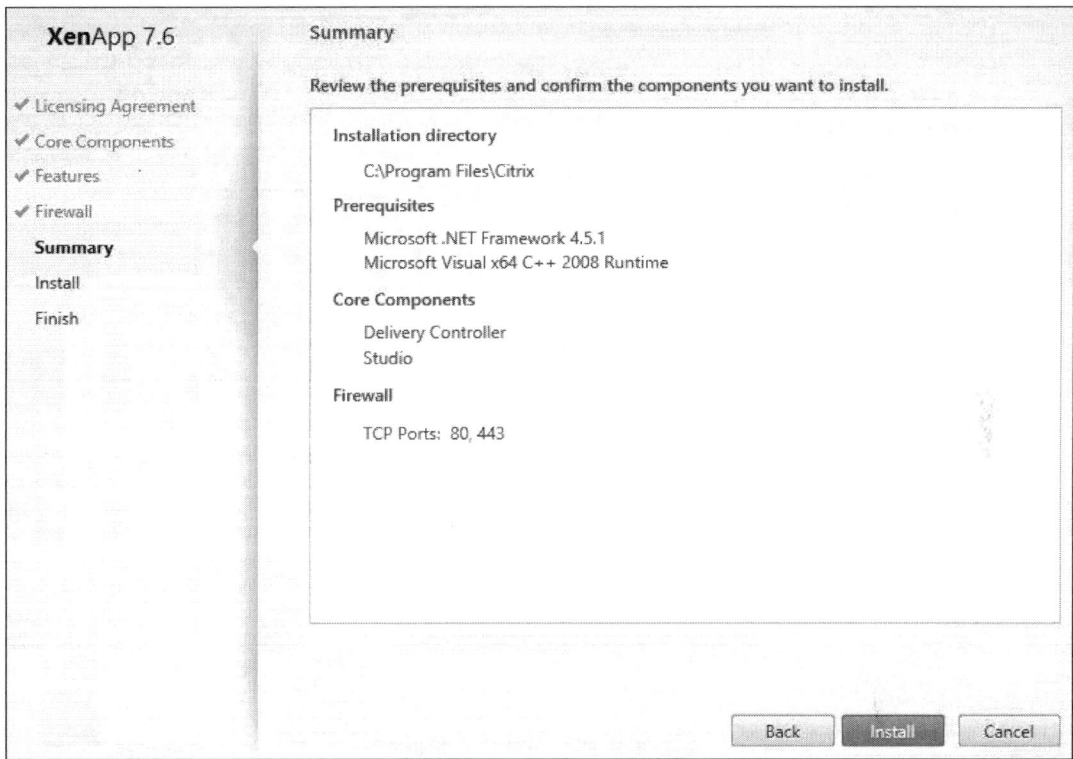

9. When the installation is complete, click on **Finish** and reboot the server if prompted. Once rebooted, log back in and go to the Windows 2012 Start menu. In the search bar, type in `Studio` and click on the green icon returned by the search to launch the Citrix Studio console, which, as mentioned in the previous chapter, is used for managing XenApp and XenDesktop 7.6 environments. Optionally, right-click on the Studio icon and select **Pin to Start Menu** or **Pin to Taskbar** for easier access. When you launch Studio for the first time, you are presented with three configuration options—**Site setup**, **Remote PC Access**, and **Scale your deployment**:

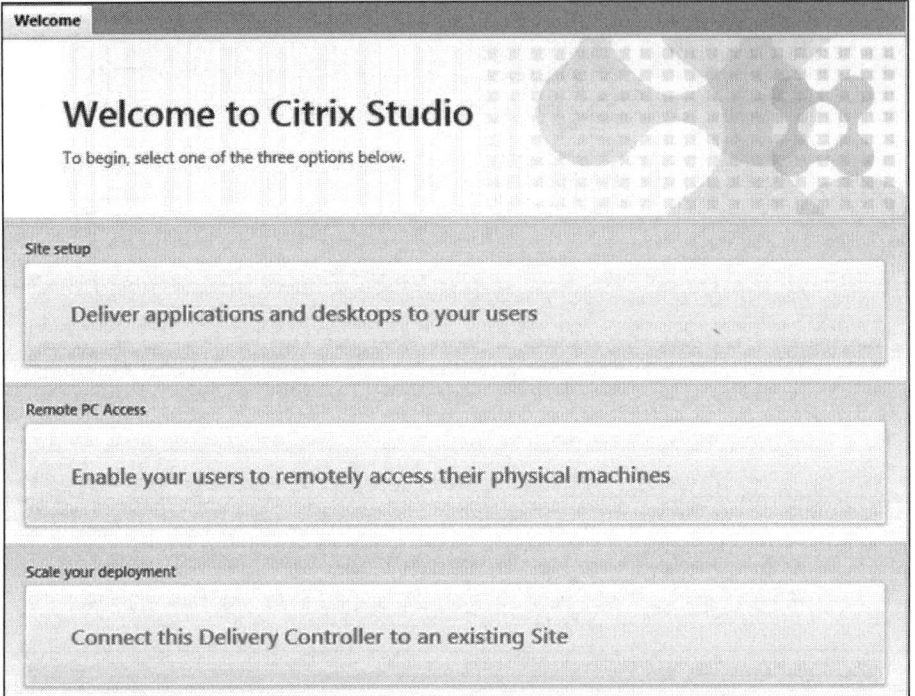

Site setup

The first option in Citrix Studio is to configure a new Citrix XenApp site. This option allows the IT administrator to give the site a name, set up a new site in the environment, and set up database, licensing, host connection, network, storage, and App-V resources on the Delivery Controller. This chapter provides a step-by-step configuration with the **Site setup** wizard.

Remote PC access

The second option in Citrix Studio is to configure the remote access to physical machines via Remote PC. It is a type of deployment where physical computers running the **Virtual Delivery Agent (VDA)** can be added to a XenApp or XenDesktop site to enable users to access them remotely through a Citrix HDX (ICA) connection. These machines cannot be power-managed by the Delivery Controller and no hosted applications can be published from them. They are usually office PCs that users need to connect to remotely and are very much like RDP, but with the added performance, security, and manageability of the Citrix ICA protocol.

Scale your deployment – existing site

Choosing to join an existing site means that, based on the size of the environment, you may need to configure multiple Delivery Controllers. For HA purposes, at least two are recommended even in small-size environments. In our case, we will have two controllers, so we will come back to this option after installing the second one. Note that the first controller always creates the new site and the second one is just added to the existing deployment.

Installing Citrix License Server 11.12.1

To manage licensing in a XenApp environment, Citrix requires the installation of a license server. The Citrix License Server 11.12.1 is a software component included in the XenApp 7.6 ISO image and it can be installed before, during, or after the Delivery Controller deployment. For example, if you are just trying out XenApp or conducting a Proof of Concept, you can choose to install the license server locally on the controller and use the 30-day free trial to evaluate the solution. On the other hand, if you have already purchased licenses and have received your license keys, you can build a dedicated VM, install Citrix License Server 11.12.1 on it, and point the controller to the license server during the site setup or later from the Citrix Studio Console. In an enterprise environment, it is always recommended to have the license server on a separate VM to avoid a single point of failure and minimize overhead for the Delivery Controller. Use the following instructions to deploy the Citrix License Server:

1. Use the same methodology from the very first section (*Creating a VM in XenCenter®*) to create a new VM on XenServer. Assign 1 vCPU and 2 GB of memory. For storage, allocate one 32 GB hard drive. Install Windows 2012 R2 as a guest OS.

2. Upon completion of Windows 2012 R2 installation, XenServer tools deployment, static IP assignment, and domain enrolment, mount the XenApp 7.6 ISO media in the CD/DVD drive of the VM.

3. Browse the CD/DVD content in **Windows Explorer**, double-click on **AutoSelect**, and choose to install **License Server**.

4. Accept **CITRIX LICENSE AGREEMENT** and click on **Next**.

5. Since **License Server** is the only option under **Core Components**, no further selection is required. Now click on **Next**.

6. Leave the default ports (TCP 7279, TCP 27000, TCP 8083, and TCP 8082), select the option to allow Citrix to configure firewall rules **Automatically**, and click on **Next**.

7. Review the **Summary** page to ensure the information is the same as displayed in the following screenshot. Click on **Install** and finally click on **Finish** once the installation is complete:

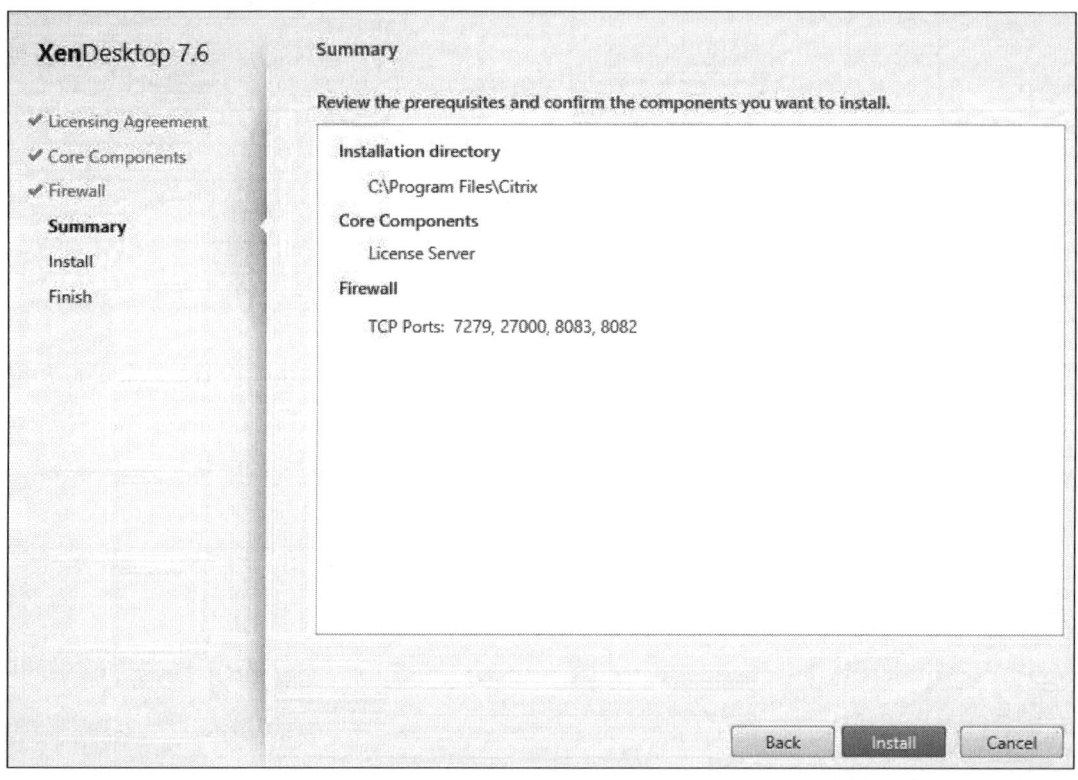

When the installation process is finished, open the Start menu in Windows, and in the search bar, type in `Simple License Service` and press *Enter*. In the web browser that opens up, there will be a search box to enter your **License Access Code** provided by Citrix when you purchased your licenses. Type in that code and click on **Display Licenses**. You will now be able to see all your licenses by product and count and you can choose to download and allocate the XenApp licenses to the Citrix License Server. It is important to have those files allocated so that when the Delivery Controller queries the **License Server (LS)** for licensing data, LS can report the correct information back to the Controller. On the same machine, you can launch the **License Administration Console (LAC)** by typing it in the Start menu or by navigating to `http://localhost:8082`. LAC will show your current license count, subscription advantage status, expiration dates, and any warnings or errors reported with licensing:

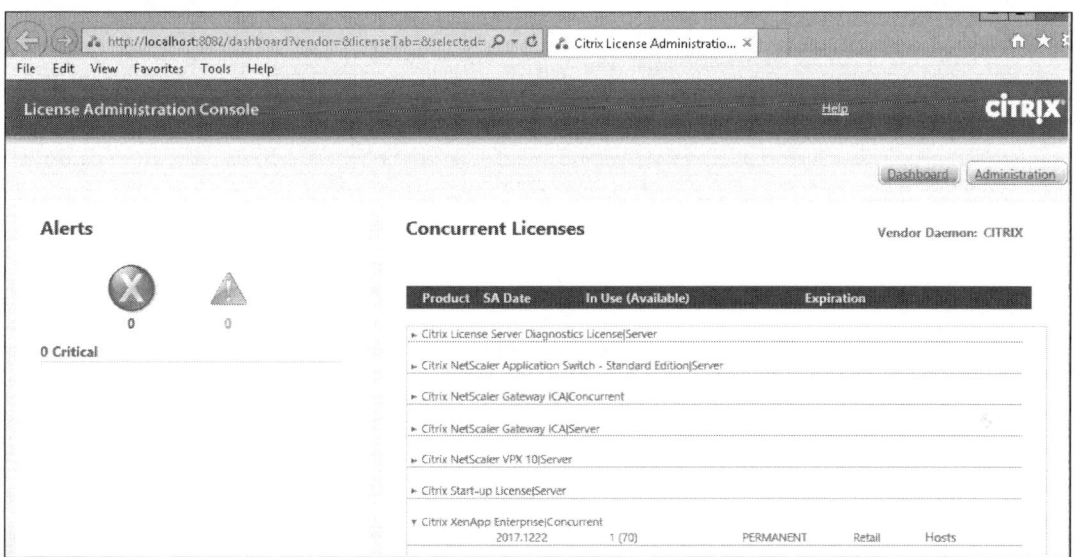

Configuring Citrix XenApp® 7.6

In this section, we are going to configure the XenApp site on the newly-installed Delivery Controller. However, before we proceed with the setup, we need to ensure we have the required hypervisor information, a service account with sufficient privileges on the hypervisor to establish a host connection from the Delivery Controller to the host, and the correct certificate if SSL is a requirement. Let's make sure we cover these prerequisites before we move forward with the XenApp configuration.

Hypervisor support

In step 5 of the *Configuring Citrix XenApp® 7.6* section, you will need to establish a connection from the XenApp Delivery Controller to your hypervisor or hypervisor console, depending on the backend host solution in use. If using XenServer, this will either be a standalone host or the **pool master** if multiple hosts are combined in a pool. You will need to obtain the DNS name, **Fully Qualified Domain Name (FQDN)**, or IP address of the host. In the case of VMware vSphere, you will need the same information, but for the vCenter server (not the ESX or ESXi host!). Yes, vCenter is a requirement because it exposes the management APIs to the XenApp Delivery Controller to be able to create and manage VMs on the hypervisor. VCenter does require a separate license from ESX, and companies do need to consider the extra costs associated with that product. Fortunately, most enterprise organizations, who use VMware solutions for server virtualization, already have licenses for vCenter, which is an essential component for host management and resource provisioning in the VMware world. However, if you are working for or consulting a smaller company with a limited budget, you may want to consider some of the more cost-effective solutions out there such as XenServer, which, at the time this book was written, was available for free with the option for paid support by Citrix. If you have a Hyper-V shop, you will need to have a server running the **System Center Virtual Machine Manager (SCVMM)** admin console and the SCVMM client console on all the Delivery Controllers installed.

XenApp® Service Account

In addition to the URL of the backend hypervisor node, in step 5 of the *Configuring the Delivery Controller* section, you will need to enter a username and password for an account with a certain level of access to the hypervisor. For this reason, it is recommended to create a service account in Active Directory that doesn't expire because it will be used not only during the initial site setup, but also continuously later on when creating and power-managing VMs and adding host resources such as storage. Then, that account can be granted the required permissions depending on your hypervisor solution.

For XenServer, using root will guarantee a successful host connection from a permission standpoint. In environments with high security restrictions, however, exposing root may not be suitable or permitted, and a service account, specifically created for XenApp, can be assigned with **VM Power Admin** rights in XenCenter.

For vSphere, there are many permission levels available in vCenter that allow a very high degree of granularity often seen in large environments. Even though a **Full Administrator** access would surely do the trick, your vSphere engineer will probably want to assign only the minimum required privileges for your service account to be able to perform the Delivery Controller tasks. Here is the full list of SDK permissions required for the XenApp 7.6 user account in vCenter:

SDK	GUI
Datastore.AllocateSpace	**Datastore | Allocate space**
Datastore.Browse	**Datastore | Browse datastore**
Datastore.FileManagement	**Datastore | Low level file operations**
Network.Assign	**Network | Assign network**
Resource.AssignVMToPool	**Resource | Assign virtual machine to resource pool**
System.Anonymous	Added automatically
System.Read	Added automatically
System.View	Added automatically
Task.Create	**Tasks | Create task**
VirtualMachine.Config.AddRemoveDevice	**Virtual machine | Configuration | Add or remove device**
VirtualMachine.Config.AddExistingDisk	**Virtual machine | Configuration | Add existing disk**
VirtualMachine.Config.AddNewDisk	**Virtual machine | Configuration | Add new disk**
VirtualMachine.Config.AdvancedConfig	**Virtual machine | Configuration | Advanced**
VirtualMachine.Config.CPUCount	**Virtual machine | Configuration | Change CPU Count**
VirtualMachine.Config.Memory	**Virtual machine | Configuration | Memory**
VirtualMachine.Config.RemoveDisk	**Virtual machine | Configuration | Remove disk**
VirtualMachine.Config.Resource	**Virtual machine | Configuration | Change resource**
VirtualMachine.Config.Settings	**Virtual machine | Configuration | Settings**
VirtualMachine.Interact.PowerOff	**Virtual machine | Interaction | Power Off**
VirtualMachine.Interact.PowerOn	**Virtual machine | Interaction | Power On**
VirtualMachine.Interact.Reset	**Virtual machine | Interaction | Reset**
VirtualMachine.Interact.Suspend	**Virtual machine | Interaction | Suspend**

SDK	GUI
`VirtualMachine.Inventory.Create`	**Virtual machine	Inventory	Create new**
`VirtualMachine.Inventory.CreateFromExisting`	**Virtual machine	Inventory	Create from existing**
`VirtualMachine.Inventory.Delete`	**Virtual machine	Inventory	Remove**
`VirtualMachine.Inventory.Register`	**Virtual machine	Inventory	Register**
`VirtualMachine.Provisioning.Clone`	**Virtual machine	Provisioning	Clone virtual machine**
`VirtualMachine.Provisioning.DiskRandomAccess`	**Virtual machine	Provisioning	Allow disk access**
`VirtualMachine.Provisioning.GetVmFiles`	**Virtual machine	Provisioning	Allow virtual machine download**
`VirtualMachine.Provisioning.PutVmFiles`	**Virtual machine	Provisioning	Allow virtual machine files upload**
`VirtualMachine.Provisioning.DeployTemplate`	**Virtual machine	Provisioning	Deploy template**
`VirtualMachine.Provisioning.MarkAsVM`	**Virtual machine	Provisioning	Mark as virtual machine**
`VirtualMachine.State.CreateSnapshot`	For vSphere 5.0, Update 2 and vSphere 5.1, Update 1: **Virtual machine	State	Create snapshot** For vSphere 5.5: **Virtual machine	Snapshot management	Create snapshot**
`VirtualMachine.State.RemoveSnapshot`	For vSphere 5.0, Update 2 and vSphere 5.1, Update 1: **Virtual machine	State	Remove snapshot** For vSphere 5.5: **Virtual machine	Snapshot management	Remove snapshot**
`VirtualMachine.State.RevertToSnapshot`	For vSphere 5.0, Update 2 and vSphere 5.1, Update 1: **Virtual machine	State	Revert to snapshot** For vSphere 5.5: **Virtual machine	Snapshot management	Revert to snapshot**

For tagged VMs, add the following permissions for the service account:

SDK	GUI
Global.ManageCustomFields	**Global	Manage custom attributes**
Global.SetCustomField	**Global	Set custom attribute**

Beware that there are two permissions on the list that were not required in XenDesktop 5.x. So if you've managed a 5.6 environment in the past and you are now building a new XenApp/XenDesktop 7.6 solution using the service account from your old environment, it will not work. The VirtualMachine.Config.AdvancedConfig (**Virtual machine | Configuration | Advanced**) and VirtualMachine.Config.Settings (**Virtual machine | Configuration | Settings**) permissions should be added now for the 7.6 Delivery Controller to be able to manage VMs in vSphere.

Securing the host connection with SSL

SSL-encrypted communications are a requirement for many IT organizations nowadays, and the Citrix infrastructure is no exception to the rule. For the hypervisor connection to be secured, you need to have an SSL certificate in place (preferably, from a trusted Certificate Authority, such as GoDaddy or Verisign) for your hypervisor. You then need to install that certificate on the XenApp Delivery Controller. There are a few methods for doing that. My personal preference is to download the certificate to the Delivery Controller from a browser and install it locally using the following steps. I will use vCenter as an example:

1. From the Delivery Controller open a web browser, such as Google Chrome, and navigate to the SSL URL of the vCenter server (https://vcenter.yourcompany.com).

2. A security warning will be displayed. Accept the warning and click on the certificate error to view the certificate.

3. In the **Details** pane, click on **Copy to File...** and export it to a new .cer file.

4. Create a new folder called c:\SSL on the Delivery Controller and save the file there. If multiple Delivery Controllers are in use, copy the certificate to all of them.

5. Double-click on the file and proceed to install the certificate for **Local Machine**.

6. Choose **Place all certificates in the following store** and then **Browse....**

7. If your Delivery Controller is running Windows 2012, select the **Trusted People** container and click on **OK**. Note that if the OS is Windows 2008 R2, you need to check the **Show physical stores box**, expand **Trusted People**, and use **Local Computer** when browsing the stores. Then, click on **Next** and finally, on **Finish**.

8. To verify that the SSL certificate was correctly installed, click on the **Start** menu and type in MMC.exe to launch the **Microsoft Management Console (MMC)**. In the console, go to **File | Add/Remove snap-in....**Under **Available snap-ins**, add **Certificates** and select to manage **Computer account** in the first prompt and specify **Local computer: (the computer this console is running on)** in the second prompt and then click on **OK**. Expand **Certificates** and navigate to the **Trusted People** container. Verify that the SSL certificate with the name of your vCenter server is there and has not expired.

9. Repeat steps 5 to 8 on each Delivery Controller in the site.

Configuring the Delivery Controller

Now that all the prerequisites have been met, you are ready to configure the XenApp Delivery Controller and site as a secure solution with only the level of access that is needed to communicate with the backend resources and manage the VMs. Let's proceed with setting up the new XenApp site from the Citrix Delivery Controller:

1. From the **Citrix Studio** welcome page under **Site Setup**, choose **Deliver applications and desktops to your users** to launch the XenApp site configuration wizard.

2. In the **Introduction** section, select **A fully configured, production-ready Site (recommended for new users)**. This will allow you to leverage the wizard to create the site database, establish licensing, and connect to the hypervisor, network, and storage resources. Under **Site name**, choose and define a name for the new XenApp site to your preference; something short but descriptive is usually good. You may want to base it on the type of environment (`lab` versus `production`), geographic zone (`NA`, `EMEA`, `APAC`), or another factor. In our case, the site will be called `GA-Prod`. When ready, click on **Next**:

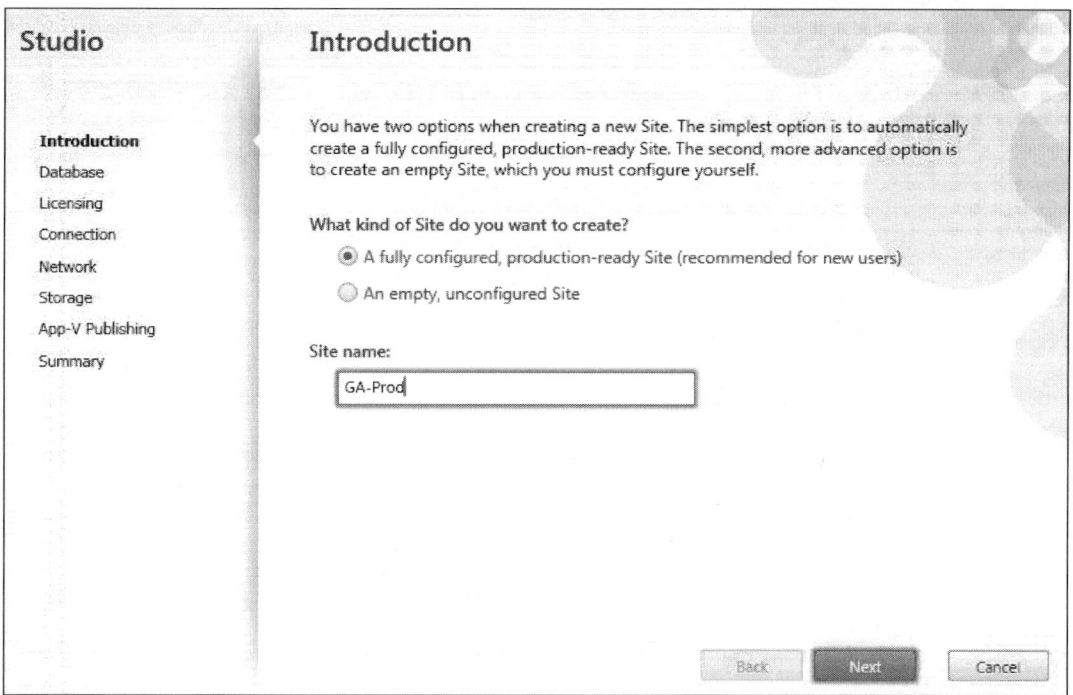

3. Next, in the **Database** screen under **Database server location**, type in the name of your SQL server. Under **Database name**, enter a name for your database or leave the default that appends your site name with a **Citrix** prefix. Click on **Test connection...** to validate permissions and SQL server connectivity. A pop-up window may appear, letting you know that **No database was found on the database server**. This is an expected behavior during a first-time install, so click on **OK** and wait for Studio to show a successful validation message. Note that your Windows account needs to have the correct permissions in SQL as defined in *Chapter 3, Preparing Your System for XenApp® Deployment*. If, due to security concerns, your account cannot be granted *sysadmin* rights, you can click the **Generate database script...** button to create database scripts manually. This option allows you to generate two scripts—database creation and database mirror. Give these to your DBA to create the XenApp SQL database manually. Now click on **Next**:

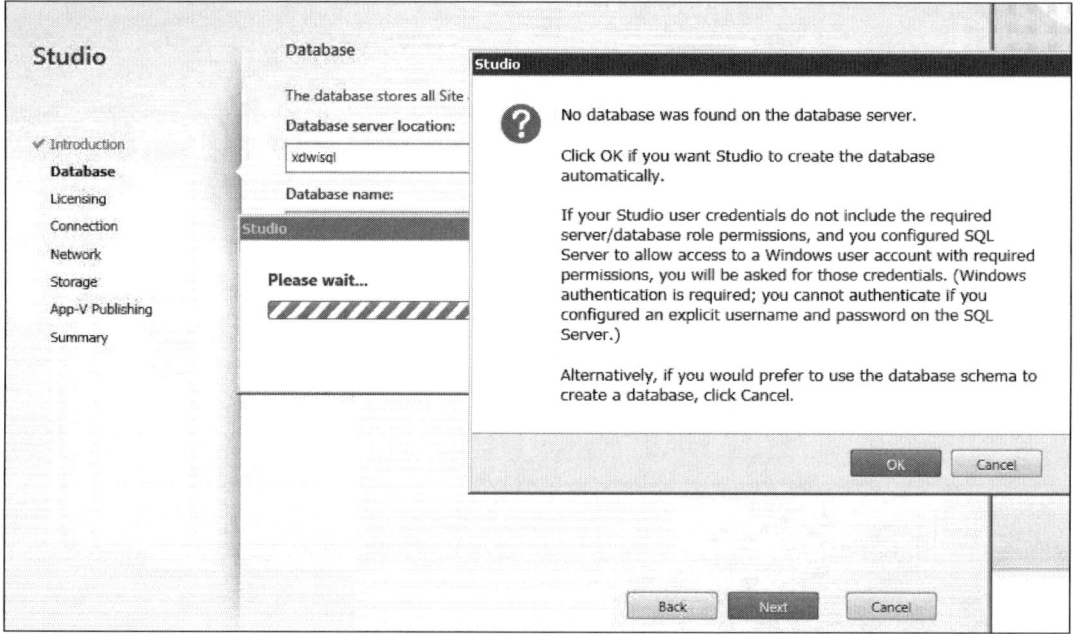

4. Under **Licensing**, specify the name or IP address of your Citrix License Server on default port `27000` and choose the license file you were issued by Citrix. Alternatively, you can choose the 30-day free trial to skip to the next stage and configure licensing later. Now, click on **Next** to proceed:

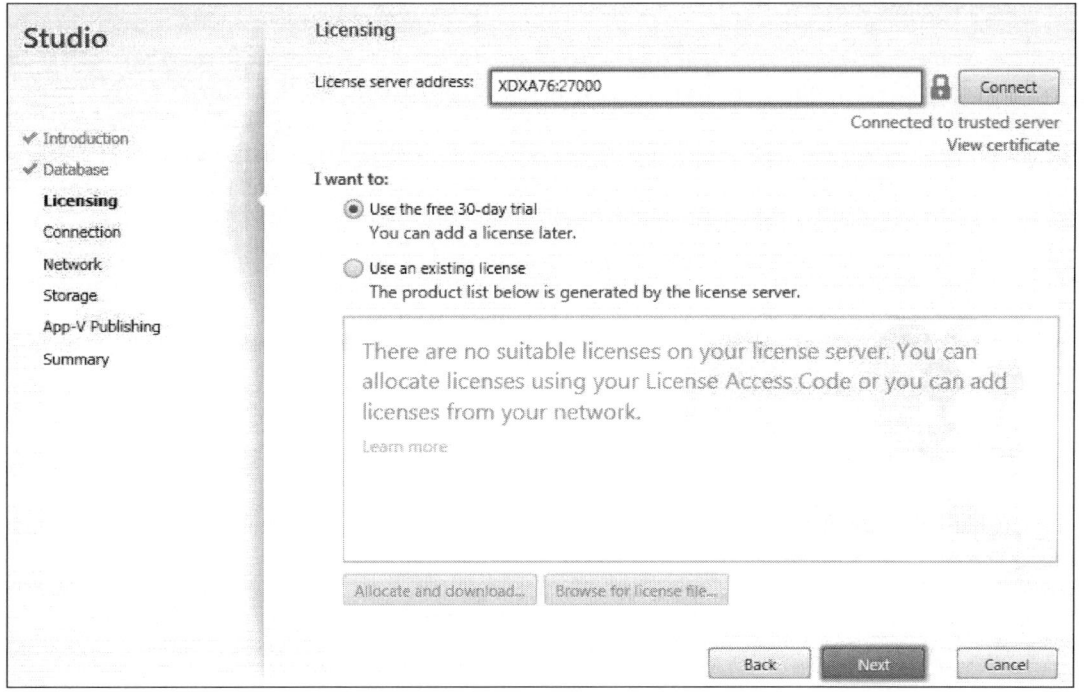

5. Next, define your host connection details. In XenApp 7.6, host connection is established to a pool of hypervisor resources that the Delivery Controller will use to communicate with for machine creation, power management, and storage. Under **Connection type**, choose your hypervisor (Citrix XenServer, VMware vSphere, Hyper-V) or your cloud provider service (Citrix CloudPlatform, Amazon EC2). You can also select Microsoft Configuration Manager Wake-on-LAN or no machine management at all (applicable if the VDA machines will be physical). Under **Connection address**, type in a URL for your hypervisor. In our case, this is `http://procenter-cx01`. This should work with the FQDN, NetBIOS name, or IP address of the hypervisor. For VMware, you have to add the */sdk* suffix to the address. For **User name** and **Password**, enter credentials with administrative privileges to the hypervisor and give the host connection a name. Select **Studio tools (Machine Creation Services)** as the VM provisioning methodology:

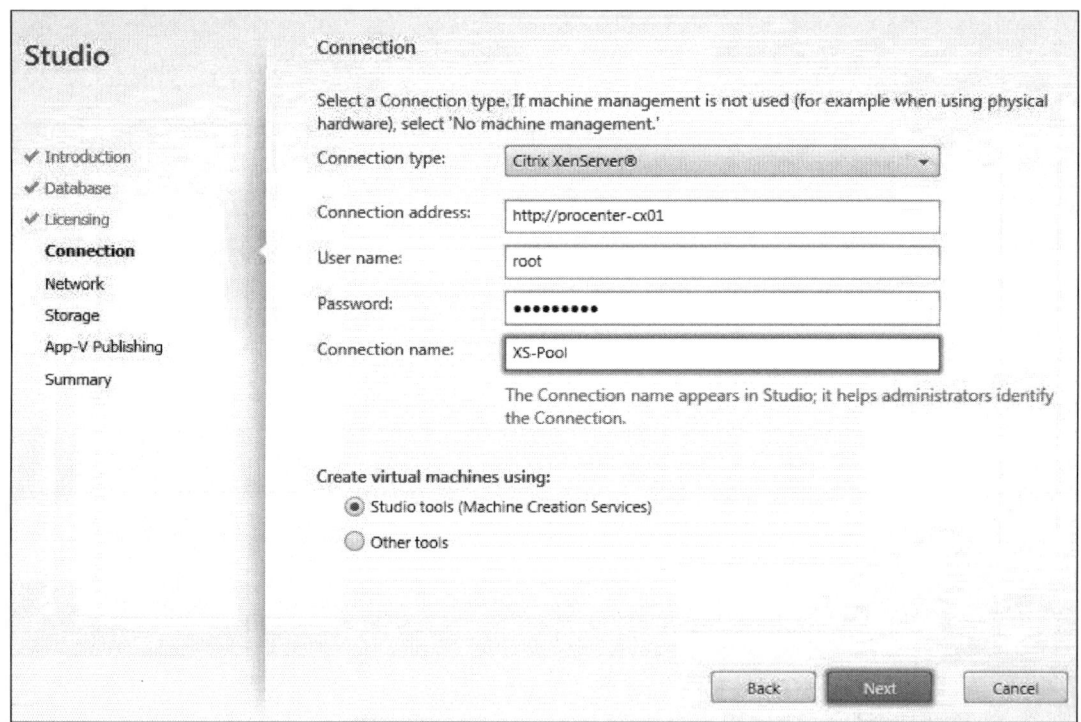

6. Next, select the network interface that the XenApp VDA servers will be attached to. Note that Studio sees all the networks available on the hypervisor and allows you to select multiple NICs in the host connection. Additionally, define a name for this resource category (for example, VM-Cluster) and proceed to **Storage**:

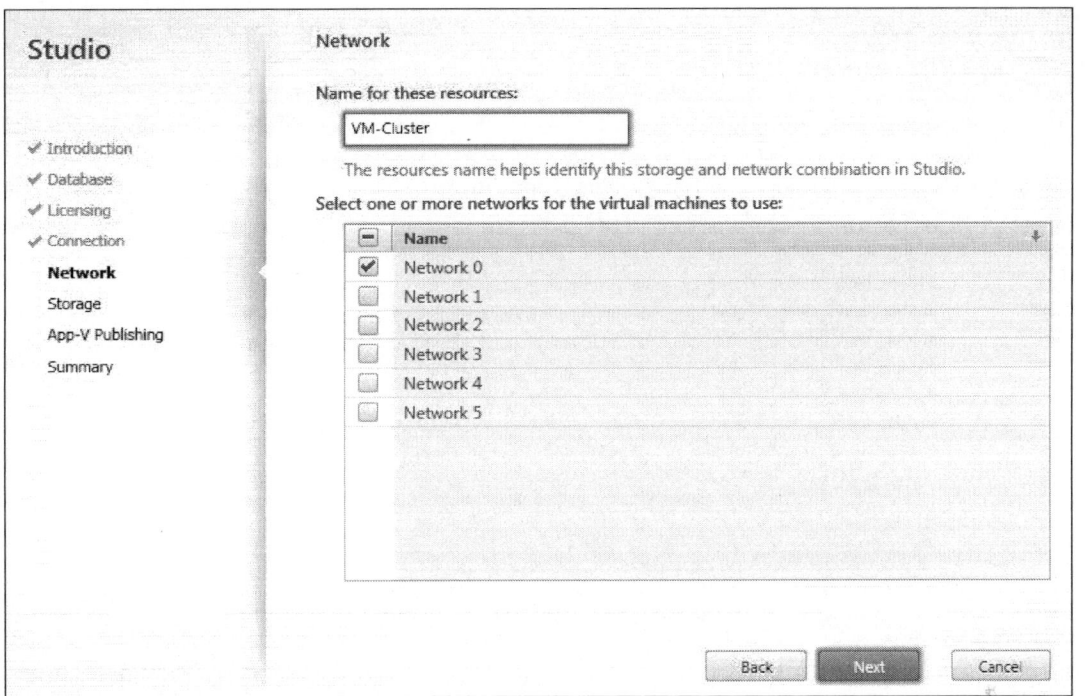

7. Next, select the storage devices available for newly-created VMs. This can be local storage on multiple hypervisor hosts or a shared repository from a SAN. Since we will be deploying server OS VDA machines (XenApp), there will be no need for **Personal vDisk (PvD)**, so leave the default setting to use the same storage for VMs and PvD and then click on **Next**:

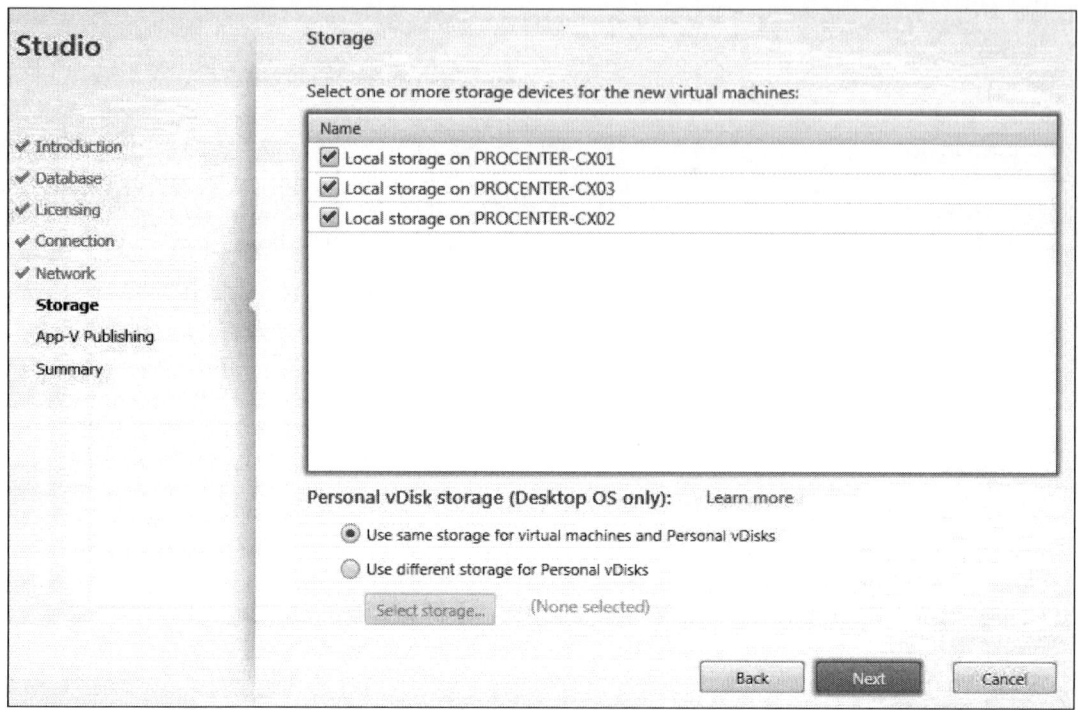

8. We will discuss this in detail in later chapters, but if you already have an App-V infrastructure in place, you can integrate it with XenApp to stream application packages to users. All you need to do is select **Yes** and enter the URL of your App-V management and publishing servers. If you do not plan to deploy App-V in this environment or you would like to do it later, choose **No** and hit **Next**:

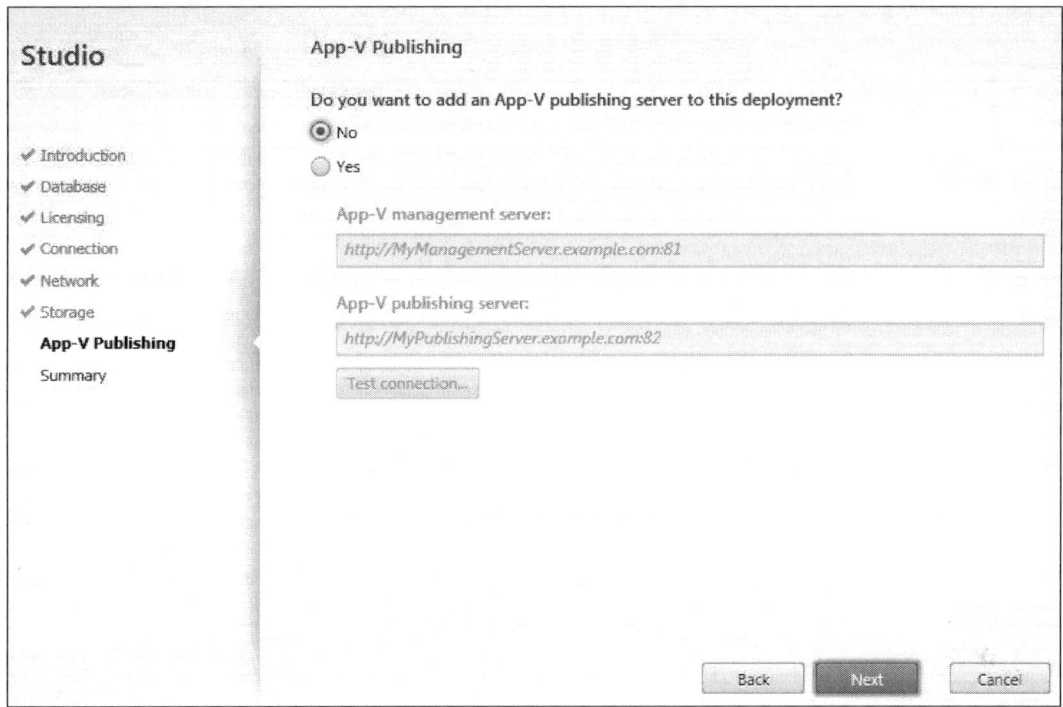

9. Under **Summary**, review your configuration, optionally opt in to participate in the **Citrix Customer Experience Improvement Program (CEIP)**, and click on **Finish**:

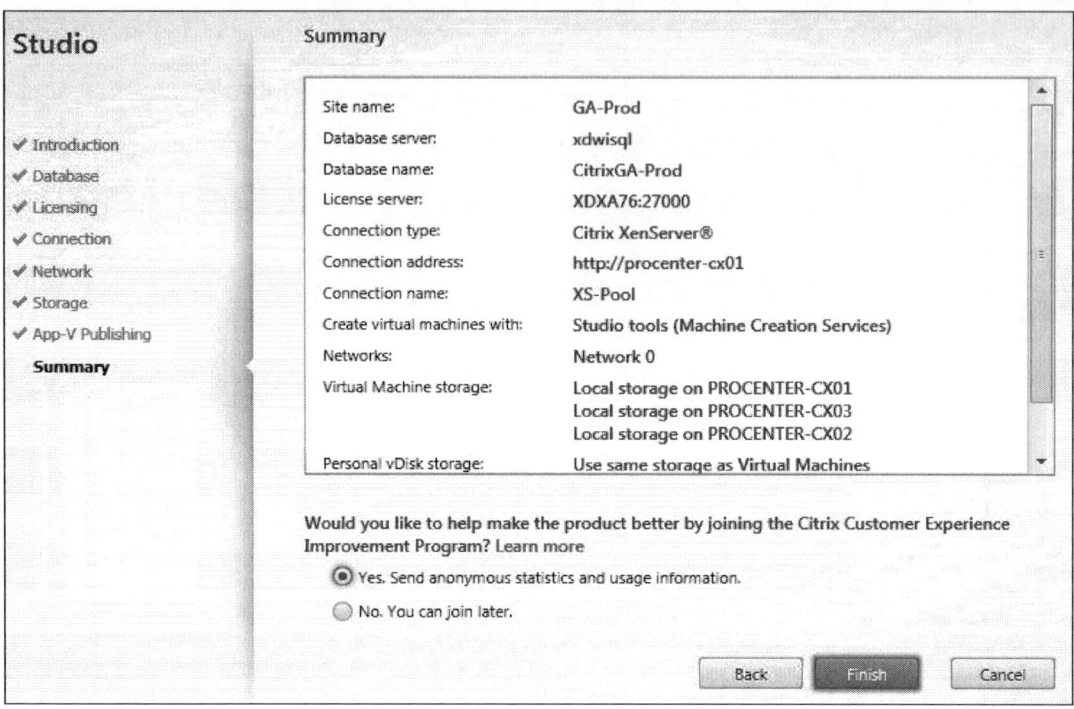

Upon the completion of the site setup, you get redirected to the **Full Deployment** page in Studio where step 1 shows as complete. There is a very useful feature in Studio that can be leveraged to make sure the site was configured properly, and all the components such as database connectivity, state of the services, and logging are functioning as expected. This test also generates an HTML report to visualize the results. To take advantage of this feature, under step 1, **Configuration**, simply click on **Test site configuration**, as shown in the following screenshot:

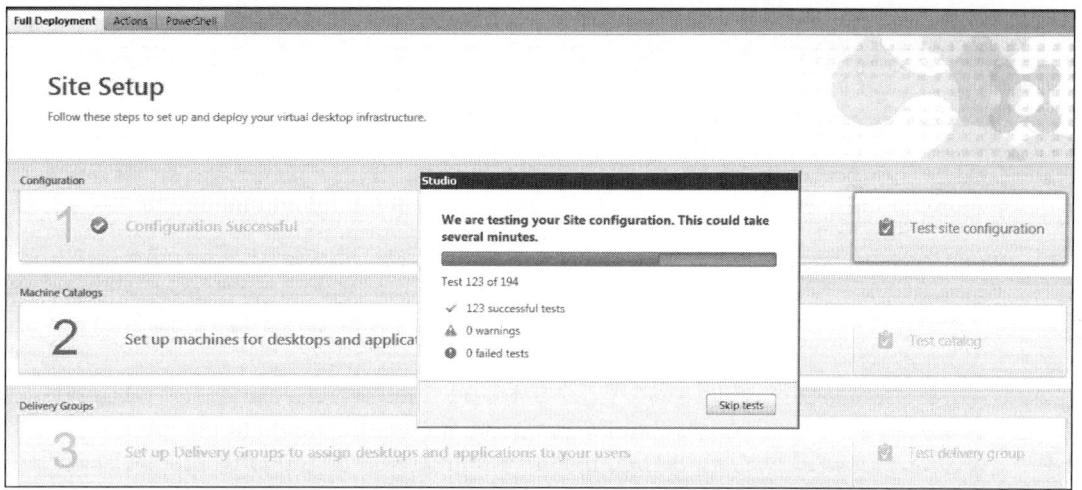

If there are any warnings or failed tests detected, be sure to examine the HTML report and investigate the areas at fault.

Observe the following screenshot and take a few moments to review all the nodes in Citrix Studio:

Later in the book, you will learn each component in more detail.

Machine catalogs

A machine catalog is a collection of virtual or physical machines managed by the XenApp Delivery Controller. In virtualized environments, a machine catalog is also the general container where the Delivery Controller puts VMs such as the XenApp application server OS machines running the Citrix VDA created by **Machine Creation Services (MCS)**, **Provisioning Services (PVS)**, and other technologies. On the catalog level, IT administrators can define what kind of machines are being created (random, static, streamed, and so on). In *Chapter 8, Building Your First XenApp® Farm – Machine Creation Services*, you will learn how to build VMs using MCS, and knowing the concept of machine catalog, will help you in making the right decision as to what type of VMs would be the most useful in achieving your business goals.

Delivery Groups

One level lower in the hierarchy are Delivery Groups. A Delivery Group in XenApp is a portion of the VMs that share the same properties in terms of user assignment, power management, and application hosting. For example, if an IT administrator created a machine catalog of thirty identical application server VMs and wants to assign ten of them to each department (accounting, sales, and HR), then they will create three Delivery Groups and add ten VMs to each of them from the machine catalog. With a separate Delivery Group for each department, the administrator will be able to publish only the applications needed for that user group, efficiently monitor active sessions, and reduce footprint by supplying only the amount of servers needed by those users. By leveraging the **Applications** tab of the **Delivery Groups** node in Citrix Studio, the IT administrator can publish new instances of applications installed on **Master Image** and associate them with specific users or user groups:

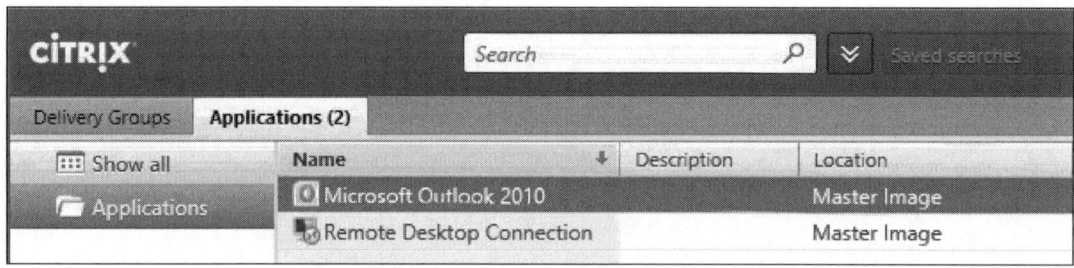

Policies

Studio Policies are a rich collection of Group Policies similar to Active Directory GPOs but tailored specifically to the Citrix environment. Some examples include clipboard redirection in virtual sessions, HDX Flash-based content control, printer autocreation and driver behavior, and many others. Citrix Policies are largely employed to secure and optimize virtual sessions by limiting how different virtual channels within the ICA protocol are used for managing user experience. Policy templates are available in Studio for a quick on-the-go optimization of LAN and WAN deployments. The following screenshot illustrates the templates for Citrix Policies in Studio:

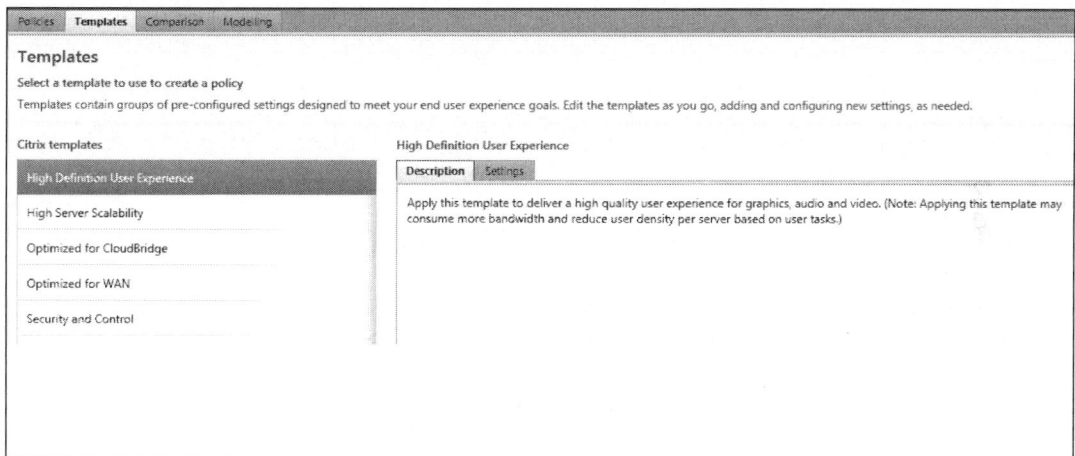

Templates for Citrix Policies in Studio

Logging

Logging (also known as **Configuration Logging**) is a very useful feature that provides XenApp administrators with the ability to track configuration changes in the XenApp site made by other (or any) administrators in the organization. This type of auditing capability was inherited from older versions of XenApp and revived in 7.x to maximize the change control transparency.

Configuration

The **Configuration** node in Studio allows you to view the list of **Administrators** authorized to manage the XenApp site and the permissions level each of them has. For example, if you have a group of help desk technicians that you want to give read-only access to monitor VM states and sessions, you can assign that type of permission in Studio. From the **Configuration** node, you can also see a list of all the Delivery Controllers in the site, the host connection created during the initial site setup and all the backend hypervisor resources defined within it, information about license count and license server connectivity, StoreFront server list, and App-V publishing. We will come back to this node in *Chapter 11, Administering a XenApp® Environment – Server Management*, when we will talk about XenApp server management and support:

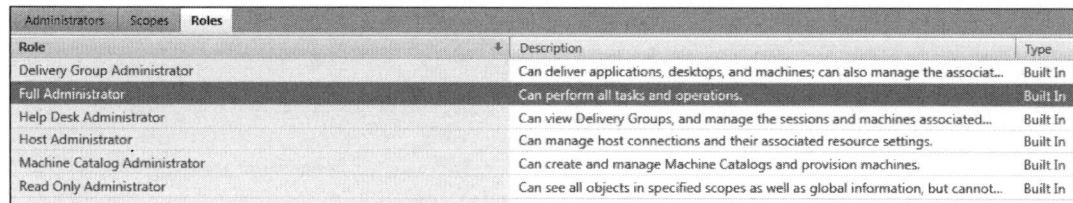

Role	Description	Type
Delivery Group Administrator	Can deliver applications, desktops, and machines; can also manage the associat...	Built In
Full Administrator	Can perform all tasks and operations.	Built In
Help Desk Administrator	Can view Delivery Groups, and manage the sessions and machines associated...	Built In
Host Administrator	Can manage host connections and their associated resource settings.	Built In
Machine Catalog Administrator	Can create and manage Machine Catalogs and provision machines.	Built In
Read Only Administrator	Can see all objects in specified scopes as well as global information, but cannot...	Built In

Administrative Roles in Studio

Joining a second controller to the XenApp® site

In Citrix (or any other environment for that matter), it is critically important to have an HA solution in place to prevent major outages from severely disrupting business operations. To achieve such a state, we will deploy a second Delivery Controller and join it to the existing site. Use the following steps for joining a second controller to the XenApp site:

1. Create a new virtual machine using the instructions in the *Creating a VM in XenCenter®* section. Assign the same compute, network, and storage resources as the first Delivery Controller and append the name to differentiate from the latter. For instance, if your first one was named CTX-DC-01, this one can be CTX-DC-02. In my case, I've got XADC76 as primary and XADC76-02 as secondary.

2. Install Windows 2012 R2 as a guest OS, deploy XenServer Tools, and apply the latest updates from Microsoft.

3. Assign a static IP, enroll in the domain, and reboot the VM when prompted.

4. Mount the XenApp 7.6 ISO media and use the instructions from the *Installing the Citrix XenApp® 7.6 Delivery Controller* section to install the XenApp DC software.

5. Once complete, launch the **Citrix Studio Console**.

6. Under **Scale your deployment**, click on **Connect this Delivery Controller to an existing site**.

7. Enter the DNS name, FQDN, or IP address of the primary Controller configured in the *Configuring Citrix XenApp® 7.6* section and then click on **OK**.

8. To verify that the operation was successful, in Citrix Studio, go to the **Configuration** node and click on **Controllers**. Both of your Delivery Controllers should be listed there.

Summary

In this chapter, we laid the foundation of the Citrix infrastructure by building out the control layer. You learned how to install Citrix XenApp 7.6 Delivery Controller and configure your first XenApp site. You also installed Citrix License Server 11.12.1 and allocated your licenses for use by the XenApp environment. You finalized the site setup by enrolling a second controller for HA. This allows us to proceed with deploying the access layer, which includes Citrix StoreFront, NetScaler, and NetScaler Gateway in the next few chapters. As we move forward with the implementation, you will start to see how the different components fit in together, and the business value of the XenApp solution will become much more evident. Stay tuned!

5
Installing and Configuring Citrix® StoreFront™

In the previous chapter, we installed our first Citrix Delivery Controller and configured XenApp 7.6, which represents the Control Layer in our Citrix infrastructure. The next step in implementing the Citrix solution is to go ahead and build the access layer, which begins with Citrix StoreFront. StoreFront is a piece of software installed on a web server based on the Microsoft **Internet Information Services (IIS)** role in Windows 2008 or 2012. The purpose of StoreFront is to authenticate users and aggregate XenApp applications and desktops into a unified web portal (Receiver for Web) or a native Receiver store where users can easily access their hosted resources. With StoreFront, IT administrators can also provide access to the same resources to users who do not have Citrix Receiver installed on their endpoint device via the Receiver for HTML5 option—a concept demonstrated later in the book. In this chapter, we will accomplish the following objectives:

- Installing and configuring Citrix StoreFront on a VM in XenCenter
- Importing and managing SSL certificates
- Joining a second StoreFront to the server group for redundancy and propagating changes from the primary server

At the end of the chapter, we will have a highly available StoreFront system that is fully integrated with the Delivery Controllers built in *Chapter 4, Installing and Configuring Citrix XenApp®*.

Installing Citrix StoreFront™

To install Citrix StoreFront, we first need to create a new VM in XenCenter using the same methodology from *Chapter 4, Installing and Configuring Citrix XenApp®*. Start by assigning 2 vCPUs, 4 GB of RAM, and a 40 GB hard drive (specifications may vary based on workload). Employ a naming convention in compliance with your company policy; in our case, it is StoreFront-01. Once created, install Windows 2012 and hypervisor tools onto the VM, apply recommended updates to the OS, and join the server to the domain. With StoreFront 2.6, the prerequisites for installing the Citrix software are enabled automatically by the wizard, but if you want to enable them manually prior to the StoreFront installation, you can always refer to *Chapter 3, Preparing Your System for XenApp® Deployment*, for a list of requirements (in this case, IIS and .NET). Use the following instructions to install Citrix StoreFront:

1. Mount the XenApp 7.6 ISO media to the VM's CD/DVD drive, double-click on AutoSelect, and under **XenApp 7.6**, click on **Citrix StoreFront**:

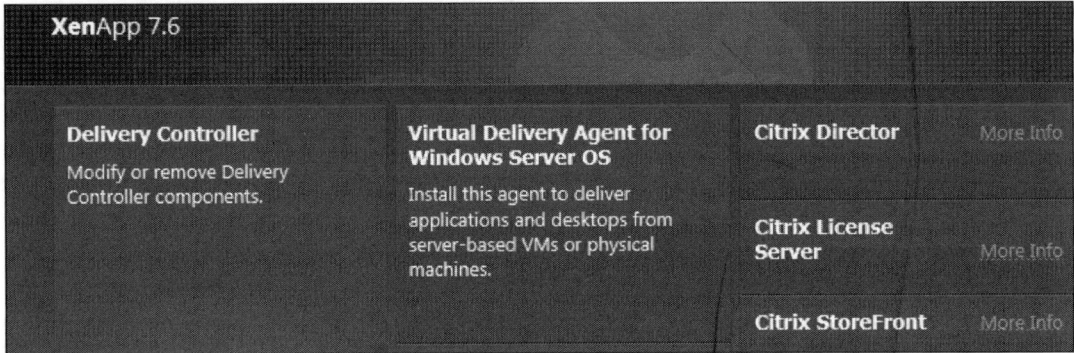

2. This lets the StoreFront installation wizard start. Read **CITRIX LICENSE AGREEMENT** and select **I have read, understand, and accept the terms of the license agreement**. Now click on **Next**:

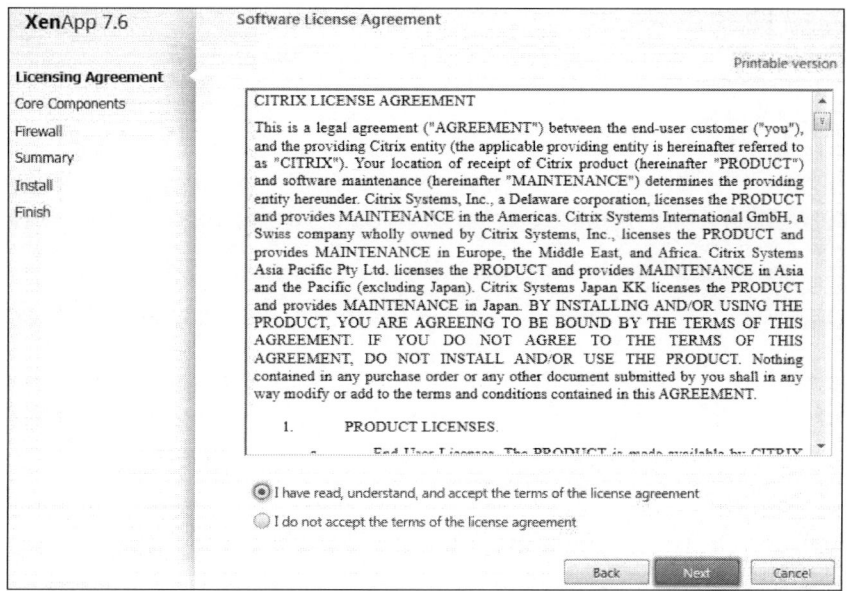

3. Under **Core Components**, note that **StoreFront** is listed as a required component and click on **Next**:

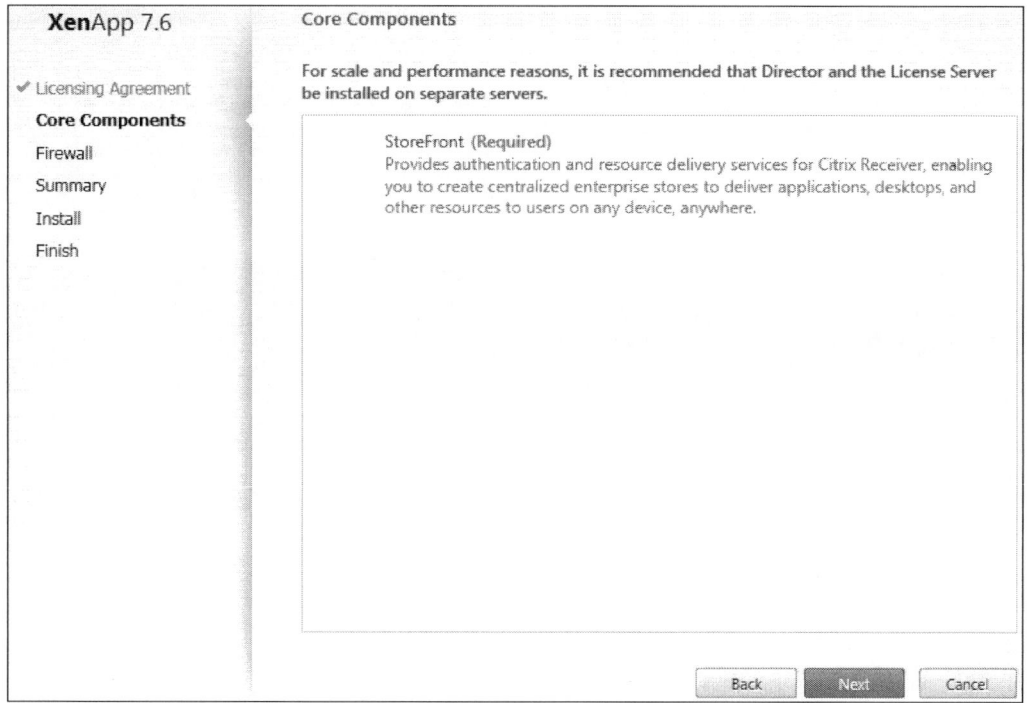

4. Under **Firewall**, choose to configure firewall rules **Automatically** for TCP ports 80 and 443 and click on **Next**. This option will create the rules in Windows Firewall on the localhost. Remember that you still need to allow these ports from your corporate firewall for users to be able to access the StoreFront resources:

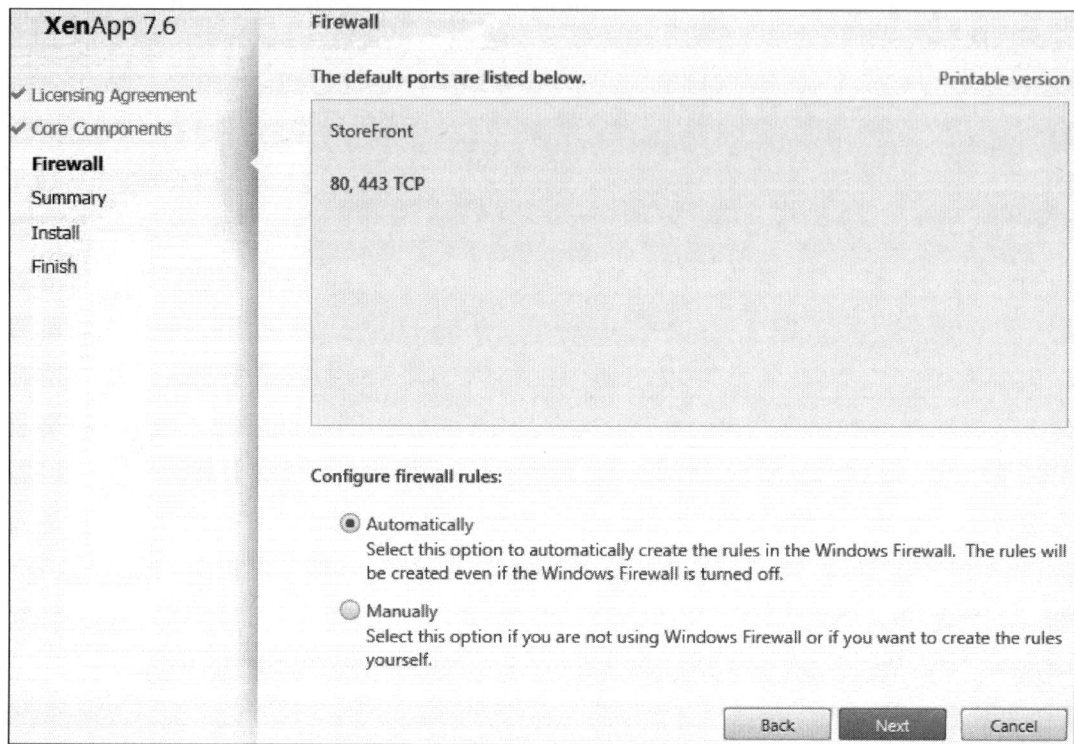

5. Under **Summary**, review and ensure that the correct installation settings and requirements (path, prerequisites, core components, and firewall ports) are applied and click on **Install**:

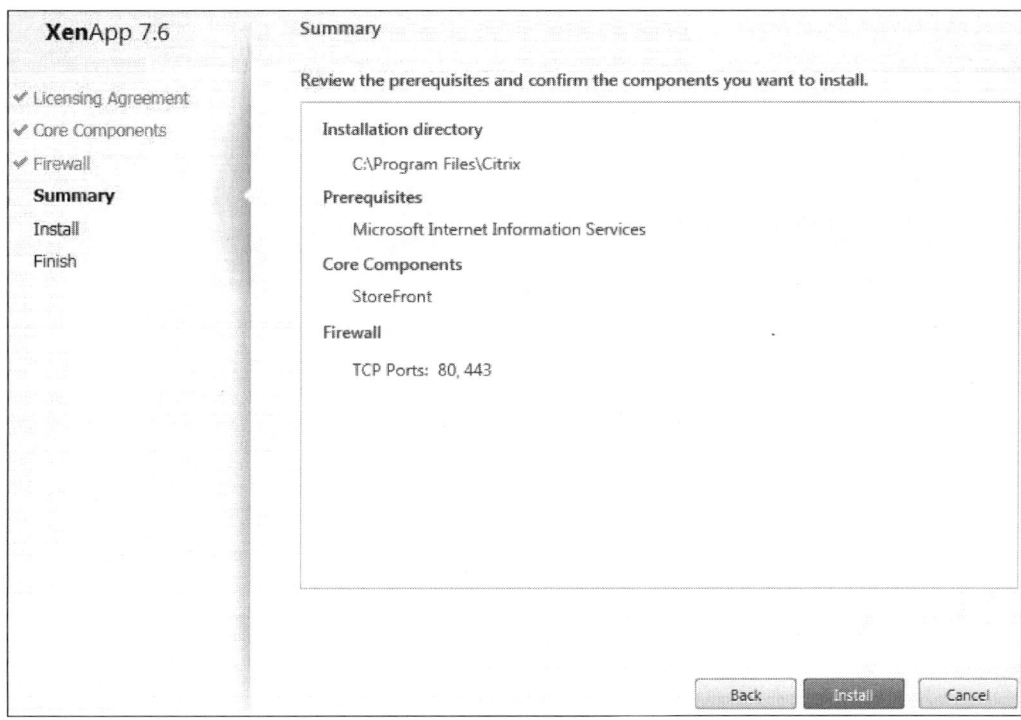

6. Once the installation process is complete, click on **Finish** to open the StoreFront management console.

Configuring Citrix StoreFront™

Configuring StoreFront for user authentication and application delivery using the latest StoreFront 2.6 software (part of XenApp 7.6) is a simple wizard-based process. It allows us to create a StoreFront site and integrate it with the Delivery Controllers in a matter of minutes. Here are some things to consider when deploying StoreFront:

- Are my users going to be connecting to their applications from both internal and external networks?
- What endpoint devices are in use?
- Am I using NetScaler for load balancing or a third-party solution?
- Is SSL a requirement for internal communications or can I use HTTP?

These are all valid design questions that are needed to be answered to determine the right StoreFront configuration for a particular environment. As this book is based on a real-world deployment for an enterprise company, we will have both internal and external users, a variety of endpoint devices such as PCs, iPads, and thin clients, NetScaler as both a load balancing and a Gateway solution, and SSL certificates across the board with the latest supported encrypted algorithms. The following sections will demonstrate how to configure Citrix StoreFront.

SSL certificates

To create a solution that is fully secured up to Citrix best practices, you will need to start with creating, importing, and binding an SSL certificate in IIS on the StoreFront server:

1. Request a new SSL certificate from your preferred trusted **Certificate Authority (CA)**, for instance, GoDaddy, VeriSign, and so on, or your domain CA to the hostname you've chosen for StoreFront.

2. On the StoreFront server, open IIS Manager and under the local server, click on **Server Certificates**:

3. Under **Server Certificates**, click on **Import...** and browse to the certificate file you obtained from your CA. Type in the certificate password in the **Password** field, if required, and then click on **OK**:

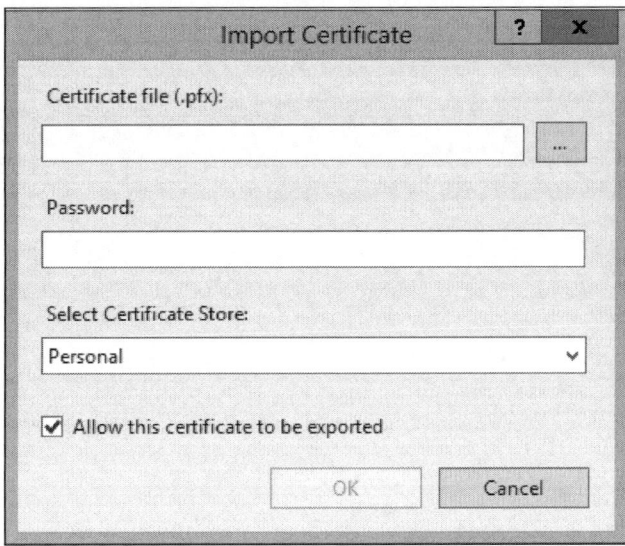

4. Under the local server node, expand **Sites** and then select **Default Web Site**. On the right-hand side under **Actions**, click on **Bindings....** The default **Site Bindings** window will be displayed; note that there is no SSL binding yet:

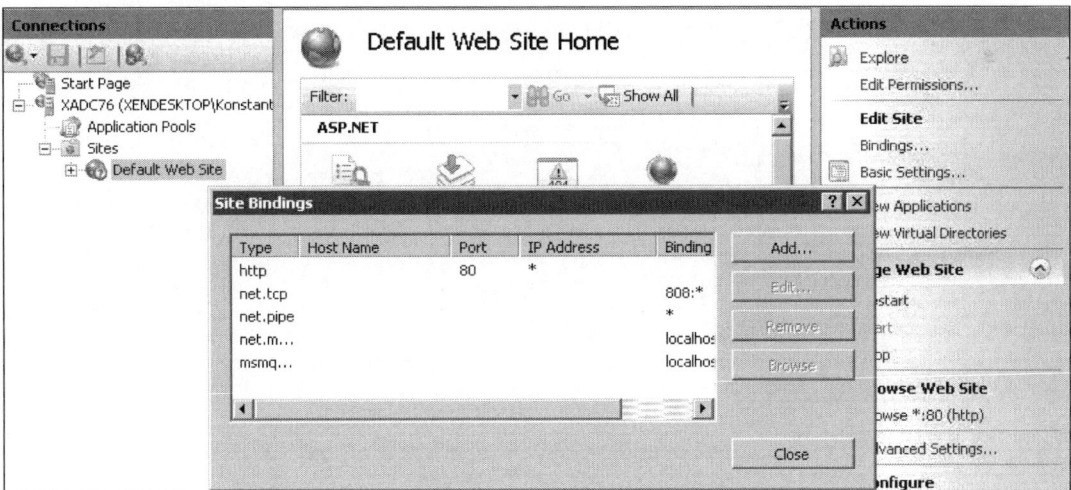

5. Click on **Add...** and then select **https** as **Type**. For **SSL certificate**, choose the certificate imported in the previous step and then click on **OK**:

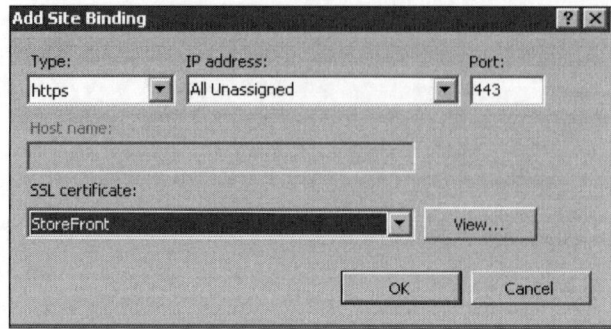

The SSL certificate called **StoreFront** is now bound to the website in IIS, and we are now able to configure Citrix StoreFront for secure connectivity.

Setting up the StoreFront™ site

Now that the SSL certificate has been imported and bound in IIS, we can proceed with creating a new site in StoreFront for secure access to applications and desktops. Let's use the following step-by-step guide to deploy this configuration:

1. Launch the StoreFront management console by typing in StoreFront in the Windows 2012 Start menu:

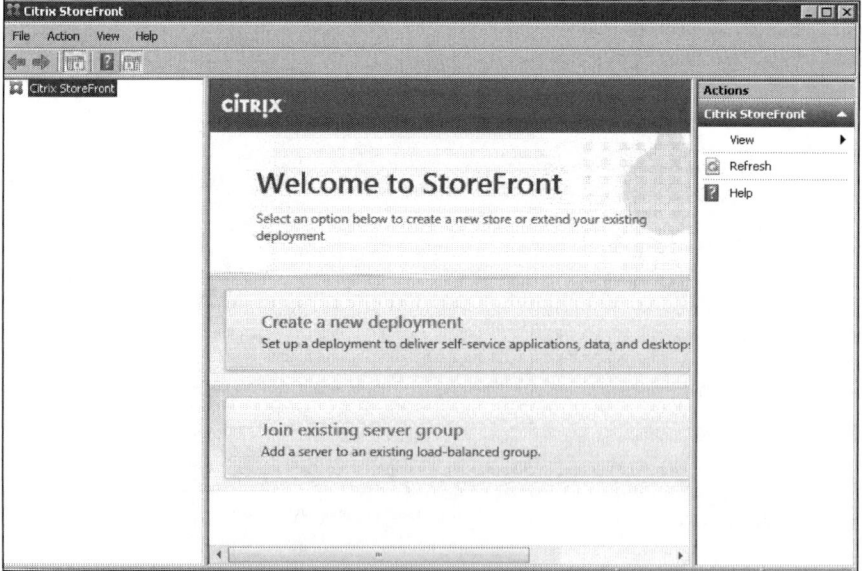

2. Click on **Create a new deployment** and wait for the configuration wizard to launch.

3. Type in the **Base URL** of your deployment (for example, `https://storefront`). In the case of multiple StoreFront servers, the **Base URL** is the name of the load-balanced vServer address that users will connect to for getting access to their applications. When ready, click on **Next**:

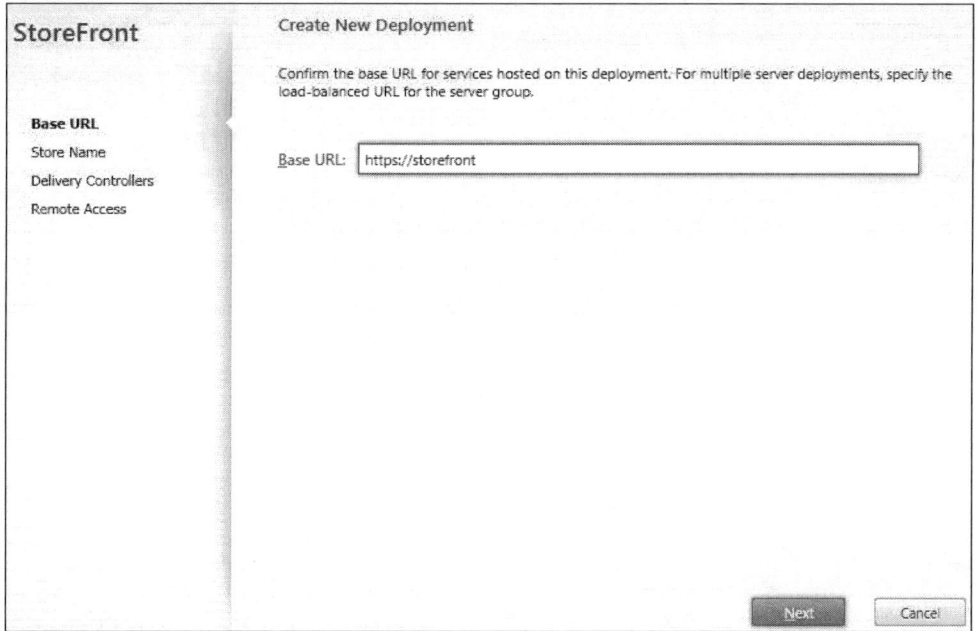

4. Under **Store Name**, define a name for the store that will contain the XenApp applications and desktops (for example, Citrix-Store) and then click on **Next**:

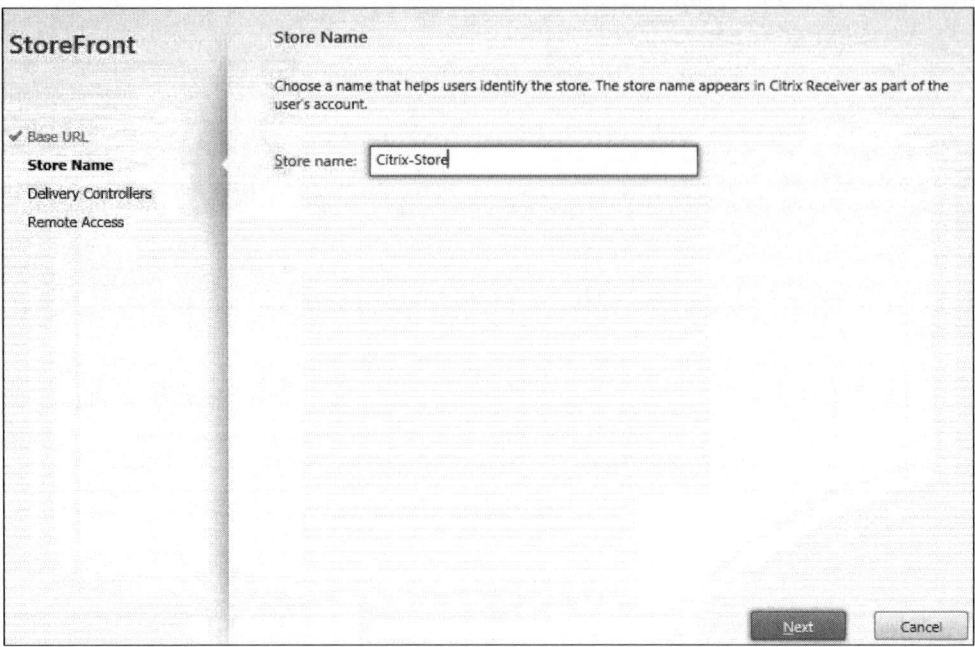

5. For **Delivery Controllers**, click on **Add** and in the resultant prompt, add the names of the two Delivery Controllers we created in *Chapter 4*, *Installing and Configuring Citrix XenApp®*. Also, define **Display name** for this resource group in StoreFront (it can be something generic such as XenDesktop). Note that port 443 is already selected. Leave everything else as default and then click on **OK** to close the prompt. Then, click on **Next**:

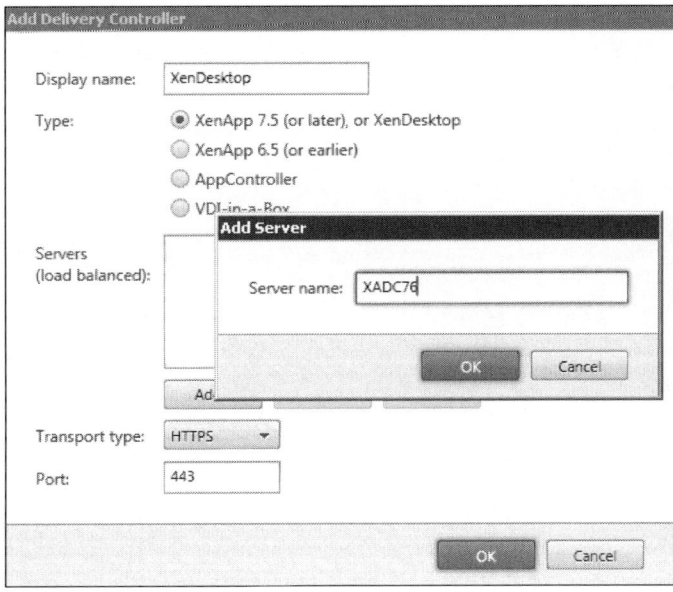

6. For **Remote Access**, leave the default setting of **None** for now. Later, when we deploy NetScaler Gateway in *Chapter 6, Installing and Configuring NetScaler Gateway™*, we will come back and change this setting from the **StoreFront** management console for external access. Next, click on **Create** to complete the StoreFront deployment:

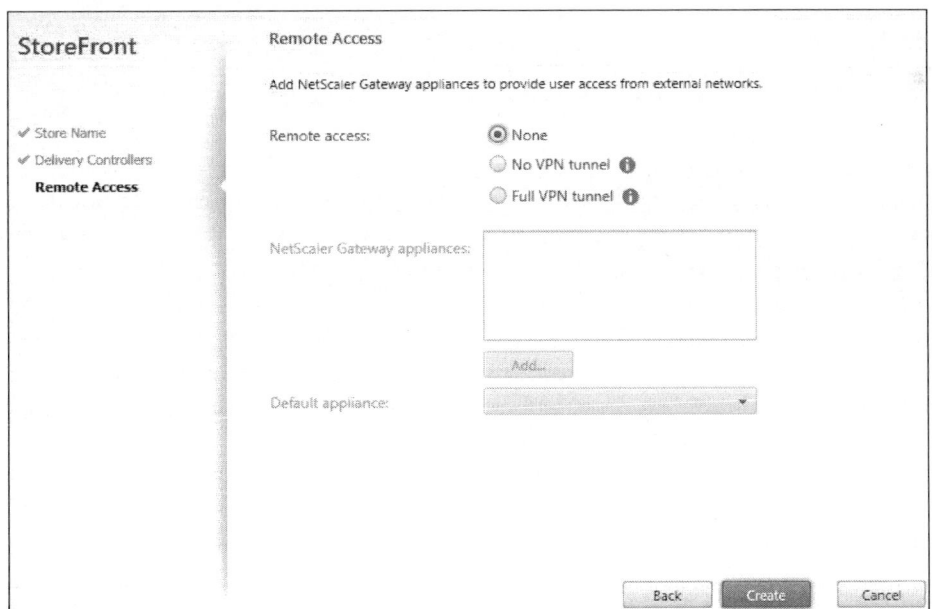

7. When the Store creation process is complete, a verification screen will appear to inform you of the successful configuration. Click on **Finish** to exit the wizard:

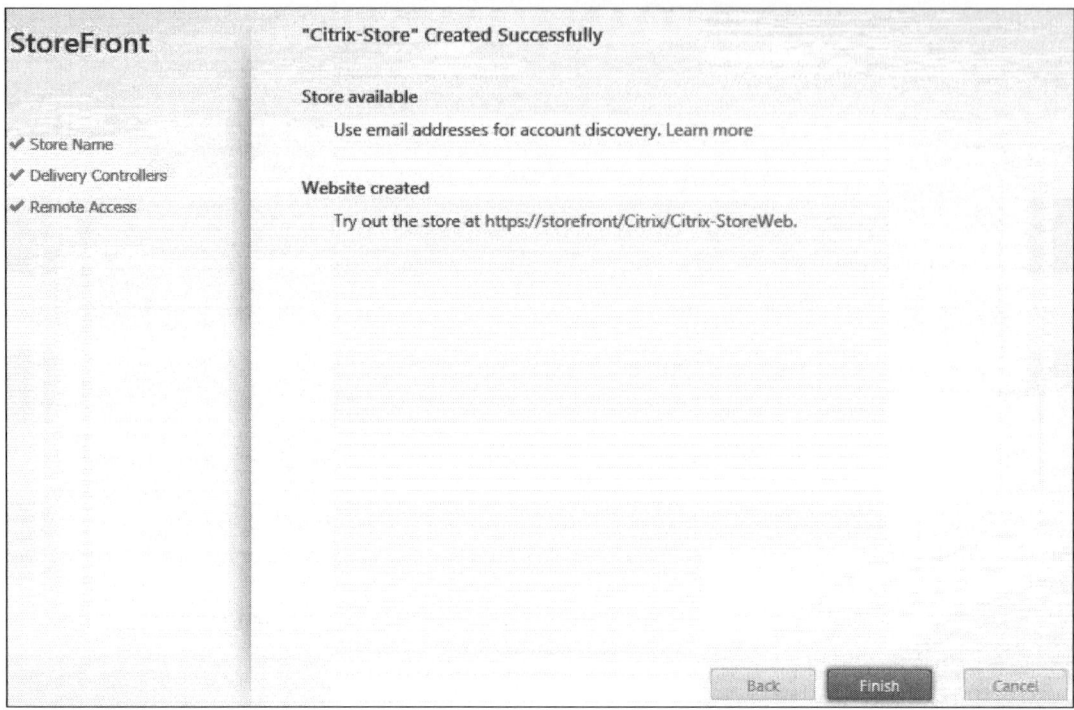

Configuring authentication methods

Five authentication methods are available in StoreFront depending on the type of connection and user requirements—**User name and password**, **Domain pass-through**, **Smart card**, **HTTP Basic**, and **Pass-through from NetScaler Gateway**. The default method for authenticating users to XenApp stores is by explicitly typing in their **User name and password** when connecting to StoreFront. Thus, this method is enabled, by default, upon setting up the site. If you enable **Domain pass-through**, the Active Directory credentials from the endpoint device (in this case, the Windows computer) are used to log in the user automatically to Citrix Receiver on their endpoint device. If smart cards are a requirement in the environment, the **Smart card** method should be selected. If a third-party web portal or SSO solution is in use, then **HTTP Basic** can be leveraged to transmit the credentials to the StoreFront IIS web server. Last but not least, the **Pass-through from NetScaler Gateway** is mandatory if the goal is to achieve SSO from the NetScaler appliance.

For example, when a user is authenticated on NetScaler and SSO is enabled on the Gateway VIP, the user is logged in to their apps and desktop store without being prompted to log on again on the StoreFront level. The **Remote Access** feature should be enabled as well for the latter method to work:

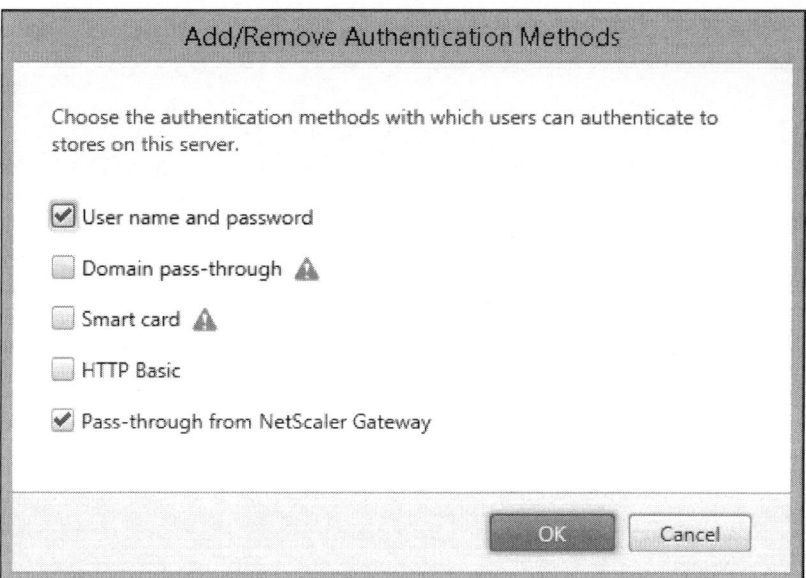

Joining a second ary server to the StoreFront™ deployment

For **High Availability (HA)** and load balancing purposes, it is highly recommended to add a second server to the StoreFront configuration. Unlike the Delivery Controller setup, which only requires the FQDN of the primary controller to join a secondary one to the XenApp site, StoreFront additionally requires an authorization code generated by the active StoreFront server in order to join another server to the site. The following steps will guide you to join a secondary server to the StoreFront deployment:

1. Apply the same instructions used to create StoreFront-01 to provision a new VM in XenCenter and install Windows 2012 R2, XenServer Tools, and the Citrix StoreFront software from the XenApp 7.6 ISO media. For ease of deployment, StoreFront-02 is the hostname defined for the new server.

2. Log on to the primary server (StoreFront-01) and launch the StoreFront management console. Select the **Server Group** node on the left-hand side and under **Actions** on the right-hand side, click on **Add Server**. Leave the prompt open:

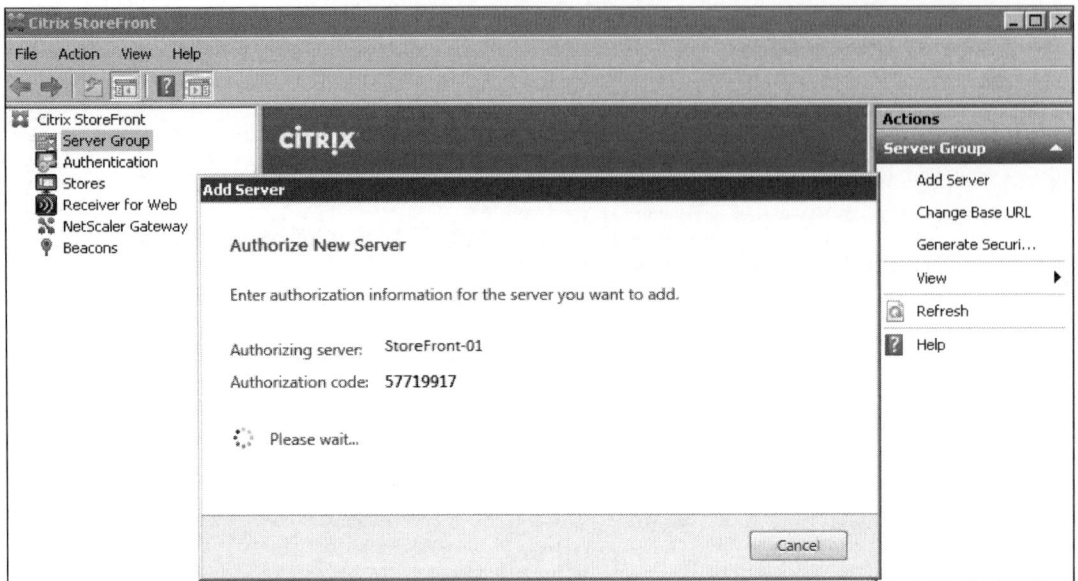

3. Copy **Authorization code** and log back in to StoreFront-02. Launch the **StoreFront** management console and select **Join existing server group**.

4. Populate **Authorizing server** and **Authorization code** with the information from step 2 and step 3 and then click on **Join**:

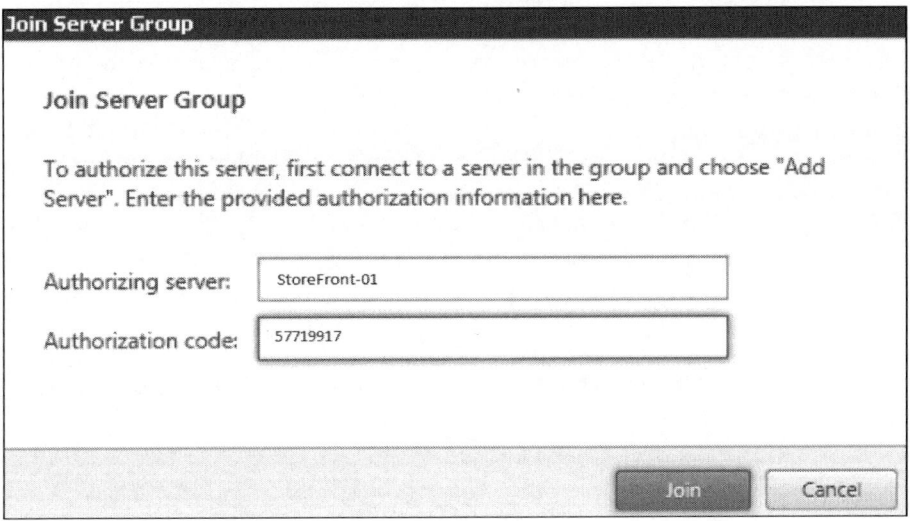

StoreFront will display a **Join Server Group** window with a progress bar and will typically take a few minutes to add the secondary server and synchronize all the settings between the two machines. Once that is complete, a message should be displayed that StoreFront-02 has been joined successfully and is now part of a multiple server deployment. Next, we will test the new Citrix StoreFront environment.

Testing the StoreFront™ user access

In this section, we will test the currently empty application store from a web browser, precisely the same way a user would do. This access method is known as **Receiver for Web** and it is an easy way to verify whether StoreFront was configured correctly:

1. First, log on to a client machine with network access to the StoreFront subnet.

2. Launch a web browser, such as **Internet Explorer (IE)**, and navigate to `https://YourPrimaryStoreFrontFQDN/Citrix/Citrix-StoreWeb`.

For this simulation, since we are yet to implement the load-balanced vServer in NetScaler for the two StoreFront machines in *Chapter 7, Load Balancing with Citrix® NetScaler®*, we will hit the `StoreFront-01` server directly to see whether we receive a valid web page. Where did we get this from? In the console on the StoreFront server, go to **Receiver for Web**. A web address such as `https://storefront/Citrix/Citrix-StoreWeb` should be displayed but the *storefront* string, which comes from **Base URL**, is the load-balanced vServer in NetScaler that has not yet been created. Thus, in order to test connectivity, we just replace that string in IE with the FQDN of the primary StoreFront server and leave the rest of the URL the same. In our case, the resultant address is `https://StoreFront-01.xendesktop.poc/Citrix/Citrix-StoreWeb`, which returns the user-facing web portal in the default Green Bubble theme:

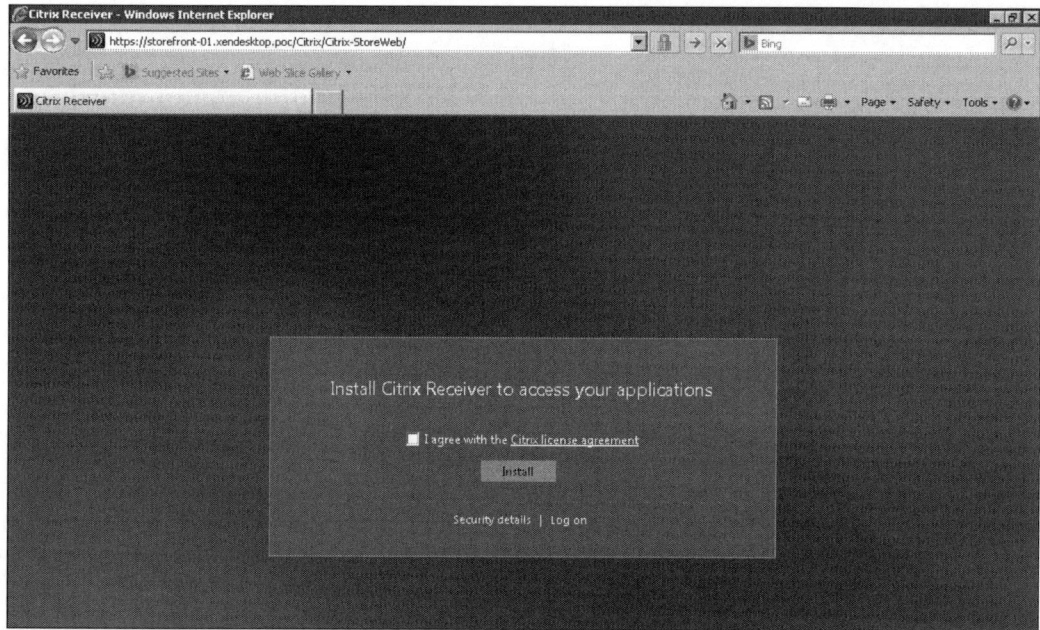

The user is now prompted to install **Citrix Receiver** to access Citrix-hosted applications and desktops.

3. Since we don't have any applications configured yet, we can click on **Log on** to skip this step (application publishing is covered in detail in *Chapter 10, Administering a XenApp® Environment – Application Management*).

   A **Cannot Complete Your Request** error will now be displayed. Why? In the current configuration of StoreFront, **Base URL** (`https://storefront/`) points to a load-balanced virtual server that we will create when we install the NetScaler load balancer in *Chapter 7, Load Balancing with Citrix® NetScaler®*. However, at the moment, this vServer does not yet exist. Since this URL is the entry point to the XenApp store for the user, the request cannot be processed. Keep in mind that this error message can also occur for a variety of other reasons such as wrong certificates, services not running, incorrect StoreFront information in NetScaler, and others (check the article CTX133904 on the Citrix Support site).

4. Let's go back to the console on the StoreFront server and change **Base URL** to `https://YourPrimaryStoreFrontFQDN/` (in this case, `https://storefront-01.xendesktop.poc/`):

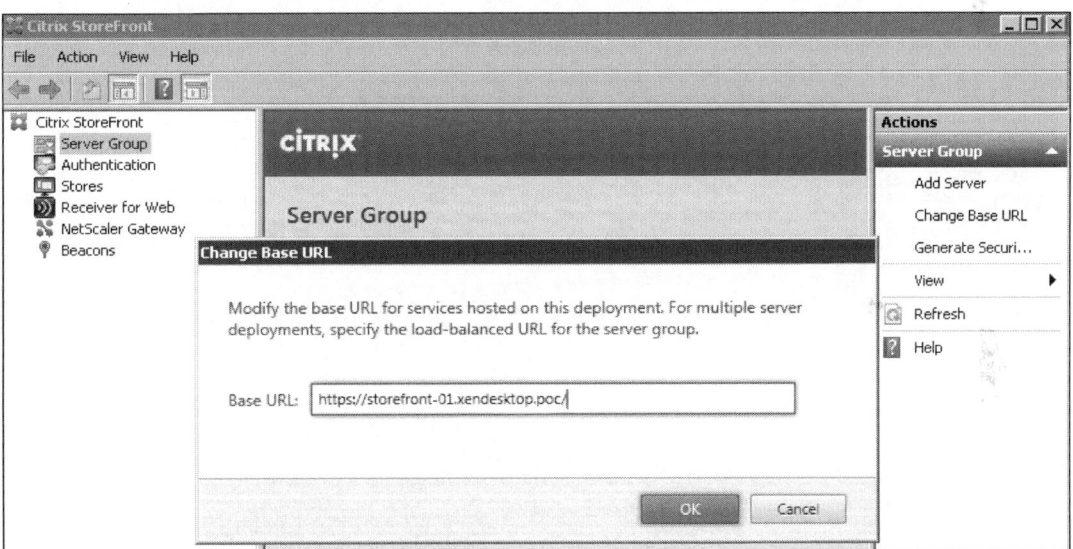

Notice that under **Receiver for Web**, the full URL has also changed.

5. On the client machine, launch a new web browser instance. Navigate to the new **Receiver for Web** URL https://YourPrimaryStoreFrontFQDN/ Citrix/Citrix-StoreWeb (in this case, https://storefront-01. xendesktop.poc/Citrix/Citrix-StoreWeb). The browser should now return the following Citrix Receiver authentication page:

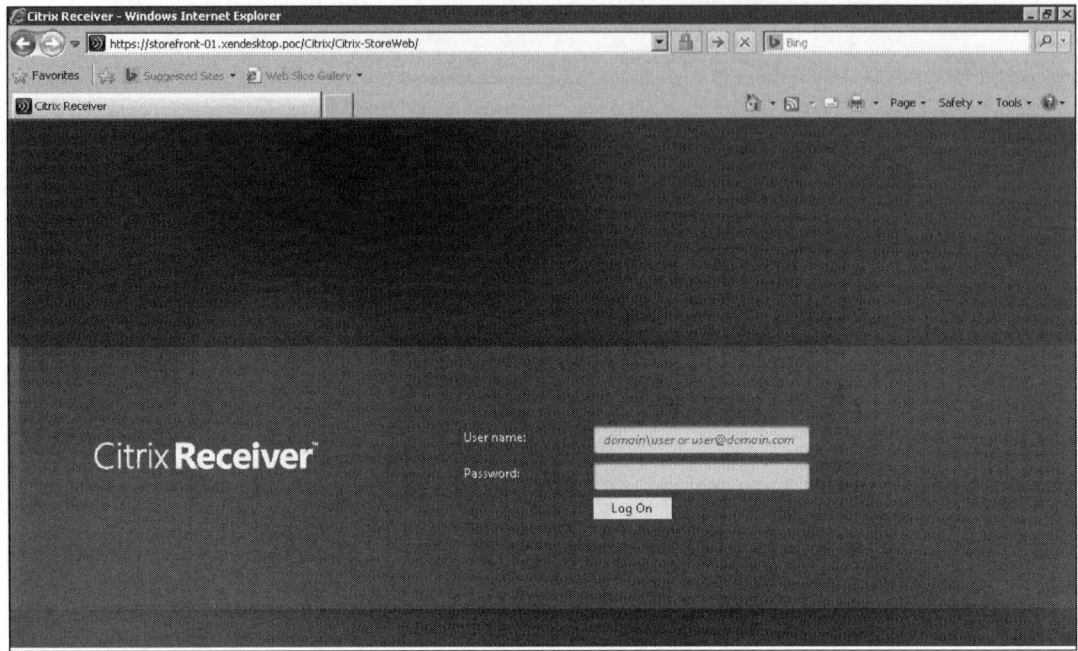

6. Type in your **User name** and **Password** in the credential fields and click on **Log On**. The user should now be redirected to their web store, which, at this point, is empty as no applications or desktops have been published yet. This test demonstrates that StoreFront is configured correctly:

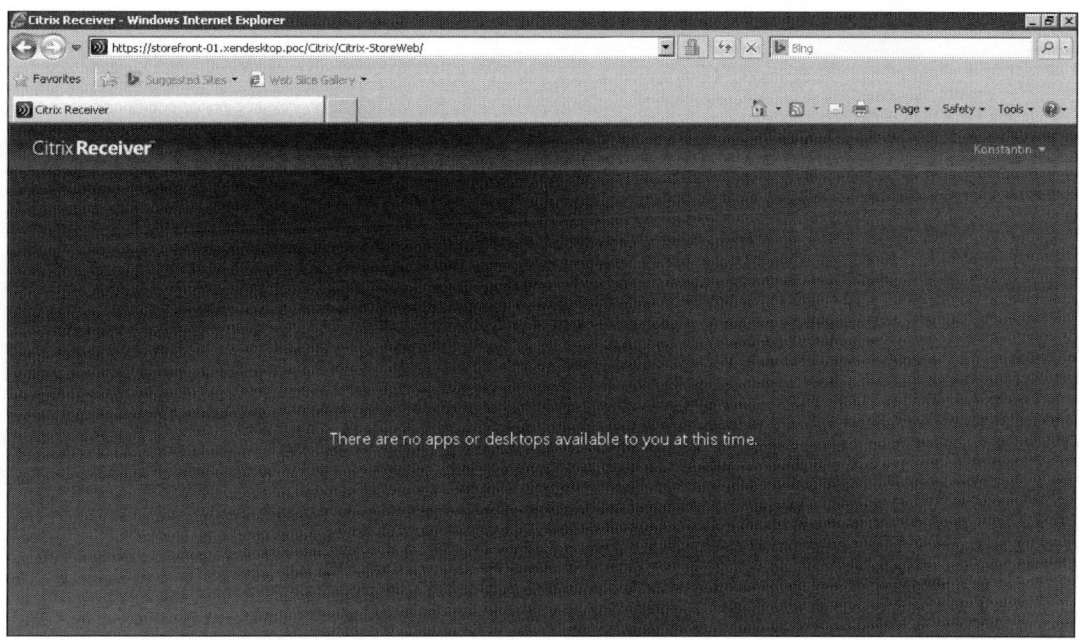

7. Log on to the StoreFront server and change **Base URL** back to the load-balanced vServer address (`https://storefront/`).

8. In the **StoreFront** management console under **Server Group**, click on **Propagate Changes** to synchronize the two servers.

Summary

In this chapter, you installed and configured your first StoreFront deployment. This highly available setup is the foundation of the access layer in the Citrix XenApp infrastructure, and can readily be used to test internal access to user stores via Receiver for Web. You also used SSL certificates in IIS to secure communications to the two servers and tested the validity of the certificates by connecting to the StoreFront HTTPS URL from a client computer.

In the next chapter, we will introduce NetScaler Gateway (formerly known as **Access Gateway**)—a powerful frontend solution by Citrix that, in external networks, enables secure access for users to applications and desktops hosted by XenApp. See you in a bit!

6
Installing and Configuring NetScaler Gateway™

For a number of years, IT administrators used Secure Gateway to frontend inbound traffic from external users. However, Secure Gateway is now obsolete and Citrix has shifted their development focus to a more robust and enterprise-scale solution. In recent years, Access Gateway Enterprise (available as both a physical MPX device and virtual VPX appliance) has been widely used by bigger companies to secure external access to Citrix XenApp and the XenDesktop environments. Access Gateway Standard and Advanced Edition, on the other hand, was the more popular product among small to midsized businesses. This was until recently when Citrix completely integrated the Gateway portion with the NetScaler appliance and renamed Access Gateway to **NetScaler Gateway (NGW)**. NGW can still be licensed as a standalone VPX product, but there is a big benefit in getting it along with the core NetScaler because of the enhanced functionalities that the latter adds, such as load balancing, traffic optimization, security, and other features. In this book, we use the NetScaler VPX, running as a virtual machine inside XenServer. If you have a physical appliance, the configuration would pretty much be the same at the software level, and you would only need to skip the part where we import the VPX instance to XenCenter. In the next two chapters, we will be working on NetScaler, configuring both Gateway and load balancing. If you are a seasoned NetScaler engineer, please excuse the very basic nature of this setup as this is only intended to complement the XenApp environment. For more advanced configurations, I recommend *Implementing NetScaler VPX™*, *Marius Sandbu*, *Packt Publishing*, which is a book solely dedicated to NetScaler and is also a great read for new and experienced engineers.

The following topics are covered in this chapter:

- Installing the NetScaler Gateway VPX, which includes virtual appliance deployment and specifications
- Configuring the NetScaler Gateway VPX, which includes a basic setup and virtual server configurations

Installing the NetScaler Gateway VPX™

Even though the NetScaler appliance is extremely scalable and feature-rich, the installation is not overly complex and can be done in a fair amount of time, provided that we have all the information readily available. The following table illustrates the prerequisites to be satisfied before starting the installation:

Resources	Resource count and memory requirements
Memory on a hypervisor host	2 GB
vCPUs	2
vNICs	2
Minimum storage	12 GB

The following IP addresses need to be configured on NetScaler for management, backend communications, and gateways:

- **NetScaler IP (NSIP)**: This is the management IP that administrators will use to access an appliance from SSH and the web GUI. In a traditional enterprise environment, the NSIP is typically an IP on the DMZ between the external and internal firewall. Besides, for management, the NetScaler also uses its NSIP to authenticate gateway users with the LDAP servers.

- **Subnet IP (SNIP)**: This is the IP that NetScaler uses to communicate with backend servers, such as StoreFront, Exchange, SQL, and others, to redirect and load balance connections to them. In a traditional enterprise scenario, the SNIP is typically an IP on the internal subnet where load-balanced servers are located, and NetScaler uses it as a source IP for the packets that it sends to these internal servers.

- **Virtual IP (VIP)**: This is the IP that a gateway virtual server resolves to. The public IP that users first hit to access the Citrix environment is translated via NAT by the external firewall to this VIP in the DMZ. One VIP will be needed for the gateway mentioned in this chapter and another one will be needed for the load balancer mentioned in *Chapter 7, Load Balancing with Citrix® NetScaler®*.

Last but not least, we need an account with administrator access to LDAP and the address of your LDAP servers to add to NetScaler once it is configured for management access. This way, we can enable the LDAP authentication for administration and end user traffic. Ideally, having at least two LDAP servers is recommended for redundancy.

Once we have obtained this information, we can proceed with installing and configuring NetScaler Gateway using the following step-by-step guide:

1. Log on to your MyCitrix account at `http://www.citrix.com/` and download the NetScaler Virtual Appliance 10.5 (or latest) to your local computer or network share accessible through XenCenter.

2. Launch XenCenter, right-click on the XenServer host, and click on **Import...**:

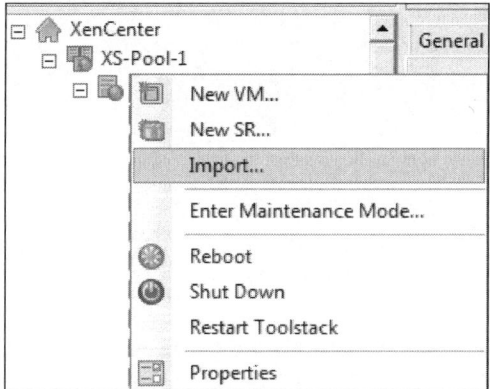

3. Follow the wizard to import the NetScaler XVA file and assign a home server, network adapter, and storage to the new VM.

4. When the VM starts automatically, open the **Console** tab in XenCenter and observe the FreeBSD boot process. When the virtual appliance is fully booted, you are prompted to configure an IP address for the management, subnet mask, and gateway. Assign a value from your network for each item and press *Enter* after each line. Use a static IP address for the appliance. Confirm the configuration if required:

```
The key's randomart image is:
+--[ DSA 1024]-----+
|                  |
|                  |
|                  |
|     .            |
|   +   S          |
|  + . .   .       |
|  o .. ...o       |
|  Eo+ +o=o..      |
|   o+B++==.       |
+------------------+

sysctl: unknown oid 'machdep.cpu_idle_hlt'
Start daemons: syslogd Feb 17 01:33:23 <kern.info> ns syslogd: kernel boot file
is /flash/ns-10.5-55.8
inetd cron httpd monit sshd .

!There is no ns.conf in the /nsconfig!

Start Netscaler software
tput: no terminal type specified and no TERM environmental variable.
Enter NetScaler's IPv4 address []: 172.30.185.7
Enter Netmask []: 255.255.255.0
Enter Gateway IPv4 address []: 172.30.185.10
```

5. Launch a web browser and navigate to the NetScaler management IP address that you assigned in the previous step using HTTP (for example, `http://YourNetScalerIPAdddress/`). A Citrix authentication page like this should appear on the screen:

6. Log on to the NetScaler web console using `nsroot` as both **User Name** and **Password**. These are the default root credentials and they should be changed at the very first login. Verify that the logon has succeeded and the NetScaler **Dashboard** page has appeared.

Configuring the NetScaler Gateway VPX™

Now that we have installed the NetScaler Gateway virtual (VPX) appliance onto the hypervisor and connected it to the network, we can leverage the management GUI to configure licensing, modes, features, and virtual servers to integrate and provide access to the XenApp environment.

Licensing your NetScaler® appliance

Like any other Citrix product, you need to license NetScaler to take advantage of its functionalities. For free trial and Proof of Concept, Citrix offers an Express edition, which you can download for free for a specified period of time to test the full set of features available with a NetScaler Platinum license. In this scenario, we demonstrate the allocation and import of license files. Specific licenses are required to unlock certain features, such as SmartAccess and the SSL VPN, which are not required for the solutions in this book. For this exercise, you will need the host ID (also known as the Flexnet ID and native MAC address) of the appliance and your MyCitrix credentials. Here is how you can get the host ID information:

1. Use a SSH tool, such as PuTTY, to connect to the NetScaler **command-line interface (CLI)** on the management IP.

2. After you are prompted to authenticate, enter the `nsroot` username and password to gain *sudo* access.

3. In the CLI, type in `shell` and press *Enter* to switch to the shell mode in BSD.

4. In the shell, run `lmutil lmhostid -ether` to get the host ID of the appliance.

Here is how you can allocate a license for the NetScaler VPX using the host ID:

1. Navigate to `https://www.citrix.com/` and log on to your MyCitrix account using the credentials supplied to you by Citrix.

2. Under **Licensing**, click on **Activate and Allocate licenses** and populate the information required.

3. Upon receiving a confirmation, download the available license file from your MyCitrix portal.

4. Log on to your NetScaler appliance using a web console (`http://NetScalerManagementIP`).

5. Open the **Configuration** tab and the **System** node. Select **Licenses** and click on the **Manage Licenses...** button:

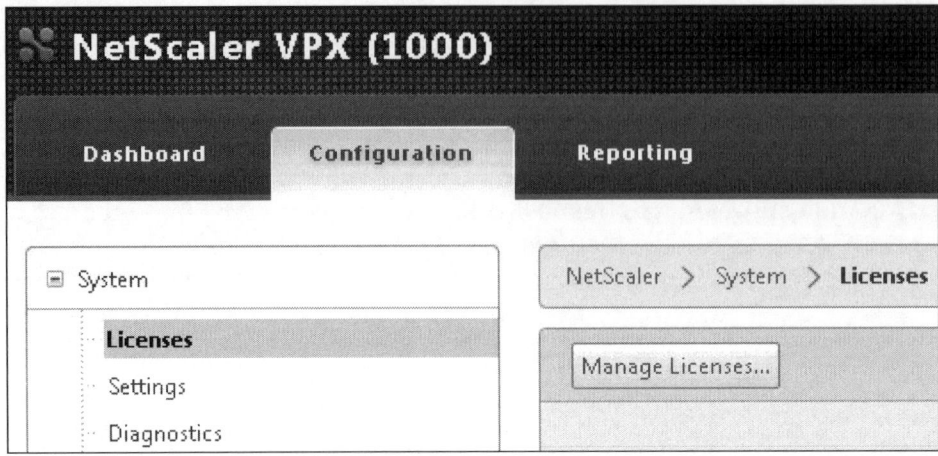

6. Click on the **Add New License** button and select **Upload license files from a local computer**. Upload the file(s) you've downloaded from the Citrix portal for your appliance:

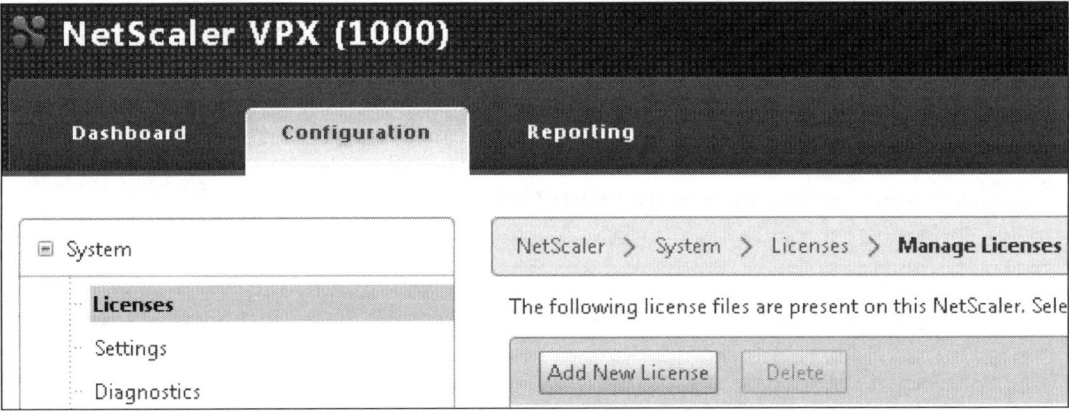

Once this is complete, go back to the **Licenses** node under **System** and check your license edition (Standard, Enterprise, or Platinum). There should be a green checkmark next to each licensed feature.

Basic modes and settings

As a multitiered appliance, NetScaler can assume various roles on the network and perform a wide variety of functions to direct, optimize, and secure traffic. Apply the following modes and settings to prepare the appliance for gateway and load balancing:

1. Under **System**, click on **Settings** and open **Configure Modes**. Choose **Fast Ramp**, **Edge Configuration**, **Layer 3 Mode**, **Use Subnet IP**, and **Path MTU Discovery**, and then click on **OK**:

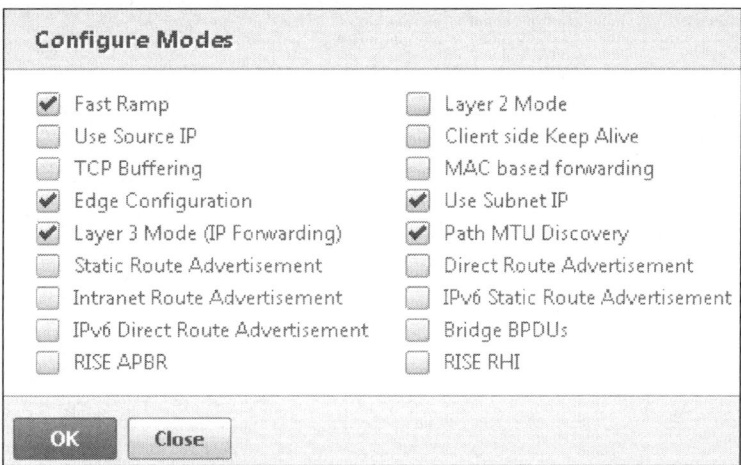

2. On the same node, open **Configure Basic Features**. Select **SSL Offloading**, **Load Balancing**, **Rewrite**, **Authentication, Authorization and Auditing**, and **NetScaler Gateway**. Now, click on **OK**:

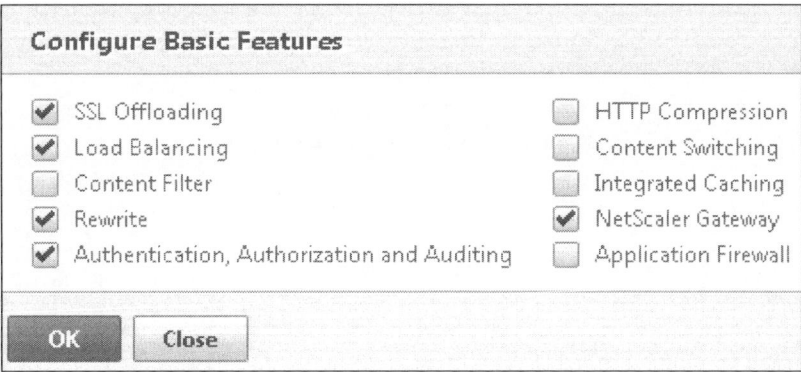

3. On the same node under **Settings**, open **Change TCP Parameters**. Select **Use Nagle's Algorithm** and **Selective Acknowledgement**. Leave everything else as default:

☑ Selective Acknowledgement	☑ Use Nagle's algorithm
☐ Immediate ACK on receiving packet with PUSH	☐ SYN Attack Detection
☐ Down service reset	☐ Limit Persist Probes
☐ Learn Virtual Server MSS	

4. On the same node under **Settings**, open **Change Global System Settings**. Select **Use Proxy Port** and **Enable RNAT TCP Proxy**:

☑ Use Proxy Port
☑ Enable RNAT TCP Proxy
☐ Enable RNAT Source IP Persistency
☐ Use in-built system user to communicate with other appliances
☐ Enable Client TCP/IP Header Insertion

5. On the same node under **Settings**, open **Change HTTP Parameters**. Enable **Drop invalid HTTP requests** and **Log HTTP error responses**:

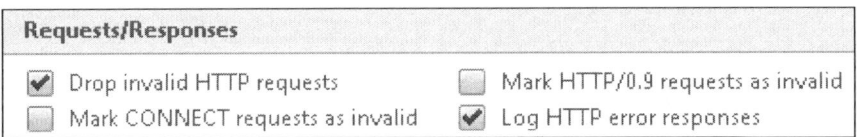

Requests/Responses

☑ Drop invalid HTTP requests	☐ Mark HTTP/0.9 requests as invalid
☐ Mark CONNECT requests as invalid	☑ Log HTTP error responses

The NetScaler system settings can be further tweaked and more advanced configurations can be introduced to take maximum advantage of the capabilities of this product. The scope of this book, however, is focused around a load-balanced Citrix XenApp solution for internal and external users, so some of the more advanced NetScaler settings are not explored in this case.

Configuring High Availability

High Availability (HA) is a feature of NetScaler that allows you to pair two devices or appliances of the same model, version, and firmware build in an active-passive configuration to provide quick failover in case of an outage. HA between the primary and the secondary node is maintained via a heartbeat sent every 200ms over the UDP port 3003. Other ports related to HA that need to be open between the two NetScalers are TCP 3010 for synchronization and replication, 3011 for command propagation, and 22 for file sync. To configure HA, simply log on to the management GUI of the primary NetScaler, and under HA in the **System** menu, add the IP address of the secondary appliance and provide credentials with an administrative access to it. Before adding HA, the passive device has to be configured with an IP address accessible from the first one for successful pairing:

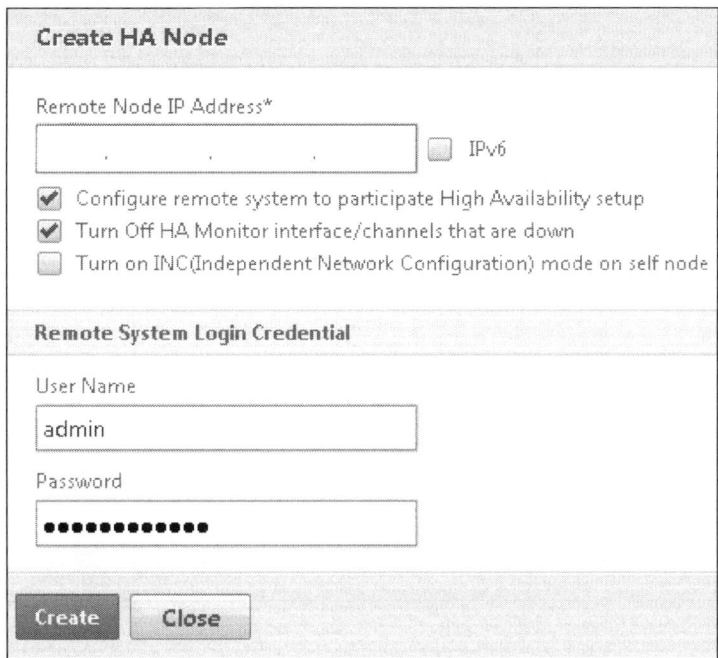

Note that if the NetScalers are different from each other in terms of model, version, or firmware, pairing is likely to fail, and currently, Citrix does not support such configuration.

Configuring the LDAP authentication

To add one or more LDAP servers to the NetScaler configuration for the Active Directory authentication, complete the following steps:

1. Log on to the NetScaler web GUI and expand the **System** node.

2. Expand the **Authentication** node and click on **LDAP**. Switch to the **Servers** tab and add your LDAP servers to the list. Ensure that you populate LDAP **Connection Settings** (**Base DN** and **Administrator DN**) as configured in Active Directory. When you've finished, click on **Create**.

3. Switch to the **Policies** tab and add a new policy. Define a name, your LDAP server and an expression, which for this setup is ns_true. When you're done, click on **Create**:

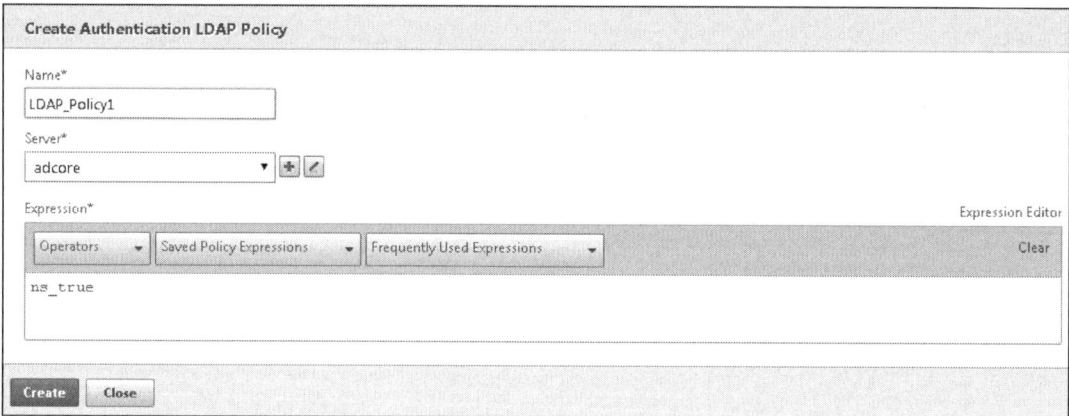

4. Verify that the policy is listed under **LDAP** as shown in the following screenshot:

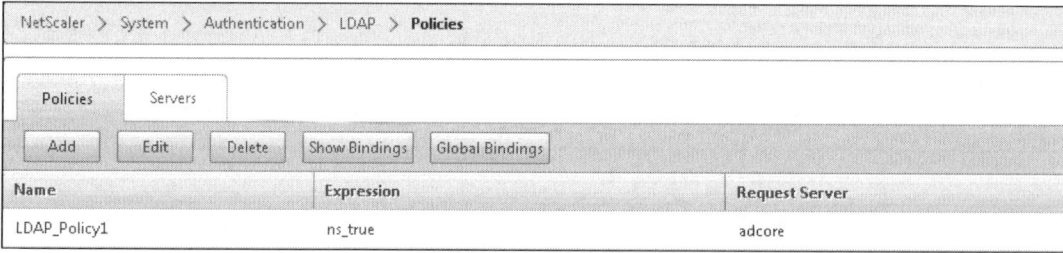

Adding a Subnet IP

To add a **Subnet IP (SNIP)** for NetScaler to be able to communicate with internal (backend) networks, complete the following steps:

1. In the **Configuration** tab, expand **System**, and then **Network**. Click on the **IPs** node and verify that the management IP you assigned in the previous section matches the **NetScaler IP (NSIP)** displayed here.

2. Click on **Add...** and type in **IP Address** and **Netmask** chosen for the SNIP. In a traditional enterprise scenario with external DMZ and internal networks, the SNIP should be a member of the internal network where the StoreFront servers reside. A static IP should be used here as well to avoid unexpected changes in configuration. Under **IP Type**, select **Subnet IP**. At the bottom of the page, for security purposes, uncheck **Enable Management Access control to support the below listed applications**:

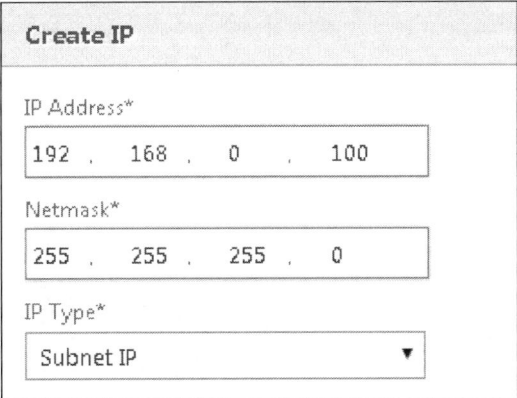

3. Leave everything else as default and click on **OK** to create the SNIP.

4. Expand the **Network** node again, and click on **Routes**. Verify that a new DIRECT route was created automatically pointing to the new SNIP.

Managing SSL certificates

In order to access a gateway URL over SSL, you will need to have an SSL certificate in place on the NetScaler Gateway to secure traffic coming in externally. To do this, we would need to create an RSA key and a new **Certificate Signing Request (CSR)** to be submitted to a trusted CA. Complete the following steps to create the CSR and import a new certificate:

1. Under **Traffic Management**, click on the **SSL** node, and on the right-hand side, under **SSL Keys**, click on **Create RSA Key**:

2. Populate the required fields to define the name, bits, format, and passphrase for the new private key as shown in the following table:

Fields	Values
Key filename	NS-key
Key size(bits)	2048
Public exponent value	3
Key format	**PEM**
PEM encoding algorithm	DES3
PEM passphrase	A password of your choice
Confirm PEM passphrase	The same PEM passphrase

3. Under **Traffic Management**, click on the **SSL** node, and on the right-hand side, under **SSL Certificates**, click on **Create CSR (Certificate Signing Request)**:

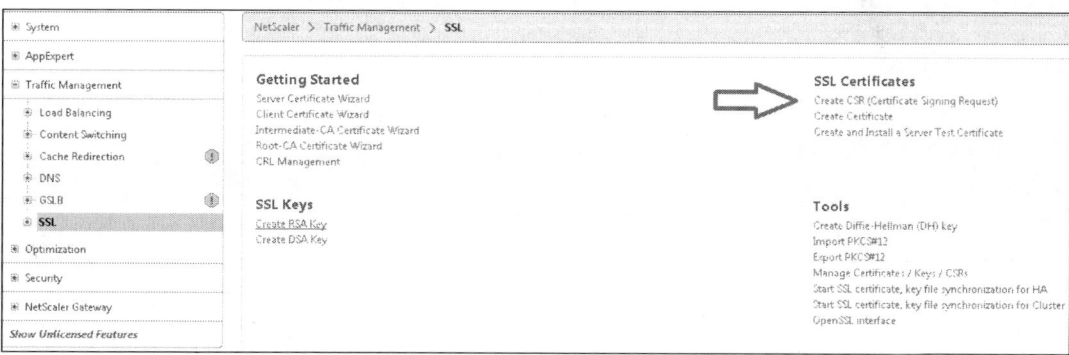

4. Fill in the required fields as shown in the following table:

Fields	Values
Request filename	A name of your choice
Key filename	NS-key
Key format	**PEM**
PEM passphrase (for an encrypted key)	The password from the RSA key
Country	Your country
State or province	Your state or province
Organization name	Your company name
Common name	FQDN of your gateway URL

Once created, use the option to download the CSR and submit it to your trusted CA to be issued an SSL certificate. After the CA verifies your authenticity, they will send you a certificate bundle, which you will upload to NetScaler via the **Manage Certificates/Keys/CSRs** option in the **Tools** section of the **SSL** node under **Traffic Management** or directly from the **Certificates** menu under **SSL**:

Also, now would also be a good time to upload your root and intermediate certificates signed by your trusted CA to the NetScaler appliance.

Configuring session policies and profiles

Session policies are a great way in NetScaler to configure granular access to the Citrix environment for users from specific endpoint devices, geographical regions, and other factors. For the purpose of this environment, we are going to configure and apply a single session policy, giving access to all users to Receiver for Web.

Follow these steps to configure a NetScaler session profile and policy:

1. Log on to the NetScaler web console.

2. Go to NetScaler Gateway and under **Policies**, select **Session**. Open the **Profiles** tab and click on **Add**.

3. Enter a name for the profile (for example, `Citrix_Prod`) and go straight to the **Published Applications** tab.

4. Apply the following settings for **Published Applications**:

Fields	Values
ICA proxy	ON
Web interface address	`https://storefrontlb.xendesktop.lab` (This is the future URL that resolves to NetScaler load balancing virtual IP for StoreFront that we will configure in *Chapter 7, Load Balancing with Citrix® NetScaler®*)
Web interface address type	IPV4
Single sign-on domain	`xendesktop.lab` (This is the domain that users are authenticated to)

5. Switch to the **Client Experience** tab and apply the following settings:

Fields	Values
Session time-out (mins)	30
Clientless access	ON
Clientless access URL encoding	Clear
Clientless access persistent cookie	DENY
Plug-in type	JAVA
Credential index	PRIMARY

6. Leave all other settings at their default values and click on **OK**.
7. Switch to the **Policies** tab and click on **Add**. Create the following values:

Fields	Values
Name	`General_Policy` (or any name of your preference)
Action	`Citrix_Prod` (or the name that you've assigned to the session profile)
Expression	`ns_true`

When you're done, click on **Create**. Verify that the new policy and profile are present in the list under their respective tabs.

Creating a virtual server

Ultimately, the purpose of NetScaler Gateway and its predecessor, Access Gateway, is to provide a frontend authentication point for external users to be introduced to the network and directed properly to their XenApp, XenDesktop, and XenMobile resources. NetScaler Gateway can also be set up for internal users if this extra layer of security is required. However, internal access is often set up to bypass the gateway and connect directly to the NetScaler load balancer VIP pointing to the backend StoreFront servers. In this case, we will create a virtual server in the DMZ. When users connect to the outside URL, the connection will be translated to this DMZ IP, which in turn will use the session policy to direct the user to the StoreFront load balancer vServer on NetScaler, and ultimately to the StoreFront server itself:

1. Expand the **System** node and navigate to **NetScaler Gateway**.

2. Open the **Virtual Servers** node and click on **Add....**

3. Give the virtual server a name, an IP address from the DMZ, define 443 for the port, and then click on **Continue**:

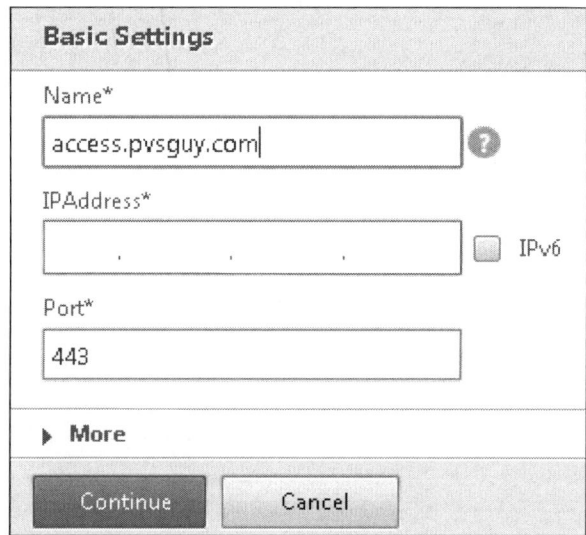

4. Under **Certificates**, click on **No Server Certificate**, and bind the SSL certificate issued for your NetScaler Gateway vServer.

5. Next, click on **Authentication**, and for **Policies**, choose **LDAP** and the **Primary** type:

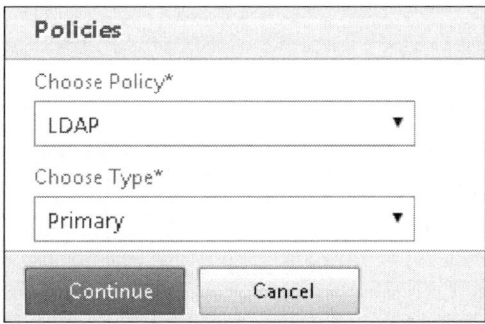

6. Click on **Bind**, select your LDAP policy, and click on **Insert**:

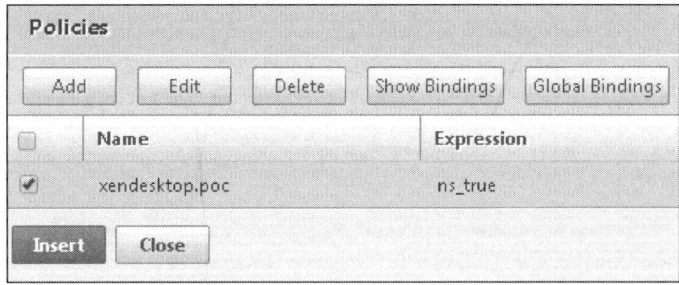

7. On the right-hand side panel, click on **Published Applications**, and then click on **No STA Server**. Under **Secure Ticket Authority Server**, click on **Bind**, and populate the URL of your STA machine (this can be the new Delivery Controller that you created for XenApp or you can use another STA host, such as your old Zone Data Collector if you are still running XenApp 6.5 or earlier versions of it). When you've finished, hit **Insert**:

8. Scroll down the vServer configuration page and click the **+** sign next to **Policies**. From the dropdown, select the **Session** policies and for the **Policy** type, choose **Request**:

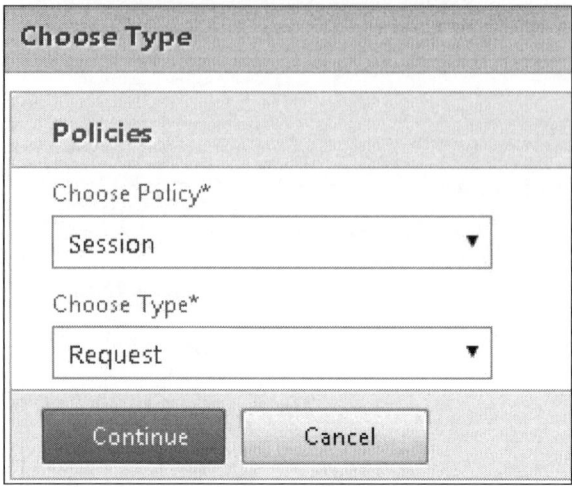

Click on **Continue** and then bind the Session Policy you created earlier in the chapter (General_Policy) to the new gateway virtual server. When the task is complete, click on **Done** on the vServer configuration page and verify that it is listed under NetScaler Gateway Virtual Servers and has a green **Up** circle, indicating that the vServer is functional.

The NetScaler Gateway setup can now be tested by browsing to the external HTTPS URL of the gateway vServer from a web browser. Before you do this, add an entry to the host file on your local machine to map the public IP assigned for the vServer to the FQDN. Of course, the load balancer virtual server that will be serving the connection to one of the StoreFront servers running in the backend is not yet configured and no applications have been published from the XenApp Delivery Controller. However, when you connect to that URL, the user login page should come up asking for credentials. This would mean that NetScaler Gateway was configured correctly at least at the virtual server level:

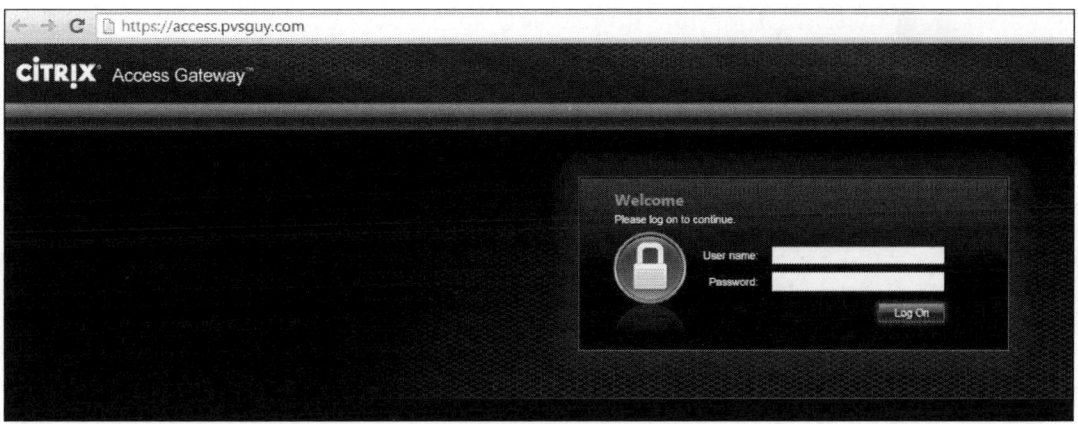

In an enterprise environment, it is very likely that internal users are required by a security policy to remain internal when connecting to the XenApp resources. In order to achieve this without being routed externally, you can create a second NetScaler Gateway virtual server with an internal VIP address to act as a callback URL and add an entry to the host file of the StoreFront server to point the gateway FQDN to the internal VIP. The same instructions from earlier in the section can be used to create the secondary vServer in NetScaler. There is, however, an additional step that needs to be taken on the StoreFront server to enable this dual-homed scenario. On the StoreFront server, using the management console, we need to navigate to the **NetScaler Gateway** node and add NetScaler Gateway to the StoreFront configuration using the following parameters:

Fields	Values
Display name	This is a name of your preference that's defined for the NetScaler appliance
NetScaler Gateway URL	This is the URL of the vServer as defined in NetScaler Gateway
Version	Choose the correct version level of the NetScaler device
Subnet IP address (optional)	The SNIP as defined in NetScaler
Logon type	Choose a domain for this configuration
Callback URL	Type in the URL pointing to the internal NetScaler Gateway vServer or VIP

For StoreFront to work properly with the NetScaler Gateway virtual servers, we also need to ensure that **Pass-through from NetScaler Gateway** is enabled from **Add/Remove Methods** under the **Authentication** node in the StoreFront console. In addition to this, **Remote Access** needs to be enabled with no VPN tunnel from the **Stores** menu:

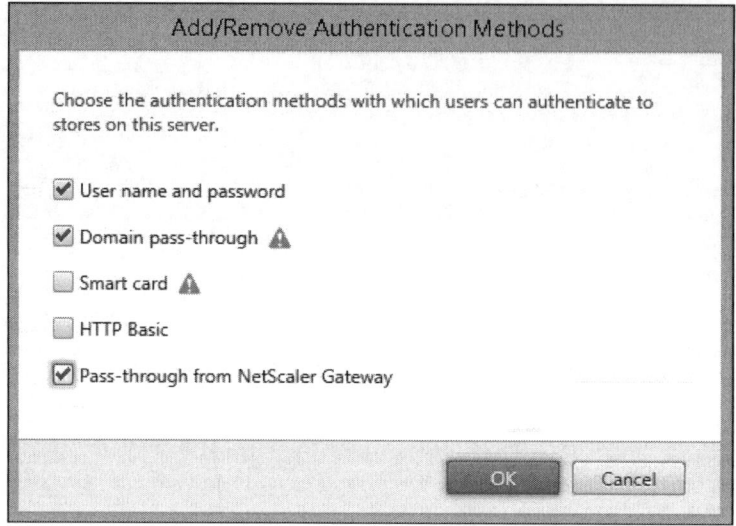

Enabling authentication methods in StoreFront

Summary

In this chapter, you learned how to quickly install and configure NetScaler Gateway from scratch to serve as an authentication and redirection point for inbound connections to the XenApp environment. Now, with the new gateway in place, users will be able to connect from outside networks via a secure protocol and get redirected to the internal StoreFront (web) servers where they will gain access to the resources assigned to them. The only missing piece before we can mark the access layer as complete is the load balancer, which logically stands between the gateway and StoreFront but is really part of the same NetScaler appliance residing in the DMZ. In the next chapter, we will build on the current configuration and implement load balancing to achieve maximum performance and overhead reduction with Citrix NetScaler. Don't go anywhere!

7
Load Balancing with Citrix® NetScaler®

Today's IT organizations are a complex ecosystem of well…expectations. Performance is treated as a commodity and nothing short of the fastest is acceptable by enterprise software, data centers, and services. Not only do systems need to deliver quickly but they also have to be highly available with no single point of failure. As a product that impacts your entire IT infrastructure, Citrix XenApp is expected to provide high performance for end users, while also keeping an environment secure and easy to manage for system administrators. Over the years, Citrix has acquired and developed a number of products that add value to its core solutions. One such product is NetScaler, part of which we already deployed in the previous chapter. Now that we have an authentication point in place for XenApp, we are going to set up load balancing for StoreFront. NetScaler can be used to load balance a multitude of services not just from the Citrix perspective, but also applications or web servers that handle a high number of connections. It is also a popular solution for Exchange and SharePoint due to a wide variety of load balancing options and optimization mechanisms that it has in place.

In this chapter, you will learn how to implement the following solutions:

- NetScaler load balancing for StoreFront
- HTTP and HTTPS load balancing services and Service Groups
- SSL certificates for StoreFront
- Load balancing monitors

Configuring Citrix NetScaler® for load balancing

The configuration of NetScaler load balancing can be done via two methods—from the GUI and the CLI. Now, if you have been in IT for a while, you know that GUI versus CLI is one of the most ancient debates of all times in both the Windows and the Linux world. Some people simply refuse to use GUIs because, as they say (and rightly so), the command line gives you a lot more control over an OS and filesystem, and the ability to script and automate tasks. Others stay as far away from CLIs as possible and prefer GUIs because of their visual presentation, which is generally more intuitive to new users. Throughout this chapter, we mostly use the graphic interface, but if you want to dive deeper into the various things that the NetScaler command shell can do for you, I suggest that you take a look at *Implementing NetScaler VPX™, Marius Sandbu, Packt Publishing*, which, in my personal opinion, is a great cookbook to get started with NetScaler. For the purpose of our deployment, we will take a step-by-step approach to check the prerequisites and configurations needed to load balance our backend StoreFront servers.

Network requirements

In most enterprise implementations, IT is somewhat departmentalized so there is a networking person who is involved in routing and switching, a firewall admin who maintains firewall rules and prevents intrusion, a security specialist who takes care of antivirus, and the list goes on. Often, as a Citrix administrator or consultant, you will find yourself in a situation where you have to request changes from people in different teams in order to get things working in your environment. A prime example of a potential situation such as this is when you configure NetScaler to route traffic properly to your internal network. The following list of requirements will help you explain what needs to be in place to the right teams and avoid fiery debates with your network folks:

- **Subnet IP (SNIP)**: This requests an IP address on the same subnet as your StoreFront servers and add it to the NetScaler IPs under **System** to create a direct route from NetScaler to this subnet.

- **Port 443**: This requests that port 443 be opened from the DMZ where the NetScaler Load Balancer service resides to the internal network where the StoreFront servers are located.

- **Port 389**: This requests that port 389 be opened from the NSIP to the LDAP server for NetScaler Gateway authentication. Alternatively, port 636 can be used for Secure LDAP.

- **Port 8080**: This requests that the STA port 8080 be opened from the NetScaler Gateway DMZ to the internal network where your Delivery Controllers reside. This is an alternative port that can be used intentionally to avoid any conflicts that may arise due to sharing the default port 80 with IIS. For ease of deployment, you could use port 80 (or 443 if required by security), which would need to be allowed to the Delivery Controllers' subnet.

With these requirements in place, we should have no problem routing traffic from the NetScaler Gateway and Load Balancer to the internal networks where our Citrix infrastructure resides.

Verifying settings and licensing

First, we need to ensure that load balancing is included in our license and that the actual feature is enabled on NetScaler. To verify this, open the NetScaler web console by browsing to the NSIP and authenticating with the help of either the root or Active Directory credentials. Once inside the console, go to the **Configuration** section and expand the **Systems** node to find **Licenses**. Verify that there is a green checkmark next to **Load Balancing** as shown in the following screenshot:

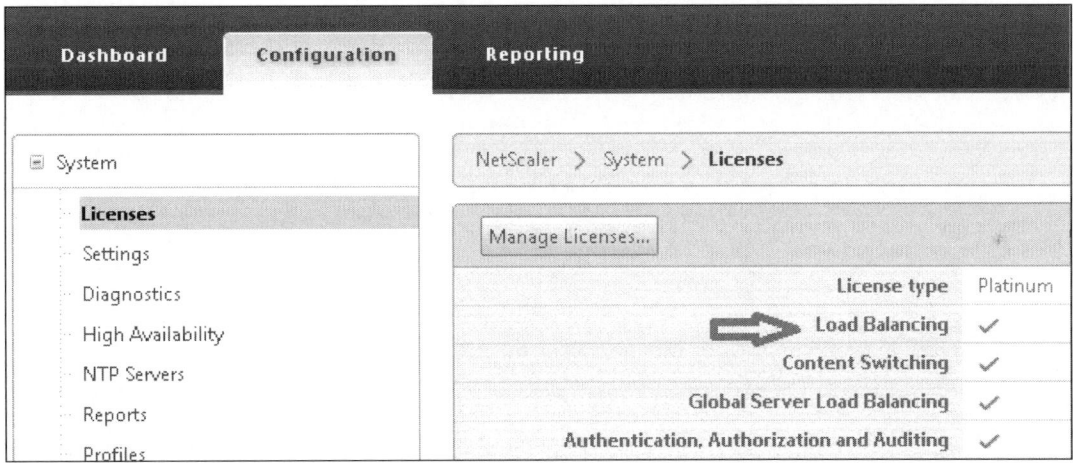

If the license file was correctly allocated and uploaded to the appliance but you still don't see the **Load Balancing** feature as licensed, be sure to consult Citrix or the vendor you've purchased licenses from to obtain more information on this issue.

Obtaining SSL certificates

Now that we know that NetScaler is licensed and ready to be used for load balancing, we need to ensure the correct SSL certificates are in place. In the previous chapter, where we deployed the gateway feature of NetScaler, we created a **Certificate Signing Request (CSR)**, which was sent to a trusted Certificate Authority. A certificate bundle was then received and bound to the gateway virtual server so that users could navigate to `https://<YourExternalURLforXenApp>`. Let's go ahead and use the same methodology to get an SSL certificate for the load balancing virtual server we are about to create. The only thing we need to change is the **Common Name** of the certificate that matches a FQDN of your choice. Some examples are `citrixlb.yourdomain.com`, `storefrontlb.yourdomain.com`, and so on (the logic here is to give it a short but descriptive value).

Adding StoreFront™ servers in NetScaler®

The first step towards configuring load balancing is to actually add the name and IP address information of the StoreFront servers to the NetScaler appliance so that they can later be referenced by the load balancing service. To accomplish this, log in to the Web GUI and perform the following tasks:

1. Under **Configuration**, expand **Traffic Management**, and click on **Servers**.

2. Click on **Add...**, populate the name and IP address of your primary StoreFront server, and then click on **Create**:

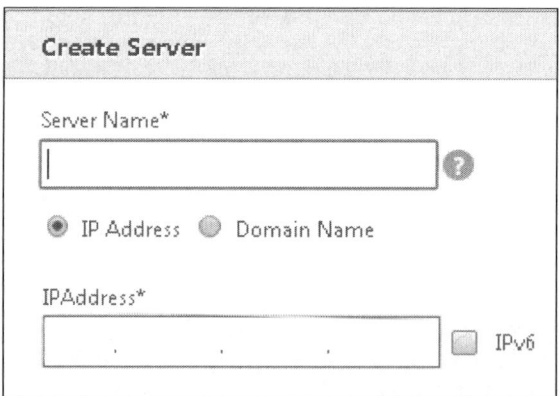

3. Click on **Add...** again, populate the name and IP address of your secondary StoreFront server, and then click on **Create**.

Creating Service Groups

The next step in enabling load balancing is to create a Service Group. In Citrix NetScaler, a service is a virtual mechanism that uses different algorithms to load balance backend servers in order to enhance session performance and improve system reliability. More than a dozen network protocols can be used for load balancing, including HTTP, HTTPS, FTP, DNS, and others. In this case, we are interested in HTTPS because this is the protocol used for communicating with the StoreFront machines. Sometimes, it is more desirable to create a Service Group instead of a standalone service as you can manage multiple services as part of this group. Use the following instructions to create a Service Group in NetScaler:

1. Under **Configuration**, expand **Traffic Management**, and click on **Service Groups**.

2. Click on **Add...**, assign a name for the load balancing service (for example, XA_SF_HTTPS), select **SSL** for the protocol, and click on **Continue**:

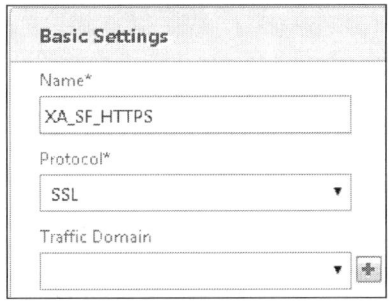

3. On the right-hand side of the screen, click on **Service Group Members**, select **Server Based**, add the primary StoreFront server from the drop-down menu, and specify port 443. Click on **Create** and then repeat the same step for the secondary StoreFront server:

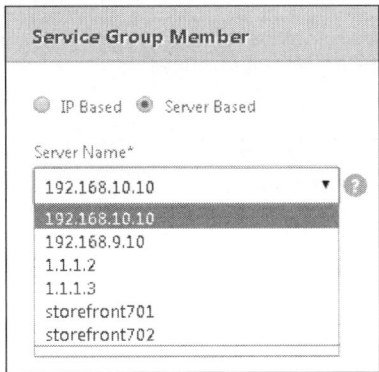

4. On the right-hand side, in the **Advanced** menu, click on **Monitors**, and add a Monitor binding to the **Service Group** of the **https-ecv** type. Alternatively, we can create a custom monitor for StoreFront to poll the backend StoreFront services.

A Monitor will regularly check the health of the backend StoreFront servers and mark them as **Down** if it doesn't receive a response from the specified protocol. There are plenty of built-in template Monitors on NetScaler that you can use to poll load-balanced servers and also create customized Monitors to fit the needs of your specific scenario. Some people have asked me why we can't just select ping as a Monitor for StoreFront servers? The answer is simple. A backend Windows machine, such as StoreFront, may be reachable on a network but this doesn't mean that IIS is actually working. So, in order to request specific information related to web traffic from the StoreFront boxes, we are better off with a more intelligent Monitor, such as **https-ecv**, which specifically probes for HTTPS availability. We can also create a new monitor from the **Load Balancing** menu in **Traffic Management** and leverage the **STOREFRONT** type to specifically check for the availability of store and services on the StoreFront servers. This is demonstrated in the following screenshot:

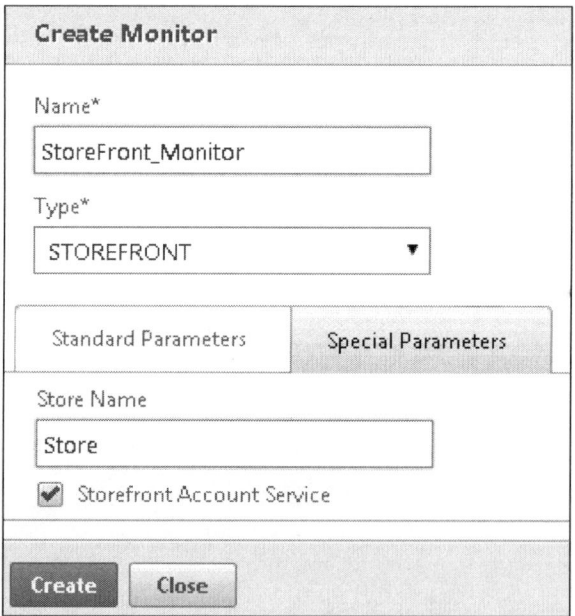

Now that we have a Service Group for HTTPS that point to the two StoreFront servers, we are ready to create the load balancing virtual server (also known as vServer) in the next section.

Configuring a load balancing VIP

The last step in configuring load balancing on NetScaler is to create a virtual server and associate it with the HTTPS Service Group that we created in the previous section. To accomplish this, we need to reserve an IP from the DMZ and make sure that it's mapped to the load balancer FQDN in DNS. For example, if we assign `citrixlb.xendesktop.poc`, it needs to resolve to this new IP address. Here are the steps to create the load balancing vServer and a **Virtual IP (VIP)**:

1. Under the **Configuration** tab in NetScaler, expand **Traffic Management**, select **Virtual Servers** that falls under **Load Balancing**, and click on **Add...**.

2. Assign a name, IP address, and **SSL** for **Protocol**, as shown in the following screenshot, and then click on **Continue**:

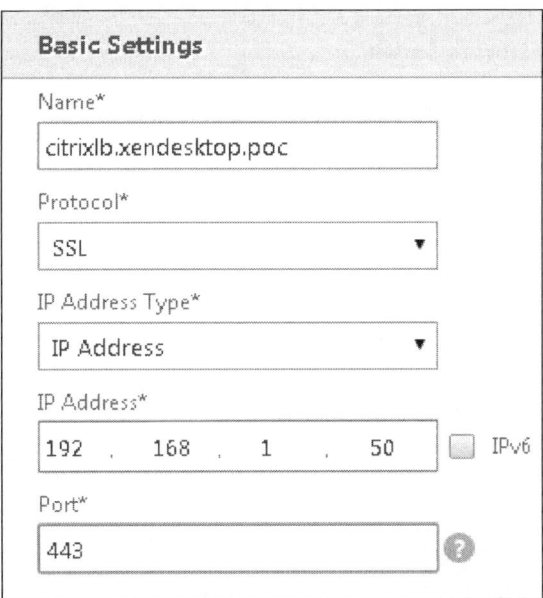

3. On the right-hand side, under **Advanced**, click on **Service Group**, and then click on **Bind**. A list of available Service Groups will show up. Select the one you created in the previous section, and then click on **Insert**:

4. Click on **Save** and verify that one Service Group is now assigned to the vServer.

5. Click on **SSL Certificates** in the **Advanced** menu of the vServer properties and bind the SSL certificate obtained previously for that virtual server. In addition to this, bind the Root Certificate as well to maintain the trust hierarchy of the SSL chain. After the full configuration of the vServer is complete, we shouldn't forget to import the SSL certificate in IIS on the StoreFront servers in order to avoid any SSL trust issues.

6. Next, click on **Method** in the **Advanced** menu of the vServer properties and choose a load balancing algorithm for StoreFront. There are more than a dozen available algorithms, including **ROUNDROBIN, LEASTCONNECTION, LEASTRESPONSETIME, SOURCEIPHASH, LEASTPACKETS,** and others. Choose the one that makes the most sense for your particular environment. For this scenario, we can select **LEASTCONNECTION** so that the service sends connections to the StoreFront server that has the least amount of connections at the time:

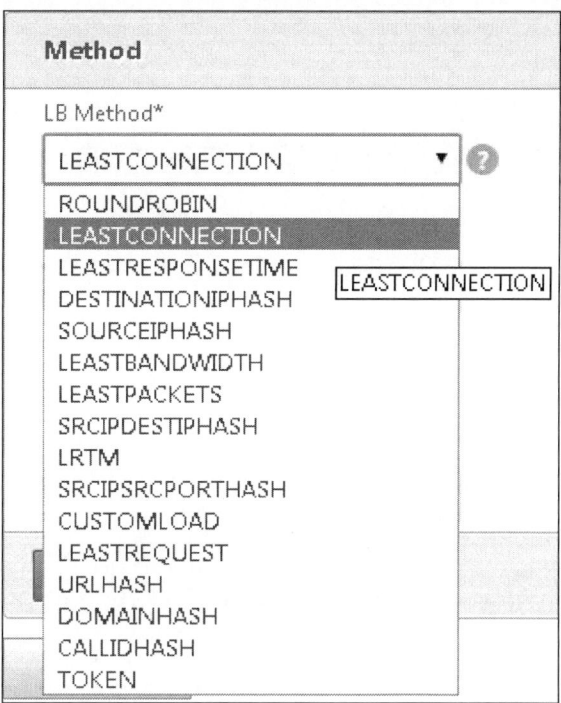

7. Optionally, we can configure **Persistence** (again from the **Advanced** menu of the vServer properties). The purpose of **Persistence** is to prevent client transactions from changing backend servers, but rather stick with the same server through the duration of the established session. Several **Persistence** methods are available in the dropdown. Since client computers will be connecting to an HTTPS load balancing vServer, we can choose **COOKIEINSERT**. With **COOKIEINSERT**, NetScaler will insert a cookie in the packet header of the first client request containing the IP address and port information of the load balanced service:

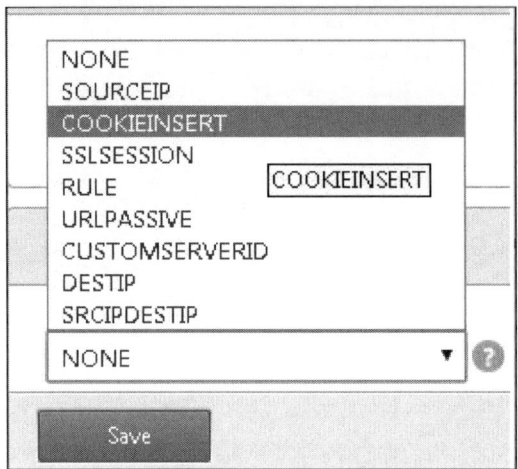

When you've finished, click on **Save** and then **Done** to finalize the virtual server configuration. Verify that the new vServer is in an **UP** (green) state in the GUI.

Testing NetScaler® load balancing

Now that we have a fully configured load balancing service on NetScaler, we should test to see if it works. The following two criteria need to be met before we can conclude that it's configured correctly:

1. The load balanced URL returns an IIS page when accessed from a browser.

2. Load balancing takes place on the basis of the algorithm we've selected.

To test against the first condition, we need to navigate to
`https://<YourLoadBalancedURL>` from a web browser. If an IIS page, such as the
one shown in this image is returned, then the request has reached one of the two
StoreFront servers and is deemed successful:

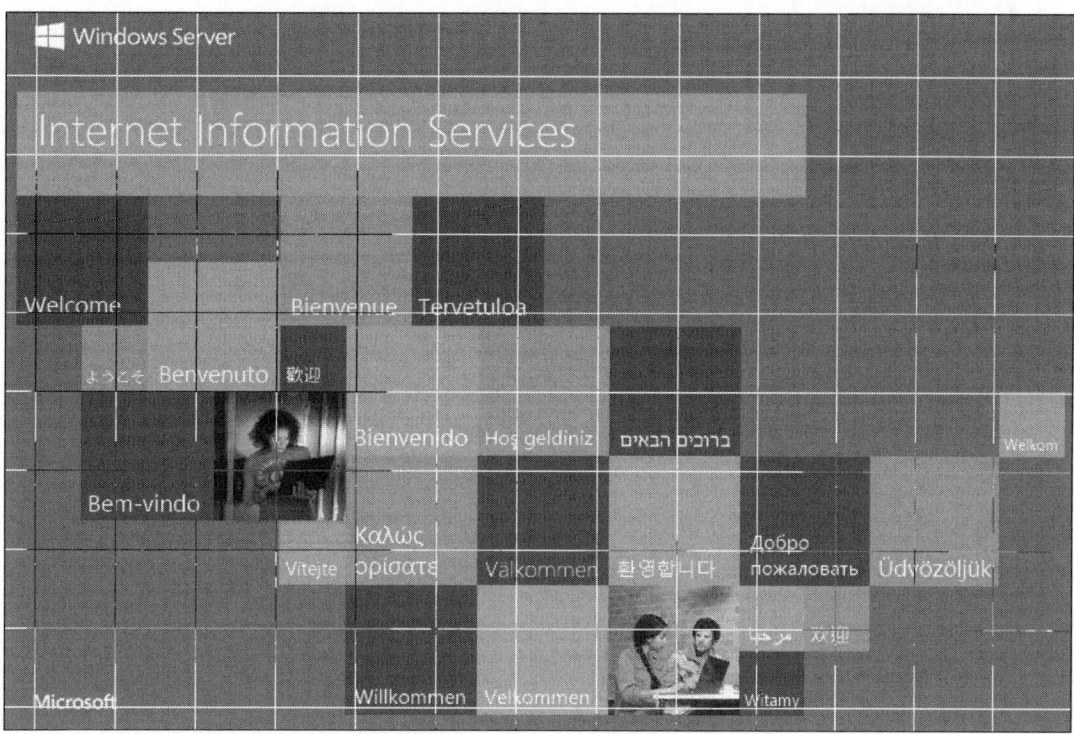

To test against the second condition, we need to download PuTTY from
`http://www.putty.org/` and log in to the CLI of the NetScaler appliance via an
SSH session. When you run PuTTY, use the NSIP as a destination point, and when
prompted, enter your credentials to enter the CLI. Once the connection is established,
run the following command to display statistics for the current vServer:

```
stat lb vserver YourLBvServerName
```

Initially, you should see zero hits on both service members. To generate more
requests, navigate to your load-balanced URL from a browser several times and run
the same command after each request to observe the hits. The expected result is to
have an equal distribution of connections between the two services. This is proof that
load balancing takes place using the algorithm method we configured in NetScaler.

Summary

In this chapter, you gained a solid understanding of what load balancing is and why we need it for our XenApp implementation. In the field, I often work with customers who upon seeing NetScaler in action immediately find many other use cases for it in their existing infrastructures just because it's so versatile and feature-rich. In this particular scenario, you learned how to configure load balancing services in Citrix NetScaler to enhance performance and avoid single points of failure in the StoreFront environment. With this setup in place, we have completed the access layer. In the next chapter, we will go back to our Delivery Controller to start building XenApp workloads for application and desktop delivery. Stay tuned!

8
Building Your First XenApp® Farm – Machine Creation Services

Before we begin, I will admit that I am purposefully using a slightly wrong terminology in this chapter. For those of you that have dealt with XenApp before the 7.x release, you are probably well aware of and have been using the jargon *farm* when referring to a group of XenApp servers. Many people in the field have continued to use this term, including me. However, the merging of XenApp with XenDesktop in 7.x has truly changed everything. People who have been working with XenApp for a long time since the Presentation Server or even the MetaFrame days have had to adopt to a certain extent the new terminology marketed by Citrix, which comes from the XenDesktop world. For example, instead of the word *farm*, you should use *site*. However, this is not entirely correct because for some people, farm is a group of Terminal Servers and now this group is actually called a machine catalog, and Citrix refers to *site* as the full set of data (machine catalogs, Delivery Groups, applications, administrators) that comprises the controller database, in other words, the full XenApp/XenDesktop environment from the point of view of the controller. I am sure that some of you would gladly debate me on this, especially folks with a solid background in Citrix XenApp and XenDesktop. So, before we get too distracted with wording, I will just state once again that I will be using *farm* to define a group of cloned RDS-enabled Windows 2012 VMs with user applications and the VDA installed on them. In this chapter, we will provide a step-by-step guide on the following subtopics:

- Preparing a master image for the XenApp deployment
- Creating XenApp Machine Catalog
- Adding, updating, and deleting VMs from a machine catalog

Explaining Machine Creation Services

Machine Creation Services (MCS) is a concept that started in the days of XenDesktop 5 and is now fully utilized as a machine provisioning technology in XenApp and XenDesktop 7.6. MCS uses the notion of cloning virtual machines from a master image, which can be a server OS, such as Windows 2012, or a desktop OS, such as Windows 8. An administrator will typically install applications that users need locally, such as Word, Excel, Outlook, QuickBooks, and so on. MCS, which is run on the Delivery Controller, will then use a snapshot of this master image to create a specified number of cloned VMs on a hypervisor and add them to the XenApp site as a machine catalog (a pool of desktops). After the machine catalog is created, the administrator creates a Delivery Group to publish the applications and desktops to users. During the creation of the Delivery Group, the controller reads the applications available on the Windows 2012 server VMs created by MCS and presents a list to the administrator to choose from. We will explore the internals of application publishing in more detail in *Chapter 10, Administering a XenApp® Environment – Application Management*. Whenever a change needs to be made to these machines, such as applying a patch or installing a new application, the administrator only needs to update the master image and then the machine catalog from the Citrix Studio console on the controller. In this chapter, we will prepare a master image for the MCS deployment and create a new catalog of Windows 2012 XenApp server VMs that are ready for hosted application and shared desktop delivery.

MCS server machines can be persistent or nonpersistent depending on the requirements of the environment. Nonpersistent VMs do not retain changes made by a user on the machine itself, so, in order to push updates out, they need to be installed on the master image first and then the entire machine catalog can be updated from the controller. Persistent VMs do retain modifications made by the user, and once created, they need to be managed as standalone computers and updates need to be made on every one of them individually. Nonpersistent machines (also known as nonpersistent VDIs) are a very popular method of machine provisioning due to the added benefit of centralized management and the ability to flush any unwanted changes or suspicious programs by just performing a reboot on the affected VM.

Once the VMs are deployed on the hypervisor by MCS and added to the catalog, they can (and should) be power-managed strictly from and by the Delivery Controller. One of the reasons for this is the unique routine that a broker goes through when powering on VMs. When a VM is turned on from Citrix Studio, the controller sends a request to the hypervisor using XenServer, vSphere, or Hyper-V APIs (depending on the hypervisor) to perform an operation and a new virtual hard disk (also known as differencing disk), which is an exact copy of the master image hard drive, is attached to this VM from a local storage or SAN repository. The old differencing disk from the previous boot is deleted and any changes made in a previous session are gone. If thin provisioning is supported on the storage side, the differencing disk will also be thin provisioned and will grow up to the full size of the master image hard drive. This is how the nonpersistent model is enforced. Besides the differencing disk, MCS VMs also have a 16 MB identity disk containing information about the unique identity of the VM as defined by the controller. We will demonstrate the notion of differencing and identity disks later in the chapter when we implement a machine catalog.

Preparing your master image

In the previous section, we briefly touched on the concept of VM provisioning, but what is a master image, anyway? It is the guest operating system on the hypervisor that serves as a template for creating multiple virtual XenApp servers with MCS. The administrator will typically install all the applications that users need and the required Citrix VDA software on the master image. They will also apply the latest Windows patches, security updates, and any drivers that might be needed for the applications to work properly. A great deal of planning needs to go into the preparation of the master image according to the business purpose of the environment. In our case, the goal is to provide applications to accounting, sales, and human resources users, so we will need to install these apps on a Windows 2012 R2 master image and enable RDS to allow app hosting and remote delivery.

Designing your master image VM

Designing a master image VM involves collecting requirements from stakeholders, such as system administrators, IT managers, and end users to understand what a business needs from the Citrix environment. In a XenApp solution, users launch applications and desktops on shared servers enabled for RDS. These servers are actually the VMs created by MCS on a hypervisor and added to a machine catalog on a controller. Hence, it is highly important to size up the compute resources, storage, and the number of servers needed to sustain the number of users that will be connecting to the environment and the type of workload (light, medium, or heavy) expected by the business. There is no magic number when it comes to the number of connections that a server can support as each environment is different and testing is the best way to find out where the sweet spot is in terms of how many actively connected users you can have per XenApp server. The following specifications provide a general starting point to build a master image, which does not guarantee, by any means, the level of performance you expect in your environment. Post deployment testing is highly recommended and adjustments in compute are almost always necessary to fine-tune the environment:

Components	Number of components/storage space required
Guest CPU	4
CPU topology	4 sockets with 1 core per socket
Guest memory	16 GB
Storage	64 GB
Virtual NICs	1
Guest OS	Windows 2012 R2 SP1

To create a master image, first we need to provision a new VM in XenCenter with the aforementioned specifications. If you have a preexisting template on the hypervisor, you can use the **Quick deploy** option to speed up the process. Once it's created, connect to the VM console in XenCenter, follow the required steps to install Windows 2012 R2, and configure a local administrator account for initial access.

Configuring your master image for Citrix XenApp®

Using your local administrator account on the master VM, perform the following steps to do the initial configuration of the machine:

1. Log on to the master image VM, mount, and then install the XenServer tools.
2. In **Control Panel**, configure a dynamic IP address and DNS assignment.

3. In **Computer Properties**, change the machine name (for example, Win2012-Master or CTX-Master-01).

4. Join the machine to a domain (you will get some added benefits, such as domain admin access, but be sure to remove any nonlocal profiles from **Advanced system settings** before using the image with MCS to keep it as clean as possible). Reboot if prompted.

5. Apply all the Windows updates available in **Server Manager** and reboot if necessary.

6. In **Server Manager**, enable the **Remote Desktop Services** role:

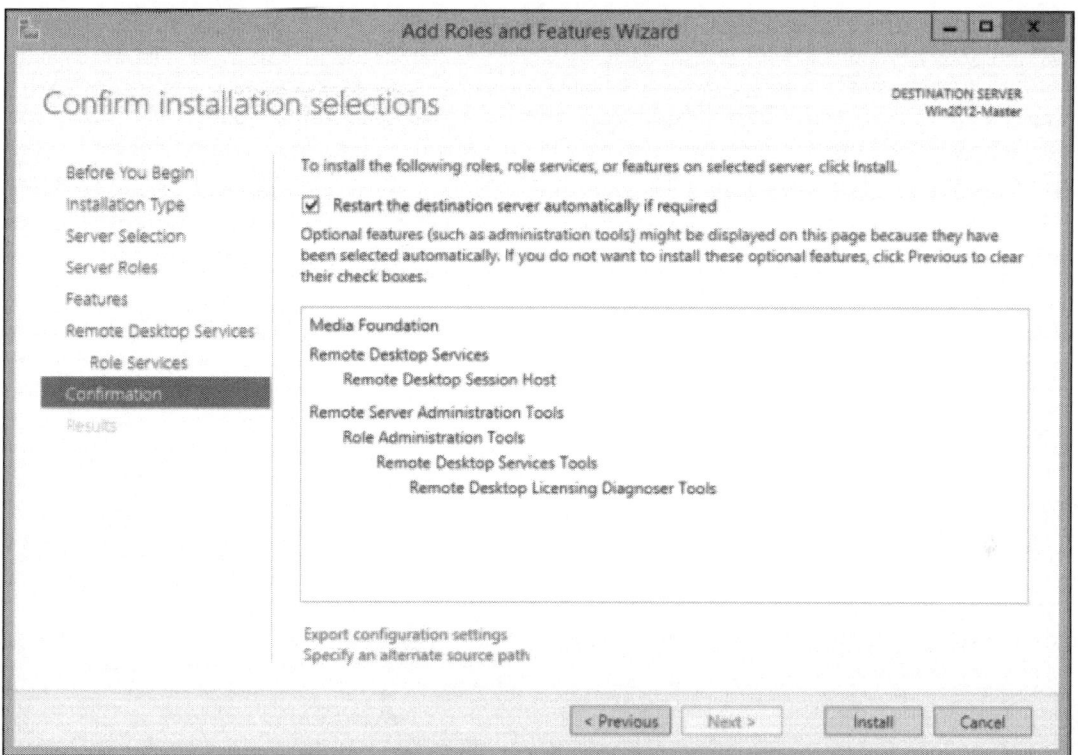

Enabling RDS in Windows 2012 R2 Server Manager

7. Create a folder in the root of C:\ called Apps.

8. Download the applications you want to present to your users to C:\Apps and install them (the program executables will be deployed in other directories such as C:\Program Files). In our case, we have three apps, QuickBooks, Excel, and an Internet Explorer URL to the UltiPro web portal for HR.

Installing the Citrix® VDA on the master VM

Here are the steps for installing the Citrix VDA on the master VM:

1. Mount the XenApp 7.6 installation media to the VM and proceed to install the Citrix VDA for the Windows Server OS.

2. In the XenApp ISO autorun window, click on **Virtual Delivery Agent for Windows Server OS** and wait for the VDA installation wizard to launch.

3. On the **Environment** page, select **Create a Master Image**, and then click on **Next**:

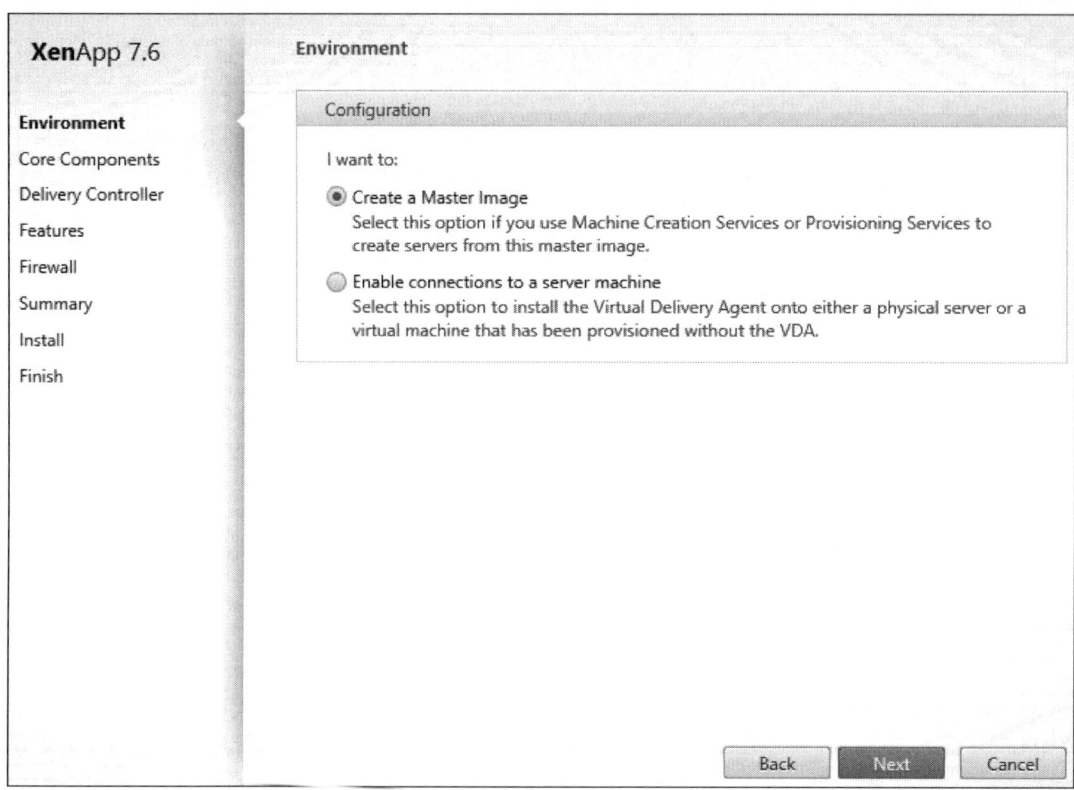

4. Under **Core Components**, note that the VDA is mandatory. You can optionally install **Citrix Receiver**, which is required on the master image if you plan to provide your users with the ability to launch XenApp hosted applications within a hosted shared virtual desktop. This is certainly a possible scenario and it is also known as a double-hop session. If this is not the case and your users will only launch hosted applications or shared desktops with locally installed apps, then you don't need Citrix Receiver on the master image. Citrix Receiver is still required, however, on the user's physical device in order to launch a Citrix ICA session (apps or desktops):

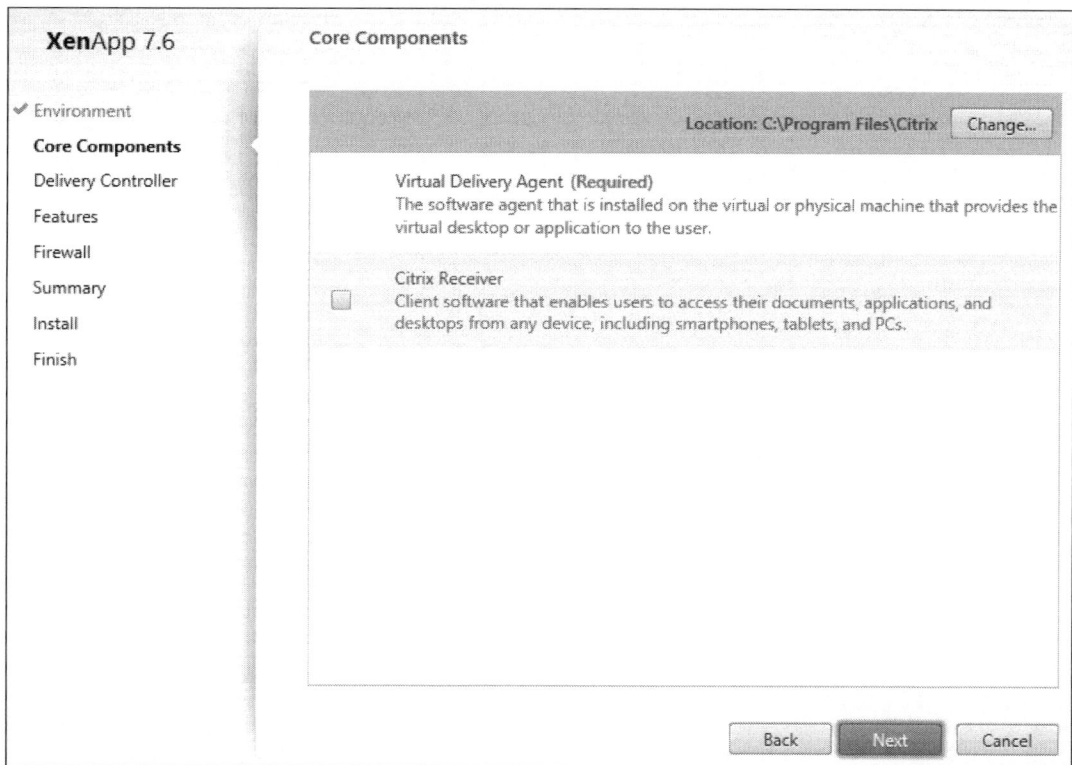

5. On the **Delivery Controller** page, select **Do it manually**, add the FQDN of your two Delivery Controllers one at a time, and verify that no errors are generated upon testing connectivity:

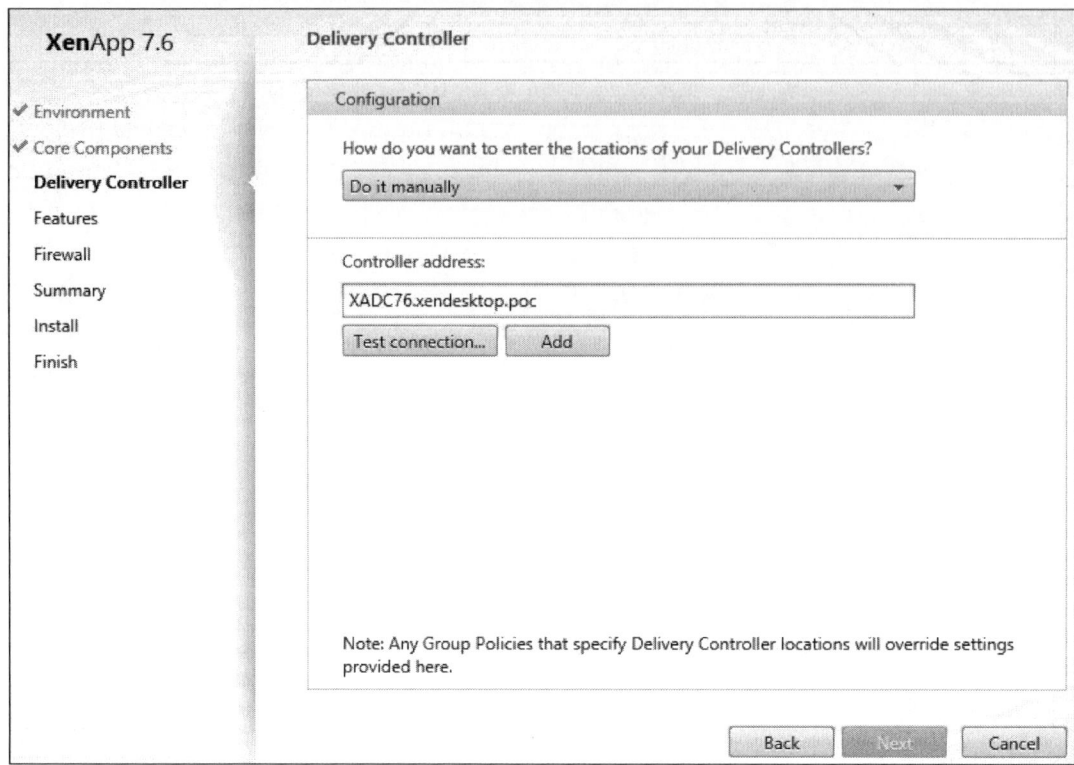

6. Under **Features**, verify that the first two checkboxes are selected to automatically optimize the image for desktop performance and enable **Use Windows Remote Assistance** to shadow users. Select **Use Real-Time Audio Transport for audio** to reduce latency on the network if **Voice-over-IP (VoIP)** is used in the environment:

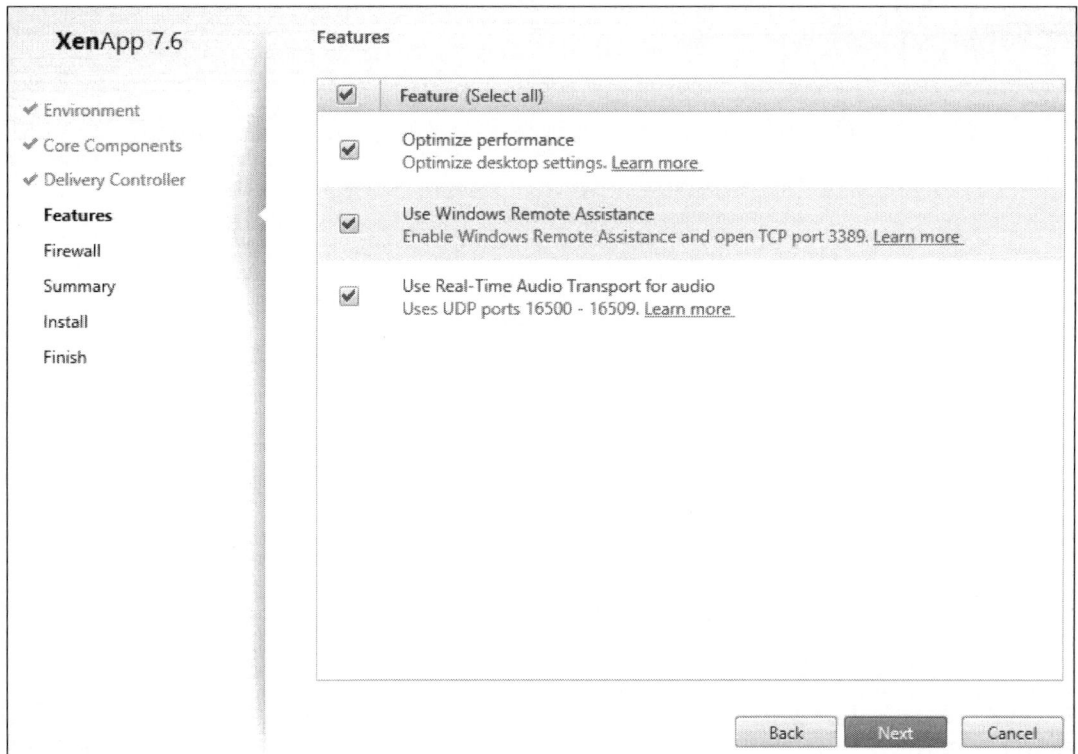

7. Under **Firewall**, verify that **Configure firewall rules** is set to **Automatically** and the listed ports are TCP 80, 1494, 2598, and 8008 for Controller Communications, TCP 3389 for WinRM, and UDP 16500 to 16509 for real-time audio. These ports will be opened on the image automatically with the help of the VDA installation:

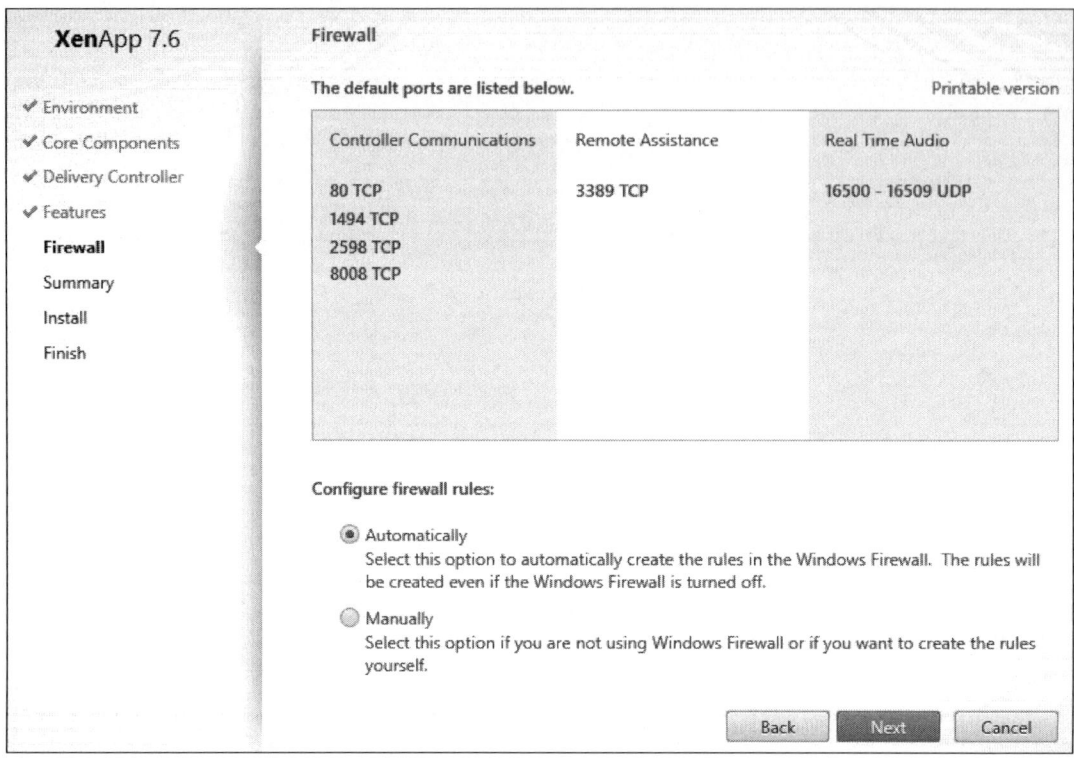

8. On the **Summary** page, scroll down to review your configurations and click on **Install**:

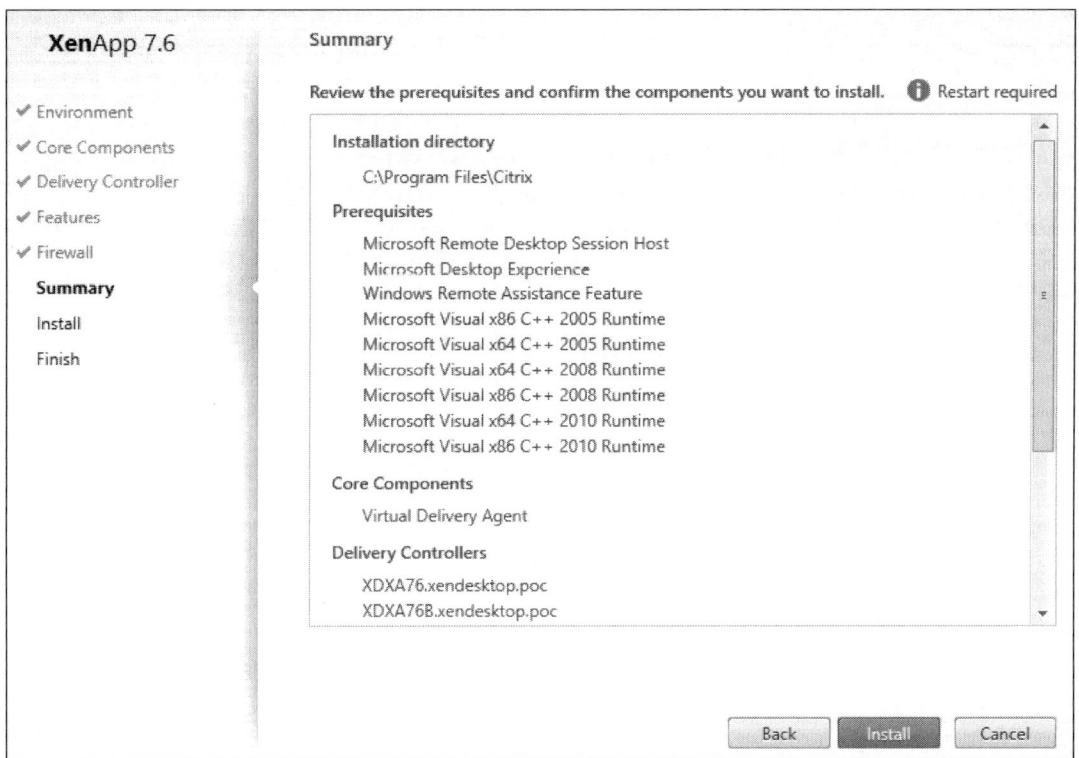

When finished, you will be prompted to restart the VM. After the machine comes back up, ensure that the VDA is registered with the Delivery Controller by going to the Windows Event Viewer and filter the **Application** log with the **Citrix Desktop Service** source to see a successful registration message (Event 1012).

If so far you have been logging on with a domain account, it is recommended to log off and log back in with a local administrator and delete any residual profiles. The logic here is that we want our master image to be as clean (or as they say, "as vanilla") as possible before it is used by MCS for cloning of VMs. The easiest way to do this is to go to **Computer Properties**, click on **Advanced system settings** on the left-hand side, go to the **User Profiles** settings, and delete any domain (nondefault/nonlocal) profiles currently residing on the system. You can now proceed to shut down the machine and take a snapshot in XenCenter. Call the snapshot Master_Snapshot_<Date> where <Date>, which refers to the current day, month, and year on your calendar.

Building XenApp® Catalogs with MCS

In this section, we will learn how to use the MCS provisioning methodology in XenApp 7.6 to create Windows 2012 R2 VM servers. These run the Citrix VDA software that is ready to accept user connections to the applications that we've installed locally on them or share a full desktop session. These desktops will be nonpersistent and any changes made to the underlying OS components by end users will be flushed upon reboot. This model allows us to manage a single master image and create as many machines as we have computing resources for from the Delivery Controller. Any application or Windows updates can also be applied on the master image and then we only need to update the machine catalog from Citrix Studio with a few clicks of our mouse. Let's now go ahead and create our first machine catalog:

1. Log on to Delivery Controller and open Citrix Studio console.

2. On the left-hand side pane, click on **Machine Catalogs**. Note that at the moment, the node is empty.

3. On the right-hand side pane, click on **Create Machine Catalog** to launch the MCS wizard.

4. On the **Introduction** page, click on **Next**.

5. Under **Operating System**, select **Windows Server OS**, and then click on **Next**:

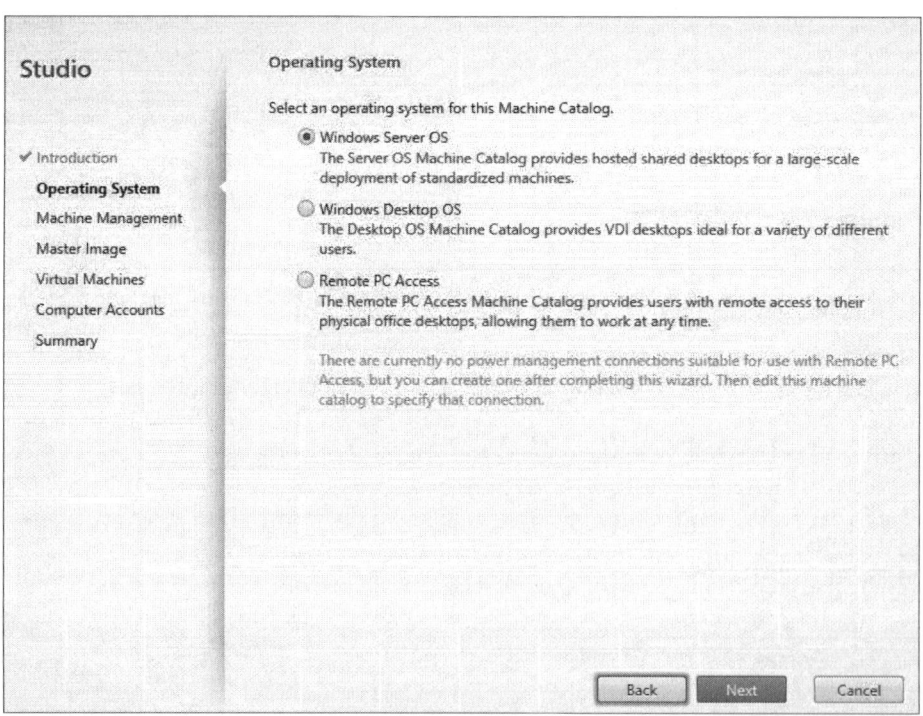

6. Under **Machine Management**, choose **Machines that are power managed** and **Citrix Machine Creation Services (MCS)**, and click on **Next**:

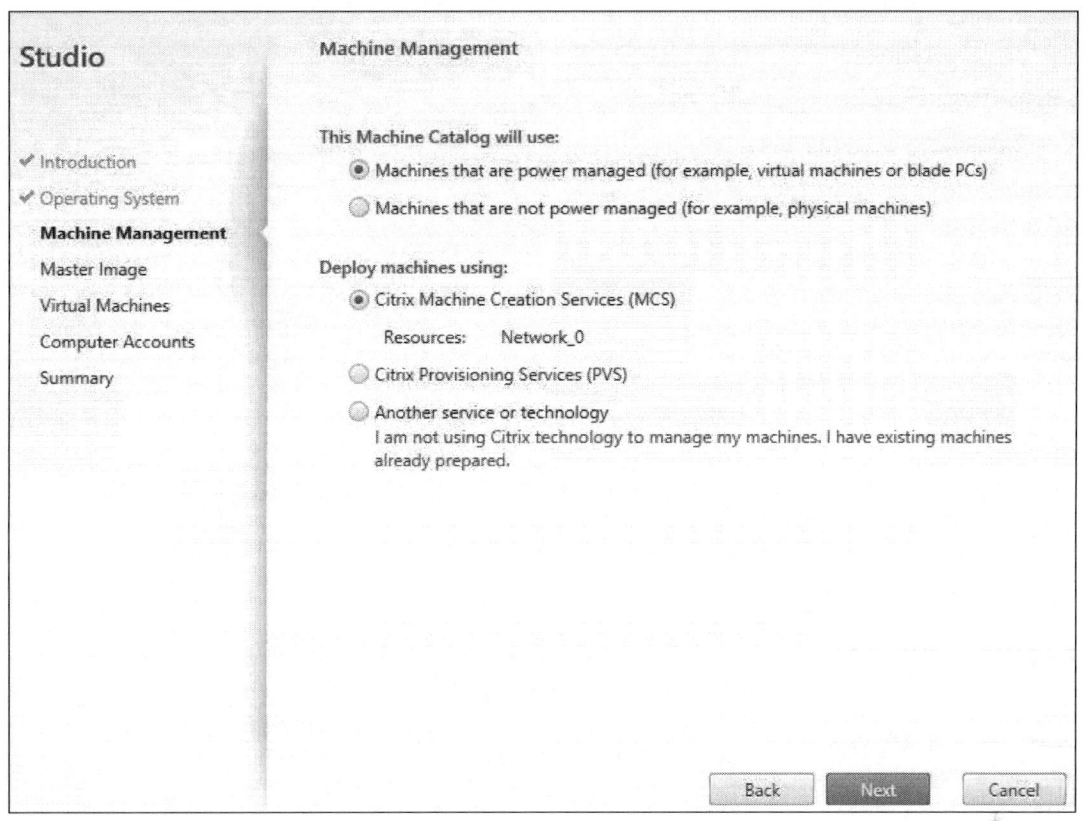

7. For **Master Image**, scroll down the list of VMs and choose the master image that you created previously. If you took a manual snapshot, expand the VM node, and highlight the correct snapshot. When done, click on **Next**:

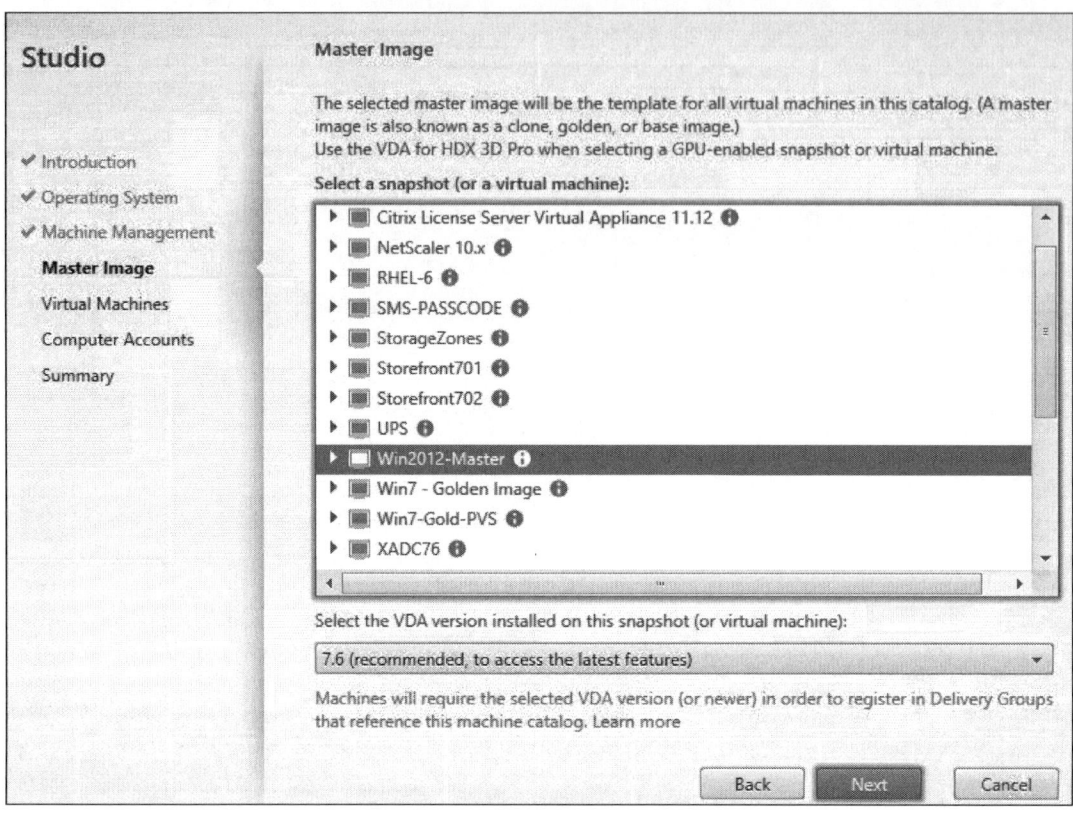

8. Specify the number of machines that you would like to create. In our case, this is 12. Optionally, you can specify the different values for the CPU and memory, otherwise, leave the default numbers to create exact replicas of the master image:

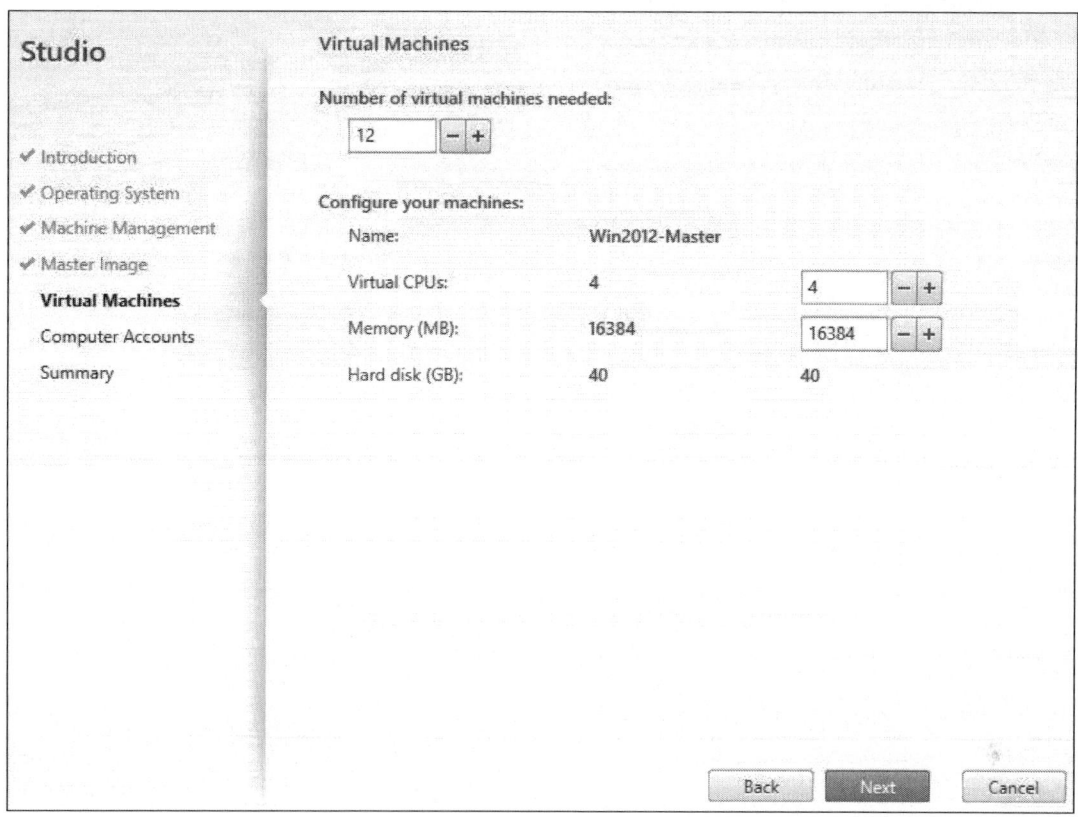

9. Click on **Next** and select the Active Directory OU where you want MCS to put the computer accounts of the machines being created. On the same page, specify the **Account naming scheme** for those VMs in the *Name-##* format. MCS will increment the numbers automatically (for example, *Name-##* will be equal to Name-01, Name-02...Name-12):

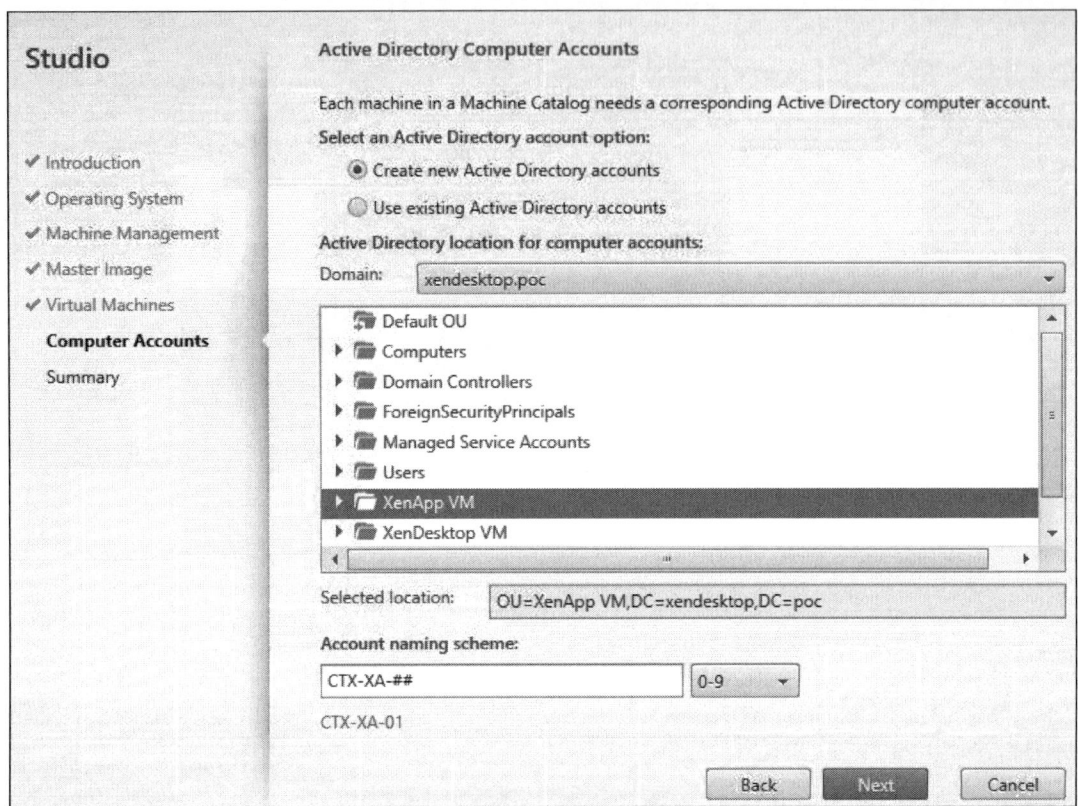

10. Click on **Next** and assign a name for the machine catalog (for example, `XenApp 2012 R2 Catalog`) and a description for administration purposes. When done, review the configuration and click on **Finish** to create the machine catalog:

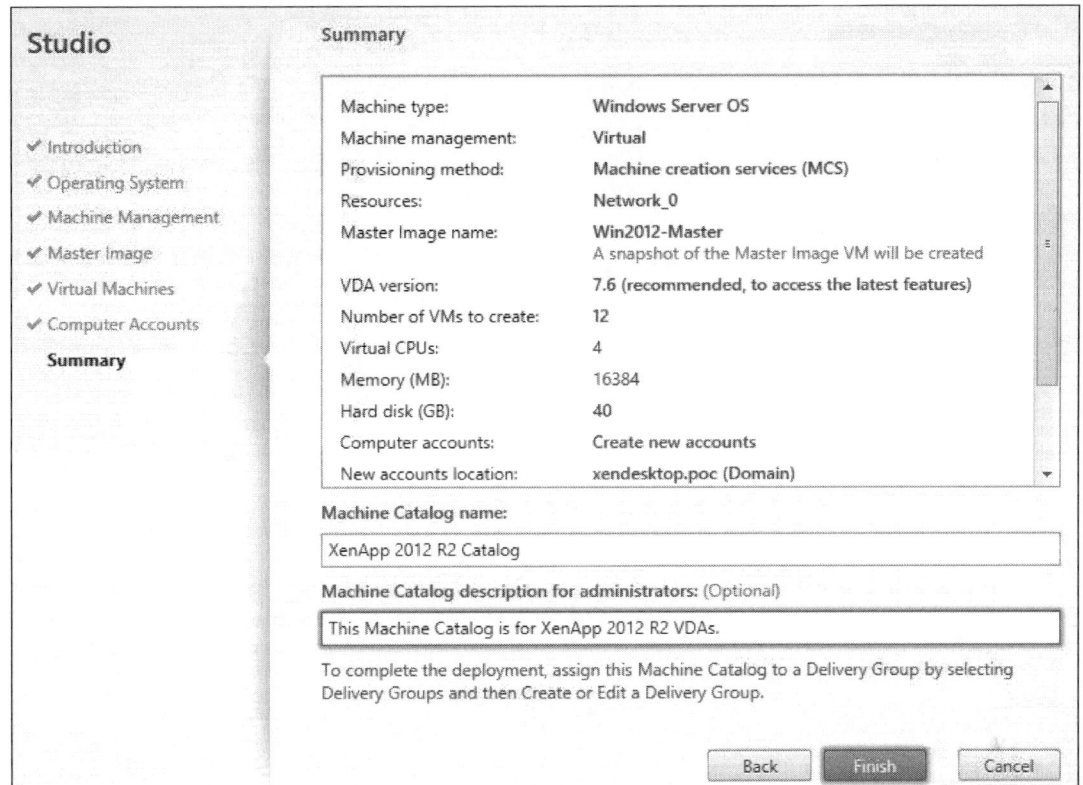

Once the machine catalog is created, you can see all twelve VMs listed in Citrix Studio. The VMs will be powered on automatically by the controller. They should also be visible from the hypervisor console, as shown in the following screenshot, as long as the MCS process is completed successfully:

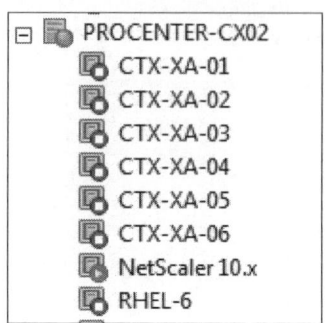

While logged into the XenServer pool, we should explore the structure of our newly created guests—the information that XenCenter offers can be extremely valuable to understand the backbone of the environment. The following eight tabs are available when you click on a VM in XenCenter:

- **General**: This provides descriptive information about the VM, such as name, OS version, boot order, XenServer tools state, High Availability, and CPU settings.

- **Memory**: This provides information about the amount of memory allocated to the VM by the provisioning technology

- **Storage**: This lists all the virtual hard drives attached to the machine. In the case of VMs created by MCS in XenApp, two devices are enumerated: the differencing disk and identity disk. The differencing disk is an exact copy of the master image hard drive and has the same size (or its thin provisioned equivalent). Every time a machine boots up, the old differencing disk gets disconnected and a fresh one is attached (thus, the VMs don't retain any changes from previous usage). The other device listed under **Storage** is the identity disk, which contains machine metadata.

- **Networking**: This lists all the network adapters available for a VM. When the machine is on and the XenServer tools are running, you can see the IPv4, IPv6, and MAC address for each port.

- **Console**: From this window, IT administrators can connect to the VM and initiate a session on the guest OS.

- **Performance**: As long as the XenServer tools are running, you can see historical information about the CPU, memory, network, and disk utilization on the VM, which is extremely useful during troubleshooting.

- **Snapshots**: This refers to points in time when the state of the machine was captured for rollback purposes.

- **Search**: This provides a resource overview of the XenServer pool, including current utilization.

The following screenshot illustrates the storage structure of MCS VMs in XenCenter:

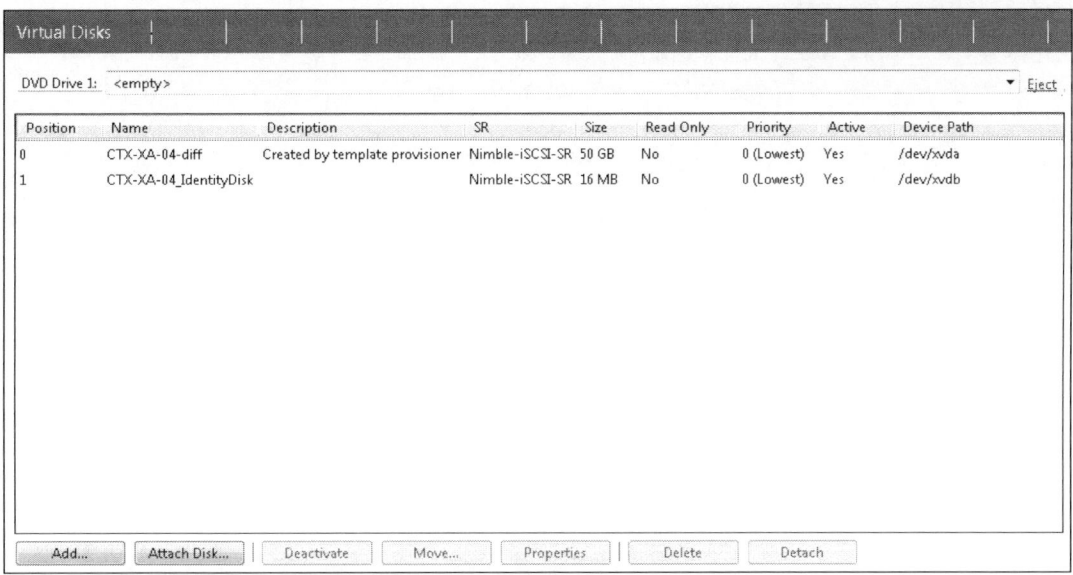

The storage structure of MCS VMs in XenCenter

At this point, all VDA machines should be managed by the administrator from the Delivery Controller, including power management operations and deletion, to ensure differencing disk consistency and avoid orphaned accounts in Active Directory and the SQL database. In *Chapter 10*, *Administering a XenApp® Environment – Application Management*, we will create Delivery Groups to departmentalize our organization and associate users with applications and desktops. With Delivery Groups, we will also be able to leverage the power management capabilities of the controller to set up machine availability for on-peak and off-peak times.

Adding, updating, and deleting VMs with MCS

Okay, but what if at some point in the future our workloads change and all of a sudden, we need more XenApp servers to sustain an expansion in user base? Luckily, adding machines with MCS has been made extremely easy. You don't need to build any Windows 2012 virtual servers from scratch and you don't need to do anything on the hypervisor. All you have to do is (again) log on to the Delivery Controller and in Citrix Studio, right-click on a Machine Catalog and select **Add Machines**. Then, specify the number of machines you want to add and choose to create new accounts in Active Directory as shown in the following screenshot:

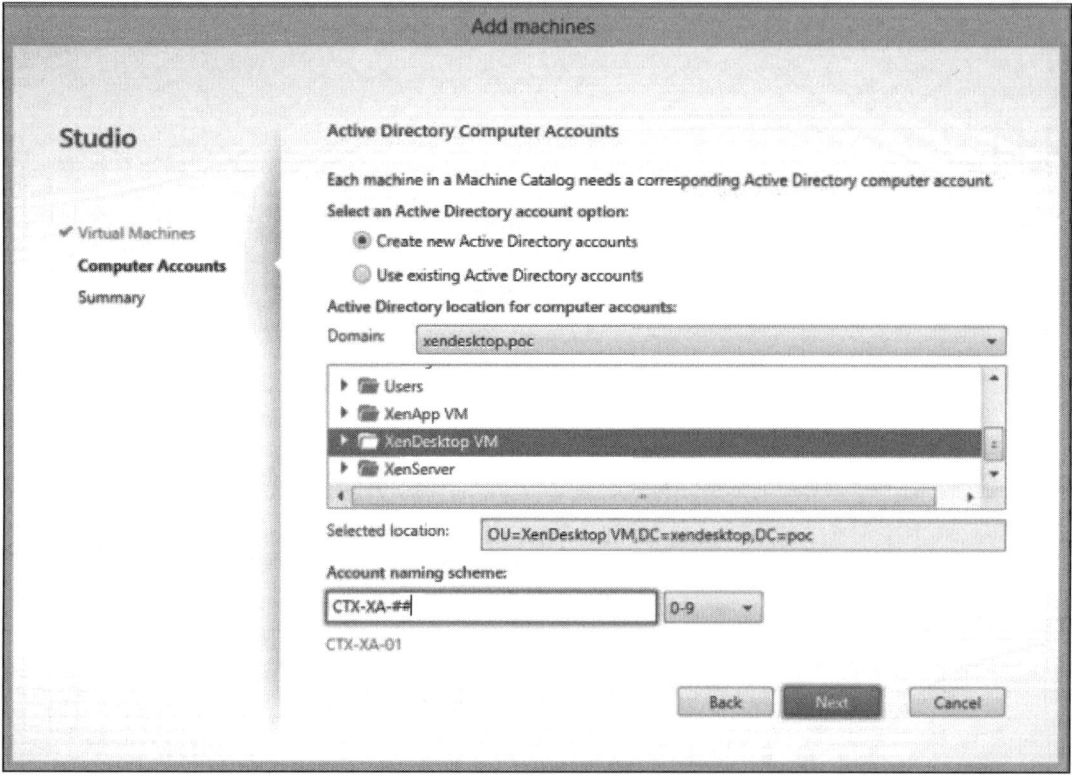

Once you go to **Summary** and click on **Finish**, the specified number of VMs will be created on the hypervisor and added to the corresponding catalog in Studio.

Besides adding machines, we can also apply updates to the catalog. This is once again a quick and easy process. The only difference here is that we first need to change the master image. For example, let's say a new update is released by Intuit that fixes a known bug in the QuickBooks code. Since we've installed QuickBooks on our master image, we need to power on the master VM in XenCenter (remember that the master is not part of the XenApp site and, thus, cannot be managed from the controller) and log on to install a software update. Once this is complete, you can optionally take a manual snapshot of the VM in XenCenter and label it `QuickBooks_Update_<date>`. This way, you can track what kind of change you've made for reference. If no snapshot is taken, MCS will create one automatically with the latest state of the VM. Then, all you need to do is log off from the master and log on to the XenApp Controller to launch Citrix Studio. You then right-click on the machine catalog and click on **Update Machines**. Select the Master Image from the list of VMs, as you did when you first created the catalog, and then choose the **Rollout Strategy** as shown in the following screenshot. XenApp allows us to be pretty flexible as to how we decide to apply the update and the impact that it's going to have on any actively connected users:

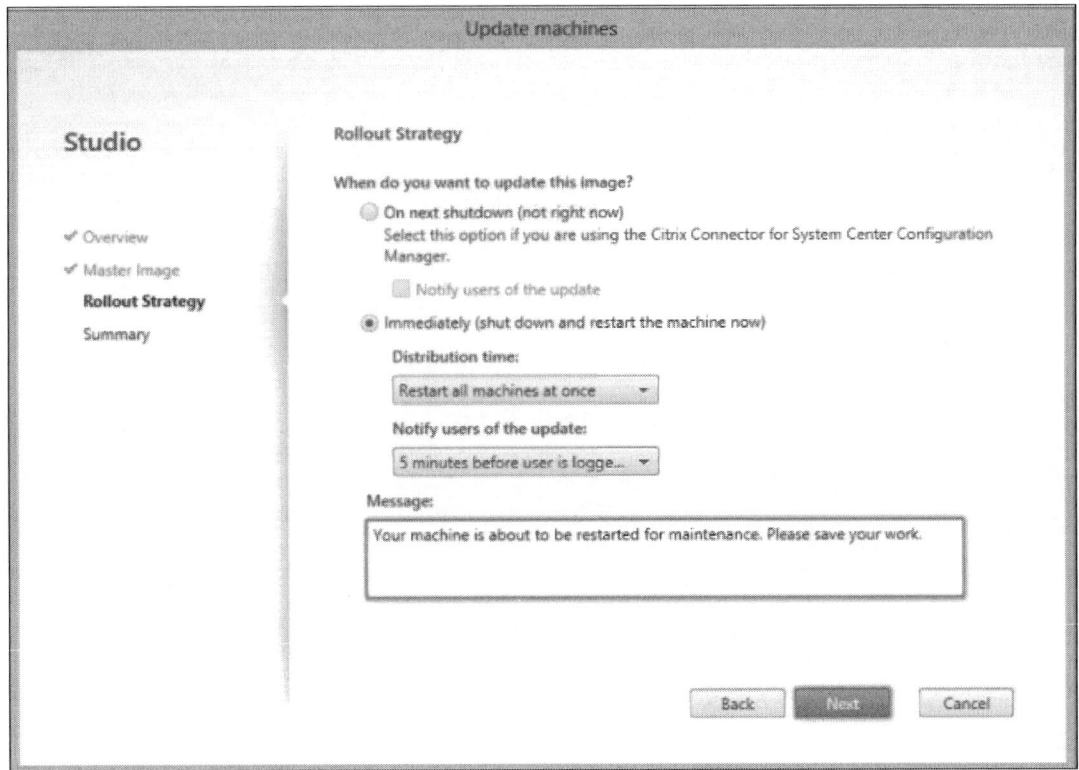

Once you review the **Summary** and click on **Finish**, MCS kicks off the update process and several minutes later, all your XenApp servers are up to date with the latest QuickBooks software. This, of course, is only true for pooled (nonpersistent) machine catalogs. Any persistent desktops would have to be updated on an individual basis.

At this point, we know how to create, add, and update XenApp servers on the fly. However, what if for some reason our user base shrinks and we don't need all twelve servers anymore? Saving memory, CPU, and disk space on the hypervisor is important because we can use the extra capacity to host other workloads such as Exchange. In this case, we can employ the MCS technology in XenApp to delete virtual servers from the site, database, Active Directory, and hypervisor. All you need to do is simply right-click on a VM in Machine Catalog in Studio, click on **Turn On Maintenance Mode** and then right-click once again to hit **Delete**. In the **Delete Options**, you can select several combinations for what to remove. I typically recommend that if you have decided to delete a VM permanently, then go with **Remove the accounts from the Catalog and delete them from Active Directory** as shown in the screenshot. This is generally the cleanest option because it doesn't leave any residual items in XenServer and Active Directory:

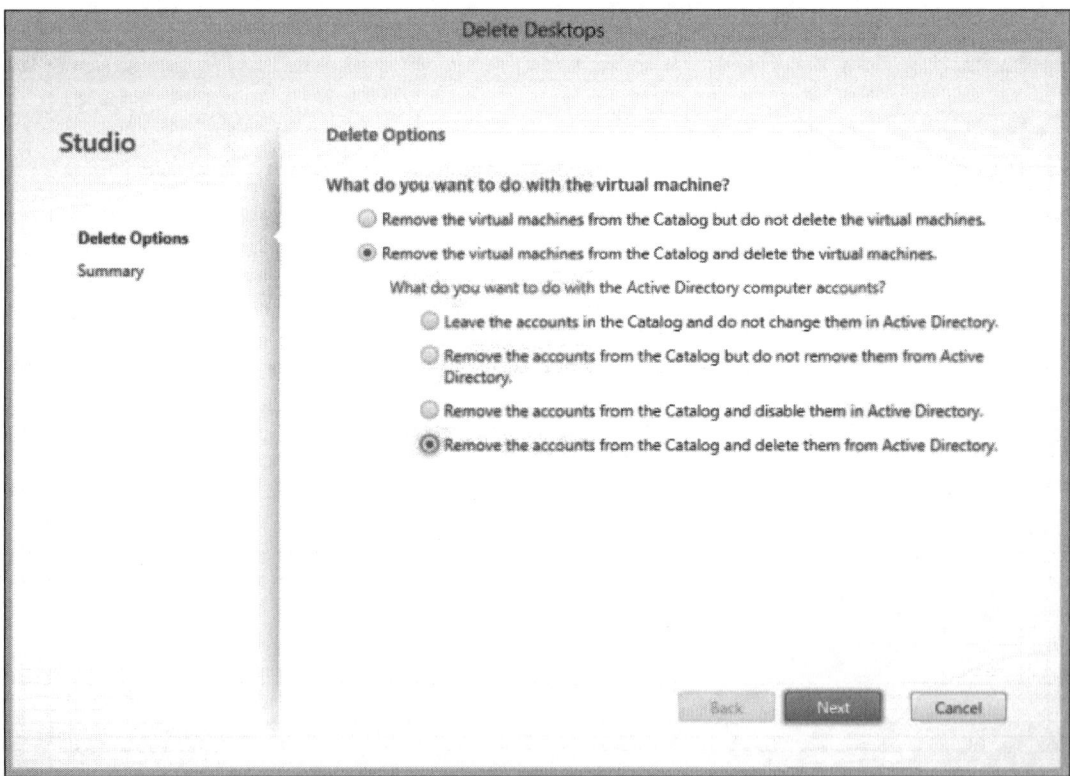

Being able to remove machines and their associated attributes throughout the IT infrastructure from a single pane of glass, the XenApp Controller can be a very useful feature for day-to-day administration because it makes resource utilization and management a lot more efficient.

What is the maintenance mode, anyway?

If you've paid close attention to the previous section, you are probably wondering why we went the extra step to turn on the maintenance mode on the VM in Citrix Studio before we proceeded with deleting the machine. This is actually a protective mechanism of the Delivery Controller. If you go ahead and delete a VM from Studio without turning the maintenance mode on, you run the risk of corrupting user data. The Delivery Controller always assumes that there may be active connections to these VMs and Studio doesn't allow you to perform a delete operation unless you have the maintenance mode on, which prevents users from connecting to this machine.

Summary

In conclusion, MCS is a very solid mechanism for server and desktop provisioning. You can create, add, and update XenApp servers from a single image. With MCS, you can also remove machines from the XenApp site with the capability of totally eliminating footprints on the IT infrastructure. In addition to this, all management tasks are done from Citrix Studio, which facilitates maintenance and it gives IT administrators a single control point for the environment. However, MCS is not the only method to build virtual machines in XenApp. There is another technology called Citrix PVS, which can deploy and manage both Citrix (XenApp/XenDesktop) and non-Citrix workloads in both physical and virtual systems. In fact, PVS is so widely popular in enterprise environments today that I will dedicate the entire next chapter to teaching the use case and deployment of this technology that many customers choose to leverage as an alternative to MCS. In contrast to MCS, PVS requires a separate server, which we will configure and integrate with the XenApp site in the next chapter. Stay tuned!

Building Your First XenApp® Farm – Provisioning Services™

In the previous chapter, we learned how to create XenApp server VMs using the MCS technology. MCS, however, is not the only way to create and manage your machine catalogs. To add flexibility for their customers, Citrix offers another software called **Provisioning Services (PVS)**. In this chapter, we will explore the following topics to help us understand PVS better:

- What is PVS and how does it work?
- The pros and cons of using PVS in an enterprise environment
- PVS versus MCS
- Design considerations for PVS
- Installing and configuring PVS to serve a XenApp solution

Getting started with PVS

Before we delve into the integration of PVS and XenApp, especially if this is the first time we've dealt with the product, it's important that we understand what PVS actually does and how it works. PVS is a UDP-based streaming technology that is designed to deliver an operating system (vDisk) to client devices over a network. PVS uses PXE protocol specs, such as UNDI, to boot a target device (such as a PXE client) and deliver a bootfile program that contains the instructions necessary to log in to a Provisioning Server and start streaming the vDisk over the network. The OS itself is contained in a VHD file, which can be delivered to virtual and physical machines. In the case of virtualization, we can command the Provisioning Server to create VMs on the hypervisor or we can add pre-existing ones to the PVS farm and assign them a vDisk. But this is not all. All PVS clients, also known as target devices, will boot to a read-only image unless an administrator wants to make changes to the OS, in which case they can choose to boot from a read/write version of the VHD.

So, what are some of the pros and cons of PVS? Let's start with the pros first.

Single image management

Imagine that you have a datacenter with 100 XenApp servers. Using traditional methods of server management, you would need to log in to each and every one of them to make changes, such as application updates and Windows patches. You may be able to use GPOs or customer scripts to enforce certain modifications but it would still require additional effort on the infrastructure end. With Citrix PVS, you can use a designated machine as a golden (master) image, create a virtual disk from its hard drive, and assign it to hundreds or even thousands of servers for OS delivery. Since a vDisk has two modes, read/write and read-only, you can modify the image in read/write (private) mode from one device and then stream it to all your devices in read-only (standard) mode. This way, all the changes made in the private mode will update the VHD and can then be streamed to the rest of your devices in the standard mode, propagating the changes you made instantaneously! The newer versions of PVS starting with 6.0 have versioning available as well so that changes can be made to a maintenance version in real-time without the need to shut down any live connections and all deltas can be kept as part of the vDisk chain.

The power of read-only

The read-only VHD is a truly powerful feature of PVS. Every time a machine is connected to a virtual disk from PVS, any changes made by users to the OS (outside their roaming profiles) are flushed upon reboot! So, let's say for instance, user John logs into a provisioned target device (for example, XenApp server, XenDesktop, Windows endpoint, and so on) and changes the network adapter settings, clock, registry, and so on. With PVS, these changes are gone once the machine is shut down. Also, any viruses that John picked up during his session are immediately erased upon reboot.

Scalability

PVS is fully enterprise-ready. Not only do you have the option of adding pre-existing machines to Device Collections in the PVS console, but in a virtual environment, you can deploy them automatically from PVS! The XenDesktop Setup Wizard and Streamed VM Setup Wizard are at your disposal to help you quickly create new VMs on the fly when you need them.

But what about the cons?

Infrastructure needs

A possible downside to PVS is the need to deploy a separate infrastructure. At least one dedicated server (virtual or physical) is needed and two are recommended for HA to install the Provisioning Server and console software. Also, an additional PVS agent is required on the vDisk to be able to create a bootable image. These items will require additional time to deploy.

Licensing

Another downside of using PVS is that it does not come bundled with XenApp Advanced Edition, and it currently requires a minimum of XenApp Enterprise licensing with unlimited capability, which is only allowed in the Platinum Edition. The following table illustrates the pros and cons of Citrix PVS:

Pros	Cons
Storage efficiency	Infrastructure needs
Single image management	Licensing costs
Read-only mode	
Scalability	

The pros and cons of Citrix Provisioning Services

MCS versus PVS

There has been an ongoing and very heated debate among Citrix professionals over which technology is better and the answer always remains the same: it depends. It depends on the size of the environment and the budget limitations of customer. From a technical perspective (and this is strictly a personal observation), PVS scales better when deploying target devices in the thousands. Creating VMs seems to be a faster process mainly because of minimized storage footprints. Since a single image is streamed over the network, the target VMs only need a hard drive to write caching, which is significantly smaller than your regular c:\ drive on the vDisk image. So, PVS can save you over 50% of space right off the bat and sometimes even up to 90% depending on the target architecture.

The main benefit of MCS is the fact that it is native to the XenApp Delivery Controller and does not require additional components and infrastructure costs. For small to midsize businesses, this is actually a pretty big advantage, which is why you would normally see MCS deployments in these environments.

Designing the PVS environment

Due to the multitude of moving parts in a PVS environment, there are design considerations that have to be addressed before the PVS servers and target devices can actually be deployed. The main point of interest here is the architecture of the customer's network. The following questions should be asked before choosing the PVS configuration for a particular system:

- Is the customer's environment fully virtualized or are they planning to stream a XenApp image to physical servers (also known as bare metal)?

- Where is the DHCP server located? Is it possible to have a dedicated DHCP server on the same subnet as the PVS environment?

- Is **Preboot eXecution Environment (PXE)** a supported communication protocol in the customer's network?

- What is the throughput of the network interface attached to the VMs or physical servers? Is it a 1 Gbps or 10 Gbps link?

- Is the customer using a local storage or SAN to store VM hard drives? Or, are they considering going for a hyper-converged architecture?

These are just a fraction of the questions that need to be asked so that we, as architects, can make informed decisions on how to deploy PVS. More importantly, we also need to consider what else we would need to do outside the purview of PVS or Citrix in order to have a successful implementation. For example, if we don't have a dedicated DHCP server for PVS, but we are given an IP range on a production DHCP server in a different subnet, we need to bring up the importance of having IP helpers and DHCP Relay configured on routers to ensure that the PVS target devices can obtain an IP address during the PXE boot. We will delve further into this topic in *Chapter 11, Administering a XenApp® Environment – Server Management*, where we will discuss server management and system administration, and also in *Chapter 13, Troubleshooting Tools, Tips, and Tricks*, where we'll discuss some concrete examples of issues seen in the field Escalation Support.

Write caching in PVS

So, at this point, you might be wondering about how it's possible to stream a read-only image when the OS constantly writes data to the hard disk? The answer is **write cache**. This is the core of the PVS design. On a read-only target device, every bit of data written to the c:\ drive is a data write to the write cache. The cache itself can be placed on the hard drive of the Provisioning Server (or another shared storage brokered by the PVS server), locally on the target device's hard drive, or in the RAM of the target device. Starting with PVS 7.0, a new write cache type was released by Citrix called **Cache in device RAM with overflow on hard disk**. This hybrid mode combines the speed of RAM caching with the option of using local storage on the target VM, should the write cache ever outgrow its allocated memory. We will take advantage of this recent development to boost the performance of our XenApp targets.

Building the PVS infrastructure

Building out the PVS environment is not a difficult or lengthy task, but selecting the right settings during the initial setup is absolutely crucial in achieving a successful deployment. For this particular scenario, the following infrastructure components need to be in place:

- A new VM on your hypervisor that serves as the first Provisioning Server (the same virtual hardware specifications as the Delivery Controller can be used). PVS and console software will be installed here. We can name it CTX-PVS-01.

- A new VM on your hypervisor to serve as the second Provisioning Server (use the same virtual hardware specifications as the ones used previously). PVS and console software will be installed here. We can name it CTX-PVS-02.

- A new VM on your hypervisor to serve as your master image (the same master as the one used in the MCS chapter could be reused as well; however, it is highly recommended that you keep PVS and MCS deployments separate). Since this is a Windows 2012 R2 server and business-critical applications will need to run on it, we should assign at least a 40 GB hard drive. We can use the same specifications as the ones used for the MCS deployment in the previous chapter as far as memory and CPU are concerned. The target device software of PVS will be installed here. We can name this `PVS-Master-Win2012`.

Installing Citrix® PVS

PVS has three installation components—console, server, and target device software. The console and server software are installed on the Provisioning Servers, and the target device goes on the VM used to create a master image. To install the server and console software, download the PVS installation media on `CTX-PVS-01` from the Citrix downloads page and run the installer, filling out the information requested, such as user and company name.

Configuring Citrix® PVS

There are two phases of the PVS configuration—server side and target side. Once the server and console software is installed, from the PVS server, we need to run the **Provisioning Services Configuration Wizard** to create a farm, database, and Windows services. On the master image, after installing the PVS target device software, we run the **Imaging Wizard** to create a new vDisk. Using this step-by-step process, we can configure PVS starting with the server side:

1. On the first Provisioning Server, run the **Provisioning Services Configuration Wizard** (available in the Windows 2012 Start menu search or under the Citrix installation folder). On the first screen, click on **Next**:

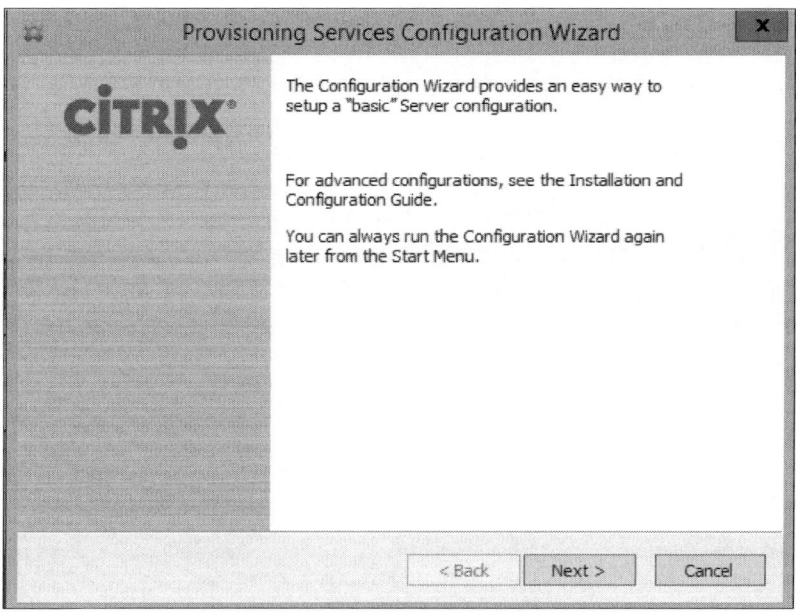

2. Under **DHCP Services**, select **The service that runs on another computer**. Keep in mind that DHCP can be configured directly on the Provisioning Server from the Windows 2012 **Server Manager**, but it is highly recommended to have a dedicated machine for DHCP to avoid putting extra overhead on the PVS server:

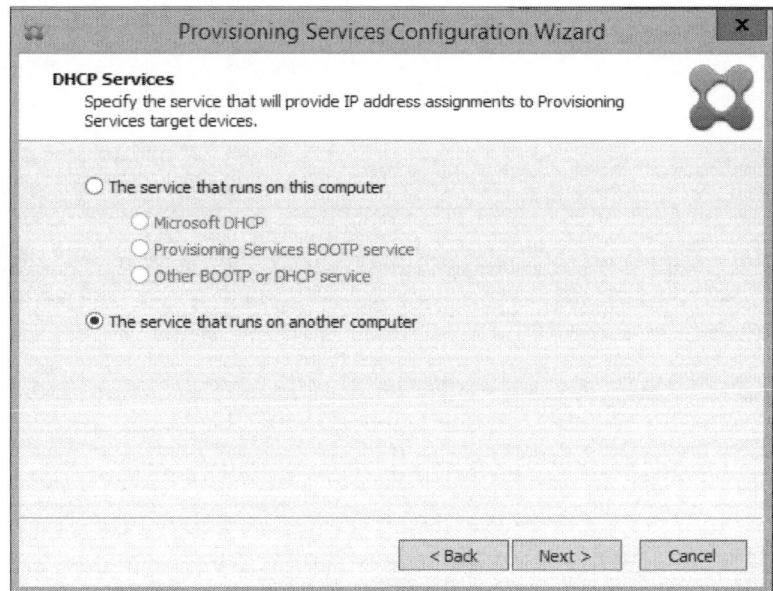

3. Next, select a service that will deliver bootstrap information to the target device. Two options are available for this purpose—**DHCP Scope Options 66/67** or **Citrix PXE Service**. Unless you are working in a completely isolated environment where PXE service broadcasting is not an issue, the recommended choice is the DHCP Options. With Options 66/67, you can specify the PVS login server name and the name of the ARDBP32.bin bootstrap file. Your DHCP server will then encapsulate this information in the Offer packet when extending an IP address to the target device. If you choose to go with the built-in Citrix PXE capability, PVS will install this service on the Provisioning Server and it will broadcast the same information to the booting target device. The unintended consequence of enabling a PXE service in PVS is that target devices from other PVS farms on the same subnet may pick up the same information which, of course, would be incorrect for them:

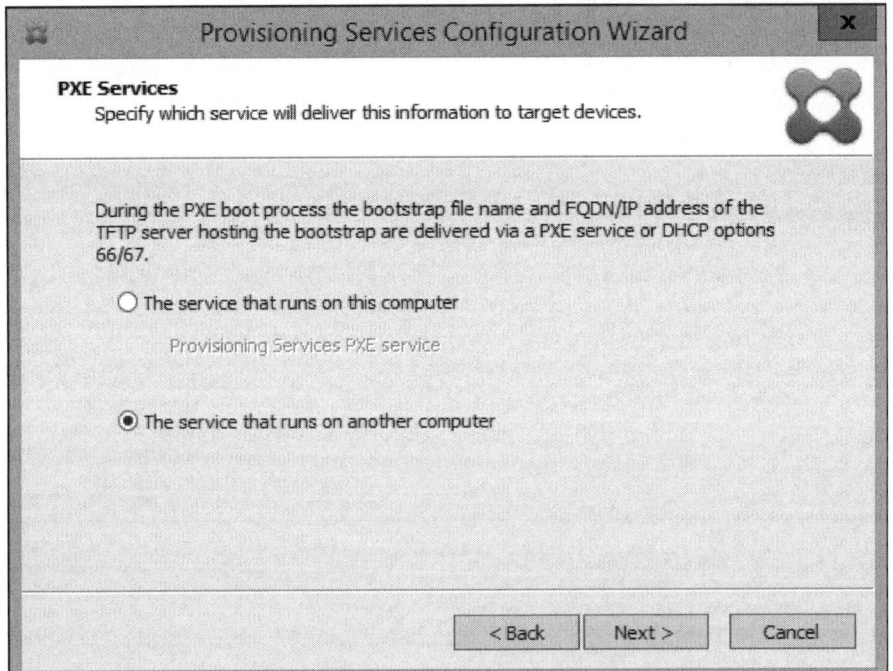

4. Next, choose to create a new farm and proceed to the next step:

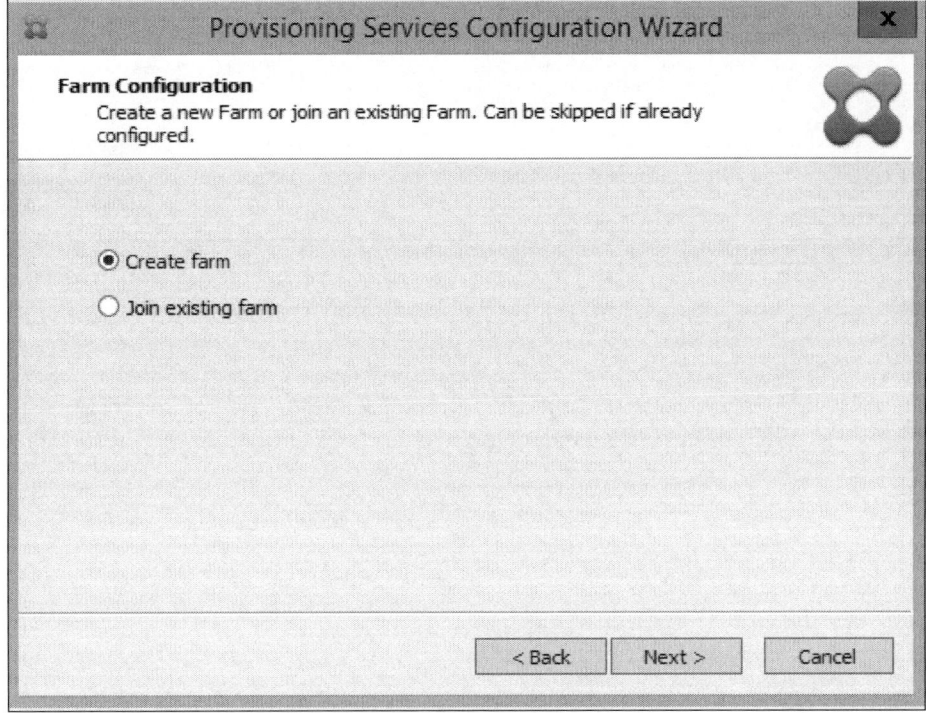

5. Then, specify an SQL server and a mirror partner if applicable. An instance name is only needed if the SQL database is not in the default instance (for example, SQLEXPRESS):

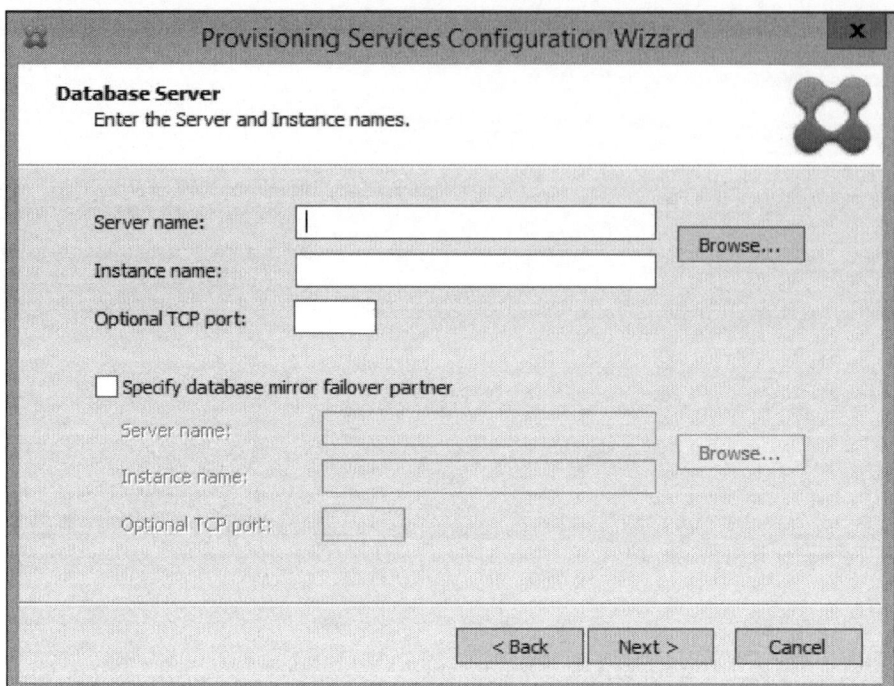

6. Next, specify the name of the database you would like to create and the name of the farm, site, and device collection (see examples in the following screenshot). Also, define the **Farm Administrator group** in the Active Directory if it's different from the default built-in administrators container:

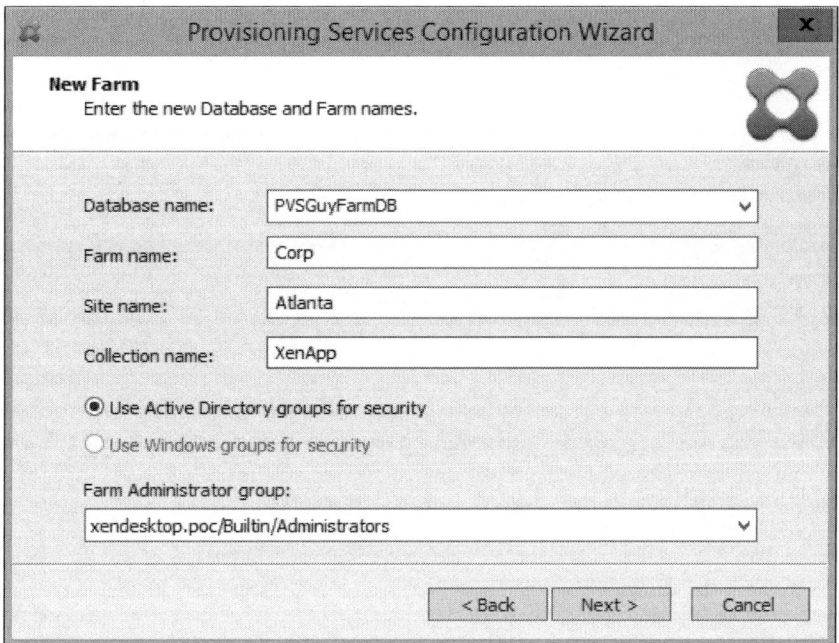

7. To create a new store for vDisk files, specify a name and a path to your VHD store. It can be a local directory, such as `C:\vDisks`, or a network path if you're using shared storage:

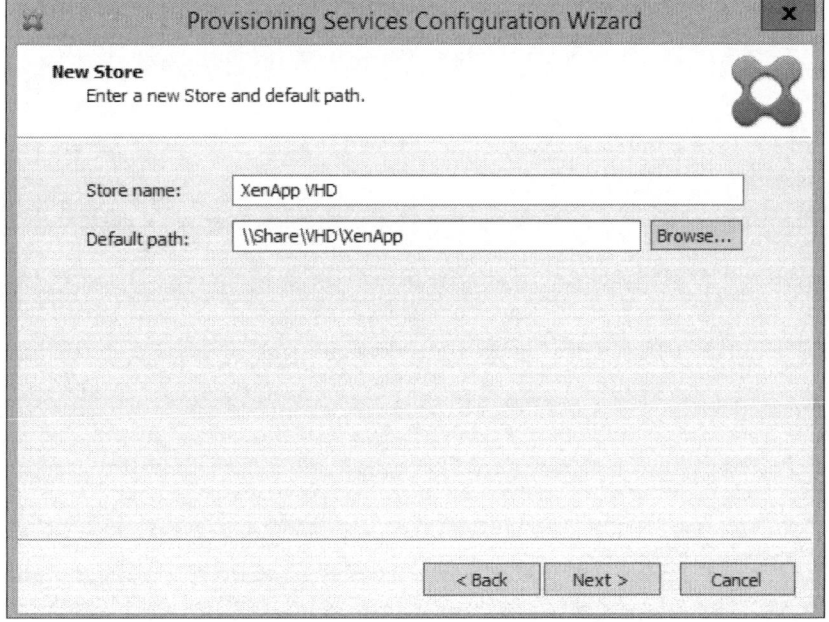

8. To configure licensing, specify the name of your Citrix License Server and a port to obtain licensing information from that machine. The default port is 27000:

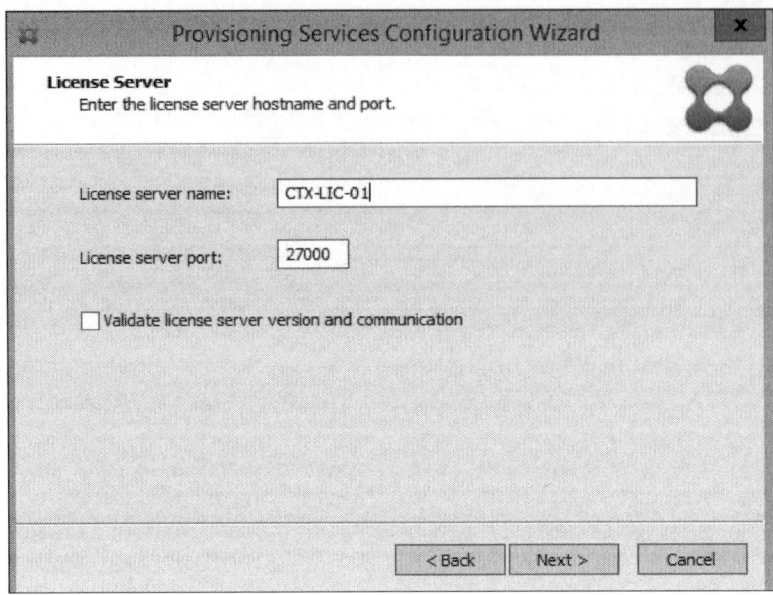

9. Enter a user account that will run the PVS Windows services (Soap and Stream). It is highly recommended that you create a service account that does not expire:

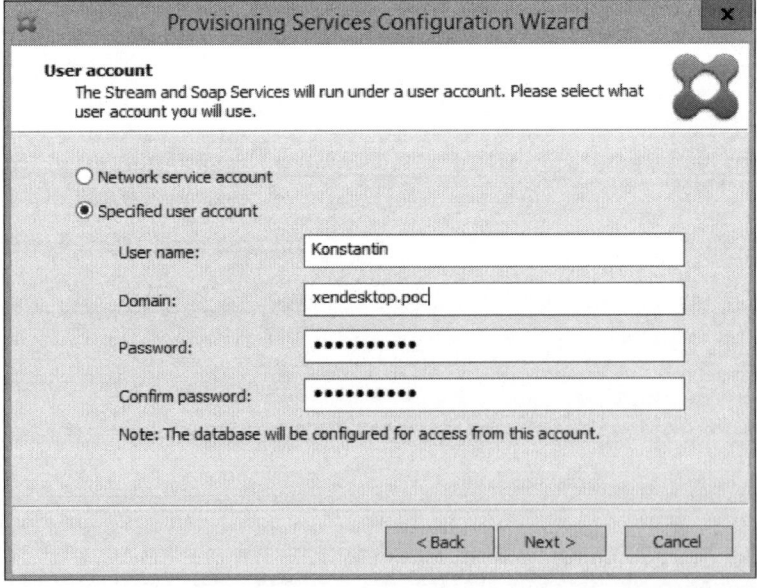

10. Leave the machine account password setting at the default value of 7 days to enable the Provisioning Server to manage the Active Directory machine accounts for the PVS target devices:

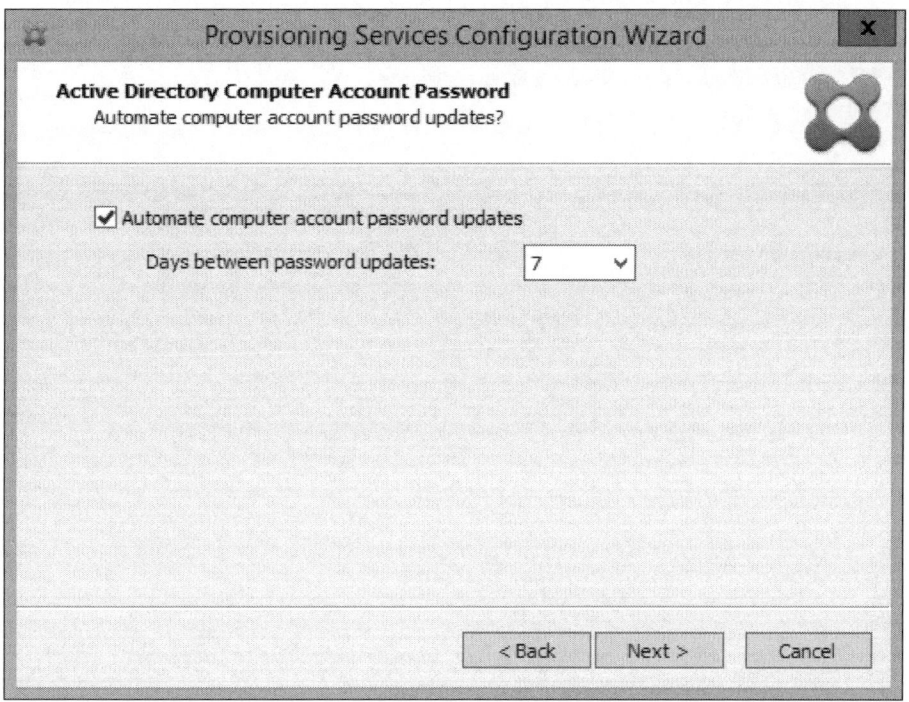

11. For **Network Communications**, select the network adapter for vDisk streaming and PVS server management. Since we have a 10 Gb connection, there is no need to isolate the streaming traffic into its own NIC. Traffic isolation can be beneficial if you have 1 Gb NICs in place to avoid network bottlenecks:

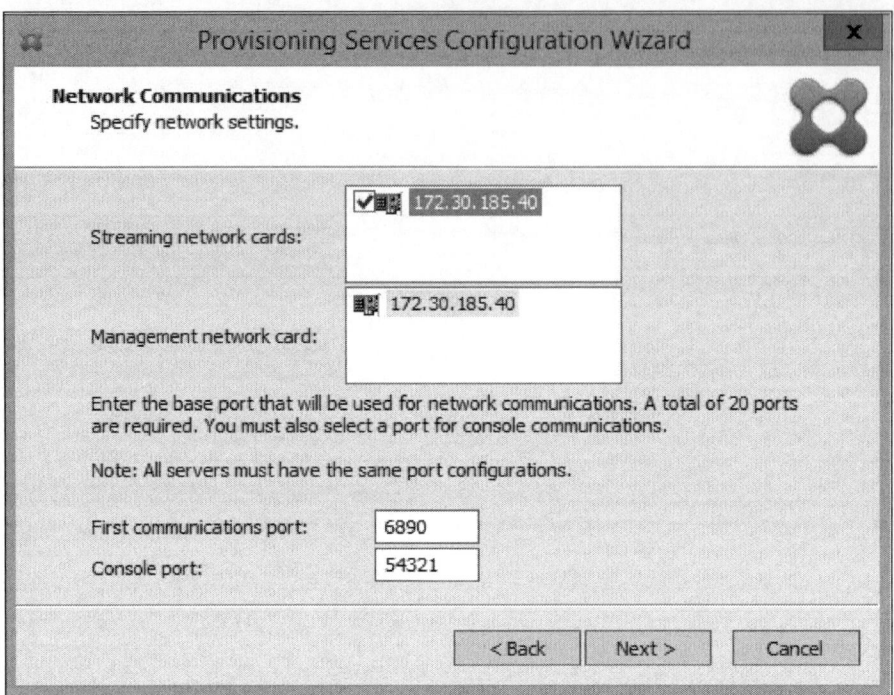

12. For TFTP, choose **Use the Provisioning Services TFTP service** to supply the bootstrap file to the target device. Alternatively, a third-party enterprise product, such as **SolarWinds**, which allows additional customizations and tuning, can be used to distribute the bootstrap:

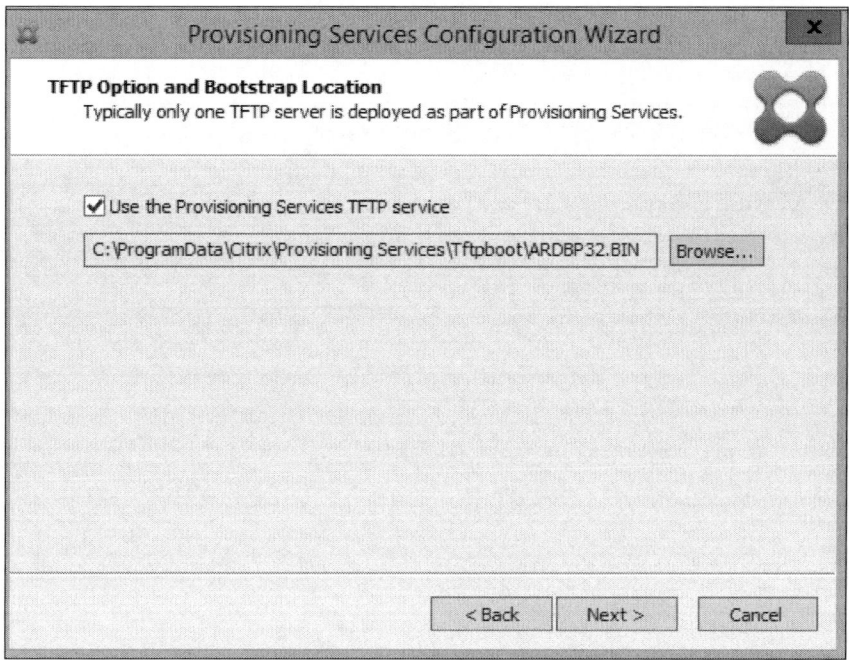

13. Next, the Provisioning Server should detect itself as an available boot server so that everything can be left at default there:

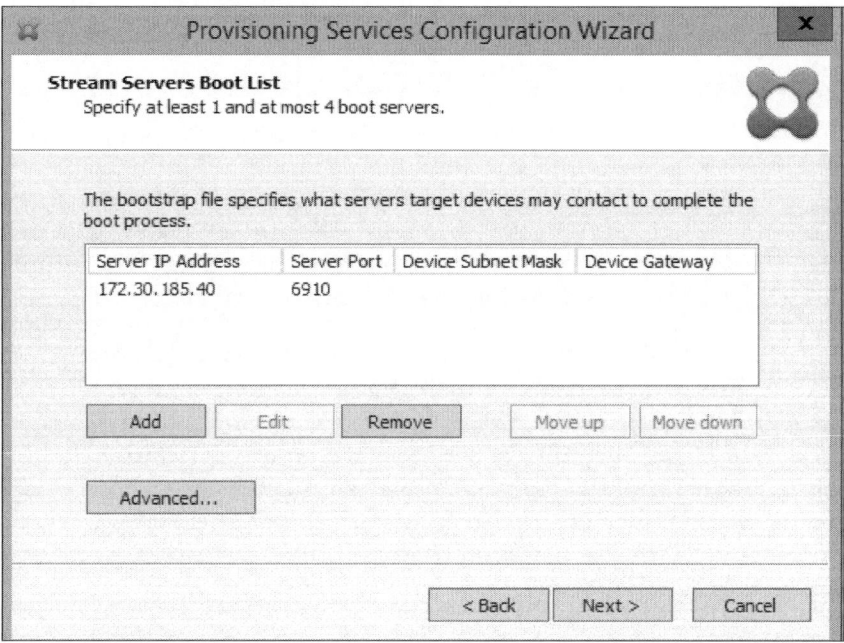

14. As a last step, review the configurations that have been put in place and click on **Finish** to configure the new PVS farm and Windows services:

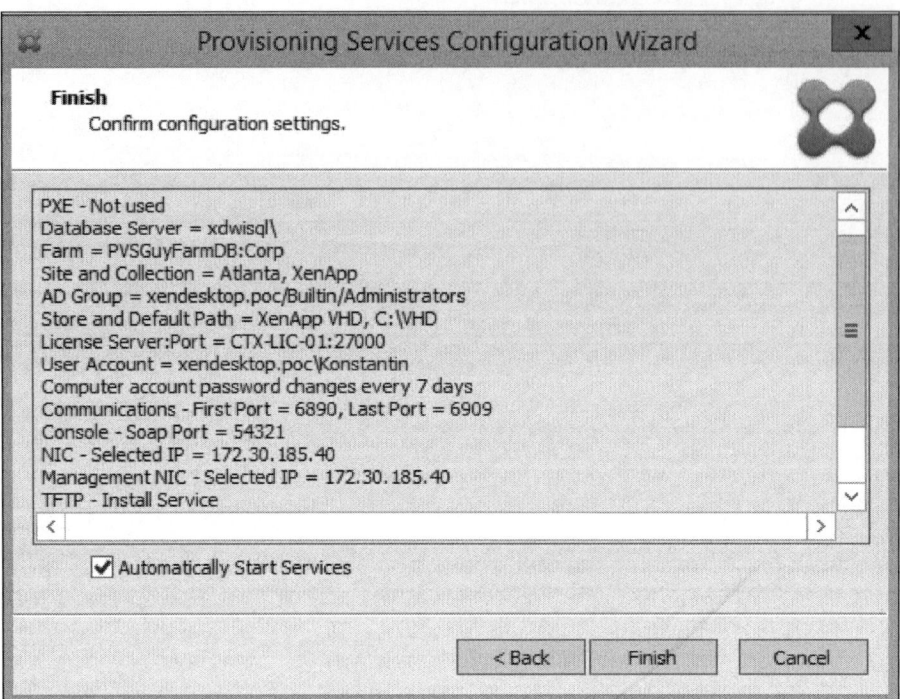

Configuring the PVS target device software

In order to create a virtual disk image of an OS, we need to install the PVS target device software on the master image from the PVS 7.6 ISO and then launch the Imaging Wizard to set up the VHD conversion. The Imaging Wizard is a built-in utility that comes with the PVS target device software, and it has greatly enhanced the administrator's capability to create a successful image by adding optimizations. Use the following steps for configuring the PVS target device software:

1. From the Start menu, launch the **Provisioning Services Imaging Wizard**. On the introductory screen, click on **Next** and specify the name of the primary Provisioning Server. The default farm communication port is 54321. If you've logged in with an account that has administrative rights to the PVS server, leave **Use my Windows credentials** selected, otherwise, choose **Use these credentials** and specify such an account:

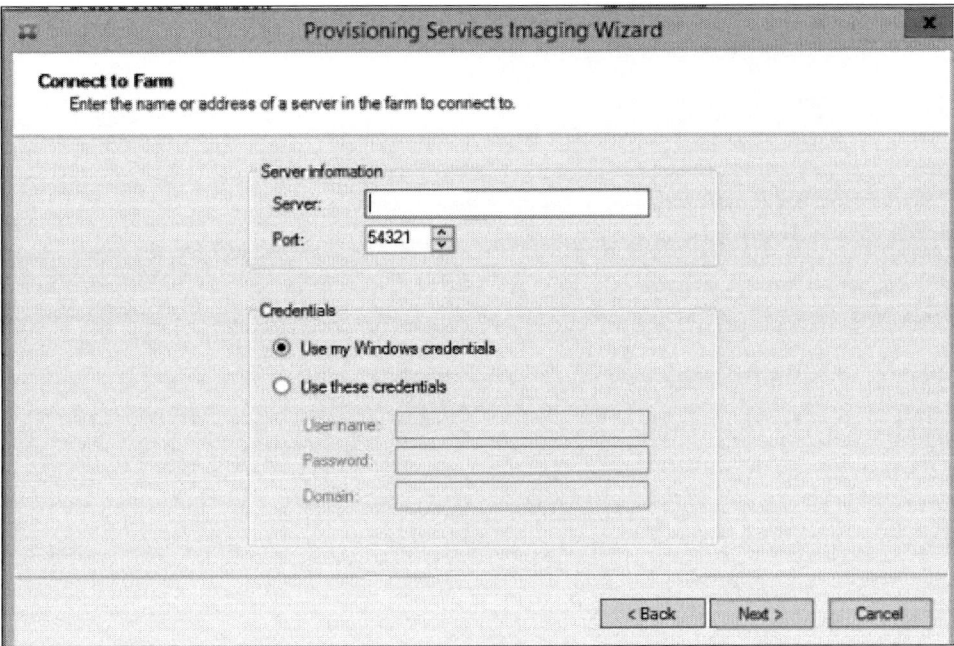

2. Next, give the new vDisk a name and choose the store where the vDisk files will reside. Leave the vDisk file as **Fixed**:

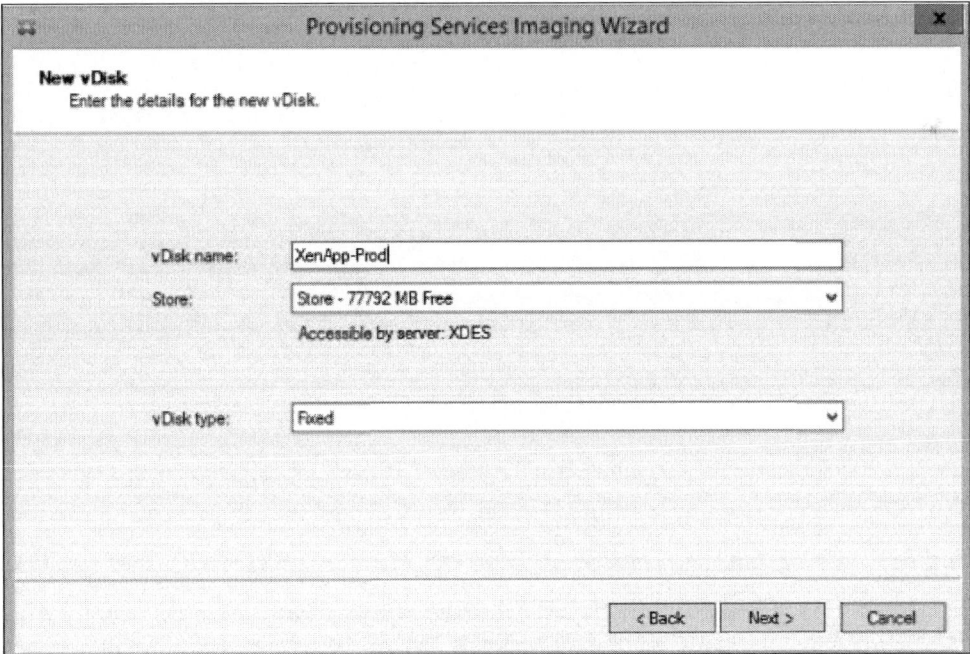

3. Then, choose to create a new vDisk. You can alternatively reuse an existing vDisk if one already exists and it is not in use:

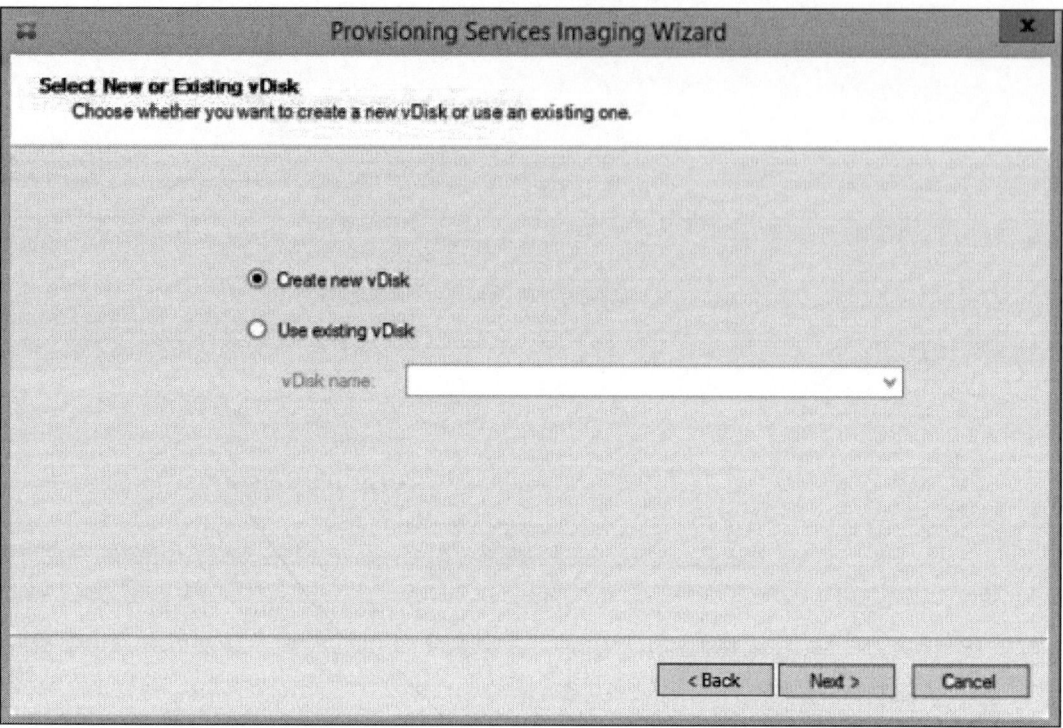

4. For Microsoft Volume Licensing, select **None** for the time being. We will revisit this setting and configure KMS in *Chapter 11, Administering a XenApp® Environment – Server Management*, where we'll take a deeper dive into server administration.

5. Next, configure the destination volumes to be imaged by PVS. By default, the first volume is **System Reserved** and the second one is the c:\ drive referred to as **C: Boot**:

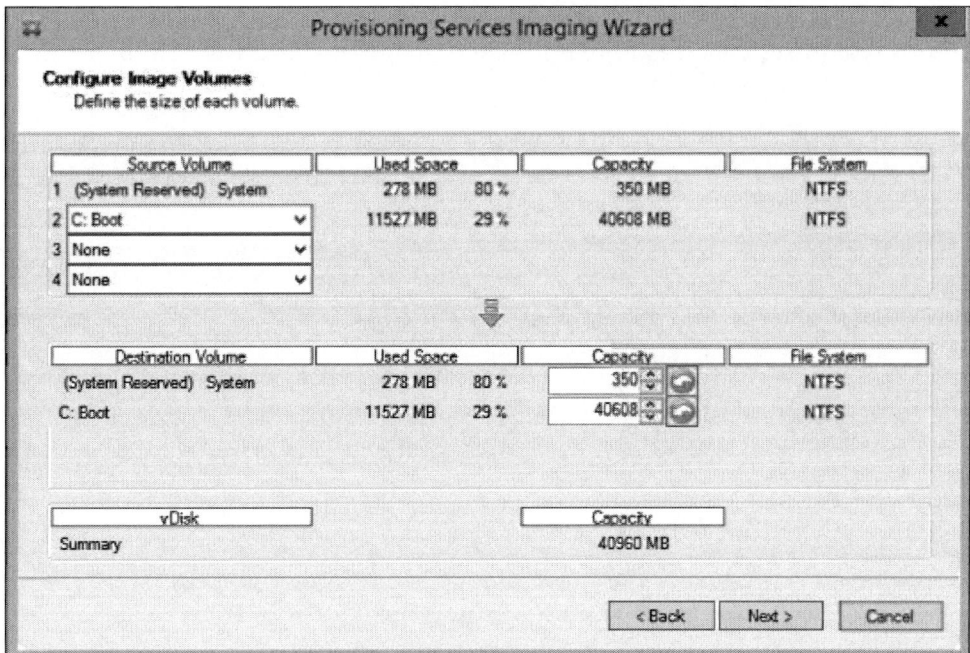

6. Create a name for the target device as it will appear in the PVS console. Note that this is different from the Active Directory computer name of this machine:

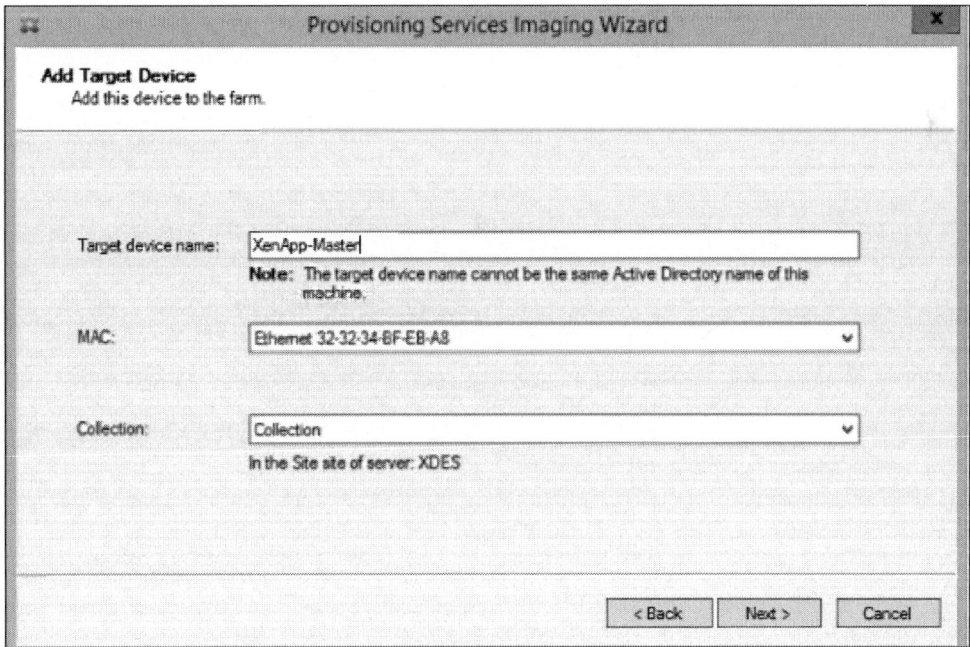

7. As a final step, review the configuration and click on **Optimize for Provisioning Services** to fine tune the image by disabling certain services that add overhead to the system:

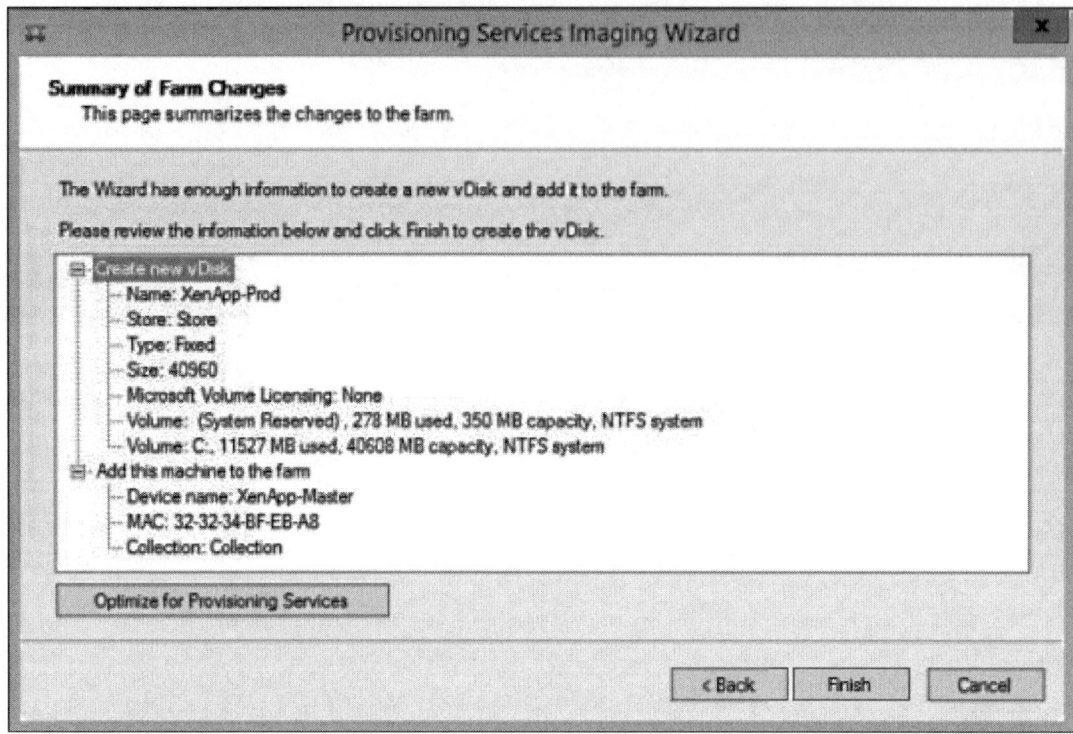

8. Once the vDisk creation is complete, a prompt will appear to change the VM boot device to a network adapter (PXE) in the BIOS and reboot the machine. If you're using XenServer, go to the VM **Properties** in XenCenter in the **General** tab, and under **Boot Options**, select **Network** and move it up to the first place in the order shown in the following screenshot:

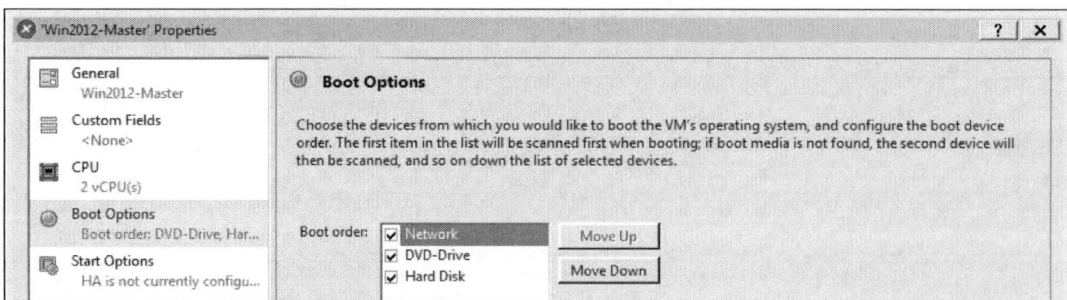

Upon restarting the machine and logging into Windows, the Citrix P2PVS (previously known as XenConvert) utility is automatically started and it converts the C:\ drive of the master target device to a VHD file. The new vDisk also appears in the PVS console on the Provisioning Server, and the VHD file is created on the shared storage under the store path specified in the imaging stage. Once the conversion finishes, we can go to the PVS console on the PVS server and under **Device Collections**, change the master target device boot mode from hard drive to vDisk to test streaming the new image by PXE by booting the target VM again, this time to the vDisk as set in the PVS console. Once we verify that the vDisk has streamed successfully and the operating system comes up in a useable state, we can create a template on the hypervisor with the same CPU, memory, and NIC specifications but without the main hard drive that we had on the master device as this would be streamed from a shared VHD. If we decide to put the write cache on a virtual hard disk, we would need to add this disk to the template VM. For a XenApp target server that will accept multiple user connections at the same time and will generate a lot of writes, it is advisable to put at least 16 to 20 GB of storage, especially if we use the new hybrid cache type called **Cache in device RAM with overflow on hard disk**, which uses different block sizes than traditional hard drive caching. Once the template is created in XenCenter, we need to log in to the PVS console and under **vDisk Pool**, change the vDisk mode from **Private** (exclusive) to **Standard** (shared).

Running the XenDesktop® setup wizard in PVS

There are two ways of provisioning new machines in PVS: the **XenDesktop Setup Wizard** and the **Streamed VM Setup Wizard**. They have very similar roles in PVS as far as creating new machines. The main difference, however, is that the **Streamed VM Setup Wizard** deploys VMs directly on the hypervisor and creates a **Device Collection** in PVS without making any contact with the XenApp Delivery Controller. This wizard is still widely used for pre 7.0 XenApp deployments, where XenApp itself wasn't integrated with XenDesktop and had a completely different infrastructure from XenDesktop. Now that XenApp and XenDesktop are basically two sides of the same product and the XenApp functionality is fully administered by the controller, it makes much more sense to use the **XenDesktop Setup Wizard** to create VMs from PVS using the XenApp host connection because it also adds machines to a new machine catalog on the controller so that we don't have to do that manually. To access the **XenDesktop Setup Wizard**, simply logon to the PVS console, right-click on the **Site** to launch the utility, and perform the following steps to create VMs on the hypervisor:

1. Enter the Delivery Controller address in the post-introductory screen.

2. Next, choose the host connection that we created on the Delivery Controller from the resource list. Submit the hypervisor connection credentials when prompted.

3. Select the PVS template created in the previous section from the template list.

4. Choose the option to create a new catalog and name it appropriately.

5. For the OS type, choose **Windows Server** and proceed to the next step.

6. Specify the number of VMs to create and resources assigned to each machine using the same specs as the template. Leave the PXE boot selected.

7. In the next two screens, choose to create new machine accounts and select an Active Directory container to store the accounts. Also, define a naming convention for the targets. When done, finalize the configuration and let the wizard do the deployment.

Once the **XenDesktop Setup Wizard** displays a message that the VM creation has been successfully completed, we should double-check the hypervisor to make sure that the VMs were indeed provisioned as expected. Also, on the XenApp Delivery Controller in Studio, a streamed catalog should automatically be created that contains entries for those VMs that were deployed on the hypervisor by the **XenDesktop Setup Wizard** in PVS. This way, those VMs can be power managed from the XenApp side and apps can be published and associated with users in a Delivery Group. A streamed catalog can also be created manually on the Delivery Controller and populated with existing streamed VMs by pointing it to a Device Collection on the Provisioning Server. This is often done for testing and troubleshooting purposes.

Summary

In this chapter, we learned about the nature of the Provisioning Services technology and how to deploy it in our XenApp 7.6 implementation to facilitate administration and reduce storage footprints in IT organizations. PVS, if deployed correctly, can make your life as a system administrator or consultant a lot easier — think about the ability to test changes in your environment without disrupting the work of your users. PVS makes it possible to push out updates on the fly and store an OS in a single file that can reside on shared storage and be replicated to your DR site. This doesn't mean, however, that this technology should be deployed in every environment. Some customers with smaller IT infrastructures may not be able to allocate the extra resources needed to build and license the Provisioning Servers and would be better served by the built-in MCS component of XenApp. Detailed planning should be done in advance and decisions should be made on a case-by-case basis. PVS is here to stay and we will revisit the topic later when we get into the nitty-gritty of XenApp administration. The next step of our journey will take you right into XenApp application management and testing. Stay tuned!

10

Administering a XenApp® Environment – Application Management

Alright! We've built the backbone of our solution, but how do we make it work to our advantage? How do we solve our business challenge and justify the cost of our investment as nicely and as quickly as possible? In the upcoming chapters, we'll discuss these and other topics of interest, and we'll focus on the hands-on administration and delivery of the XenApp environment to serve end users.

First, let's recap what we've implemented so far. The following table shows each component of the Citrix infrastructure and the quantity of units deployed for redundancy:

Citrix component	Quantity
XenApp Delivery Controller	2
Citrix StoreFront Server	2
Citrix Provisioning Server	2
Citrix NetScaler appliance	2
Master image	2

As you can see, we have two of each component so that if one member experiences an unforeseen crash, the other one can continue to operate the environment. The reason we have two master images is because we've configured both MCS and PVS as a machine deployment methodology, where one has both the PVS and the VDA agent installed on it and the other one only has the VDA, which is sufficient for MCS. We've used these images to deploy a machine catalog on the Delivery Controller and a Device Collection on the Provisioning Server, both containing six XenApp agent servers with Microsoft Office, QuickBooks, and Internet Explorer on them.

The XenApp software provides us with two main methods of delivering these applications to an end user under XenApp licensing terms: **hosted applications** or **hosted shared desktops**. Hosted applications are programs that are installed and run on the XenApp agent server but through the Delivery Controller and StoreFront, they can be presented to users via a web browser or a native store on Citrix Receiver, which is running on an endpoint device. With the help of this model, each time a user requests a session, a new instance of the application is launched on the XenApp agent server, which uses the CPU and memory of this server for app execution. This is probably the most widely used method of application delivery in enterprise environments because it allows the user to launch business-critical apps presented to them by an administrator from anywhere and any device that runs Citrix Receiver. The other method of application delivery is by actually giving the user a full desktop with their apps installed and launched locally on it (also known as hosted shared desktop or hosted shared VDI). With this model, the XenApp agent server is actually presented as a desktop that can be shared by multiple users at the same time, while still running securely in the data center. Hosted shared desktops are a lower cost alternative to traditional VDI desktops that run an end-user OS, such as Windows 8, which, unlike a Windows 2012 RDS server, doesn't support session sharing and requires XenDesktop licensing.

In this chapter, we will cover the following topics to explore and demonstrate both methods of application delivery in XenApp:

- Understanding hosted applications
- Updating hosted applications via MCS and PVS
- Accessing hosted applications via NetScaler Gateway and StoreFront

Application delivery – hosted apps

As I've hinted previously, this is by far the most important feature of XenApp and it has been at the core of the product line for the past decade. Even with recent changes in architecture and going from IMA to FMA, the concept of being able to present a business-critical application to a massive number of end users without having to maintain it on each device has grown more and more influential over time. This has also continued to drive interest in the product from customers around the world. However, in the context of our technical implementation, the big question at this point is how do we get from a bunch of XenApp servers deployed on the hypervisor to a meaningful set of applications being accessed by end users and managed by administrators? The following is a step-by-step procedure needed to publish the applications that we currently have installed on the XenApp agent servers to our users. This is accomplished by deploying Delivery Groups in Citrix Studio on the XenApp Delivery Controller. What are Delivery Groups? They are sets of VMs extracted from a machine catalog that can be associated with Active Directory user groups for the purpose of application and desktop delivery. Power management is also configured on the Delivery Group level and applications are selected and published there as well.

Creating Delivery Groups

The creation of Delivery Groups is accomplished through Citrix Studio on the Delivery Controller in a similar fashion to how machine catalogs are formed. Since in our deployment we have three departments of employees—sales, engineering, and HR—it makes sense to create three Delivery Groups for each department even if they use the same master image and machine catalog. This way, we can publish only the applications relevant to a particular user group and users will not have visibility into other application environments. Follow these specified steps when you're ready to deploy the first Delivery Group and repeat the same process for each subsequent one:

1. Log on to Citrix Studio on the XenApp Delivery Controller and select the **Machine Catalogs** node. Observe the machine catalog we created with MCS in *Chapter 8, Building Your First XenApp® Farm – Machine Creation Services*.

2. Select **Delivery Groups** and click on **Create Delivery Group** on the left-hand panel of Studio.

3. Skip the **Introduction** page and choose the number of machines to add to the Delivery Group from the current Catalog.

4. Under **Delivery Type**, choose **Desktops and applications** and click on **Next**:

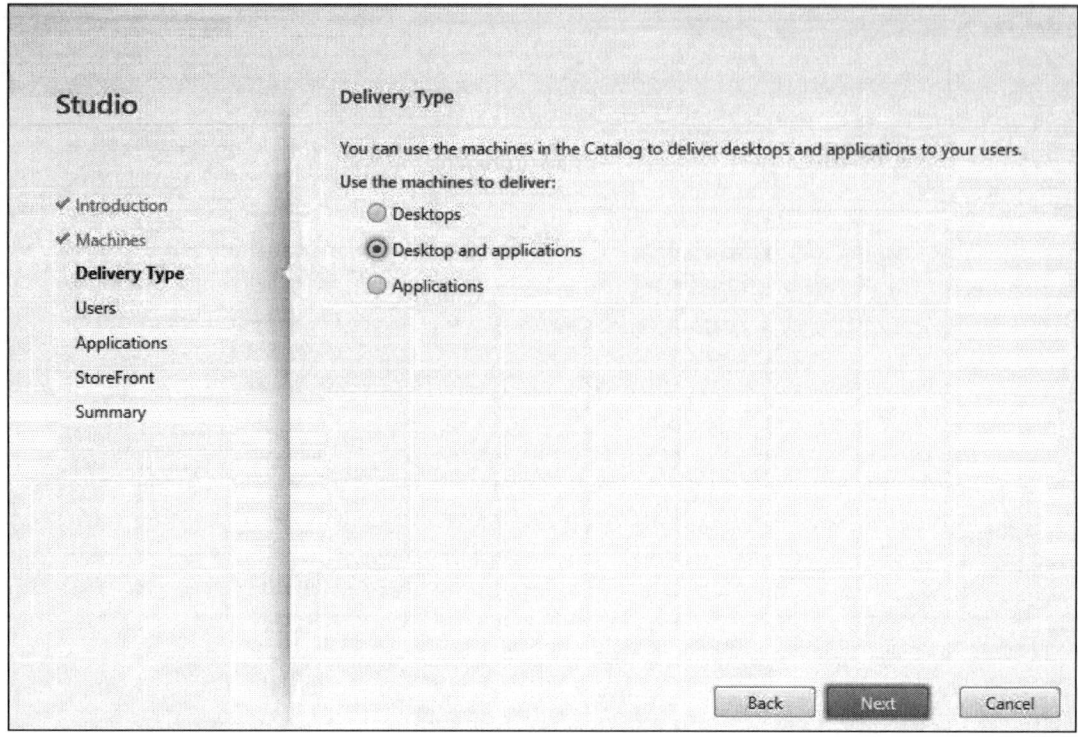

5.   At this point, we will associate the engineering group in Active Directory with the new Delivery Group:

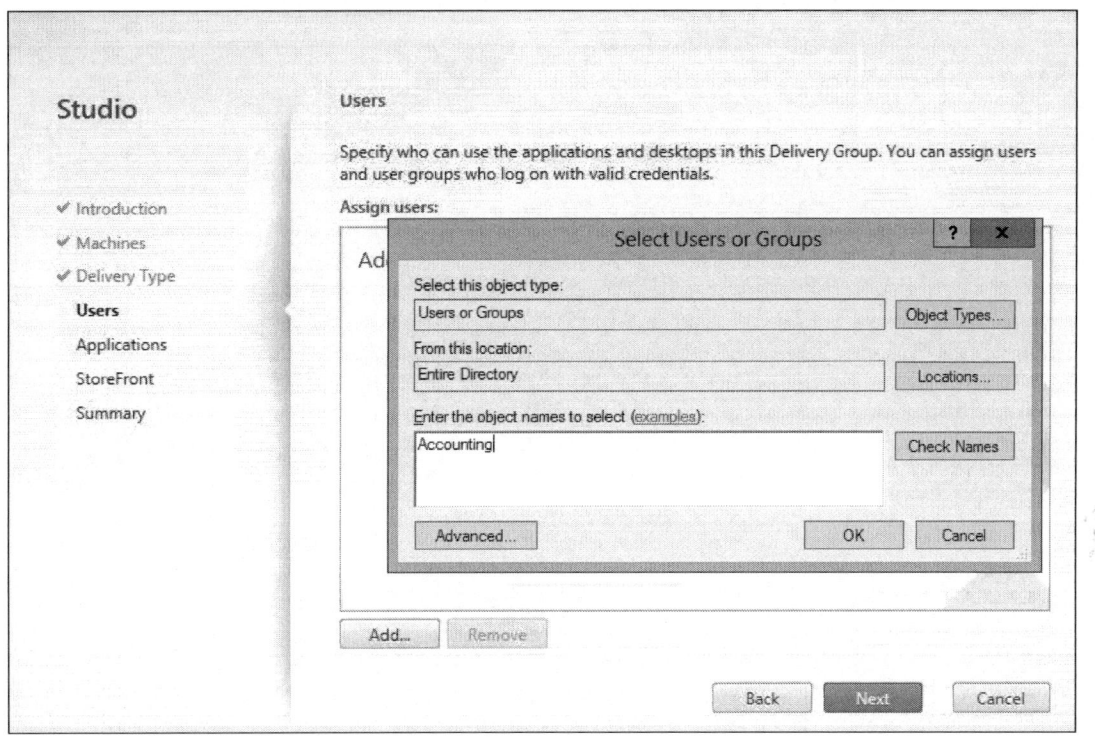

6. Under **Applications**, click on **Add applications manually...** and fill in the path to the application executable for Google Sketch and the working (parent) directory, as shown in the following screenshot:

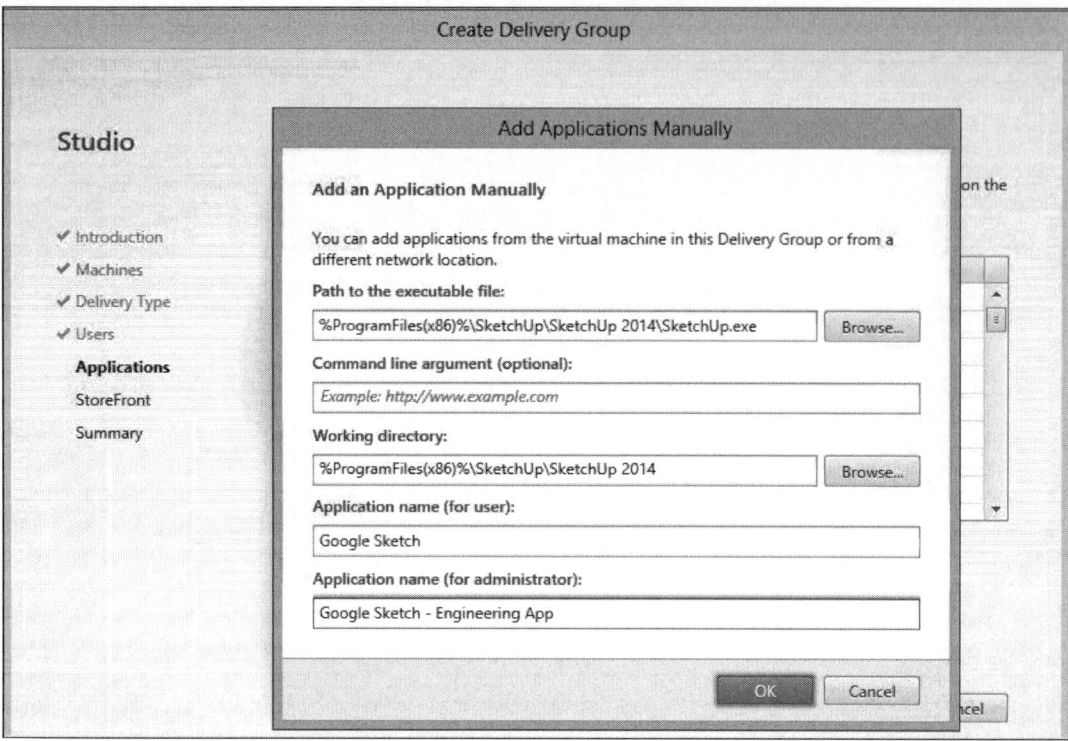

7. Next, leave the Receiver StoreFront URL as manual and go to **Summary** to review the configuration:

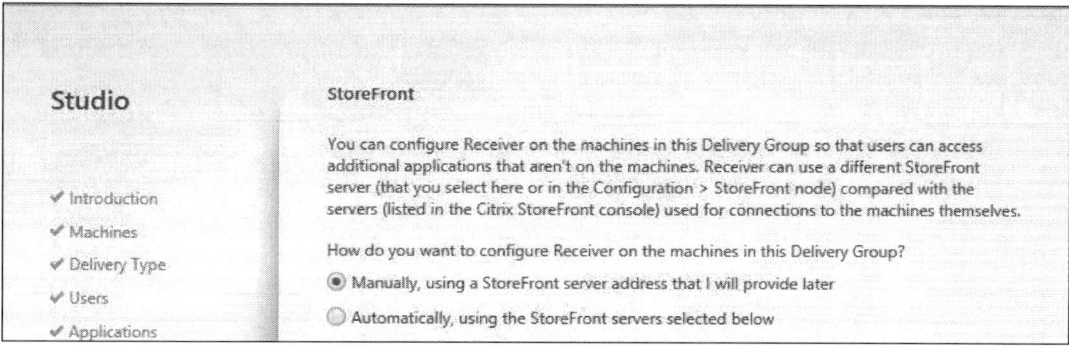

8. Give the Delivery Group a name and an optional description, and then click on **Finish**.

The newly created Delivery Group will have the number of machines that we've specified in the configuration and the Google Sketch application will be published to the Engineering users group. All the applications selected during the creation of the Delivery Group will be visible in the **Applications** tab of the **Delivery Groups** node in Studio. They can also be structured in folders for ease of management. If at any point in time, we need to add a new application to the published list, there is an option in the left-hand side pane in Studio to add applications.

Updating hosted applications – MCS

The process of updating an existing application depends on the technology used to create the XenApp agent machines, such as MCS or PVS. In the case of MCS, updating applications is fairly easy—all you need to do is log in to the master image, perform the required task, shut it down, optionally take a snapshot (or let MCS handle this), and select the option in Studio to update the catalog from the machine catalog level. When the catalog update is finished, all we need to do is restart the VMs from Studio if the rollout strategy was to restart them manually. Otherwise, they will reboot on their own once the process is complete.

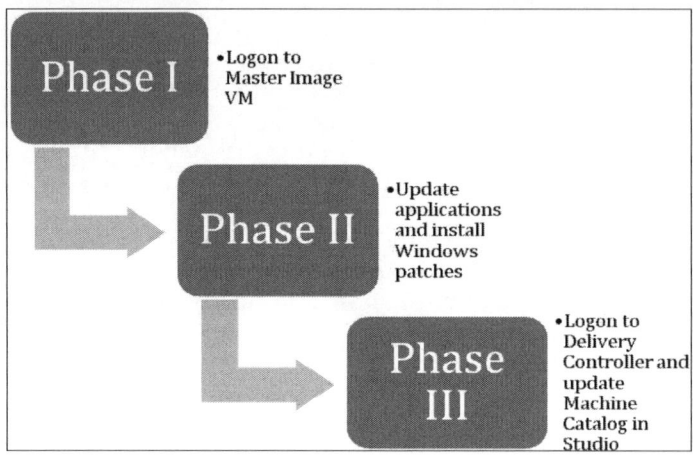

As seen in the flowchart, when using XenApp and MCS, the process of updating applications involves updating the master image first and then the machine catalog in Studio. When the VMs are done rebooting, they will have the latest software that was installed on the master image and will be ready to accept connections from end users. There is also a feature available in Studio to put machines or entire **Delivery Groups** in **Maintenance Mode**. What this means is that when an administrator performs maintenance on the VMs, they will not accept user connections during this time. This feature doesn't really impact the update process because all the changes are made on the master image and are later propagated to the VMs by the administrator from the Delivery Controller. The true value-add from **Maintenance Mode** is derived during troubleshooting. If you are working on an issue that's impacting one or more VMs and you want to do testing without impacting users, you can simply put either that particular VM or the entire Delivery Group into **Maintenance Mode**, which will ensure that users will not be able to connect until the issue is resolved and the feature is turned off.

Updating hosted applications – PVS

PVS, on the other hand, takes a different approach. Since the OS image is contained in a VHD file that gets streamed to target devices, we need to put the vDisk in the read/write mode first by changing the properties of the base or create a new maintenance version and boot a VM to this image to make the necessary changes. So, let's take Internet Explorer, for example, which is the supported platform for many web-based applications. When a new **Knowledge Base (KB)** update from Microsoft comes out for IE11 and we need to update the vDisk, we can either put it in the read/write (also known as private Image) mode or create a maintenance version of this vDisk from the PVS console and boot a target device to the vDisk in order to modify the content of the OS. Introduced in PVS 6.0, versioning is a great method to make changes while keeping several copies of the vDisk for rollback purposes. The way it works is that it creates an AVHD file, which contains a delta of the original base and the first version, or if multiple versions have been created, then AVHD is the delta between the previous and the next version. The following flowchart illustrates the steps involved in modifying a vDisk using versioning:

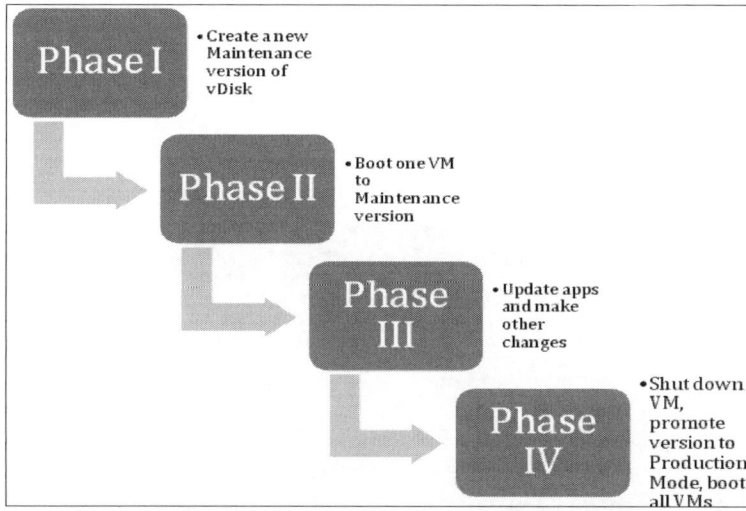

Even though versioning is the preferred and recommended method of updating an image in PVS 6.0 and later versions(in our case 7.6), there is also an alternative option, which was primarily used before this feature was released. The other method involves putting the vDisk in the private mode from the vDisk Properties in the PVS console and booting the target device to the base image to make necessary changes to it. This way, only the VHD file is modified and no new AVHD files are created. Even though this is a simplified way of updating the image, it comes with one big disadvantage. Much like a maintenance version, private mode is one-to-one read/write relationship, so only one target device can be booted to the vDisk at any given time. However, because we directly modify the base VHD, we have to end all other connections to this vDisk prior to changing the mode to private. This means that we need to pause production for a certain period of time until the changes are made and the vDisk is switched back to standard. With versioning, the production devices continue to be operational since they are connected to the most current point-in-time version before the maintenance version, which doesn't affect production. The following chart illustrates the workflow of an image update using the old private mode method:

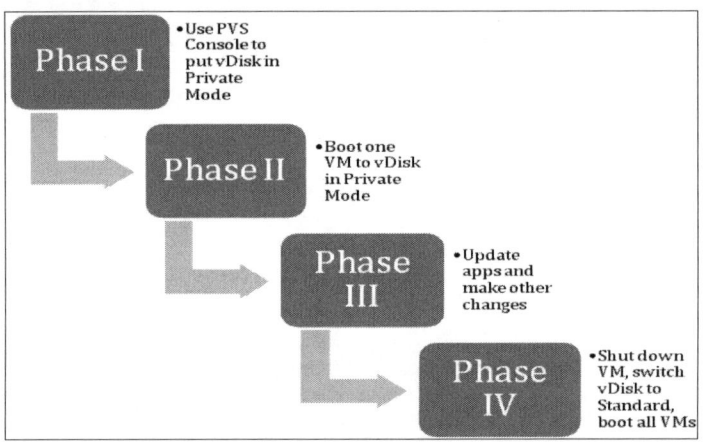

In conclusion, private mode takes the same amount of steps as versioning. However, versioning offers a lot more flexibility as it is natively non-disruptive to production and can be leveraged for testing at any point in time. The duration of the impact from private mode can be mitigated by making a copy of the VHD file, renaming it to something else (for example, vDisk-Test), and importing it to the vDisk pool using the PVS console. This way, you can play around with a copy of the production image without disrupting the current connections because as long as the file is named differently, PVS will treat it is a separate vDisk altogether. Once the application updates on the second image are complete, target devices can be unassigned from the production image and reassigned to the other one. They would still need to be restarted to connect to the new vDisk, but if done in batches, user activities will most likely remain uninterrupted.

Accessing hosted applications via NetScaler Gateway™

Application accessibility is the main objective of users along with performance. As such, XenApp-hosted applications need to be available to users at all times but they also need to be presented in an intuitive way so that employees spend the majority of their time using the actual programs rather than learning how to access them. As shown in the preceding section, Active Directory user groups and individual users are added to the Delivery Group level either while creating it or editing the group properties. More often than not, administrators will create the Group and only add a few test users and then go back later to add real users during production rollout. This way, they ensure that the apps can be accessed rather than give production users direct access into the environment without prior testing. Thus, as a first step, I typically either add myself or a test account that is a member of the domain to the Delivery Group from the **Edit Delivery Group** menu in Studio as shown in the following screenshot:

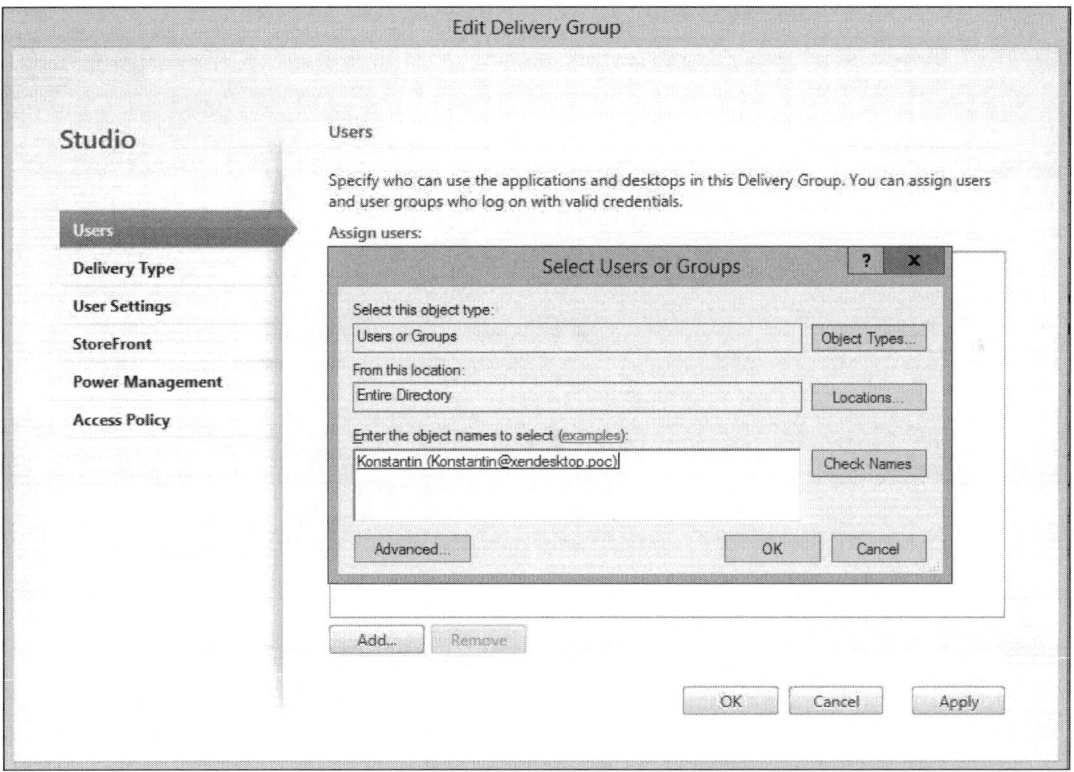

At this point, you should be able to connect to the NetScaler Gateway URL and access your Receiver for the web store. Now if you didn't have Citrix Receiver installed on your computer, you would be prompted by StoreFront to download the software from `http://www.citrix.com/` and install it locally on your machine. When you connect to your application store for the first time, you are presented with a pointer to add your apps, as shown in the following screenshot:

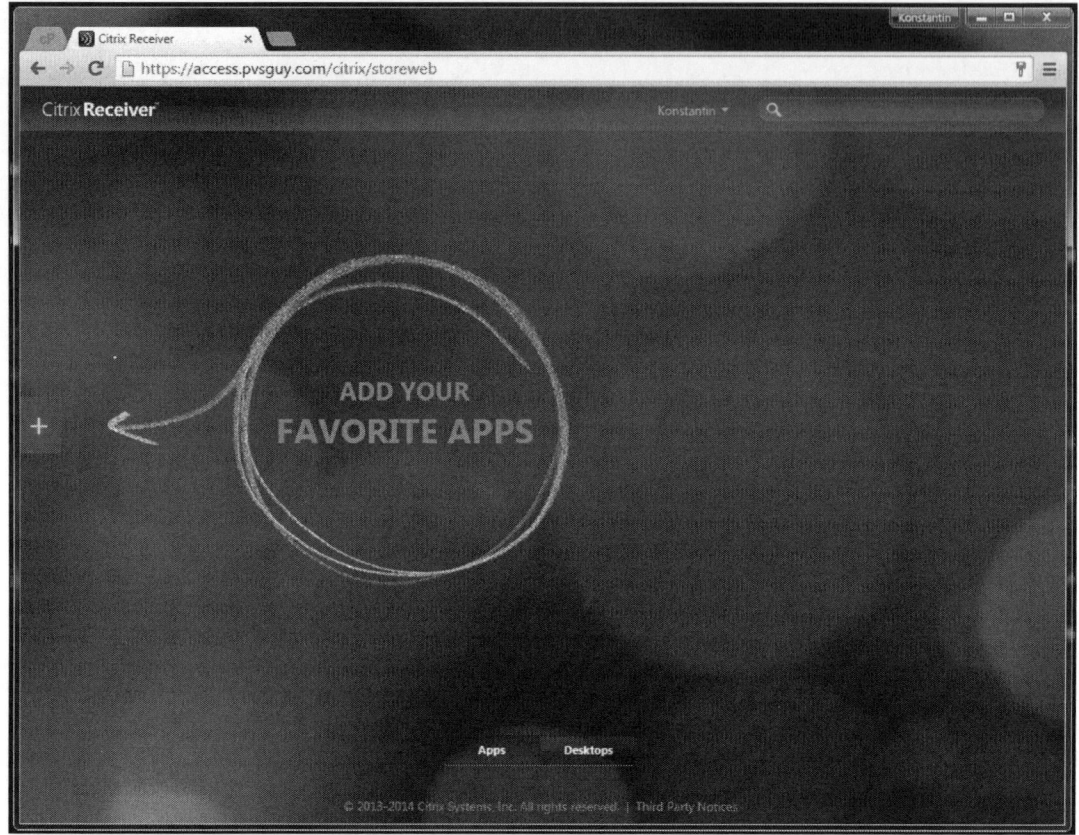

Upon clicking the **+** sign on the left-hand side, you are presented with a list of applications assigned to your user account on the Delivery Group level. This is where users can pick both applications and desktops depending on the resources that the administrator has assigned to them:

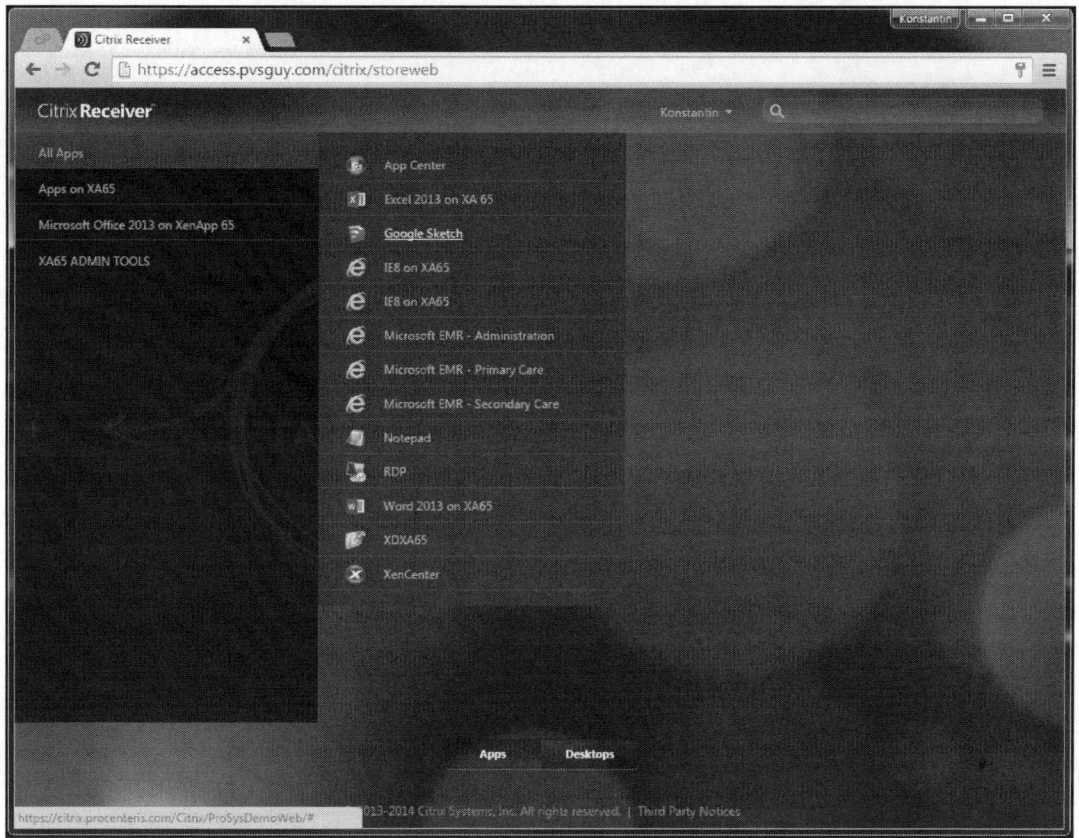

After choosing **Google Sketch**, the app is moved to the center of the screen from where the user can launch it with a single mouse click and start using it as if it was running locally on their machine.

Using the same methodology, a user can be added to all three Delivery Groups for testing, thus gaining access to applications from all three departments of a company. For instance, when we publish Internet Explorer with a prepopulated URL pointing to the UltiPro login page for HR, once a user is added to the Delivery Group properties on the controller, the app should become available in the application store as shown here:

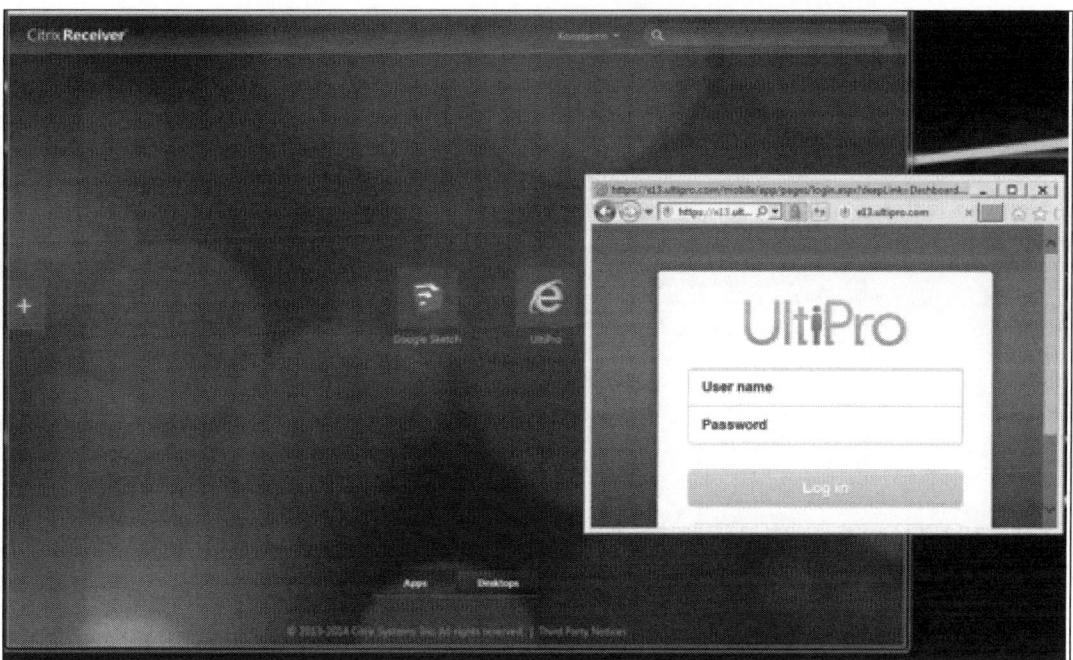

The concept of publishing Internet Explorer URLs is very popular and widely used by customers due to its ease of use and the fact that many of today's enterprise apps are hosted on web servers and their databases are accessed through a web portal. For security purposes, many companies don't allow access to those websites from external networks and the only way to access them is through either via VPN, which may not always be reliable, or via a hosted application running securely on a server in the data center but available through Citrix XenApp. With the right Group Policy settings in place, the administrator can completely lock down the browser in a way that users cannot access other websites or local drives on the XenApp server. All of a sudden, you can gain access to your business-critical software from anywhere without exposing the company's internal network to outside risks.

So, how do we publish an Internet Explorer link rather than just the browser itself? Just like user associations, new apps are published on the Delivery Group level in Citrix Studio by either creating a new Delivery Group (for example, XenApp Human Resources Group) or creating a new application under the **Applications** tab of the **Delivery Groups** node:

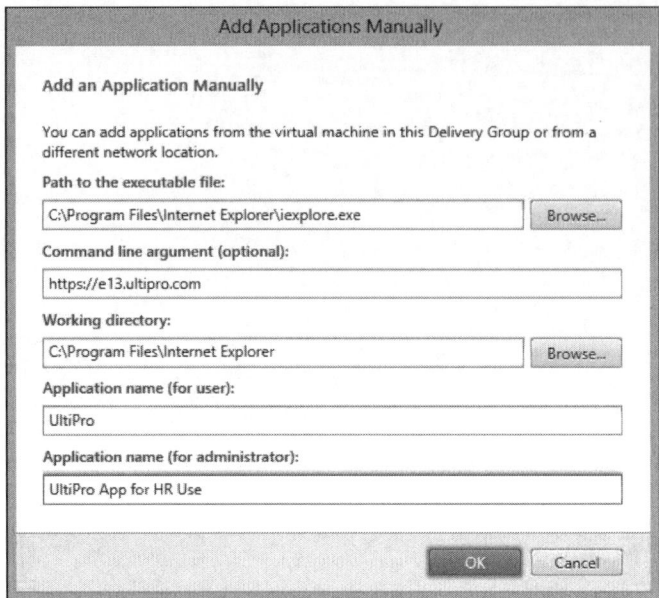

As shown in the preceding screenshot, the application executable is published with the URL of the UltiPro login page as a command-line argument. Any other browser-based application would be presented in the same way. For instance, the sales department will get their Salesforce portal as a published Internet Explorer executable that automatically redirects them to `https://login.salesforce.com` upon a session launch.

Accessing hosted applications via StoreFront™

Sometimes, for simplicity or troubleshooting purposes, it might make sense to connect users directly to StoreFront instead of a NetScaler Gateway virtual server. This way, they would put the URL of the Receiver in their browser for the web address configured in StoreFront. An example scenario of this is when a NetScaler appliance has crashed and a secondary node is not available, administrators will want to test the internal URL of the StoreFront store and provide it to some users as a temporary measure. However, using StoreFront directly means that you would not be able to take advantage of session policies on the NetScaler that can be configured to make intelligent decisions about your connection request based on geographic location, endpoint device, packet content, and other factors.

App-V integration

An important feature of older XenApp versions, such as 6.5 was **Application Streaming**. With the help of this technology, applications could be installed in a single repository known as **Application Hub** and streamed to client devices with only the required portion of the code being executed on a local system. This was very beneficial to a lot of customers because they only needed to install and maintain the applications in a centralized file server and network overhead was kept to a minimum. However, in later versions of the product, such as 7.5 and 7.6, Citrix has retired the Application Streaming feature and has instead decided to integrate XenApp with Microsoft App-V. This is a result of a collaboration effort between Citrix and Microsoft where a mature technology, such as App-V, which is widely used by many enterprise customers, can now be leveraged to provide the same functionalities as Citrix Application Streaming within the Citrix environment. App-V applications can be accessed via Receiver or StoreFront (aggregated in the same store as regular XenApp hosted apps) or locally on a VDI image. At the same time, they are completely isolated and independent from XenApp servers and all the packaging and optimization is done in the App-V environment.

To integrate your existing App-V infrastructure with XenApp, all you need to do is go to Citrix Studio and add your management and publishing servers in the **App-V Publishing** node, as shown in the following screenshot. The same task can be accomplished during the initial site creation wizard if an existing App-V solution is available at that time:

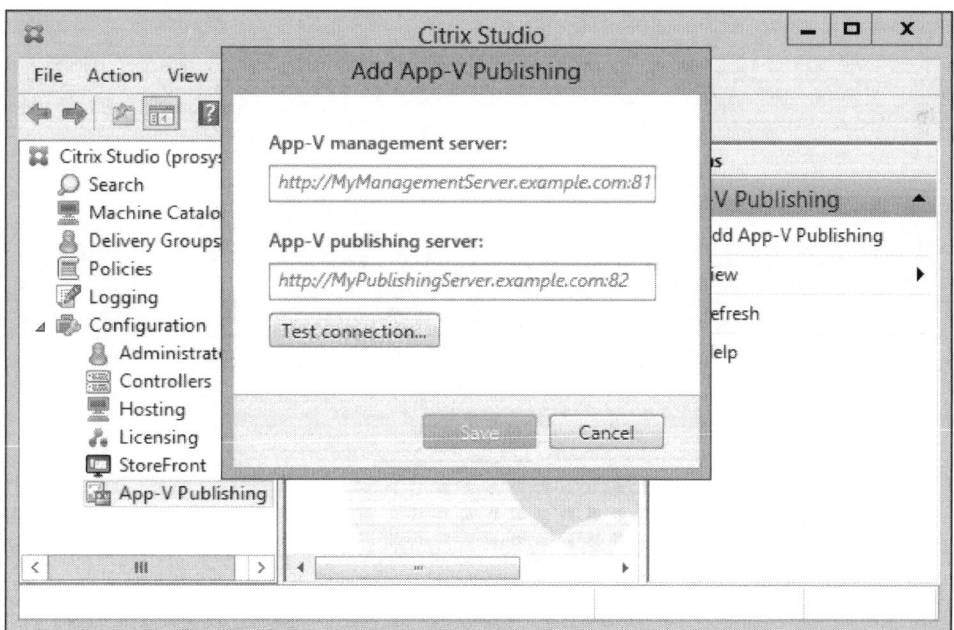

From that point on, App-V applications can be published in the Delivery Group just like regular XenApp apps. When creating a new app in Studio, both types of apps are enumerated from the master image. Once publishing is completed, all apps will be listed in the **Applications** tab of the **Delivery Groups** node and ready for use by the associated user groups.

Summary

In this chapter, we learned how to publish applications hosted on the Windows Server OS and manage virtual machine resource pools on the Delivery Controller to unlock the powerful features of Citrix XenApp. From the next chapter onwards, we will learn how to manage licensing, Group Policy, and profile management for this freshly built environment of XenApp machines. We will also learn how to optimize user experience and security based on the type of network that incoming connections are generated from. In other words, lots of interesting stuff is coming up shortly. Stay tuned!

11
Administering a XenApp® Environment – Server Management

Long gone are the days of WinFrame when Citrix used to be just a server where multiple users executed applications at the same time. In the 21st century, Citrix's portfolio has grown to include virtualization, networking, mobility, and cloud space and every bit of Citrix infrastructure is full of moving parts. Managing a XenApp environment can sometimes prove challenging, so having a good understanding of the different procedures involved in the XenApp administration is pivotal to your organization's success. In this chapter, we will explore the following topics with a focus on system management:

- Licensing your XenApp environment for **Remote Desktop Services** (**RDS**)
- Facilitating profiles with Citrix Profile Management
- Benefiting from Session Prelaunch and Lingering
- Managing Citrix policies and Active Directory GPOs in the XenApp environment
- Upgrading the VDA and PVS target device software
- XenApp permissions and delegated administration
- Monitoring solutions

RDS licensing

Why do we need RDS licensing for XenApp? Recall from *Chapter 1, Why Citrix XenApp® – Making the Case for App Virtualization*, how the XenApp VDA requires that the underlying Windows server also be a Remote Desktop Session host. By leveraging the RDS (formerly known as **Terminal Services**) framework, Citrix can deliver a vast majority of today's enterprise applications to any device, while at the same time enhancing security, overhead control, and user experience. In order to achieve this, customers need to purchase RDS Licensing from Microsoft or an authorized reseller of Microsoft. As these licenses are per user and not concurrent, the sensible thing to do from the planning perspective is to buy as many licenses as there will be users with access to the XenApp environment. There are a few options when it comes to RDS licensing. However, what I've mostly observed in the field is that customers go with OPEN Licensing. With this approach, you don't have to physically download any licenses from your Microsoft account. Instead, you need to go through a license verification process initiated by your system. The easiest way to do this is to designate an RDS license server (the Citrix license server can also be used for this as long it is a Windows machine and not a Linux appliance) and enable the Remote Desktop Services License Manager from the **Add Roles** function of **Server Manager**. Then, from the RD Services License Manager console, activate the Open License by filling out all the required customer information. Once Microsoft verifies the request, the number of licenses available will be imported into RDSLM and will be ready for distribution to RDS-enabled XenApp agent servers. However, how do we tell these machines to go out and request licenses from the RDS License Server? It's actually pretty straightforward—all we need to do is create a GPO or add this setting—`Computer Configuration\Policies\Administrative Templates\Windows Components\Remote Desktop Services\Remote Desktop Session Host\Licensing`—to an existing GPO and apply it to the XenApp machine OU:

The following two values need to be set:

Fields	Values
RDS per user	**Enabled**
License server name	The DNS name of of your RDS license server

Once these GPO settings are applied to the XenApp agent machine OU, remote connections are allowed as far as Windows is concerned. If configured incorrectly, users will be prompted with a license grace period notification when launching a shared desktop session.

Citrix® Profile Management

Profile management has been a challenge for IT for quite a while and even though there are several robust solutions on the market that facilitate administration, user profiles have remained somewhat complex, prone to data corruption, and are a major cause for delays in user login times to physical and virtual desktops alike. To tackle these challenges, Citrix has bundled into the XenApp product a free profile solution called Citrix Profile Management, also known as **User Profile Management (UPM)**. This product combines the level of granularity and control needed by IT administrators to keep user profiles efficient, while avoiding the need to deploy a separate infrastructure for profile solution. UPM profiles can be configured to function as roaming or mandatory depending on the need of the environment (UPM does not officially use these terms as they are widely used in the Microsoft community). With roaming profiles, data saved in the profile is copied to a central repository, such as a file share, and it follows a user by synchronizing back to a machine the next time they log in. Optionally, a template profile can be prepared and enforced the first time the user logs in. If none is specified, a profile is created for the user automatically from the machine's default (local) profile. Mandatory profiles, on the other hand, do not get copied back to the central share and the user gets the same profile every time they log in. This means that the profile is deleted upon logoff and a new one is created from a template during next logon. Mandatory profiles are mostly used in environments where users are not allowed to save anything in their profiles for security purposes. This type of solution also helps prevent network bottlenecks as no data is transferred over a network and it helps avoid profile bloating.

So, why UPM profiles?

Many people have asked me the same question over the years: why even bother with UPM? After all, don't native Windows profiles provide the same functionalities without the need to configure anything extra? This is a valid question and many times the answer may even be, "Sure, you don't really have any use for UPM," especially if you are managing a very small environment. However, on the other hand, if you think about it, UPM is a virtual profile solution that allows you to isolate XenApp/XenDesktop user profiles into a dedicated profile share and because the UPM Group Policies are only applied at the computer level, the service kicks in only when a user logs on to their virtual session (be it an application or a desktop). This way, any profile settings and, for that matter, issues and corruptions on the physical machine don't carry over to a virtual session. Now, hopefully, a user will be connected to a XenApp application or desktop for a majority of their workday, so administrators can see exactly what's in their profile and avoid any misconfigurations or security vulnerabilities potentially present on the endpoint device. With profile management, profiles from active sessions are temporarily stored on the XenApp agent server hosting the session.

UPM also provides a Group Policy template with very granular settings that can be applied to minimize overhead. The following are some great examples of how UPM can be efficient:

- File exclusions
- Directory exclusions
- Active write back
- Delete profiles at logoff

The GPO template also provides logging settings so that if any issues occur in the environment, administrators can get extensive data to troubleshoot the issue.

Configuring profile management in a XenApp® environment

Back in the 6.5 days, we used to have to install the profile management agent on each XenApp server—not anymore. Starting with 7.x, UPM is part of the VDA, so there is no need to install additional software on your XenApp agent servers. Once the VDA is present on an image, everything else at the profile level is controlled via Group Policy objects and settings, including enabling the UPM functionality itself. The administrative (ADM) template for the **Group Policy Management Console (GPMC)** is available for download from CTX125494 and is also included in the XenApp 7.6 installation media. Once a policy template is imported into GPMC on your Domain Controller, the GPO settings are located in `Computer Configuration\ Administrative Templates\Classic Administrative Templates (ADM)\ Citrix\Profile Management`:

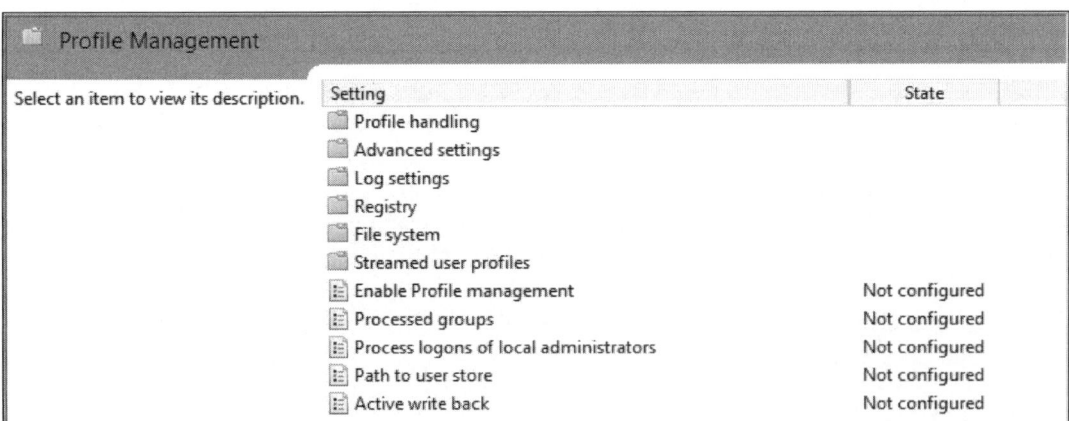

Depending on the use case of the environment, some settings may not be relevant and do not need to be configured.

The first step in integrating Citrix Profile Management to the existing XenApp or XenDesktop system is to enable **Profile Management**, which is the first individual object in the Profile Management Group Policy settings. Secondly, under **Path to user store**, specify the UNC path to the file share you want the profiles to reside in. In the `Profile handling` folder, a recommended setting to enable is **Delete locally cached profiles on logoff**. With this setting in place, profiles from active sessions are purged from the XenApp agent server when a session is over. Another popular GPO setting is **Active write back**. AWB allows changes in the profile to be dynamically written back to the file share during a XenApp session instead of waiting until the user logs off. This solves the so-called "last writer wins" problem. What this challenge constitutes is a discrepancy from a user's point of view. For instance, a user has three application sessions open at the same time from three different XenApp servers. Let's say that they change an application setting on the first two sessions and then log off of these two servers. If they then make a change to an application setting in the third session and log off of it, the first two changes in the previous sessions will be ignored and only the last one will be synchronized with the profile. By using UPM with **Active write back**, not only are the changes recorded, but they also written back to the profile in real time. This feature truly differentiates Citrix Profile Management from other solutions, especially regular Windows roaming profiles. Last but not least, **Exclusion lists** of individual files and entire directories (located under the `File System` folder of the Profile Management GPO) can be put in place to prevent certain items from being copied back to the profile share. This is a very powerful setting. By excluding temporary objects, such as browser cache and other unnecessary stuff, you can control the size of the profiles. Of course, the exclusion lists setting will not prevent profile bloating on its own, but it is a definite step in the right direction.

Profile Streaming

Besides all the benefits mentioned in previous sections, a very neat feature called profile streaming is also available in Citrix Profile Management as a Group Policy setting. As the name suggests, files and folders in a profile are retrieved from the file share only when access is requested by users. In a large environment, this can save a great deal of overhead by reducing the bandwidth needed to load a profile and, respectively, the user logon time. The setting is located under the `Streamed user profiles` folder in the same ADM template as the rest of the UPM policies. The only caveat is it cannot be used in combination with personal vDisk in XenDesktop.

Taking advantage of Session Prelaunch and Session Linger

Many people found it strange when Citrix changed the XenApp architecture from the old IMA to the new FMA so much so that they could no longer use the Session Prelaunch and Session Lingering features. Session Prelaunch was a critical component of many enterprise environments because it allowed IT administrators to get application sessions ready for users when they came in the morning to avoid inevitable system bottlenecks caused by mass logons during peak hours. It also helped prevent logon delays for users because the session was already launched for them and they just needed to click on the icon in the web interface to make the application appear on their screen immediately. Session Linger, on the other hand, allows sessions to be kept alive even after users close all their applications. This way, if a user decides to open one of the previously closed applications, the delay of launching a brand new session is avoided and the old session is restored. However, when XenApp was merged with XenDesktop in 7.0, these features were no longer available. Since up to that point XenDesktop had only dealt with desktops and not applications, Session Prelaunch and Session Linger were never really included in the older versions of XenDesktop to begin with. Chances are, though, they were too important for XenApp 6.5 customers, so they were brought back to life in XenApp 7.6.

Configuring both Session Prelaunch and Session Linger is done from Citrix Studio in the **Edit Delivery Group** wizard under **Delivery Groups**. Under **Application Prelaunch**, an administrator can specify whom the prelaunch applies to and under what conditions prelaunched sessions end. For example, the feature can be enabled for any user who requests an application from a particular Delivery Group or to a specific subset of users who log on to Receiver. A prelaunched session can be scheduled to end after a certain amount of time has passed without starting an application and when machine load exceeds a certain percentage:

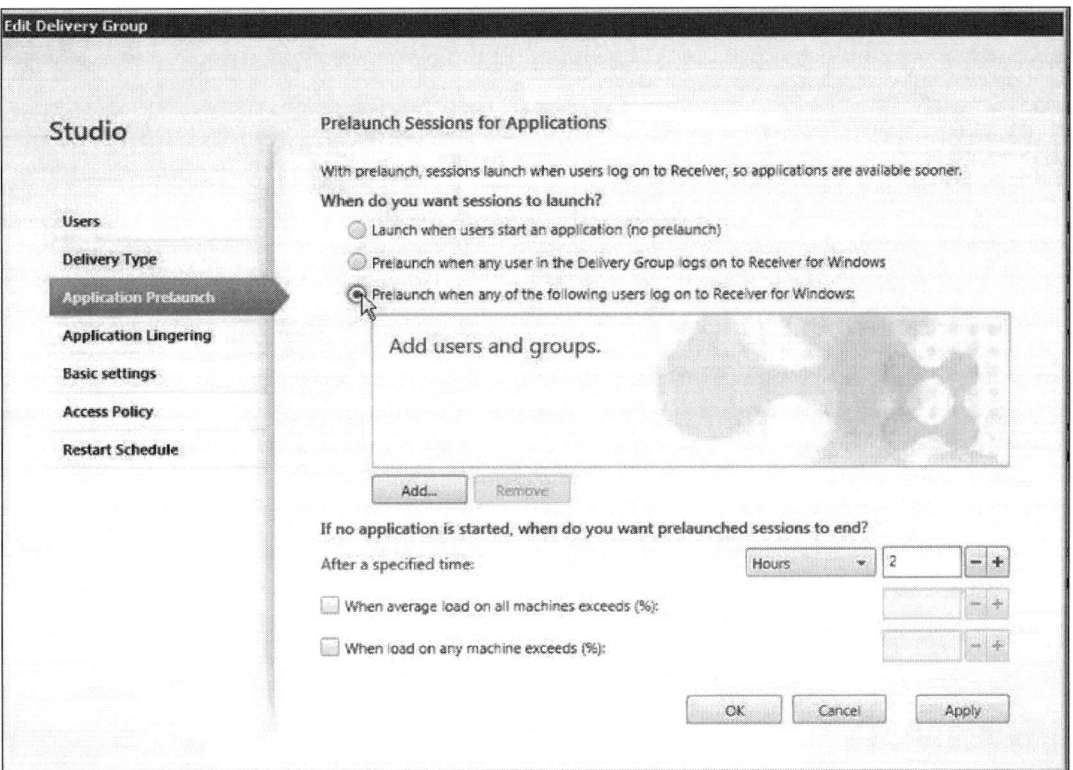

To complement Session Prelaunch, the IT administrator can configure Session Linger under the **Application Lingering** section of the **Edit Delivery Group** wizard. One of the truly powerful aspects of this feature is that it can be set up to keep user sessions alive not just for a specific period of time after all applications are closed, but also up until a certain percentage threshold of server load is met. This way, inactive sessions can be released if a XenApp server becomes heavily utilized so that more resources are freed up for incoming users.

Keep in mind that both Session Prelaunch and Session Linger are only available and supported when users launch applications via Receiver for Windows:

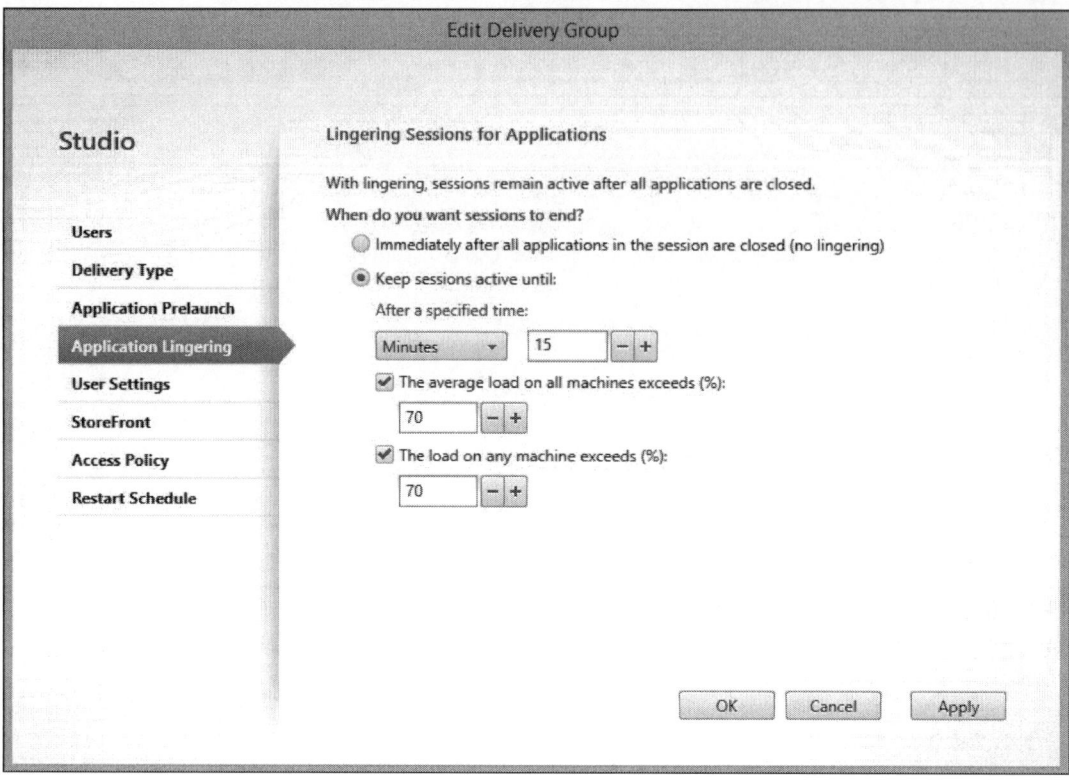

Facilitating XenApp® administration with Citrix® policies

In the IT world, Group Policies are a constant presence and a big factor when making decisions about how to manage infrastructures, especially those where the sheer number of users creates a high degree of complexity, which results in more support tickets and other hurdles for IT staff. The effective use of GPOs can greatly reduce these hurdles and facilitate management of the environment, even more so in XenApp, which has so many moving parts. To help customers achieve this goal, Citrix has provided an entire collection of Citrix policies in Citrix Studio or as an Active Directory snap-in so that administrators can have full control over things, such as virtual channels in the ICA connection and printing settings. I have actually dedicated the entire next chapter to printing just because it is such a vast topic that's very often clouded by confusion and uncertainty. Here are several examples of Citrix policy categories in XenApp that are often leveraged in enterprise environments:

- Audio
- Video
- USB
- Printing
- Flash
- Client drives

Similar to Active Directory GPOs, Citrix policies are split between user and computer policies. Several filters are available to apply settings to certain groupings. For instance, Delivery Groups can be leveraged as filters so that only users connecting to an application or desktop of a particular Delivery Group will be affected by settings applied to this group. Policy assignment can also be done based on whether a connection is coming from an external network through a NetScaler Gateway or internally. Custom tags can also be used for the most amount of flexibility.

How do you get started with Citrix® policies?

Whichever way you choose to manage your Citrix policies (whether from Citrix Studio or the Active Directory snap-in), creating policy objects is very simple. If you haven't dealt with policies in previous releases of XenApp or XenDesktop, then you may want to start by using templates. Templates are prebuilt combinations of Citrix policies designed to help you achieve a certain goal in your environment. For instance, the **Optimized for WAN** template sets the **Audio quality** to **Low** in an ICA/HDX session so that users connecting from external low-speed networks are able to perform basic functions without additional latency caused by high-bandwidth-consuming audio traffic. Another popular template, which is contrary to the WAN optimizer, is the **High Definition User Experience** template. It contains the same settings but with opposite values. For instance, the **Audio quality** is set to **High** and **Desktop wallpaper** is **Allowed**. This is to achieve the best possible user experience and session quality, and is suitable for high-bandwidth internal networks where traffic bottlenecks are not likely to hamper performance:

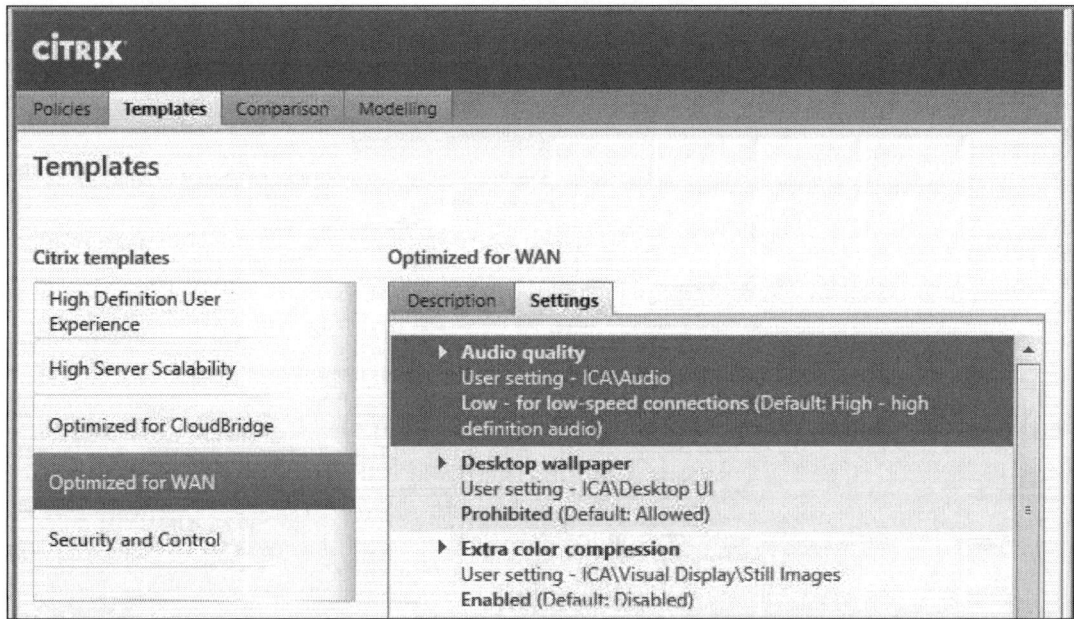

As nice and easy as the templates are, however, they are very niche and do not have a whole lot of settings in them. Even though templates are a great starting point, real-world environments are fairly complex and will require additional policy objects depending on the user base and company policy. Companies where data security is the number one priority usually put many restrictions in place to minimize the interaction between users' physical machines and their virtual applications or desktop sessions. Citrix policies allow you to put granular settings in place that will allow or disallow the use of certain devices, such as USB thumb drives inside a virtual session. So, by restricting USB redirection, IT administrators are able to prevent users from saving sensitive documents to a USB drive on their physical machines. In addition to this, client drives can be blocked from mapping to a virtual application or desktop such that users are not able to save documents on their physical machines or network shares. These sensitive pages of data can only be stored on the virtual desktop, which runs securely in a datacenter in the case of hosted shared desktops or in the Citrix profile, which operates on a virtual level. Another good example of security restrictions is disallowing client clipboard redirection. With this setting in place, users cannot copy and paste data between their physical machines and their virtual sessions.

Not all Citrix policies, however, revolve around security. There are plenty of settings directed towards user experience and bandwidth management. For example, flash and multimedia content can be rendered on the XenApp server or redirected to an endpoint device depending on the hardware specifications of each node. If a client device where a virtual session is received from has enough horse power and some sort of acceleration is embedded in its hardware, then this type of content can be processed there to alleviate the XenApp server and make it more scalable. However, if a low-end thin client is used as an endpoint device, then it makes sense for flash and multimedia to be processed by the XenApp server, which is typically provisioned with more memory and CPU. A very useful setting in the Citrix policy engine is the **Flash URL compatibility list**. As demonstrated in the following screenshot, flash behavior can actually be set based on individual websites that are preapproved or disallowed by an IT administrator.

Using this policy setting, the administrator can blacklist and whitelist URLs, and for the whitelisted ones, there is an option to specify whether the content will be rendered on the client or the server:

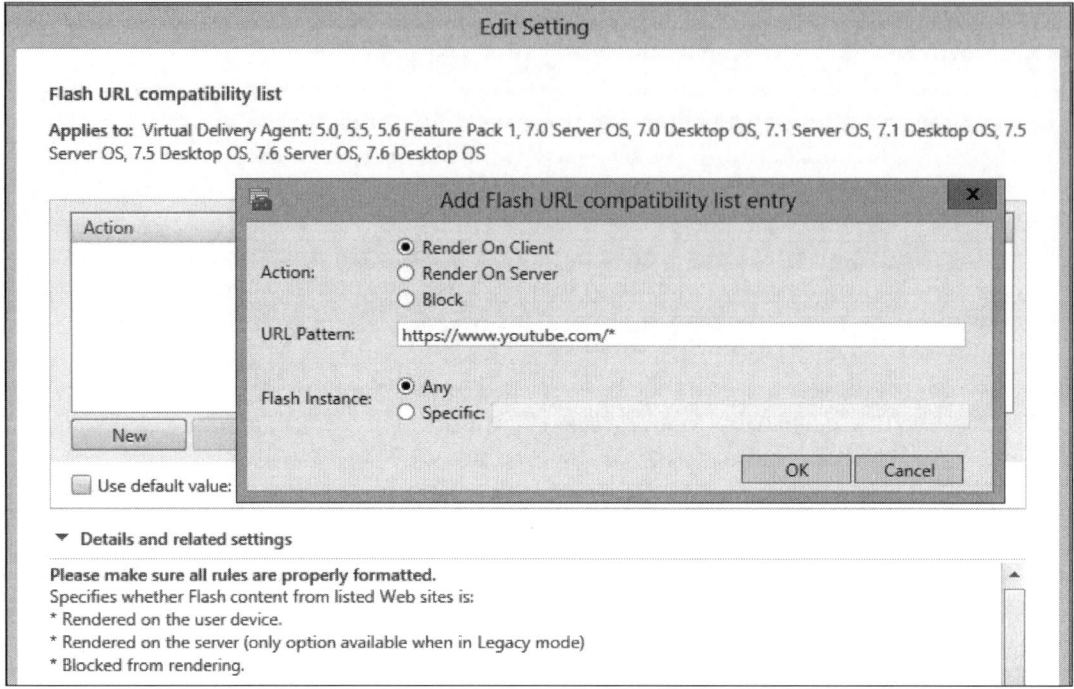

The most sensible thing to do if you are unsure which setting would provide the best experience for your users is to test both client and server rendering and monitor session performance and resource utilization on clients and servers at the same time.

The role of Active Directory Group Policies

In the world of IT, Active Directory Group Policies are the law of the land. Many people are not particularly fond of them because of the added complexity that they bring about in large enterprise environments. Like them or not, however, GPOs are absolutely indispensable for every serious IT organization and they play a huge role in combining compliance with end user experience.

It is very typical for Active Directory GPOs to accompany Citrix policies by applying settings to the same user or computer objects. In the context of highly secure environments, often times XenApp sessions are completely locked down. In the example of hosted shared desktops where every user interaction with an operating system can affect others, I have personally on many occasions recommended that a desktop experience be restricted to only what is needed for users to do their jobs. Any **Administrative Tools**, such as **Control Panel** and **Command Prompt**, should be blocked to prevent dangerous modifications by the user. Sometimes, it also makes sense to hide certain drives on the XenApp server so that users do not have access to system files. It is important to remember that even if XenApp is being leveraged to launch individual applications only as opposed to full shared desktops, the user can still run executables in the server OS. For instance, in a scenario where IE is published as an application hosted on the XenApp server and granted by the Delivery Controller, a user can still open **Command Prompt** from IE (if downloads are not prohibited) by typing in the `file:///C:/windows/system32/cmd.exe` path in the IE address bar.

These are just some examples where risk exposure can be minimized by leveraging Active Directory Group Policies. On the other hand, there is a fine line between the right amount of GPOs and excessive GPO use. Too many Group Policies can negatively affect user experience by increasing logon times to XenApp applications and desktops. These types of issues are likely to result in more help desk calls. Since every environment is different, it is nearly impossible to determine the right number of Group Policy settings without assessing customer needs and limitations first. A good rule of thumb is to have less GPOs even if more settings are in them, rather than having many GPOs with less settings in them. The following subsections explore some useful Active Directory GPO settings to get started with.

Disabling Administrative Tools

In a Citrix environment, regular users who access remote applications or desktops hosted on a XenApp server should definitely not be able to uninstall programs and run commands on this server. So, a quick and easy way to disable **Administrative Tools** is by using AD GPOs. To block access to Windows **Command Prompt** using the **Group Policy Management Console (GPMC)**, create a new GPO or modify the existing one by navigating to `User Configuration\Administrative Templates\System` and then select **Prevent access to the command prompt** and set it as **Enabled**.

With this setting in place, users should not be able to run the CMD executable from anywhere on this server. To disable user access to **Control Panel**, navigate to `User Configuration\Administrative Templates\Control Panel` in GPO setting in GPMC and select **Prohibit access to the Control Panel and PC settings** and set it as **Enabled**.

Hiding XenApp® system drives

The next category of Group Policy settings that come in handy in a XenApp environment are the ones that hide XenApp system drives from users. This is especially important for XenApp servers provisioned with PVS where the write cache is located on one of the local drives of a server because you don't want users to accidentally (or on purpose) delete the write cache file, which would cause the server to stop functioning. Active Directory GPOs offer two options when it comes to accessing drives: hide access and prevent access. Hiding a drive makes it disappear from **My Computer**, but it remains accessible if the path is put in manually in **Windows Explorer**. This option generally does the job, especially if users need access to certain drives to save data (after all, if I don't see it, then it must not exist, right?). However, if you want to ensure maximum security of a system, you may want to resort to preventing access to drives altogether. This option, however, has implications for user access that needs to be considered carefully as certain applications may become unusable in this scenario. To hide local drives on the XenApp server, add this User Configuration\Policies\Administrative Templates\Windows Components\Windows Explorer setting to your GPO and select **Hide these specified drives in My Computer**, set it as **Enabled** and select one or more drive letters from the drop-down menu.

To disable access to local drives on the XenApp servers, add this User Configuration\Policies\Administrative Templates\Windows Components\Windows Explorer setting to your GPO, select **Prevent access to drives from My Computer**, set it as **Enabled**, and choose a combination of drives.

In some environments, it might make sense to take it a step further and go as far as prohibiting right-clicking on icons and shortcuts. To enable this setting in your GPO, navigate to User Configuration\Administrative Templates\Windows Components\Windows Explorer, select **Remove Windows Explorer's Default Context Menu** and set it as **Enabled**.

Even though it sounds extreme from a user's point of view, this draconian measure will prevent users from seeing and changing file paths, properties, and other attributes of a filesystem. These are just some GPOs in addition to your default domain policy that can be leveraged to secure your XenApp environment.

Folder Redirection

Earlier in the chapter, we talked about profiles and how Citrix Profile Management can provide flexibility and isolation of user profiles in a XenApp environment. In the current configuration where UPM is enabled and profiles are stored on a file share on your network, both user settings and user files are copied to one location. However, what if you want to store files and folders in one place and user settings in another? How would you do this? The answer is simple: by separating files from settings, you reduce the size of the profile, which can dramatically improve logon times. The mechanism of sending user files and folders to a separate location independent from a user store is known as Folder Redirection and it has been around for years. Popular redirection items include **Application Data (AppData)**, desktop, documents, music, pictures, and others. Prior to XenApp 7.6 and XenDesktop 7.0, Folder Redirection could only be managed via the Active Directory GPO, but with the 7.x generation, it is now integrated in the Citrix Policies in Studio under the `Profile Management` folder. To create a Folder Redirection Citrix Policy, simply create a new policy in Citrix Studio or modify the existing one and in the policy wizard search field, type `folder redirection` to quickly see a list of settings. As demonstrated in the following screenshot, there are quite a few folders that can be redirected outside of a user's profile in Citrix Studio:

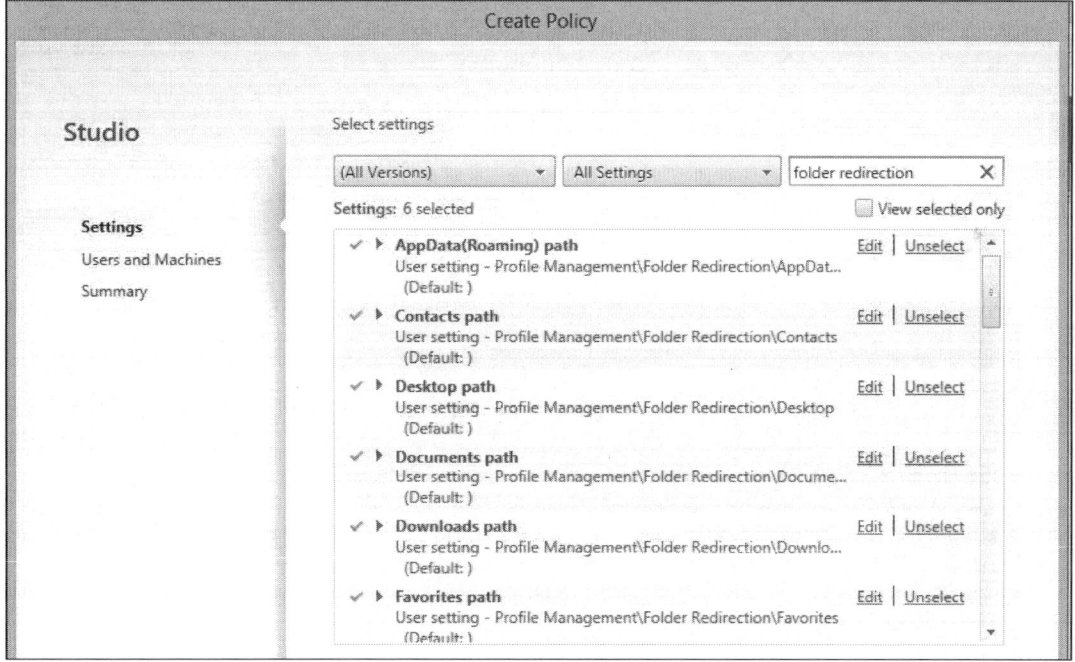

The potential drawbacks of Folder Redirection

Despite the obvious benefits of using Folder Redirection in enterprise environments, there are some disadvantages that have been noted in the field. Even though Folder Redirection tends to reduce logon times, it might decrease the overall performance in a XenApp session. Since user files are not actually transferred with a profile locally on a server at logon, when a user requests access to them during a session, they might observe a delay in response. For example, if a user opens an Excel spreadsheet in a virtually hosted desktop, even though the Excel program is installed locally on the XenApp agent server, the file is essentially *streamed* down to the desktop from a file share or a home drive, and thus the file might take longer to open. Another drawback of this technology is that redirected folders cannot be added to **Exclusion lists** in **Profile Management**. In other words, temporary objects, such as browser cookies that are typically recommended to exclude from synchronizing back to the profile share via UPM GPO, will now follow the redirected folder that they were originally downloaded to.

Upgrading VDA and PVS target device software

All of us in the IT world have to deal with upgrades—from the smallest binary on **Patch Tuesday** to complex upgrades of enterprise applications, databases, and storage. A pivotal part of administering a XenApp environment is keeping your systems as up to date as possible with the latest Citrix hotfixes and service packs. When it comes to major releases, such as XenApp 7.6, it is completely understandable and expected that companies will not migrate their production environment from 6.5 to the latest version right away. In all fairness to them, the architecture is so different between 6.x and 7.x that in some cases, it may not be recommended to do so until all applications are tested with 7.6 and newer operating systems, such as Windows 2012 R2. Since there is no upgrade path from XenApp 6.5 to 7.6, companies currently on 6.5 will need to build a brand new 7.6 infrastructure, conduct thorough testing, and slowly migrate users to a new environment. To provide time for customers to make a more comfortable transition, Citrix recently extended the end of life date for XenApp 6.5 to June 2018 with end of maintenance ending in December 2017. Keep in mind that these dates might change again in the future.

Since we've already covered upgrading XenApp catalogs with MCS and Device Collections with PVS in *Chapter 10, Administering a XenApp® Environment – Application Management*, in this section, we will focus on upgrading the two Citrix agents, the VDA and the PVS target device software, which is somewhat tricky, especially when PVS is involved.

Upgrading the VDA via MCS

For starters, let's begin with the simplest scenario. In a XenApp environment where VM deployment is done from the Delivery Controller via Machine Creation Services, if you want to upgrade the VDA software running on the XenApp agent servers, all you need to do is log on to the master image, install the latest version of the VDA, and update the catalog from Citrix Studio. Once the update process is complete, the XenApp VMs are rebooted and they immediately pick up the change because their new differencing disks reflect what is on a master image. No other actions are needed since PVS are not involved.

Upgrading the Citrix® Agents via PVS

The second scenario we need to explore is when XenApp agent servers are provisioned and stream an OS through Citrix PVS. The XenApp VMs are defined as a Device Collection on the PVS server and are also present on the Delivery Controller as a machine catalog. Any application updates, including the Citrix software, are done on the vDisk in the read/write state (the private mode or the maintenance version) as opposed to on the master image as it is the case with MCS. There are two Citrix programs that run on the vDisk in a provisioned XenApp deployment: the VDA and the PVS target device software. The VDA itself is upgraded in the same way as in the previous scenario—all you need to do is to download and run an installer for the latest version and it will walk you through the steps of upgrading. The only difference is the machine that it is run on. With MCS, there is only one master image per catalog and changes are made directly on this image. In the case of PVS, any VM from the Device Collection with the same virtual hardware as the vDisk (NIC, storage driver, and so on) can boot to an image in the private mode or to a maintenance version since it connects to a VHD file over a network. However, upgrading the PVS target device software is a much more tedious task than doing so with the VDA. Since the PVS agent actively maintains a heartbeat with the Provisioning Server and its driver is essentially responsible for communicating with the vDisk, as of this time, it is not possible to upgrade it on the fly until possibly later this year (2015) according to some announcements made by Citrix. In order to upgrade the PVS agent software, you have to perform a procedure known as reverse imaging. In other words, you need to merge your versions to the base if you have one and perform the following steps to revert the vDisk back to your hard drive to upgrade the PVS software:

1. Boot your VM to a vDisk with an additional disk attached of the same size or larger than the vDisk. Initialize the new disk and create a new NTFS volume.

2. Two conversion tools called BNImage and P2PVS are provided with the PVS agent software under C:\Program Files\Citrix\Provisioning Services. Run either one and copy the vDisk to the newly attached drive. Since the OS typically resides on C:\, choose C:\ as a source volume and the newly attached drive as a destination volume.

3. In **Disk Management**, mark the new disk as the **Active** partition.

4. On the Provisioning Server, use the PVS console to set the same VM to boot from the hard drive.

5. Back on the image, uninstall the PVS target device software and restart the machine.

6. Use the opportunity to update the hypervisor tools if a newer version is available and reboot the machine when prompted.

7. Run the PVS Imaging Wizard. Create a new vDisk or choose to reuse the existing one. Restart when prompted, log on to Windows, and finalize the conversion.

8. On the Provisioning Server, use the PVS console to set the same VM to now boot from vDisk and ensure that the correct vDisk is assigned.

9. Shut down the maintenance machine, change the vDisk from private to standard mode, and boot the entire Device Collection to this vDisk in the read-only state.

10. Check **Programs and Features** in **Control Panel** to verify the version of the Citrix VDA and the PVS target device. If no information is displayed there on the PVS agent, you can check the vDisk status tray for this and other statistics on the image.

Notice that the procedure outlined here may differ slightly from the official one from Citrix in article CTX135746, which works as well. Most information provided here is based on real-world experience and a great deal of troubleshooting.

There must be another way...

So, after going through this somewhat tedious procedure, some of you may be asking yourselves the same question that keeps coming up over and over again: isn't there an easier way? And, the answer is: yes, there is! Remember how the operating system streamed by PVS is encapsulated in a VHD file? If you have a XenServer hypervisor, you can actually copy this VHD and import it as a new VM in XenCenter as shown in the following screenshot. Once it is imported, the VHD becomes the local hard drive of the new VM and you can boot and upgrade the Citrix software without any dependency from the Provisioning Server. Once you've upgraded the software, all you need to do is export the VM generating a new VHD file or overwrite the existing one and import it to the PVS farm using the import function in the PVS console:

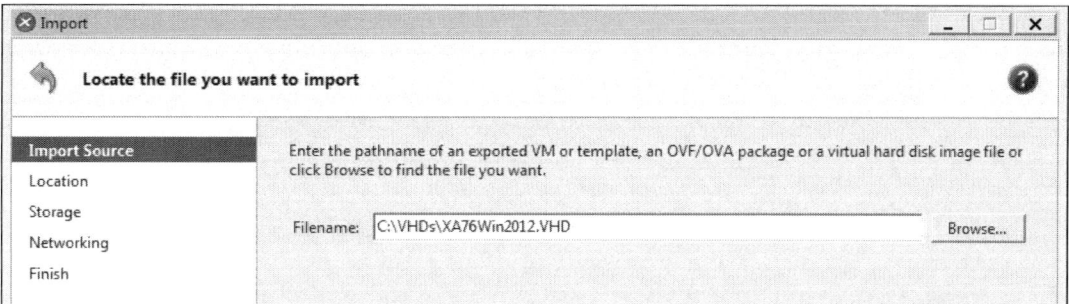

This is known as XenServer Direct VHD Boot. It is still a workaround and involves more than just upgrading the target device software but it saves you the time spent on reverse imaging and running the Imaging Wizard is not necessary. There may be some additional steps that need to be performed, such as rejoining a machine to a domain, so it is recommended to always have a backup of the vDisk files. If you are a Microsoft shop, this procedure works just as easily with Hyper-V since it uses the same VHD file format as PVS. In the case of vSphere, you can still take advantage of the workaround, but you would need to download a third-party tool to convert the VHD to VMDK and vice versa. Once again, both reverse imaging and a direct VHD boot from a hypervisor can be leveraged to upgrade the PVS target device, which cannot be modified during an active connection to the vDisk in real time. For any other image modifications, such as applying Windows patches and application updates, it is recommended to use versioning from the PVS console. With this method, the VHD file becomes the parent of the VHD chain and an AVHD file is generated every time a new version of the vDisk is created at a point in time (similar to the concept of snapshotting).

XenApp® permissions and delegated administration

To reflect the structural hierarchy of many IT organizations, Citrix XenApp 7.6 uses a model called **delegated administration** to assign permissions to system administrators and help desk personnel. The DA approach relies on three concepts: administrator, role, and scope. Administrators are employees who, at a minimum, have an Active Directory user account on a domain and are assigned one or more pairs of role and scope. The role determines the type of access that the administrators have to the XenApp site. For example, a Level 2 support analyst can be assigned a help desk administrator role, which would allow them to see the Delivery Group and machine catalog information in Studio and perform power management tasks, but they cannot modify any of the read-only settings at this level. The scope, as the name implies, is a group of objects that the administrator has visibility or control over. For example, you can assign someone a narrow scope, such as a single Delivery Group as opposed to all the objects in a site. Here is a list of all the roles available for assignment in Studio:

- Full administrator
- Machine catalog administrator
- Delivery group administrator
- Host administrator
- Help desk administrator
- Read-only administrator

With the DA approach, IT management can offload certain tasks to different people according to their responsibilities and knowledge of Citrix.

Monitoring the XenApp® site

Even though the delegated administration model adds solid structure to the XenApp permission model, no organization can function efficiently without the proper monitoring tools in place. In fact, monitoring is not just a necessity, it's an industry! Sometimes, it feels like there are so many monitoring applications that it's hard to choose the right one that combines powerful tools with cost effectiveness. Companies, such as Lakeside Software, SolarWinds, Extrahop, and ControlUp develop and sell enterprise-ready monitoring software used by many companies in the end user computing space. There is also a web-based tool called **Citrix Director** that comes free with the XenApp 7.6 ISO. Director can be installed on an IIS-enabled server and can reside on the same machine as the Delivery Controller. The console provides visibility into the entire XenApp site, including session count, user logon times, active processes and open applications, launch failures, and others. You can also configure Director to pull information about the HDX (ICA) protocol, including audio, flash, USB, and others. The following screenshot provides a sneak peek into the Director console and some of details available on the **Dashboard**:

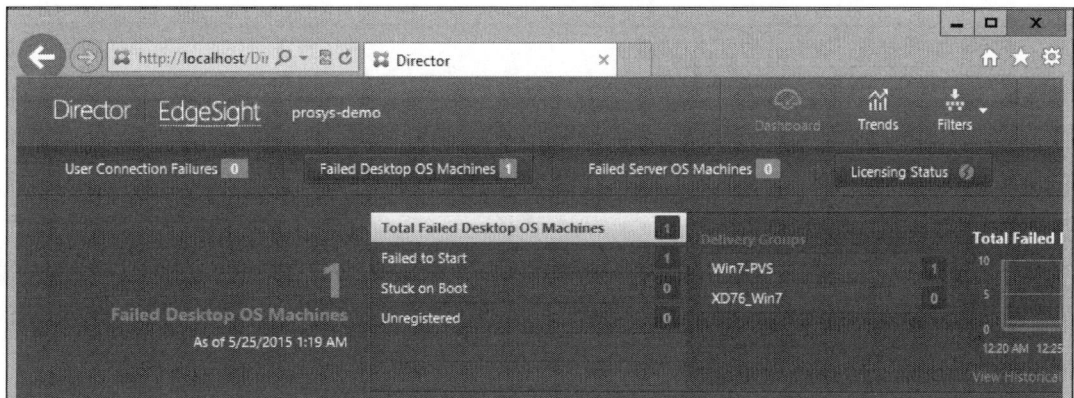

Citrix Director also includes EdgeSight, which is still available as a standalone product for XenApp 6.5 but will be reaching end-of-life at the same time as that version of XenApp. Most of the functionalities of EdgeSight monitoring are now either replaced or integrated in Director.

Summary

In this chapter, we continued to dig into the ins and outs of XenApp administration, shifting the focus from application delivery to server management, profiles, and Group Policy. We covered a spectrum of topics to help you get started with managing your XenApp environment regardless of whether you built it yourself or inherited it from someone else. By now, you should be familiar with profile management, GPO tweaks, RDS licensing, Citrix agent upgrades, permissions, and monitoring. Stay tuned for the next chapter where you will embark on the journey of…printing!

12
Printing

If you walk around your office and ask both users and IT administrators what their major pain points are, there is a 99% chance that printing will be high on the list, if not the primary hurdle for some of them. In today's enterprises, there are so many printing devices available that it has become a real challenge administering and delivering them to users where and when they need them. Besides the quantity of units, making sure that the correct printer drivers are installed and that they don't cause issues with other applications is a constant concern for system administrators. When you add a virtual layer on top of this, things can get even trickier and this is what this chapter is all about. The goal is to explain how printing works in a Citrix infrastructure and how printer objects can be managed to minimize overhead and make your life at least a little easier on the printing side of things. The following topics are examined and explained:

- Windows printing concepts
- XenApp printing processes
- Printer objects and management
- Print optimization via Citrix and Group Policies

Printing in the Windows world

The best place to embark on our printing journey is our traditional physical Windows environment that we are so painfully familiar with. In this type of scenario, we have a user who clicks on the **Print** button on an Excel spreadsheet on their PC and collects the printed document from their printer. This document is known as a print job, but the real question is what enables this print job to go to the correct printer or get printed at all? The Windows service responsible for managing not only the print job but also the printer objects and their drivers is the print spooler. Since it handles so many responsibilities when it comes to printing, any problems with the print spooler usually have a direct impact on users (for example, printer objects not being constructed properly or print jobs sitting idle in queue). The printing process in Windows can vary depending on the type of corporate IT infrastructure and the nature of client peripherals. Most printers can be categorized as local (also known as locally attached) and network, which are usually managed by a centralized system called print server. If a printer is locally attached to a client device via USB, LPT, or the COM port, upon receiving a print request from a user, the print spooler will send the print job directly to the queue of the printer. On the other hand, if the user chooses to print to a remote printer (for example, one of the devices on an office floor), the print spooler will send the job to the server that manages this particular printing device, and this print server will send the job to the actual printer. The following diagram illustrates the Windows printing communication process:

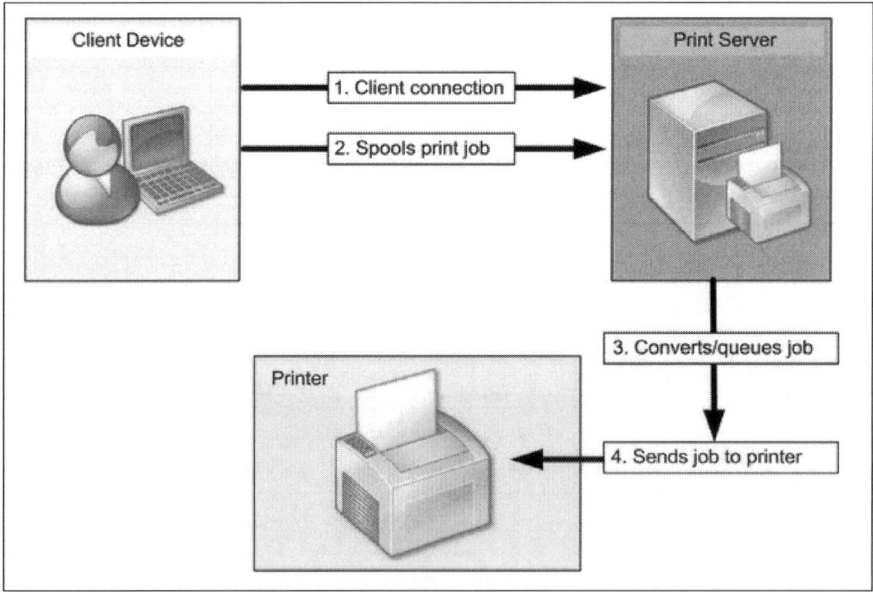

The Windows printing communication process, which can be found at http://support.citrix.com/proddocs/
topic/xenapp65-admin/ps-printing-network-basics.html. © Citrix Systems, Inc.

So, what are some benefits of using each printer type? Well, for starters, having a locally attached printer is convenient for users because it's not shared with other people, so long queues are generally not seen. Another benefit for more tech savvy users is that they may want to maintain the printer themselves, install the toner they want, and so on. However, this is rarely the case in corporate IT where executives and other users with special requirements are usually the ones provided with dedicated local printers. More often than not, though, in an office environment, you would see a majority of people using network printers because these allow them to be mobile and have access to them from any device. The latter type of scenario requires a well-thought-out infrastructure, keeping fast performance and convenience in mind.

What happens in the background?

Printing a Word document is actually a much more complex transaction than it looks on the surface. Most longtime IT administrators have had to deal with the installation, maintenance, and troubleshooting of printer drivers, which is not always a pleasant task. But, what are these drivers there for anyway? A printer driver is a piece of software that serves as an extension of an operating system, and its primary purpose is to enable applications to print independently of the model, technical specifications, and requirements of the printer. In programmatic terms, applications create print jobs by calling device-independent functions and the print driver then helps convert graphic commands from an application to a data format that the printer understands. To interface with the print driver, most Windows-based applications use the **Graphics Device Interface** (**GDI**) API, which is a set of functions, classes, variables, and constants that give a user the ability to draw objects and send them to an output device, such as a monitor or printer. To achieve this two-fold communication, GDI has components operating in both user and kernel modes. Every printer introduced on a network or a local machine will require a driver to be installed either locally on a print server or on a session host in the case of an RDS environment.

The following diagram demonstrates the interactions between of different components and processes in a client-server type printing system with the user application being at the top of the stack and the printer itself at the bottom:

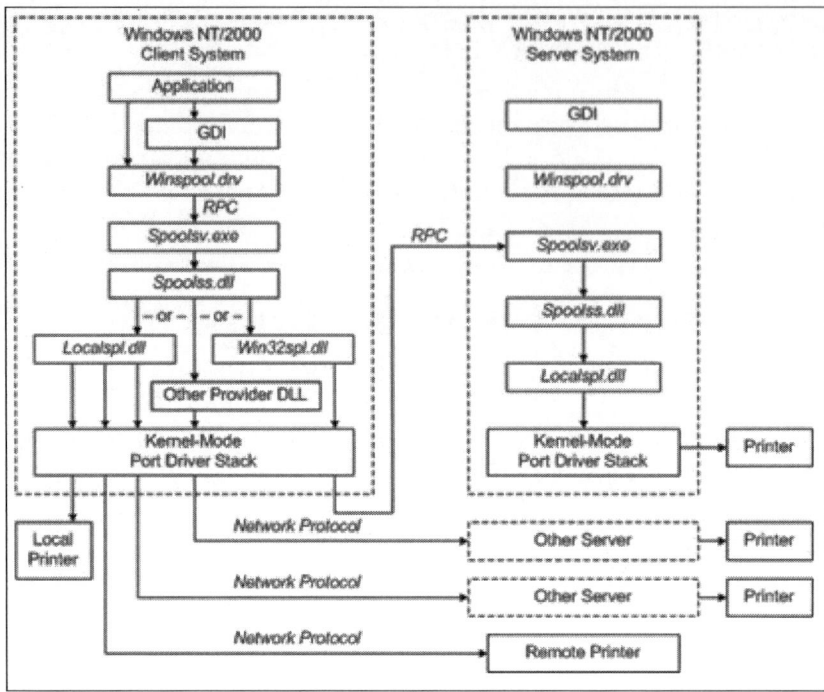

The client-server Windows printing architecture by Microsoft Performance Team, which is available at http://blogs.technet.com/b/askperf/archive/2007/06/19/basic-printing-architecture.aspx

The introduction of Windows 2012 brought about significant changes and optimizations to the Windows printing architecture, such as the V4 driver model, which supports smaller drivers and improves file isolation and printer sharing. Nevertheless, the diagram from the Microsoft Performance Team still generally holds true even with the recent modifications.

Windows Printing challenges

Printing as a concept seems very straightforward. After all, what can be so complicated about being able to print a text document? LaserJet printers have been around for over 40 years and Windows has had printing functionality since the late 80s. It's actually consumer needs that have changed. As companies embrace technology and IT infrastructures expand, an increasing number of vendors want a piece of the pie. If IBM and Xerox were the pioneers of early LaserJet printers in the 70s, you now have a long list of vendors and industry giants, such as Canon and Hewlett-Packard, manufacturing multifunctional all-in-one printers, copiers, and fax machines with Ethernet, Wi-Fi, and Bluetooth capabilities. Since pretty much every manufacturer develops proprietary drivers for every printer model and a new driver version is released periodically, it can get extremely challenging to keep up with software lifecycles and compatibility lists, let alone find documentation about best practices, troubleshooting, and vendor support.

Even though maintained by IT administrators, network printers pose their own challenges as users often times may complain about slow printing, unavailable devices, and application hangs. Similar to other computer devices, print servers are also prone to system crashes, bugs, and network-related problems. So, how do we move from a physical to a virtualized environment knowing that we already have a complex printing infrastructure in place? The first thing on the checklist should be to stabilize the current system. Obviously, there will always be users who need support but moving into such a project requires a deep understanding of our peripherals and most importantly — time. If most printers on the domain (local and network) are well maintained and functional, the implementation of Citrix XenApp applications and hosted desktops will require much less downtime for users and less troubleshooting effort for IT administrators.

Printing in a Citrix® world

Implementing a virtualized environment, such as Citrix XenApp and XenDesktop, requires planning and design for various components of an infrastructure, including networking, storage, servers, applications, profiles, and much more, as seen in previous chapters. However, in the midst of deploying XenApp, sometimes, administrators and consultants tend to overlook the printing part *just because it's working now*. Clearly, as proven by the slew of support tickets I've seen and worked on during my time as a support escalation engineer at Citrix, this is an incorrect approach that often causes project delays and customer dissatisfaction. To avoid unnecessary issues and lengthy support calls, let's start by reviewing the fundamentals of printing in a Citrix environment, how it builds upon Windows concepts, what is changed, and what stays the same after moving to a virtualized system.

The fundamentals

XenApp 7.6 printing services relies heavily on the Windows printing architecture discussed in previous sections, but has additional standards in place to accommodate user requirements in a virtualized environment. The XenApp virtual sessions are meant to provide users with a mobile workspace that gives them everything they need to do their job and boost productivity, while at the same time giving IT departments the control, transparency, and centralized management they need to support their organization. As such, XenApp applications and desktops must satisfy the following requirements:

- Session presentation of all local client printers if allowed by company policy
- Session presentation of all network client printers if allowed by company policy
- Ability of users to add printers if allowed by company policy
- Ability of IT administrators to assign printers to users for use within a session
- Seamless experience for users with maximum approximation to the printing speeds they have had when printing from their local machine
- Retention and manageability of printer properties
- Transparency of print drivers and driver consolidation (universal printing)

Printer provisioning

When a user connects to a virtual desktop in XenApp 7.6, the process that makes printers available in a session is known as **provisioning**. The dynamic nature of printer provisioning means that printer objects and properties are constructed when a user logs on or reconnects to a session as opposed to being stored locally on the XenApp VDA server. The two common provisioning methods are printer autocreation and **Universal Print Server (UPS)**.

Autocreation is the process of connecting networks and locally attached client printers to a virtual session at logon. For instance, if a user has a mix of USB and TCP/IP printers in the **Devices and Printers** subsection of **Control Panel** on an endpoint, if allowed by the Citrix policy, autocreation will attempt to map the same objects in a virtual desktop or application session. However, in order for these printers to work inside the session, the drivers have to be installed on each XenApp VDA server OS machine. This can be a daunting task and the overhead on the servers can be significant. If you're using autocreation, it is highly recommended to only pass through the user's default printer as opposed to all the printers from a client device to avoid memory and CPU utilization spikes on servers. Constructing multiple objects at session launch is likely to cause logon delays and more support calls for an IT team. The following screenshot illustrates the default printer object on a Windows PC:

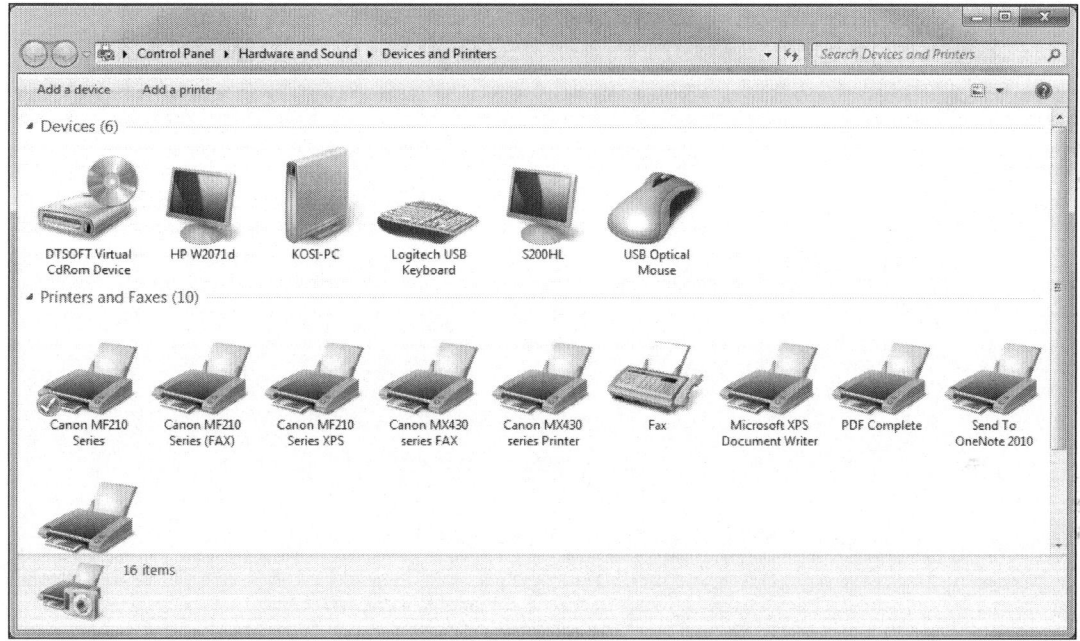

The default printer object on a Windows PC

The other popular method of provisioning is using the Citrix proprietary UPS. If you've had a print server before to manage network printers, UPS is a great addition to your environment because it uses the Citrix **Universal Print Driver (UPD)** technology. With UPD, you no longer need to worry about installing manufacturer drivers on the XenApp VDA servers because it provides vendor-independent support for session printers. As long as the printer you plan to use is certified as Citrix Ready (check `http://www.citrix.com/ready`), UPD should be able to handle print jobs in virtual sessions from any device. Besides facilitating driver management, UPS also contributes to optimizing user experience by doing a native compression of the print job, thus reducing the load on a network. To deploy UPS, you need to download the server-side and client-side components (`UPServer.exe` and `UPClient.exe`). The UPServer software is installed on a new or existing print server and UPClient is placed on the XenApp golden image. Inside a virtual session, when an application requests a document to be printed, it invokes UPD within the Windows printing subsystem. UPD then leverages UPClient to send the data over to the print server. Next, UPS invokes the UPS port monitor and the print driver to send the print job to a network printing device. The following diagram illustrates the UPS communication flow:

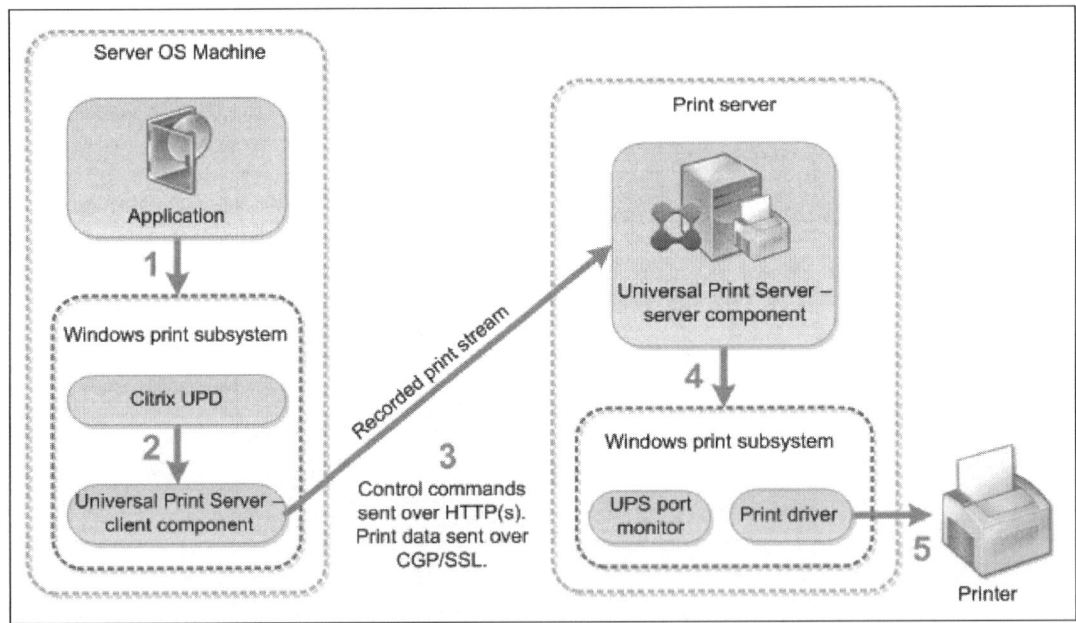

The UPS communication flow, which is available at http://docs.citrix.com/en-us/xenapp-and-xendesktop/7-5/cds-plan-wrapper-rho/cds-print-intro.html. © Citrix Systems, Inc.

Local printers versus network printers

As discussed in the *Printing in the Windows world* section of this chapter, there are two major categories of printers in both home and corporate environments. Printers that are directly connected to a client computer via the USB, LPT, or COM port cables are referred to as local (or locally attached). Printing devices that are accessible via Ethernet or Wi-Fi are known as network (or remote) printers. About 10-15 years ago most printers, especially those used for home use, were mostly locally attached via USB. However, in recent years, technological advancements and stiff competition in the market have allowed people to start purchasing more affordable network and Wi-Fi devices that often times have 4-in-1 (printing, scanning, copying, and faxing) capabilities. In corporate environments, TCP/IP printing and centralized printer management have been firmly established as the standard. The following is a high-level overview of how the different components of a print transaction communicate in a Citrix virtual session depending on the device category.

Follow these steps in the case of a locally attached printer:

1. User Sue opens Citrix Receiver on her PC and clicks on Microsoft Word to open a document.

2. After the application is launched, Sue decides to print a page that she has been previously working on. She leaves the printer selection at the default printer and clicks on **Print**.

3. The data is encapsulated in the ICA protocol on the XenApp server OS and gets sent through the virtual channel that's responsible for printing to Sue's PC, and the Windows subsystem on the client device transmits the job to the local printer.

The following diagram illustrates the locally attached printer's communication flow with ICA/HDX:

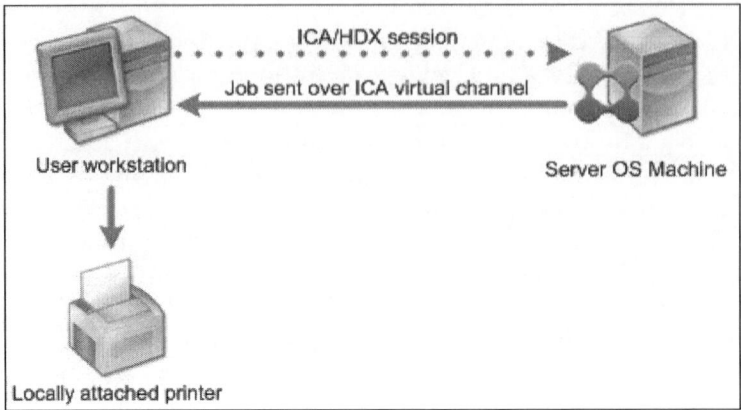

The locally attached printer communication flow with ICA/HDX, which is available at http://docs.citrix.com/en-us/xenapp-and-xendesktop/7-5/cds-plan-wrapper-rho/cds-print-intro.html. © Citrix Systems, Inc.

With this model in place, the print transaction is optimized because the data is compressed by the Citrix proprietary ICA/HDX protocol. Now, let's take a look at how the same process changes when network printers are in use.

Follow these steps in the case of a network or remote printer:

1. The same user Sue launches Microsoft Excel from Citrix Receiver. Excel is hosted on the XenApp server OS.

2. Sue hits *Ctrl+P* on her keyboard and from the available *provisioned* printers, she chooses the one that she knows is located right outside her office.

3. The XenApp server OS sends data to the print server over the network, and the print server subsystem transmits the print job to the remote printer.

The following diagram illustrates the network printer communication flow with ICA/HDX:

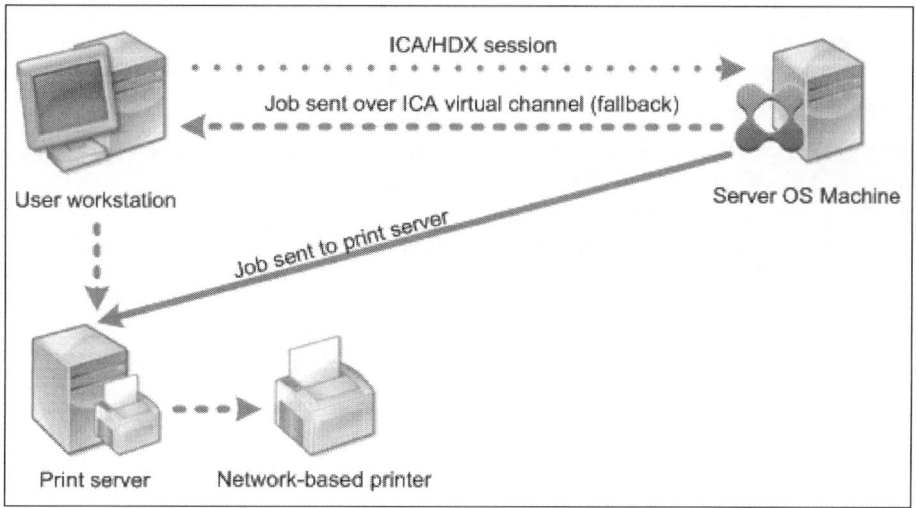

The network printer communication flow with ICA/HDX, which is available at http://docs.citrix.com/en-us/ xenapp-and-xendesktop/7-5/cds-plan-wrapper-rho/cds-print-intro.html. © Citrix Systems, Inc.

A couple of notable differences can be observed between the flowcharts for each of the two scenarios. Apart from the introduction of a print server as an additional component, in the case of network printing, the XenApp server VDA OS by default sends the print job directly to the print server over the network. In addition to this, it also has the functionality of performing fallback through the ICA virtual channel to the client device instead. This is a major difference as compared to the locally attached model, which only uses the ICA/HDX channel, bouncing back the job to the client device.

The Citrix® Print Management service

What actually carries out the printer provisioning, management, and deletion in the XenApp environment is the Citrix Print Management service, which gets installed automatically with the VDA on the XenApp server OS. The executable responsible for running the service is CpSvc64.exe, which should be visible in **Task Manager** at all times when the service is set to Automatic start. By default, Citrix Print Management is run by NT AUTHORITY\LocalService, which is a Windows account with minimal privileges over the OS:

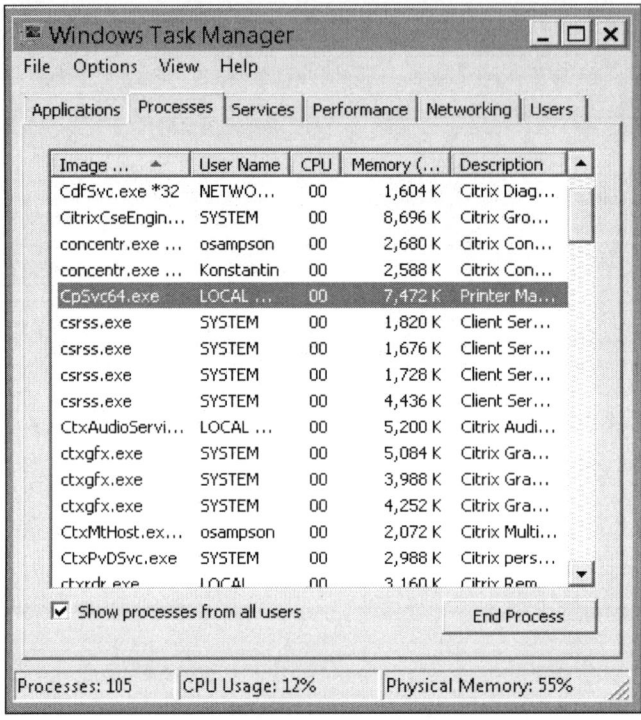

CpSvc64.exe in Windows Task Manager

The Citrix Print Management service impersonates an end user and is responsible for monitoring user logon activity to ensure that printers are presented correctly and autocreated devices are not shared between multiple user sessions. In *Chapter 13, Troubleshooting Tools, Tips, and Tricks*, we will examine some known issues with CpSvc64.exe and share some case studies from the field to show how to identify and resolve potential challenges with this service.

Citrix® Printing policies

So, assuming that you already have a XenApp environment in place (you should if you've come this far into the book!) with fully redundant Delivery Controllers, Provisioning Servers, StoreFront Servers, NetScalers, applications, and desktops readily available for use, it is the right time to go ahead and configure your Citrix policies to accommodate your users' printing needs. But, where do we start and how? I say, let's give preferential treatment to our favorite printer autocreation.

Autocreation

By default, this method is set to allow all client printers to be provisioned at session launch, but as you learned in this chapter, this is not a best practice because it can cause slow logons and reduced performance within the session. The recommended setting would be to **Auto-create the client's default printer only**. How do you achieve this? Simply open Citrix Studio on the Delivery Controller (or remotely if you prefer) and create a new **User** policy in the **Policies** node. In the **All Settings** drop-down menu, you can find **Printing**, which contains all the print settings, or simply type the word printing in the search box for all the settings to appear. Since they are listed in alphabetical order, the autocreation ones will be at the top of the list. In order for client printers to be mapped in a virtual session, client printer redirection also has to be allowed. This way, if users add additional printing objects, they would be eligible for printer provisioning within the session:

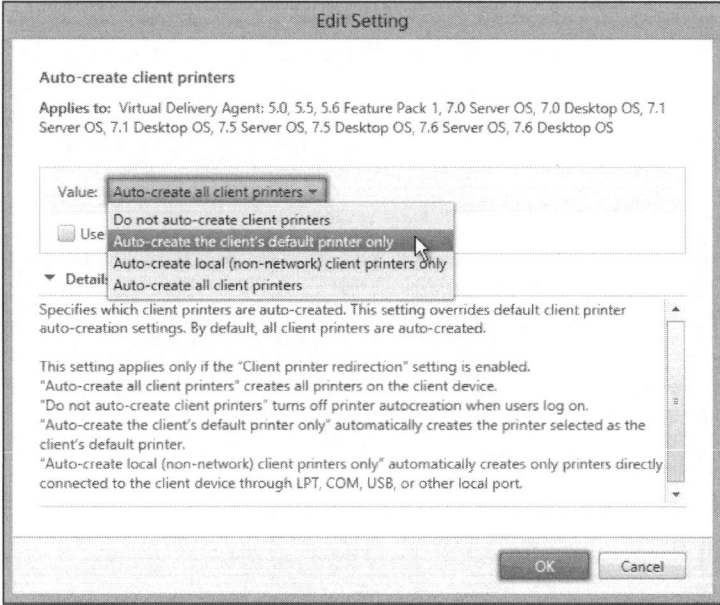

The XenApp 7.6 printer autocreation policy

Some companies and government agencies have security restrictions that don't allow any printing or printer mapping from local machines. Here are some reasons why you would want to prevent printing in a Citrix environment:

- Data exposure
- Network congestion
- Environment complexity
- Server resource utilization

As an example from the field, I recently performed an implementation for a US-based customer that had offshore locations in different parts of Asia. To stay in compliance with company policy, printing was strictly prohibited in this environment because of the limited visibility that IT staff in the U.S. had over offshore endpoints. Also, many financial institutions that deal with sensitive data every day would find it beneficial to prohibit printer redirections for some employees to prevent them from potentially exporting this data outside company premises.

UPS and UPD

UPS, which works in conjunction with UPD, is also configured on the Citrix policy level. Contrary to autocreation, though, it is disabled by default. So, if you plan on using UPS, you have to enable it explicitly in the policy settings. As seen in the following screenshot, there are two options used to enable UPS: with or without fallbacks to regular network printing. The fallback option is good in case, for whatever reason, the UPS software fails, as long as the native drivers for remote printers are in place:

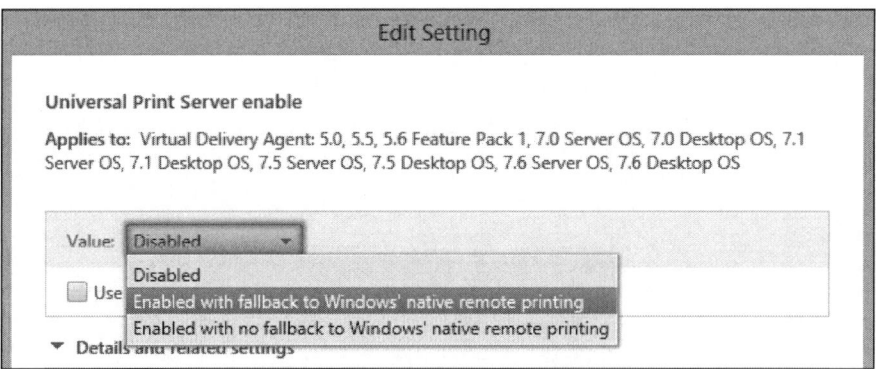

The UPS policy in Citrix Studio

Other policy settings are available in the **Printing** section of the Citrix policies to modify UPS data ports and put restrictions on bandwidth utilization. The latter can come in handy in high-latency WAN networks where users connect from different geographic locations and limited bandwidth is shared by a multitude of users.

The other recommended setting in most environments is to use UPD. As the name implies, UPD provides universal support for all printers certified as Citrix Ready and removes the need to install vendor drivers on the XenApp servers. In some cases, however, it is preferred that you have at least certain drivers installed for fallback purposes as the **Universal print driver usage** setting here suggests:

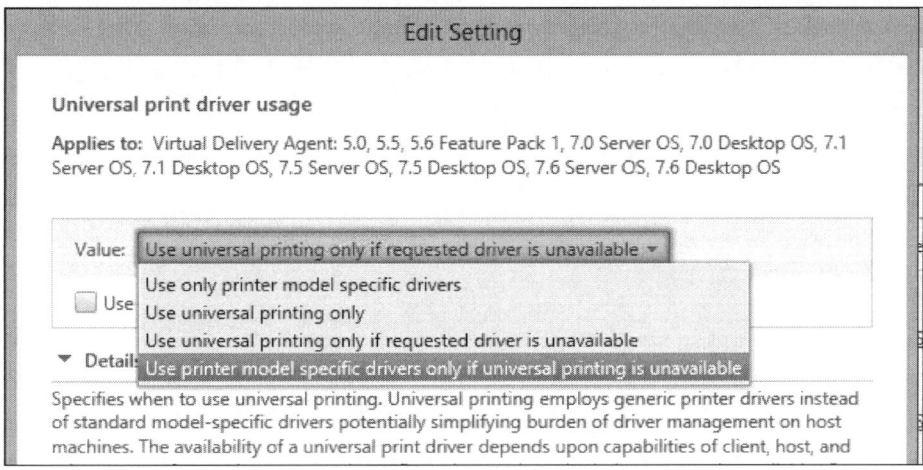

The universal print driver usage and behavior

So, how do we deploy UPS, anyway?

The following instructions provide a quick and fairly simple way of deploying UPS in your environment for the management of network-based (session) printing. This is a standard implementation leveraging UPS, UPD, and a random TCP/IP printer:

1. Create a VM to serve as a print server (only done once) and enable the **Print Management** role in Windows 2012 R2.

2. Mount the XenDesktop/XenApp 7.6 ISO to the VM's CD/DVD drive and install `UpsServer_x64.msi` (only done once).

3. Obtain the IP information of your network printer and if it's on a different, nonroutable subnet, add a static route to the print server VM using the following command:

    ```
    route add <IP> mask 255.255.255.255 <IP>
    ```

4. Add the printing device as a TCP/IP printer by right-clicking on **Printers** in the **Print Management** console and selecting **Add**. Ensure that sharing is enabled and specify the name by which the shared printer will appear to users.

5. On **UPS Firewall**, create a new inbound rule to open TCP ports 8080 (HTTP/SOAP) and 7229 (print data stream/CGP), which are the default ports used by the XenApp servers to connect to the Citrix print server. These ports can be changed from the Citrix policies on the Delivery Controller.

6. On the Citrix golden image, mount the XenDesktop/XenApp 7.6 ISO to the VM's CD/DVD drive and install UpsClient_x64.msi. Also, add a static route much like you did in step 3) to the network printer if it's on a different, nonroutable subnet and push out an update to your catalogs (only done once).

7. On the XenApp Delivery Controller, configure the following Citrix Policy settings under **Universal Printing Policy** in Studio:

    ○ **Session printers (user setting)**: Add the **Printer UNC path** by browsing to the UPS (for example, \\192.168.2.20). Click on **OK** and the policy setting should now be enabled as displayed:

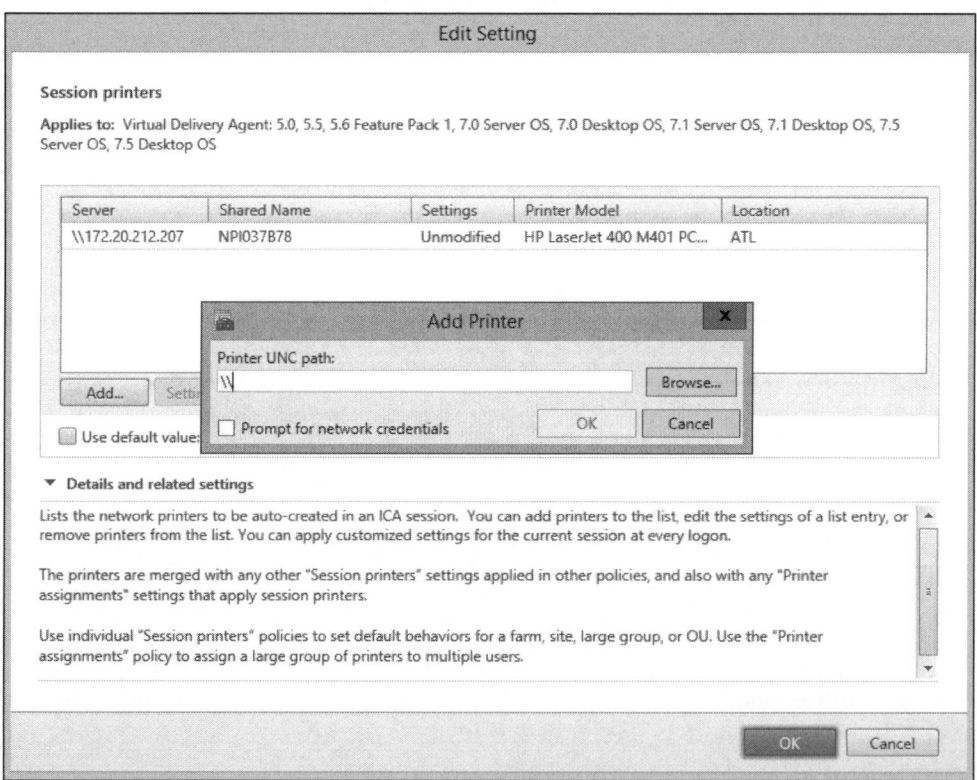

The session printing Citrix policy

- ○ **Universal driver preference (user setting)**: Add the name of the driver type (for example, **PCL6**) as displayed in the printer model information on your print server and move it up to the top of the list:

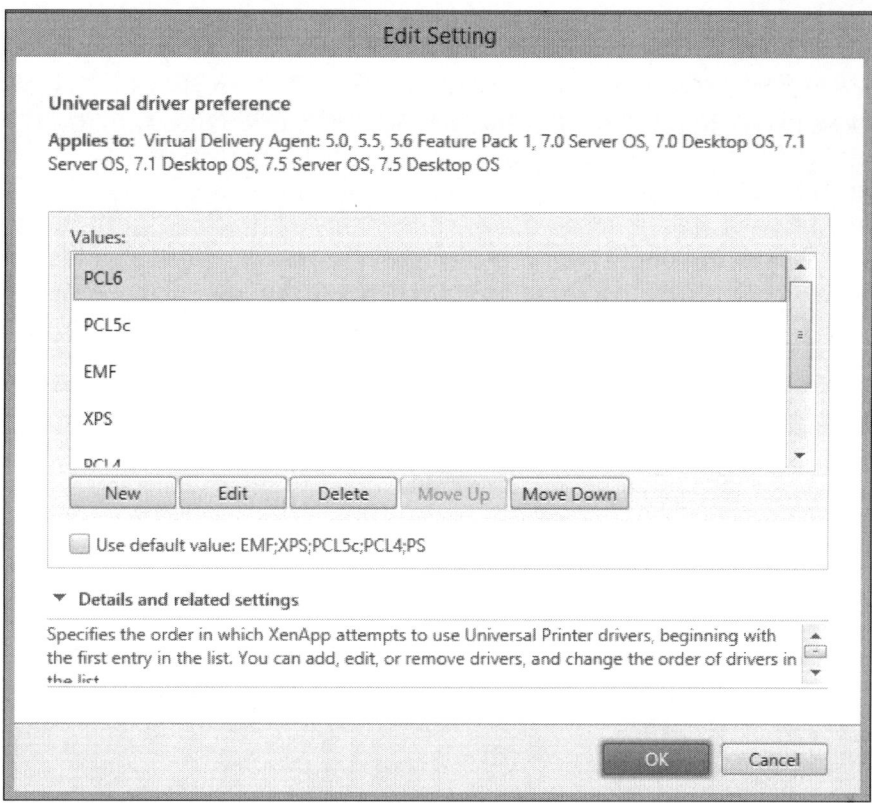

The universal driver preference

- ○ **Universal print server usage (user setting)**: Set the value to **Use printer model specific drivers only** if universal printing is unavailable
- ○ Enable UPS with a fallback to the Windows native remote printing

With this simple solution in place a user, who is assigned to a Delivery Group with XenApp server VDAs participating in the UPS configuration and printing policy settings applied to their OU, should be able to print to a remote session printer that the IT administrator has defined for them. Normally, this would be a printer next to their office or on the same floor.

Summary

This was a bit of a wild ride, wasn't it? The history of printing, software internals of printing, Windows printing, Citrix printing, universal printing, network printers, local printers, drivers and spoolers, Group Policies, and the list goes on. As challenging as printing support can be, the most important part of implementations built from scratch is to assess user needs and plan each and every step of a project around those needs. Being able to deliver a working solution means that you know your stakeholders and you employed industry best practices when executing the project. Sometimes, unfortunately, there are significant gaps in vendor documentation, so it is up to you—the admin or consultant—to test untested configurations and find out what works best for your users. Hopefully, in the process, you don't get tired and get inspired instead. There are not too many good blogs about printing (just a hint!). Stay tuned for the next chapter where we'll get into the nitty-gritty of troubleshooting Citrix XenApp with lots of case studies and other fun.

13
Troubleshooting Tools, Tips, and Tricks

Troubleshooting is an essential part of the everyday life of IT administrators and consultants. In fact, some people that I've talked to spend as much as 60-70% of their time troubleshooting issues. Whether it's helping users on help desk calls or working on a configuration problem or a bug in a production system, the time it takes to resolve these problems directly impacts the business operations of a company. On some occasions, the financial losses from system downtimes are tremendous. Companies who have tens of thousands of employees servicing millions of customers worldwide (think stock trading platforms) simply can't afford to have complete production outages in their IT environment. For this reason, as much as I love IT, being an IT administrator can be a very stressful job, especially when systems aren't performing well and users complain all the time. In this sense, supporting a Citrix environment can be challenging even for the most seasoned engineers. Also, because the Citrix infrastructure is directly responsible for delivering applications and desktops to end users, any time a user has an issue, it becomes a "Citrix issue." Even if a network or storage is down (which often proves to be the case in situations such as this), the Citrix environment and engineer responsible for it become guilty until proven innocent. However, problems in underlying components, such as network and storage, are not always the main cause of an issue. Many times, there is a misconfiguration on a Citrix owned server that doesn't project itself until later on when certain circumstances are met. Setting up a highly available environment with Citrix best practices in place is critically important, which is where consultants and architects add tremendous value (after all, if you've never performed a Citrix implementation in your life, your boss shouldn't expect you to deploy a fully redundant 50,000 user XenApp solution spanning across four continents and servicing 24/7 connections around the globe). The purpose of this chapter is to provide a series of case studies based on real-world issues that I've worked on during and after my tenure at Citrix Escalation Support.

Most importantly, though, my purpose is to arm you with a troubleshooting methodology that will help you resolve issues faster even if you haven't seen a problem before.

Troubleshooting methodology

When I worked at Citrix, I grew through the support ranks from Level I all the way up to escalation, which is considered the highest tier (Level III). During this time, I acquired many different skillsets and troubleshooting techniques and I was influenced by various engineers in my department (Christopher Asaro, Randy Johnson, Daniel Guevara, Raza Rehman, and Fernando Telleria, to name a few). If there was one thing that I learned for sure is that you can't know it all. However, with the right methodology in mind and the proper resources at hand, you can solve almost every case (unless it's a bug in which case someone from software development has to rewrite the code). With this in mind, regardless of whether you are an enterprise admin or a vendor support engineer, if you are dealing with end user computing issues in a Citrix environment, the methodologies used in this chapter will hopefully help you handle support calls more efficiently and your resolution time will be much faster.

Notes and templates

Taking detailed notes during a support call is absolutely crucial. Even if the issue is an easy fix for you, having information about it in your OneNote will help you track user activity, correlate issues to users, and form patterns that you can apply later when troubleshooting more difficult problems. Besides, some users may report the same problem but the root cause may be different, so it's always good to add more information to your own knowledge base. Taking good notes, though, can sometimes be challenging, especially if you are like me and you don't multitask very well. In this case, the best thing to do is use a template that has certain information already prepopulated. Here is a good example of a template that I used when I was troubleshooting issues every day for 5-6 different customers a day:

Environment

1. Citrix Delivery Controller
   ° Operating system version
   ° Operating system service pack
   ° Server count
   ° Citrix software version
   ° Citrix hotfixes installed

2. Citrix Virtual Delivery Agent Server
    ° Operating system version
    ° Operating system service pack
    ° Virtual hardware (CPU, memory, and storage)
    ° Are the hypervisor tools up to date?
    ° Server count
    ° Citrix software version
    ° Citrix hotfixes installed
    ° MCS or PVS?
    ° How many Delivery Groups are there?

3. Citrix StoreFront Server
    ° Operating system version
    ° Operating system service pack
    ° Server count
    ° Citrix software version
    ° Citrix hotfixes installed
    ° Are connections internal or external?
    ° Is load balancing used? What is the base URL?
    ° How many stores are being used? What is the authentication type?

4. Citrix Provisioning Server
    ° Operating system version
    ° Operating system service pack
    ° Server count
    ° Citrix server-side software version
    ° Citrix target-side software version
    ° Citrix hotfixes installed
    ° DHCP Scope Options or Citrix PXE? Is the Boot ISO being used with static IPs?

5. Citrix NetScaler
   - VPX, MPX, or SDX?
   - Firmware version and build
   - Load balancing, Gateway, or both?
   - VIPs using SSL?
   - SSL certificates public, domain, or self-signed?

6. Endpoint device
   - Thin client, PC, or mobile device?
   - OS version and service packs?
   - Citrix Receiver version?

7. SQL Server (skipped in cases where SQL does not appear relevant)
   - The OS version and service pack level
   - The SQL and Management Studio version
   - Is mirroring or clustering enabled?

8. Hypervisor
   - The server hardware model
   - The CPU/memory/storage capacity
   - Count
   - Type and version (XenServer, VMware, Hyper-V, and so on)
   - Cluster or standalone?
   - Number of NICs
   - NIC bonding or teaming enabled?
   - Are VLANs enabled?
   - Standard Switching or Distributed Switching?
   - Storage type (is it local or shared?)
   - If SAN—Fibre Channel, iSCSI, other? Vendor?
   - Is multipathing enabled?

Issue

Summarize the problem in a few sentences.

Detailed description

Provide as many details as possible about the circumstances leading to the problem and the user impact.

Troubleshooting

List all the steps you took to troubleshoot this issue (regardless of whether the steps were successful or not in resolving it). Include a path to any data collected from the environment, such as logs, traces, and screenshots.

Action items (if applicable)

List all the action items you've instructed a user or customer to use or test to resolve the issue.

Resources

Reference all the articles and documentation you followed during the troubleshooting session.

If you are a technical support engineer, you probably already use a similar template to organize your notes and gather as much information as possible from your customers.

If you are an IT administrator, your template may look something like this:

- What is the domain/username of the user experiencing the issue?
- What is the name of the Citrix application with which you are having trouble?
- How is this computer connected to the network (office/LAN/VPN)?
- Which Citrix environment are you trying to access (production or development)?
- What version of Citrix client is installed on a machine (found in **Control Panel**)?
- What is the URL of the Citrix environment?
- Have you accessed this Citrix environment and application before? If yes, when did it last work correctly?
- Did you try accessing this application from a different computer? If yes, did it work?
- Are you the only user affected?
- What is the exact error message (attach the screenshot if possible)?
- What troubleshooting steps have you attempted so far (reboot computer, restart browser, or delete temporary files)?

Obviously, this template looks different from the first one because you directly interface with the end user, but the notion is the same—collect data, do research, and deliver a resolution or escalate to the next level.

Research

Doing research is almost always a necessary step when you troubleshoot a problem. Unless it's something routine or an issue that you've already seen and resolved in the past, you will need to do research. Sometimes a little, sometimes a lot. Fortunately, in this day and age, you have access to more information than you could ever process. Search engines, such as Google, Yahoo, and Bing really are your best friends as you can easily find a ton of articles and blogs on almost every topic in technology. Sometimes, you may have to scroll through a few dozen pages of forum threads to find a resolution to your problem, but the likelihood of someone having had the same issue before is very high since most IT folks are not afraid to seek advice online. Here are some great Internet resources where you can find answers to almost any question or issue in your Citrix environment.

Citrix® Knowledge Base

The Citrix **Knowledge Base (KB)**, is a huge source of information. In fact, any time you have a problem with your Citrix environment that you are not sure how to resolve, pull Google and type in some keywords, such as `ICA session disconnect`, and you will find plenty of Citrix Support articles that offer resolutions to your issue. You can also go directly to `http://support.citrix.com` and search only the Citrix KB as opposed to the entire universe. However, I've found the Google search engine to be more optimized (after all, this is what Google specializes in, right?). The Citrix Support articles are a quick way to find a fix without having to go through hundreds of pages of documentation.

Citrix® discussion boards

Another way of finding resolutions to issues in the Citrix environment is by browsing Citrix forums. Often times, Google search results would lead you to a discussion board where people have put their own two cents on an issue. Anyone can sign up and post questions on these forums. I personally enjoy browsing the forums because I can frequently find resolutions that are not documented in the Citrix KB. The Citrix forum threads are categorized by product and can be found at `http://discussions.citrix.com`.

Community websites

Last but not least are my favorite websites from the Citrix community. This community can encompass anyone who posts articles online or blogs about the technology. Some people are very focused on certain products, such as XenApp and XenDesktop. Other folks are more generalist in their approach and write about all their products and multiple vendors. Every year, Citrix awards the best and brightest community contributors with the **Citrix Technology Professional (CTP)** award, which is the equivalent of vExpert for VMware and MVP for Microsoft. Here I will list some of my must-read blogs, but you can find a lot more by just browsing the Web and social media:

Bloggers	Links
Adam Gamble	`http://www.adamgamble.org`
Andrew Morgan	`http://www.andrewmorgan.ie`
Carl Webster	`http://www.carlwebster.com`
Ingmar Verheij	`http://www.ingmarverheij.com`
Jarian Gibson	`http://www.jariangibson.com`
Jason Samuel	`http://www.jasonsamuel.com`
Kenny Baldwin	`http://www.desktopsandapps.com`

Bloggers	Links
Marius Sandbu	`http://www.msandbu.wordpress.com`
Neil Spellings	`http://www.neil.spellings.net`
Pawel Serwan	`http://www.pawelserwan.wordpress.com`
Robin Hobo	`http://www.robinhobo.com`
Vikash Kumar Roy	`http://www.vikashkumarroy.blogsport.com`
Wilco Van Bragt	`http://www.virtualization.vanbragt.net`
The XenApp blog	`http://http://xenappblog.com/`

Case studies

The rest of the chapter is mostly case studies based on actual cases and issues that I have handled either during my time as a support engineer at Citrix or from later customer-facing projects. Keep in mind that all confidential information has been removed and these are only my own views and experiences and in no way do they represent official statements from my former or current employer. For the purpose of being consistent with my troubleshooting methodology, I have used my template; however, this is a shorter and modified version of it to avoid wordiness.

Provisioning Services™

The first series of case studies are based on Citrix Provisioning Server. PVS is a critical component of enterprises and the XenApp and XenDesktop environments and is often blamed for outages even if the root cause is different (for example, underlying network or storage issues). Problems in the PVS systems usually have high visibility within an organization because the delivery of XenApp Server operating systems and XenDesktop machines is directly affected. Hence, it's important to explore cases that you might come across in production.

Case 1 – Retries

The first case study on the **Provisioning Services (PVS)** product is about the famous issue of generating too many retries on a streamed XenApp Server OS (also known as a XenApp target device). Retries are a mechanism built into the PVS software that reflect the frequency of packet retransmissions in a PVS stream.

Environment

- Citrix product: Provisioning Services (PVS) 7.6 and XenApp 7.6
- Server OS: Windows 2012 R2
- Target device OS: Windows 2012 R2
- Hypervisor Type: ESXi 5.1 with vCenter Server 5.1
- Hypervisor platform: Cisco **Unified Computing System (UCS)** B200 Blade chassis
- Storage: EMC SAN via Fibre Channel

Issue

A customer ran XenApp 7.6 on a provisioned vDisk and experienced an unusual amount of retries almost all the time during the day.

Detailed description

The retries started to generate every morning after a nightly reboot of the XenApp servers and would go up consistently throughout the day until the next scheduled reboot. The maximum number of retries observed was close to 5000. The retry activity was monitored from the PVS console, as shown in the following screenshot, and the vDisk system tray object on the target:

Server Port	Retries	Version
6918	47	11
6913	5304	11
6924	4927	11
6928	734	11
6930	2480	11
6916	1884	11

Troubleshooting

The following steps were taken to troubleshoot the high retries based on publicly available information from Citrix and experience working with the product:

1. Test for OS-specific issues:
   - Checked other vDisks in the environment and they all seemed to have the same problem.
   - Created a brand new XenApp vDisk and configured it to provision with the existing PVS servers. The same behavior was observed.

2. Test for Provisioning Server-specific issues:

   ◦ Disabled load balancing from the PVS Console and assigned the vDisk to the first and then the second PVS server individually but no change in behavior was noticed.

   ◦ Introduced a new PVS server to the farm and spread the connection load between all three PVS servers equally. The retries were still present.

   ◦ Disabled TCP Chimney Offload via the `HKLM\System\CurrentControlSet\Services\Tcpip\Parameters\DisableTaskOffload=1` (DWORD) registry key. This, by the way, is a very common step when troubleshooting not just retries but also boot delays, OS slowness, and generally anything that is suspected to be a network-related issue. By disabling Chimney Offload, we make sure that no CPU tasks are being offloaded to the network adapter of that machine to avoid bottlenecks. In this case, however, this did not make a difference to the retry count.

3. Test for hypervisor-specific issues:

   ◦ This was the first big breakthrough in the case. Since there were four ESXi hosts in a cluster hosting the Citrix environment, we decided to migrate a couple of target VMs to the same hypervisor that housed one of the PVS servers. As soon as we did this and rebooted these machines, we noticed that no retries were generated on them anymore. In the meantime, the rest of the streamed servers sitting on different ESXi hosts still had the retry count go up to enormous levels. What we inferred from this test was that if streaming traffic never left the ESXi host, no retries were generated. However, the moment that traffic went to a different server (thus no longer being contained on the same Standard vSwitch), the retries would go up right away.

   ◦ Based on the preceding test, we immediately started looking at the hypervisor resource utilization. Strangely enough, no bottlenecks were found either on the network bandwidth, CPU, or at the memory level.

4. Verifying hardware settings and platform-specific issues:

   ° Using WireShark, we were able to correlate the retries to actual packet loss. So at that point, we knew that the issue was network-related but looking at every possible angle, the network seemed healthy and not overly utilized. The SolarWinds network monitoring tool was used to report bandwidth utilization at the Ethernet and fabric level and we hardly saw any activity above 25% of the available bandwidth. So, if it wasn't a capacity bottleneck, what could it be? The answer is in the next and final bullet point that helped us close this case.

   ° Digging deeper down the stack, we started looking at the configuration settings of the actual blade servers hosting the vSphere environment. Being a Cisco UCS platform, the physical server architecture differs from other server vendors in the way profiles are set up and managed and the way proprietary Cisco Fabric Interconnects handle network and storage communications. Within the UCS Manager, you can assign a **Quality-of-Service (QoS)** policy to a fabric and prioritize traffic based on its type. After a detailed investigation, this is exactly what turned out to be the issue. If the vNIC responsible for the PVS traffic has a drop-eligible, low-priority, or best-effort weight assigned to it, then traffic will most certainly get dropped in favor of other communication types. After disabling the QoS policy for this, UCS fabric retries were no longer seen and the performance of the streamed XenApp servers got much better.

Case 2 – BNIStack errors

If you've been playing around with PVS for a while, for sure you've come across the term BNIStack (probably in one or two **Blue Screens of Death**). To be more accurate, `bnistack.sys` is the PVS network stack driver that's responsible for the target device side of streaming traffic. If BNIStack does not function properly, the target device will either freeze or crash with a BSOD. Also, when converting an OS to a vDisk, if `bnistack.sys` fails to load at boot, the machine will fail back to the master device hard drive and the conversion will fail. Errors in the Windows Event Viewer have sometimes proven to be benign, but more often than not, there is at least some cause of concern that something wrong has happened within the operating system if an error has been generated. So, what do BNIStack errors mean? Citrix actually has a list of references (CTX126407) on the BNIStack events in the Event Viewer, but this list only cites the event and doesn't go into much explanation of the root causes.

Environment

- Citrix Product: Provisioning Services 7.x
- Hypervisor: None. Physical systems are streamed to bare metal
- OS: Windows 2008 R2

Issue

A customer saw intermittent BNIStack 85 errors in the Windows Event Viewer of a few target devices. Sometimes, these events were accompanied by BNIStack 158 errors. Users would report random session freezes on the XenApp servers but no evidence showed that the two issues were correlated.

Detailed description

The syntax of Event ID 85 is as follows:

```
[MIOWorkerThread] IOS Socket UNAVAILABLE - not counting retry.
```

The syntax of Event ID 158 is as follows:

```
[MIoProcessIosReadTransaction] Invalid reconnection handle returned.
```

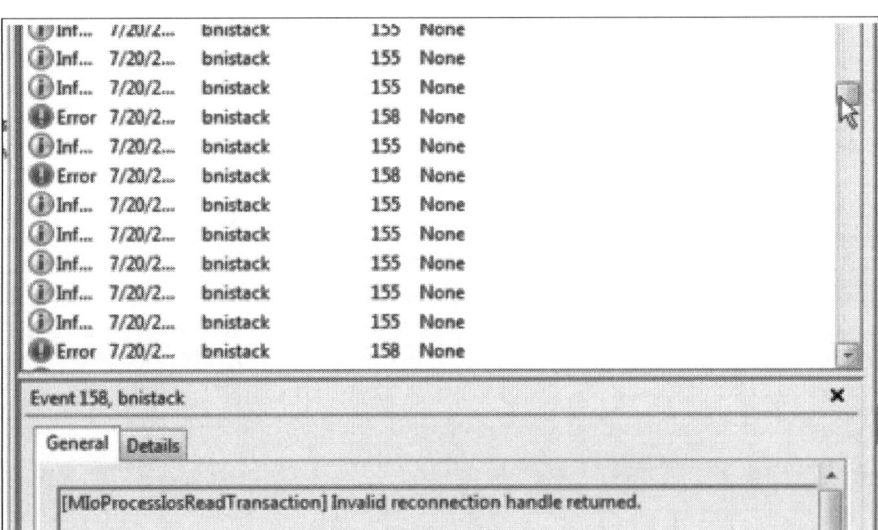

Troubleshooting

Internal research and lab reproduction (also known in the support circles as repro) showed that Event ID 85 from BNIStack is most likely a result of a network adapter disconnection that occurred in several instances in the time frame that it was tested in. During a remote session with the customer, we were not able to trace the disconnections back to particular machines as the error was intermittent and occurred on some machines only, and the Event IDs for network disconnections in Windows can come from various sources. The ones that we found during our research and lab replication for Windows 2008 R2 were as follows:

- **Event ID 15500**: This can be found at `http://technet.microsoft.com/en-us/library/dd392962(v=ws.10).aspx`

- **Event ID 4202**: This can be found at `http://technet.microsoft.com/en-us/library/dd408432(v=ws.10).aspx`

- **Event ID 4**: This can be found at `http://social.technet.microsoft.com/Forums/windowsserver/en-US/0408a28d-6ab8-4c85-8773-4bc42c2df40b/network-adapter-disabled-event-id-4-netsvc-miniport-reset`

As far as Event ID 158 is concerned, the error also seems to be generated upon a vDisk disconnection and/or due to retries.

Conclusion

In the end, it was reported that the issue turned out to be related to an out-of-date NIC driver on the underlying server platform. Updating the driver and NIC firmware corrected the problem. Other causes for vDisk freezes could be intermittent packet drops and expired DHCP leases (for the latter, setting up a DHCP reservation for the target device should resolve the issue).

Case 3 – Target device boot failure

This is one of the most common issues that almost every Citrix administrator will encounter during the lifetime of their environment. In this case study, we will take a look at how to troubleshoot target device boot failures without any dependence on the OS.

Environment

- Citrix product: Provisioning Services 7.6
- OS: Windows 2008 R2, Windows 2012 R2 and Windows 7/8/8.1

Issue

A provisioned target device fails to boot to a PVS vDisk. The problem can be observed at different stages during the boot process.

Detailed description

Multiple scenarios are possible and have been identified depending on what phase of the boot process the failure occurs and they are as follows:

1. A failure to obtain an IP address from DHCP is shown as follows:

```
Network boot from Intel E1000
Copyright (C) 2003-2008  VMware, Inc.
Copyright (C) 1997-2008  Intel Corporation

CLIENT MAC ADDR:                       GUID:
PXE-E51: No DHCP or proxyDHCP offers were received.

PXE-M0F: Exiting Intel PXE ROM.
Operating System not found
_
```

2. This is the IP address obtained either via DHCP or statically via the Boot ISO but results in a failure to download the bootstrap:

```
Found NIC @ PCI bus 2, device 0, function 0
Found PnP BIOS signature @ F000:6A70
Found UNDI BIOS signature @ C800:0020, Revision 2.2.2
Found "!PXE" @ 9C47:0000
Downloading tsbbdm.bin from              _ FAILED!
_
```

3. The IP address is obtained and the bootstrap is downloaded successfully but the target device not found in the database:

```
gPXE (http://etherboot.org) - 00:04.0 C900 PCI2.10 INT19 PMM0020010 C900

Press F12 for boot menu.

Boot device: Network - success.
gPXE (PCI 00:04.0) starting execution
gPXE initialising devices...


gPXE 1.0.0 -- Open Source Boot Firmware -- http://etherboot.org
Features: AoE HTTP iSCSI DNS TFTP bzImage ELF Multiboot PXE PXEXT

net0:                    on PCI00:04.0 (open)
  [Link:up, TX:0 TXE:0 RX:0 RXE:0]
DHCP (net0                       ok
net0:
Booting from filename "ARDBP32.bin"
tftp:/           /ARDBP32.bin. ok

No entry found in database for device.

Press any key to continue...
```

4. The target device is logged in and vDisk is found but gets stuck due to a black screen or the Windows logo, which appears during boot.

Troubleshooting

1. For the first scenario, it's clear that this is not a PVS code issue but something is preventing the DHCP server from assigning an IP address to the PXE client. In many cases, when the target device and the DHCP server are in different subnets, the Discover packet from the target never makes it to the other side because the router doesn't have the intelligence to forward the packet to other subnets. To resolve this issue, we've enabled DHCP Relay or IP Helper on the router to allow the transmittance of PXE packets to other networks.

2. In the second scenario, we have a machine that is able to obtain an IP address but the transfer of the bootstrap file from a TFTP server fails. This is most likely due to port 69 being blocked on the TFTP server (typically, a PVS server or a third-party tool such as SolarWinds). Other root causes include incorrect information in the DHCP Scope Options 66 and 67 (the server and bootstrap name) or the Boot ISO if you're using Boot Device Manager in PVS. To ensure that we cover the basics, we need to verify that the TFTP service runs in the Windows services components.

3. In the third scenario, the error means that the PVS login server received a streaming assignment request from a target device that isn't located in the PVS database. This is usually when targets are manually added to the Device Collection in PVS and some of them may have been missed—these are the ones that will error out on boot in this phase. To rectify the issue, we simply added the machine to a Device Collection using the PVS console.

4. PVS targets that get stuck during boot often do so after the vDisk has been found and an attempt to stream the operating system has been initiated. Once the vDisk is found, the target goes into a single-read mode when the PVS server transfers roughly around 300 MB of the OS, containing only the low-level drivers that are necessary to begin loading the OS. Since this is a very fast exchange of data, any bottlenecks in the network or storage will be exposed here. In one case, the problem was due to the E1000 virtual NIC in vSphere, which at the time of writing this book, was not recommended or supported by Citrix for any version of PVS after 5.6. Changing it to VMXNET3 in the VM settings can solve some performance and vDisk creation issues. In another case where the PVS server was physical, moving the VHD chain to local storage on this server as opposed to SAN alleviated the issue.

XenApp® and XenDesktop®

The second batch of case studies is focused on XenApp and XenDesktop, specifically the ICA/HDX connectivity failures, licensing issues, and console discrepancies. There are many other problem types documented by Citrix Support and the online community, so it's always fun to skim through the latest articles and forum threads when time permits.

Case 1 – 1030 error when launching the app

1030 is one of the most common and, unfortunately, generic errors encountered when launching a XenApp-hosted application or desktop. Since there is no additional explanation or syntax in the dialog box, it requires the collection of logs and traces to chase it down.

Environment

- Citrix product: XenApp/XenDesktop 7.6

- VDA version: 7.6

- OS version: Windows 2008 R2/2012 R2 and Windows 7/8/8.1

- NetScaler (is it required or not?): Yes, version 10.5 plus NetScaler Gateway are required

Issue

Users reported that on trying to launch their published application, they received an error message.

Detailed description

The issue appeared to have started occurring after some changes were made during a planned maintenance window. The syntax of the error was **The connection to "App" failed with status (1030)**:

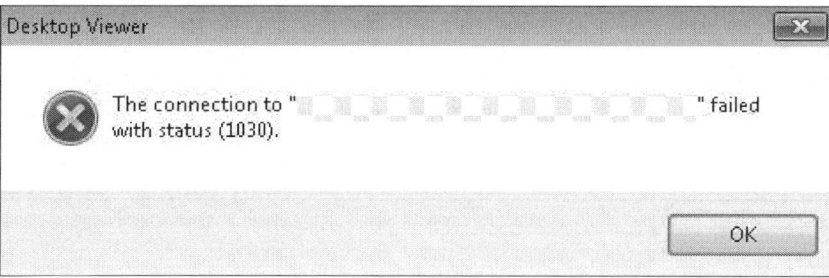

Troubleshooting

Due to the generic nature of the error, the right approach in this case was to try and narrow down the issue first. The first thing we asked was whether all users were affected and if the connections were initiated from external or internal networks. The customer confirmed that all users coming in externally had the problem but was unsure about internal connections. So, the first troubleshooting step was to test internal access when going directly to the StoreFront server. Based on these tests, we found that internally users were able to connect, so only external ones were failing. With this information in mind, it became apparent that something in the network had changed, possibly during the maintenance window the previous weekend. This sounded an awful lot like a port connectivity issue and this turned out to be the case. Looking at the network communications in a Citrix infrastructure where NetScaler Gateway is used as an external front-end and authentication point, we realized that ports 1494 and 2598 must be open between the NetScaler SNIP and the VDAs. Once a virtual session with an application or desktop is established, the ICA/HDX protocol gets encapsulated into the SSL packets between NetScaler and the user device, so only port 443 needs to be open through the external firewall. The problem in this case was that someone had removed the firewall rules on the internal firewall that sits between the Demilitarized Zone (DMZ) and the internal networks where the VDAs were, which wiped out 1494 and 2598 from the list of allowed ports, thus blocking ICA/HDX communications out to NetScaler. Recreating these rules resolved the issue.

Additional notes

Other causes for 1030 or a protocol driver error include DNS issues, where the different components in a Citrix environment cannot resolve each other, or even sometimes missing hotfixes. An out-of-date VDA can project some or all the known issues described in the hotfix article. An old version of Citrix Receiver may not even be supported by the latest XenApp software.

Case 2 – RDS license errors

Sometimes, users are able to launch a XenApp-hosted shared desktop, but a message pops up from the system tray stating that the machine has entered a license grace period for Remote Desktop Services. Even though it's not an immediate threat, if the issue is not addressed in a timely fashion, eventually the XenApp servers will stop accepting connections from end users.

Environment

- Citrix product: XenApp 7.x
- Microsoft product: Windows 2012 R2 with the Remote Desktop Services (RDS) role
- Licensing type: XenApp is concurrent and RDS is per user

Issue

Users report that on connecting to a hosted shared desktop from XenApp, they get a message in the system tray that the RDS licensing mode is not configured and has entered a grace period.

Detailed description

The issue can take place all the time or randomly depending on the circumstances. The exact error is captured in the following screenshot:

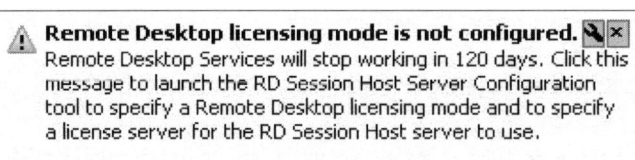

Troubleshooting

Two possible scenarios are investigated in such cases: is the issue occurring randomly for some users only or is it affecting everybody all the time? In either case, the first place we look at is the GPO, which is typically used to apply RDS configurations to a group of servers. The RDS licensing settings are located under this `Computer Configuration\Policies\Administrative Templates\Windows Components\Remote Desktop Services\Remote Desktop Session Host\ Licensing` GPO:

Two settings are of relevance as follows:

- Use the specified Remote Desktop license servers
- Set the Remote Desktop licensing mode

To define a license server for RDS, the customer simply had to enable and populate the first setting with their designated RDS license server and the second setting with the RDS license type (this is usually per user). After applying the GPO to the XenApp RDS servers, the error in this particular case was no longer present.

Other notes

This was a nice catch but what if the error was intermittent and affecting some users? Randomness suggests that the configuration must be correct in terms of the GPO setup, but maybe the policies were not applying properly to certain servers due to DNS or time synchronization issues.

Case 3 – Citrix® Studio showing incorrect VM states

Several times, I've come across an issue where the Citrix Studio console showed the incorrect registration or power states of virtual machines managed by the Delivery Controllers. Even though it seems cosmetic, this problem has a much deeper impact than expected because incorrect information can prevent the controllers from brokering user connections and issuing important power policies.

Environment

- Citrix product: XenApp 7.x
- Hypervisor: ESXi with vCenter, Hyper-V with SCVMM, or XenServer
- Catalog type: Random (Machine Creation Services)

Issue

Citrix administrators have reported that some unregistered machines appear as **Registered** in Studio and vice versa, and the power states of some VMs that are **On** show as **Off**.

Detailed description

A number of issues have been reported since the problem started occurring. For example, some users are unable to connect to their sessions—no error is displayed but the session never starts or an error, such as **Cannot start your desktop**, is displayed after a long wait. In addition to this, Citrix administrators have been unable to issue power management commands from Studio.

Troubleshooting

The way we approached this issue was by identifying problematic behavior in the Delivery Controller host connection. From the very beginning, it was apparent that the controller wasn't communicating properly with vCenter and, thus, had extremely outdated information on the states of the VMs. We leveraged PowerShell to obtain details on the status of the host connection using the following commands:

```
asnp citrix.*
```

```
Get-BrokerHypervisorConnection
```

The output for the preceding commands is as follows:

```
PS C:\Windows\system32> asnp citrix.*
PS C:\Windows\system32> Get-BrokerHypervisorConnection


Capabilities                              : {PowerOn, PowerOff, SuspendResume, Reset...}
HypHypervisorConnectionUid                : c096b94f-b455-4d96-ac06-2c6ddd2fc7e7
IsReady                                   : True
MachineCount                              : 10
MaxAbsoluteActiveActions                  : 100
MaxAbsoluteNewActionsPerMinute            : 10
MaxAbsolutePvdPowerActions                : 50
MaxPercentageActiveActions                : 20
MaxPvdPowerActionsPercentageOfDesktops    : 25
MetadataMap                               : {}
Name                                      : XenServer_Pool
PreferredController                       : XENDESKTOP\XDXA76B
State                                     : Unavailable
Uid                                       : 1
```

The first command loads the Citrix PowerShell snap-in, and the second command retrieves the host connection details. As seen in the screenshot, State shows as Unavailable, which validates the communication issue between the Delivery Controller and the hypervisor management platform. In this case, we found that the password of the XenApp 7.6 domain account that ran the host connection had expired. Whenever this happens, the Delivery Controller stops updating its information and Studio starts showing incorrect states for the VMs. Updating the host connection account password in the **Hosting** section of the **Configuration** node in Studio fixed the problem but the long term solution and best practice is to use a service account with password expiration disabled in Active Directory. This way, the risk of running into this issue is minimal unless someone manually changes the password.

Summary

In this chapter, we formed a methodology to help you stay organized and efficient when troubleshooting end user and customer issues in your Citrix environment. To cover some of the most common scenarios, we went over multiple case studies based on real-world customer issues seen in the field. These studies were broken down by product and followed a template oftentimes used by Citrix Support. Since they are only a very small fraction of all the different problem types reported by customers, hopefully, you will enjoy the amount of information available online through vendor documentation and even more so by the Citrix community of bloggers and enthusiasts who dedicate their own time to helping people adopt the technology.

14
The Big Day – Going Live with Citrix XenApp®

And, here we are! Back to where we started, but, hopefully, with a brand new infrastructure in place, one that will not only serve your users well but can make you proud as an IT manager.

The goal of this chapter is to prepare you to migrate the newly built XenApp environment to production. In most cases, this is not a very easy thing to do and requires careful planning because of the potential impact on a business if things were to go not so smoothly. Here are some scenarios that are reviewed in this chapter (note that not all potential situations are covered here and your specific use case may differ from these):

- First time adoption of a virtual environment
- Migrating from one virtual environment to another
- Upgrading to comparable versions of the same product
- Expanding existing systems and new user base accommodation

Environment must-do's

Even though every customer is different and every environment is specific to the needs of the company that will be using it, there are some general rules of thumb when a new system is built. The first one (and I can't repeat this enough) is testing, testing, and testing.

Functional and performance testing

In IT, a design is only as good as the worst possible scenario that can happen in your environment. While you cannot completely anticipate or prevent an outage before it occurs, if you do thorough testing before placing your system in production, you can rectify many issues and inconsistencies before they ever have a chance to impact your users. To start small, first you need to validate an architecture and ensure that the XenApp solution was built as designed. If any requirements have changed along the way, they need to be accounted for and the design needs to be adjusted to satisfy them. For instance, if the environment was initially built for 600 users, but all of a sudden the management of a company decides that two more departments with 200 users each need to be served by XenApp, you suddenly now need to expand the amount of XenApp server VDAs to accommodate 400 additional users. While this is easy enough to do either via MCS or PVS, it also has implications on your network, storage, and licensing. So, you have to make sure that you have enough capacity for each of these variables. Once you verify that the implementation is consistent with the design, you should test the functionalities of your XenApp site with a fictitious test user specifically created in Active Directory for this purpose. The reason why you would want to do this before you actually summon somebody from the accounting department to do it is because you need to get a feel for the environment yourself and then be able to compare it with the feedback received by a would-be production user. Using this domain account, you can test internal and external connectivity from a variety of devices. If you know that you will have users launching published applications and desktops from iPads and smart phones, you need to test every possible device (you don't want your CIO screaming that she can't connect to an app from her iPad).

Functional testing is not just about being able to connect from anywhere, anytime, and any device. It is also about how data is handled during and after a session. In other words, how will users save their files and documents when working with an application or hosted desktop, and does the chosen method work as expected? Will they be saving all their files inside their profiles (a risky business since this can lead to profile bloating and slow logons) or will they be presented with a home directory? Folder redirection can help prevent large files from being stored in a roaming or UPM profile. What about a cloud solution, such as ShareFile or OneDrive that can replace the need for on-premise storage of files? It all depends on the needs and requirements of the business, but what matters the most is that the solution be tested before it is rolled out to production. It is not unusual for profiles to become problematic in the initial stages of a live environment. For example, testing can reveal that profiles are not being saved in the UPM store after a user logs off from a virtual session. While this may be an easy fix (insufficient permissions to the profile share), it is better that it's identified in the early stages than later on when users are actually prone to losing data.

Once you verify that the environment works as expected for one user and you are able to manage it the way that it was designed, the next step is to test for performance. Performance issues often stay hidden during functional testing because the environment is not *under stress* during this time. To achieve a more accurate representation of a live production system, you need to summon many people to test hosted applications and desktops at the same time. It is fine to start small but the greater the number of test users who get closer to the actual concurrent base that will be logged into the environment on a daily basis, the more likely you are to identify potential bottlenecks and correct them in a timely manner. But, what if you can't amass the number of real users you were hoping to get for testing? Fortunately, there are plenty of tools out there that can help you simulate the load that you think accurately represents your live environment. Citrix used to have a very interesting product called **EdgeSight for Load Testing (ESLT)** that did just this. By executing a variety of scripts, ESLT was able simulate both XenApp and XenDesktop connections and help with predictive analysis. However, a few years ago, Citrix decided to retire the product and end maintenance and support for it. Since then, third-party companies emerged with their own load testing software. One such company that develops simulator software for virtual environments is **Login VSI**. Their product, also called Login VSI, is widely used to measure performance for Citrix XenApp, XenDesktop, Microsoft RDS, and VMware Horizon View. IOMeter, which is geared more towards measuring storage intensity, can also be used to produce performance metrics and is available online for free.

During performance testing and, in general, any time your users are experiencing session latency, it is *always* a good idea to check the resource utilization of your hypervisor. Host capacity is not unlimited and sometimes it is easy to get caught up in troubleshooting an application layer when maybe you've simply run out of resources on your host. Most hypervisors provide at least some basic monitoring utilities (or you can pay for the more advanced stuff). In the case of Citrix XenServer, you can go to the Performance tab of the host in XenCenter and immediately pull information on the CPU, memory, and NIC utilization. From there, you can easily identify spikes in CPU, memory, and network bandwidth bottlenecks. However, the bigger question is that how do you actually determine the root cause of a problem in order to fix it before users get their hands on the environment. In the case of hypervisor utilization, it is usually pretty straightforward and if the design was executed properly, you should not have more virtual machines than the host can sustain. In fact, you should not even get close to 100% usage of physical memory and datastore capacity. Also, if you ever do need to scale out when adding more physical hosts (rack servers or blades), make sure that you always have *N+1* (where *N* is the number of hosts needed plus at least one spare host for failover purposes).

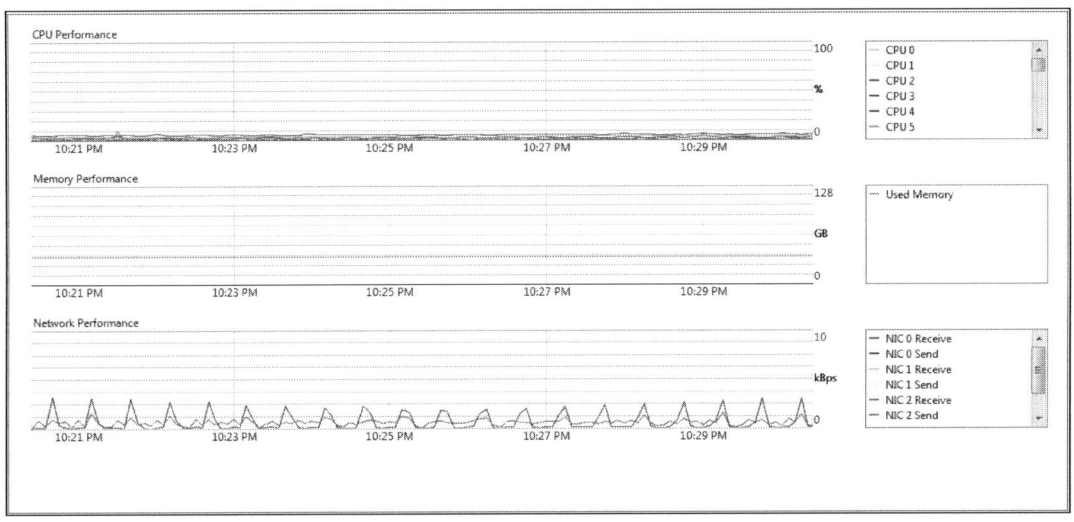

Very low resource utilization in XenCenter (CPU, memory, and network performance)

If during testing, you notice that logging into a virtual session is slow, always take a look at these two components—profiles and Group Policies. With time, if not managed properly, user profiles can become very large and this would slow down the logon process. Also, the presence of many User GPOs that get applied during logon is likely to have a negative impact; so, wherever possible, try to reduce the number of GPOs for a particular OU.

 In my testing, I have found out that it is better to have fewer policies with many settings in them than lots of small ones with one or two settings in them.

Database backups

In the XenApp 7.6 world, ever since the new FMA architecture was introduced, database availability has become one of the most critical, if not the *most* critical component of the Citrix environment. Earlier in the book, we explored different methods of making your Citrix database highly available (mirroring, failover clustering, and so on), but even then, if all your SQL nodes go down, you will not be able to manage the environment and no new sessions will be brokered. For this reason, regardless of the HA method you've chosen to employ, you should take regular backups of both the XenApp and PVS database if PVS is in use. This way, if your database gets corrupted, you can always restore to the last known good backup and revert the XenApp site using PowerShell, and the PVS farm using the PVS Configuration Wizard. You can easily take database backups from SQL Server Management Studio or you can deploy a backup script that runs on SQL Server at a specified interval. The latter option is typically better because it automates the process and frees up time for your DBA to do other important tasks. One of my favorite aspects of SQL Server Management Studio is the wealth of automation tools that you can leverage from the GUI. The aforementioned script is already available and ready to be deployed using **SQL Server Maintenance Plan Wizard** in the **Management Plans** section of the **Management** tab in SSMS. There is a short query that you need to execute first to enable the SQL Server Agent extended stored procedures:

```
sp_configure 'show advanced options', 1;
GO
RECONFIGURE;
GO
sp_configure 'Agent XPs', 1;
GO
RECONFIGURE
GO
```

Once these statements are run in the query field of SQL Server Management Studio or in the SQLCMD mode, you will be able to launch the wizard to create scheduled backup jobs for the XenApp database. Most customers do backups at night since user activity is decreased and the SQL server is not as busy at this time. Both the full database and the transaction logs should be backed up.

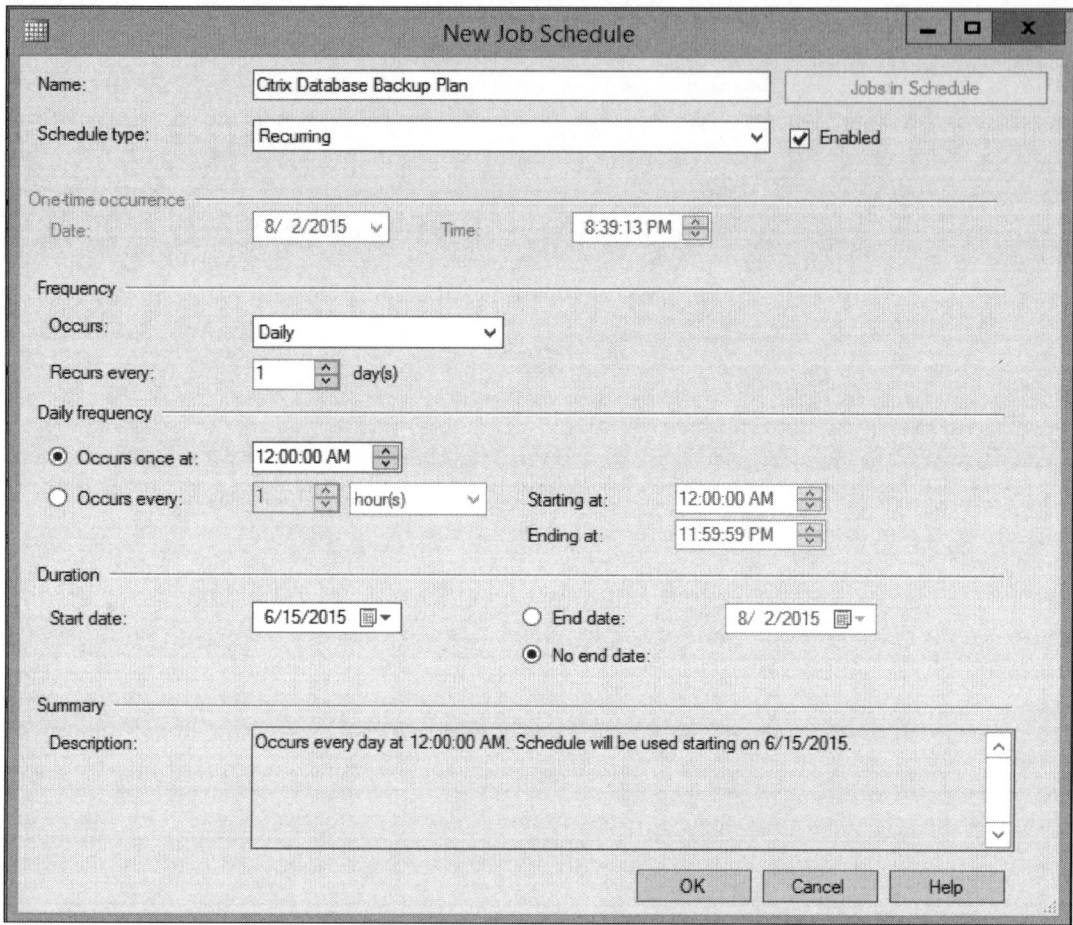

NetScaler® configuration backup

Equally as important as backing up your database is exporting the NetScaler configuration. Regardless of what model and build you have, every setting and attribute set in NetScaler resides in a configuration file called ns.conf. Saving the configuration is easy enough—all you need to do is click on the diskette button in the top right-hand corner of your NetScaler Management GUI and a new copy of ns.conf is saved on the appliance. This is only a part of the job, though. Appliances fail and files get lost, so the best way to back up your entire NetScaler configuration is by exporting all the files from /nsconfig/, /var/, and /netscaler/ to an outside location. Using a **Secure File Transfer Protocol (SFTP)** client, such as WinSCP, you can simply connect to the NetScaler appliance on NSIP using administrative credentials or root and copy the files to your machine. To perform a full backup where not just your settings and frequently used files are saved, but also your SSL certificates and license files as well, export the following directories:

- /nsconfig/|| ssl/*, license/*, fips/*
- /var/ || netscaler/ssl/*, wi/java_home/jre/lib/security/ cacerts/*
- wi_java_home/lib/security/cacerts/*

You are probably saying to yourself, "Huh?!" Okay, I will admit that this is an old school way of doing things. These days most functions are available in the GUI and you can export your configuration by navigating to **System | Backup and Restore | Backup**. Yes, I could have started with this but then it is no fun!

Testing HA

To have a redundant solution, every component of your Citrix environment should be highly available. This means that if something goes wrong with one of your Delivery Controllers, NetScalers, StoreFront servers, or even the hypervisor, a secondary one should be in place for failover purposes. The purpose is to avoid downtime during partial outages, which are fairly frequent in many IT environments. In this section, we will review how HA is deployed for the different components of the Citrix implementation and how to simulate failovers to validate redundant configurations.

NetScaler® HA

Having a highly available NetScaler configuration is absolutely crucial for your environment. Most, if not all, users who connect to XenApp applications and desktops will go through NetScaler for load balancing and gateway authentication. If you only have one appliance and the chassis experiences a power problem or network connectivity goes down, then no new users will be able to connect and business will be severely impacted. To avoid such situations, always have an HA pair of NetScalers. In case one goes down, the other can take over all user connections. This configuration is also known as active-passive, which allows for failover of one of the nodes without user impact. It is worth noting that at the time of writing this book, the HA feature is only supported if both appliances are the exact same model, version, and build. Pairing different models or two different platforms, such as physical and virtual, are unsupported and may result in the appliances not working properly. So, how do you test if your HA configuration is really working? One of the easiest ways is to force a power off on the primary NetScaler. In this situation, since most settings are the same between the two nodes, the failover should occur smoothly and users should continue to get connected to backend servers in the XenApp environment.

StoreFront™ HA

StoreFront servers are a little different from NetScaler when it comes to HA. You can have a group of servers on the StoreFront level, but ultimately, the availability is defined by using load balancing with, say, NetScaler. By creating a virtual server with a **Virtual IP (VIP)** and a load balancing service that is mapped to a pair of StoreFront servers, if any one of them is down, users will only be sent to activate one. To test the VIP, you can power off or disable the NIC on one of the StoreFront servers and ensure that you can connect through the other one.

Delivery Controller HA

Going back to earlier chapters, we talked about the roles of the different components in a XenApp environment. The Delivery Controllers receive registration requests from the VDAs and this is how the XenApp server OS machines become available to service users with applications and desktops. Also, the Delivery Controller serves as a link between users and VDAs, brokering each and every session. HA is configured during the VDA installation when all Delivery Controllers can be enumerated, thus providing more than one registration path for agents. If not configured during the installation, an administrator can create a registry key on the master image, place it there in the FQDN format, and separated by a space. The string registry value is called ListOfDDCs and is located under `HKLM\Software\Citrix\VirtualDesktopAgent` for a 32-bit OS and `HKLM\Software\Wow6432Node\Citrix\VirtualDesktopAgent` for a 64-bit OS.

Name	↓	Last Updated	Registered Desktops
XDXA76.xendesktop.poc		0 minutes ago	3
XDXA76B.xendesktop.poc		0 minutes ago	3

Equally distributed VDA registrations between Delivery Controllers

Production rollout strategies

After you've fully backed up your environment and tested it for functionalities and performance, it is time to come up with a rollout strategy to put your XenApp solution in production. Depending on your particular scenario, you can either use a phased approach or put everyone online at the same time. Here, we will review a couple of methodologies and hopefully one of them will fit your design and help you with the rollout.

Going virtual for the first time

If this is your first virtual setup and you've only served applications on physical workstations, this will be quite the change for your users. Whether you present individual apps through Citrix Receiver for the Web or Receiver for Windows or Linux, or they're connecting to a hosted shared desktop, your users will need to adjust to how they access their new workspaces. Sending out a step-by-step document to everyone is pretty much mandatory, so you won't have to answer a thousand calls a week from frustrated employees. The document should include the XenApp URL (NetScaler Gateway or StoreFront), instructions on how to install Citrix Receiver, and how to add applications to the self-service portal.

Virtual-to-virtual migration

A virtual to virtual migration scenario is true when you've had an older version of XenApp, such as 6.5, which is built on the IMA architecture and you've installed 7.6 in a parallel environment. So now you have two systems—the old one that is still in production and the new one, which was built recently. The first question that may pop into your mind is that why have we built a separate deployment instead of upgrading version 6.5? We already answered this question—we've done this due to the differences in architectures. 7.6, which is based on FMA, is a completely different software and there is no direct path to it. So, when building the new 7.6 master image, you need to ensure that all the required applications are installed so that users do not experience any functional differences. To do a cutover, you can provide a new URL leading to the new environment or change DNS to point to an external address to the new NetScaler Gateway VIP. The latter would provide a more seamless transition for users.

Upgrading to the latest version

Upgrading to the latest version is possible when you are already running a 7.x version of XenApp or XenDesktop in production but you want to upgrade to 7.6. In this case, since your deployment is already using the FMA architecture, a direct upgrade path is available via the 7.6 ISO. Once you have upgraded your Delivery Controllers, StoreFront servers, and XenApp Server OS VDAs, the environment can be readily used without any other changes. Since the upgrade process involves restarting services, it is always a good idea to perform the upgrade outside of business hours or on a weekend.

Expansion of existing systems

Another situation that you may run into is the need to expand your existing environment. This generally occurs when a company's management decides that more users or business units will use XenApp to gain access to virtually hosted applications and desktops. In this case, you may want to think about building another image, especially if the requirements of the user group that you will be accommodating are substantially different from the existing ones in terms of applications. Core programs that consume a substantial amount of resources on a VM can be isolated on dedicated master images and the servers hosting them can be put in separate machine catalogs. Otherwise, the process of expanding the environment in XenApp 7.6 is very straightforward. All you need to do if you are using MCS is add more machines to the catalog in Citrix Studio. If PVS is the preferred deployment method, then **XenDesktop Setup Wizard** in the PVS console can be leveraged to increase the number of XenApp Server OS machines. On the NetScaler side, the throughput utilization should be carefully monitored from **Dashboard**, and if it approaches the maximum specifications of an appliance as the environment expands, a license or model upgrade should be considered depending on the current configurations.

Summary

In the last chapter of *Getting Started with Citrix XenApp 7.6*, we covered performance and functionality testing, high-availability validation, and production rollout strategies for your XenApp solution. These are important checkpoints as you get ready to go live with an environment that can help you identify and resolve potential production-affecting issues early on.

Dear reader, it was a privilege to be your companion in this journey. I truly hope this book gave you something that you were missing before. Something that you can apply to make your employees happier, your data more secure, and your company more profitable. In technology, the only constant is change, and modern day IT requires us to keep up with many software and hardware products. XenApp combined with XenDesktop is one of the most mature solutions in the end user computing space and it's definitely here to stay. Whether you are building a small lab for your own development or a production deployment for thousands of users, this book is always here for you. Remember that success starts with learning the basics. Best of luck and I will see you on our next journey!

Index

Delivery Groups
about 88
creating 193-197
Demilitarized Zone (DMZ) 24, 25
Desktop Delivery Controller (DDC). *See*
XenApp® Delivery Controller
DHCP Scope Options 66/67 176
Dynamic Workload Balancing 33

E

EdgeSight for Load Testing (ESLT) 273
Electronic Medical Records (EMR) 33
end-of-extended-support (EOES) 14
end-of-life (EOL) 14
end-of-maintenance (EOM) 14
external network 25

F

failover cluster instance (FCI) 41
Fibre Channel (FC) 26
FlexCast Management Architecture
(FMA) 7, 24
Folder Redirection (FR)
about 29, 223
drawbacks 224
Fully Qualified Domain Name
(FQDN) 42, 74
functional testing 272-274

G

Graphical User Interface (GUI) 3
Graphics Device Interface (GDI) 233
Group Policy Management Console
(GPMC) 212, 221
Group Policy Objects (GPOs) 48

H

hardware layer
about 51
domain infrastructure requisites 52
host requisites 51

High Availability (HA)
about 41, 105
configuring 121
Delivery Controller HA 278
NetScaler® HA 278
StoreFront™ HA 278
testing 277
hosted applications
about 192, 193
accessing, via NetScaler Gateway™ 201-206
accessing, via StoreFront™ 206
Delivery Groups, creating 193-197
updating, for MCS 198
updating, for PVS 199, 200
hosted shared desktops (HSD) 9, 192
hypervisor support
configuring 74

I

Independent Computing Architecture
(ICA) 4
Independent Management Architecture
(IMA) 7
internal network 25
Internet Explorer (IE) 38, 107
Internet Information Services (IIS) 2, 45

K

Key Management Service (KMS) 12
Knowledge Base (KB) 199

L

LDAP authentication
configuring 122
License Access Code 73
License Administration Console (LAC) 73
License Server (LS) 39, 73
load balancing
NetScaler®, configuring 134
testing, on NetScaler® 142, 143
load balancing VIP
configuring 139-142
Local Area Network (LAN) 24

Thank you for buying
Getting Started with Citrix XenApp® 7.6

About Packt Publishing

Packt, pronounced 'packed', published its first book, *Mastering phpMyAdmin for Effective MySQL Management*, in April 2004, and subsequently continued to specialize in publishing highly focused books on specific technologies and solutions.

Our books and publications share the experiences of your fellow IT professionals in adapting and customizing today's systems, applications, and frameworks. Our solution-based books give you the knowledge and power to customize the software and technologies you're using to get the job done. Packt books are more specific and less general than the IT books you have seen in the past. Our unique business model allows us to bring you more focused information, giving you more of what you need to know, and less of what you don't.

Packt is a modern yet unique publishing company that focuses on producing quality, cutting-edge books for communities of developers, administrators, and newbies alike. For more information, please visit our website at www.packtpub.com.

About Packt Enterprise

In 2010, Packt launched two new brands, Packt Enterprise and Packt Open Source, in order to continue its focus on specialization. This book is part of the Packt Enterprise brand, home to books published on enterprise software – software created by major vendors, including (but not limited to) IBM, Microsoft, and Oracle, often for use in other corporations. Its titles will offer information relevant to a range of users of this software, including administrators, developers, architects, and end users.

Writing for Packt

We welcome all inquiries from people who are interested in authoring. Book proposals should be sent to author@packtpub.com. If your book idea is still at an early stage and you would like to discuss it first before writing a formal book proposal, then please contact us; one of our commissioning editors will get in touch with you.

We're not just looking for published authors; if you have strong technical skills but no writing experience, our experienced editors can help you develop a writing career, or simply get some additional reward for your expertise.

Citrix® XenApp® 6.5 Expert Cookbook

ISBN: 978-1-84968-522-1   Paperback: 420 pages

Over 125 recipes that enable you to configure, administer, and troubleshoot a XenApp® infrastructure for effective application virtualization

1. Create installation scripts for Citrix XenApp, License Servers, Web Interface, and StoreFront.

2. Use PowerShell scripts to configure and administer the XenApp's infrastructure components.

3. Discover Citrix and community written tools to maintain a Citrix XenApp infrastructure.

Citrix® XenApp® 7.x Performance Essentials

ISBN: 978-1-78217-611-4   Paperback: 120 pages

Tune and optimize the performance of your farms with the new improved XenApp® architecture

1. Monitor your infrastructure using the new tools, and learn how to optimize the end-user experience.

2. Discover the new FlexCast Management Architecture of XenApp 7.5 and its components.

3. Explore the new features designed for mobile and remote users.

Please check **www.PacktPub.com** for information on our titles

Getting Started with Citrix XenApp 6.5 [Video]

ISBN: 978-1-84968-936-6 Duration: 01:58 hrs

Build and manage your own fully-functioning Citrix farm based on XenApp 6.5

1. Create a basic XenApp farm quickly and easily.

2. Learn everything you need to know, from installation and configuration to HDX and virtualization.

3. Presented in a logical succession that will walk you through the entire process of getting started with Citrix XenApp 6.5.

Citrix XenApp Performance Essentials

ISBN: 978-1-78217-044-0 Paperback: 126 pages

A practical guide for tuning and optimizing the performance of XenApp farms using real-world examples

1. Design a scalable XenApp infrastructure.

2. Monitor and optimize server performance.

3. Improve end user experience.

4. Tune the farm for WAN connections.

Please check **www.PacktPub.com** for information on our titles

Printed in Great Britain
by Amazon